THE SEARCH FOR GOD

THE
SEARCH FOR
GOD

.

David Manning White

MACMILLAN PUBLISHING COMPANY

New York

COLLIER MACMILLAN PUBLISHERS

London

Macmillan Publishing Company
866 Third Avenue, New York, N.Y. 10022
Collier Macmillan Canada, Inc.

Library of Congress Cataloging in Publication Data
Main entry under title:
The Search for God.
Includes index.
1. God—Quotations, maxims, etc.   I. White,
David Manning.
BL205.S4   1983   291.2'11   83-9427
ISBN 0-02-627110-9

10 9 8 7 6 5 4 3 2 1

Designed by Jack Meserole

Printed in the United States of America

Nur eine schmale Wand ist zwischen uns,
durch Zufall; denn es könnte sein:
ein Rufen deines oder meines Munds—
und sie bricht ein
ganz ohne Lärm und Laut
Du, Nachbar Gott
RAINER MARIA RILKE

Contents

Preface

My initial purpose in compiling this interpretive anthology was to provide a synthesis of the most significant thoughts about God transcribed in the scriptures of the world's great religions and in the commentaries of many men and women of rare spiritual perception. These God Seekers, as I term them, emerged throughout all periods of human history and in every part of the world, and over the ages they have given us a spiritual treasury of immense proportion. But in the course of spending several thousand hours collecting the quintessence of their religious insights, a secondary purpose gradually manifested itself.

Somehow, the very act of contemplating, savoring, and treasuring the key thoughts of these classic God Seekers became the strongest religious emotion I had ever experienced. I began to understand, as never before, that the Creator of the Universe, although allowing us, his children, the freedom to choose the pathways of our lives, had in his eternal love and compassion purposefully sent many prophetic messengers to convey his gift of ethical wisdom.

It was as if God were doing all He could, short of creating robots who would automatically react with knee-jerk perfection, to enable us to understand and to accept the meaning of our brief cosmic moment in his Eternal Now. So, although this book was initiated out of an intellectual curiosity about the most profound ways that mankind has perceived God during the past four or five thousand years, it became something far more meaningful to me.

The collective thoughts of the God Seekers, as represented in this volume, reflect their recurring discovery that the Creator of all humankind had a plan for the survival of a world that today totters on the edge of Armageddon. Therefore, if this anthology allows me to share their remarkable insights with others, who like myself did not fully realize how much they hungered for a reaffirmation of God's love and wise rule, it will be a reward I shall long cherish.

Although I was not consciously aware of it, the genesis of this book took place forty-five years ago when some gifted professors introduced me to the works of such God Seekers as John Milton, Dante, Goethe, and Pascal. During my last undergraduate year, quite fortuitously, I also had the good fortune to enroll in a course in comparative religion. There for the first time I encountered the beauty and wisdom of the Koran, the hymns of Kabir and Guru Nanak, the sacred poetry of Jalal-ud-din Rumi, the moral revelations of Guatama Buddha, and the countless jewels of the Vedic literature of India. Reading these gems of spirituality and comparing their approaches to understanding God with those in the Old and New Testaments convinced me that one supreme creator was the author who inspired all God Seekers. Yet at that time nothing would have surprised me more than to learn that, many years later, the seed that had been planted then would become this anthology.

There are a number of people who unwittingly had a hand in my decision to attempt this book, and I would like to acknowledge them. From my immediate family there was my grandfather, Charles Kazansky, whose spiritual joy at a seder would have elicited a loving embrace from the Baal Shem Tov himself. My cousin, Anne Polland Scharf, shared her personal library with me during the formative years of my childhood. Such books as a magnificent edition of the Old Testament "Song of Songs," illustrated by Rockwell Kent, opened my eyes to the mystery of total involvement in life.

At Cornell College in Iowa, I had the great fortune to study with Howard Clinton Lane. This paragon of a teacher gave me an insight into *Paradise Lost* that sparked my need to learn how other God Seekers answered the troubling issues John Milton had raised. And I cherish the memory of Professor Frederick McGaw, who walked with me on a raw March day in 1938 into the middle of a woods until we found just the right spot to read Plato's *Phaedo* to each other.

From the world of formal religion I remember Bishops Francis J. McConnell and G. Bromley Oxnam, great liberal ministers of the Methodist church, whose eloquence sent my mind reeling when I first heard them in the mid-1930s, and later I listened to the outstanding Jewish writer, Maurice Samuels, and fell in love with his stories of Isaac Loeb Peretz. It was also my joy to know Dr. Howard Thurman during the decade from 1955 to 1965, when he was dean of the chapel at Boston University, for this man's life and work exemplified Leo Tolstoy's precept that the reason of life is for each of us simply to grow in love.

The Maharishi Sayada in Rangoon's Thathana Yeithka generously let me share his monastic regimen for two weeks in 1958, when I was an advisor to the Burmese government, thus enabling me to learn more about Buddhism than I could have ever learned from books. Nor can I forget my friend Baron William Frary von Blomberg of Hampton, New Hampshire, whose genius at bringing together people of all races and faiths to work for the ideal of the brotherhood of man under the fatherhood of God has impelled me to follow, however falteringly, in his steps. Through Baron von Blomberg I met Sant Kirpal Singh, a truly great Sikh guru, whose lifelong ecumenical work for the "unity of mankind" continues to this day to be a constant source of inspiration.

Throughout the years I have been blessed with some special friends who listened with patience and true *caritas* to my difficult spiritual explorations. Among them, I particularly recall Roy Teele, Robert Rowley, "Toppy" Tull, Ruth Mason, Helen Weston, Rosemary Shafer, Luisa Kreisberg, and Betty Friedan.

Catherine Wallerstein, by accepting my hand in 1943, brought a transcendent dimension to my life. For nearly forty years she has made me ever-mindful of Robert Burton's observation in his *Anatomy of Melancholy:* "There is no joy, no comfort, no sweetness, no pleasure in the world like to that of a good wife."

Thus, for some thirty years I collected my favorite passages from the great religious scriptures of mankind, as well as commentaries by hundreds of theologians, philosophers, poets, and clergy of all faiths. But nothing would have come of this—other than sharing my gems with a few friends and students over the years—had it not been for another longtime friend, Jeremiah Kaplan. He not only encouraged me to compile and write this anthology, but perhaps more importantly, used his good offices at Macmillan Publishing Company to enable me to undertake it. The painstaking effort of my editor at Macmillan, Charles Levine, to shape this book into its present form, puts me more in his debt than he knows.

One of the greatest of the God Seekers, the thirteenth-century spiritual genius Meister Eckhart, once wrote in his *Book of Divine Consolation* some lines that epitomize my dedication of this book to all who read it. I cannot but hope they will share in the inspiration I have felt in collecting and frequently perusing these spiritual jewels.

Eckhart said, "May the God of love and mercy, the truth grant to me, and to all who are to read this book, that we may find and become aware of the truth in ourselves."

Acknowledgments

In preparing a book of this kind, one is dependent upon the goodwill of the publishers and copyright holders of many books. I wish therefore to express my gratitude to the following distinguished publishing houses and acknowledge their gracious permission to reprint material from their books. In some instances it has proved impossible to get in touch with any individual holding proprietary rights. Moreover, if in my attempt to clear permissions I have inadvertently overlooked any matters of this kind, I wish to express my regrets and to assure any concerned parties of my readiness to rectify this in any subsequent edition.

Abingdon Press: *Prayer* by George Arthur Buttrick © *So We Believe, So We Pray* by George Arthur Buttrick; © *Religious Values* by Edgar Brightman © 1925; *Nature and Values* by Edgar Brightman © 1945; *Prayer and the Common Life* by Georgia Harkness © 1948; *The Dark Night of the Soul* by Georgia Harkness © 1945; *The Doctrine of God* by Albert C. Knudson © 1930; *Recoveries in Religion* by Ralph W. Sockman © 1938; *The Highway of God* by Ralph W. Sockman © 1942.

Allen and Unwin, Ltd., London: *Appearance and Reality* by Frances Herbert Bradley © (1916); *Brahma-Sutra* by Sarvepalli Radhakrishnan © (1960); *An Idealist View of Life* by Sarvepalli Radhakrishnan © (1933).

Andrews and McMeel, Inc.: *Dostoevski* by Nicolai Berdyaev © (1934); *The End of Our Time* by Nicolai Berdyaev © (1933).

Moses Asch: For permission to reprint passages from Sholem Asch, *One Destiny* © (1945) and Sholem Asch, *What I Believe* © (1941).

Dr. Peter A. Bertocci for permission to quote from his book, *Introduction to the Philosophy of Religion*, published by Prentice-Hall © (1951).

Geoffrey Bles, Ltd., London: *The Heart of Man* by Gerald Vann © (1944).

Cambridge University Press: *Philosophical Theology* by F. R. Tennant © (1928).

Wm. Collins, Ltd., London: *The Divine Pity* by Gerald Vann © (1972); *Stones or Bread* by Gerald Vann © (1957).

Columbia University Press: *Christianity and the Encounter of the World's Religions* by Paul Tillich © (1963).

Cornell University Press: *Faith and Knowledge* by John Hick © 1957.

Crossroad Publishing Company: From *Meditations on the Sacraments* by Karl Rahner, copyright 1975 by Dimension Books, Inc. This edition and arrangement © 1977 by the Crossroad Publishing Co. From *Foundations of Christian Faith* by Karl Rahner, English translation copyright © 1978 by the Crossroad Publishing Company. Used by permission.

Doubleday and Co. Inc.: *The Roots of Religion in the Human Soul* by John Baillie © (1926); *Under Western Eyes* by Joseph Conrad © (1921); *Notes on Life and Letters* by Joseph Conrad © (1922); *Social Life in the Spiritual World* by Rufus Jones © (1923); *Collected Poems* by Rudyard Kipling; *The Open Door* by Helen Keller © (1957); *On Being a Christian* by Hans Küng © (1976); *Seven Pillars of Wisdom* by T. E. Lawrence © (1936); *The Shoes of Happiness* by Edwin Markham © (1922); *Contemplative Prayer* by Thomas Merton © (1971); *Contemplation in a World of Action* by Thomas Merton © (1971); *Christianity and the Religions of the World* by Albert Schweitzer © (1923).

E. P. Dutton and Co. Inc.: *The Thread of God* by Arthur Christopher Benson copyright 1907.

William B. Eerdmans Publishing Co.: *The Silence of God* by Helmut Thielicke © (1962).

Epworth Press, London: *The Living God of Nowhere and Nothing* by Nels Ferre © (1966).

Fortress Press: Reprinted from *Life Can Begin Again* by Helmut Thielicke, copyright 1963; *How to Believe Again* by Helmut Thielicke, copyright 1972, by permission of Fortress Press.

Harcourt Brace Jovanovich, Inc.: *Till We Have Faces* by C. S. Lewis © (1952); *No Man Is an Island* by Thomas Merton © (1955); *The Conduct of Life* by Lewis Mumford © (1951); *Flight to Arras* by Antoine de Saint-Exupéry © (1943); *The Little Prince* by Antoine de Saint-Exupéry.

Hollis & Carter, London: *Collected Poems* by Alice Meynell copyright 1947.

Holt, Rinehart & Winston: *The Two Sources of Morality and Religion* by Henri Bergson © 1935; *The Resources of Religion* by Georgia Harkness ©. 1936; *The Presidential Papers* by

Norman Mailer © 1963; *Life, Mind and Spirit* by Conway Lloyd Morgan © 1926; *The Star of Redemption* by Franz Rosenzweig, translated by William W. Hallo © 1970.

Horizon Press: Reprinted from *Hasidism and Modern Man* by Martin Buber, copyright 1958, by permission of the publisher, Horizon Press, New York.

Judson Press: *God's Revolution and Man's Responsibility* by Harvey Cox © (1965). Used by permission of Judson Press.

Alfred Knopf, Inc.: *The Fall* by Albert Camus © (1958); *The Myth of Sisyphus and Other Essays* by Albert Camus © (1955); *The Plague* by Albert Camus © (1948); *Joseph and His Brothers* by Thomas Mann, translated by H. T. Lowe-Porter © (1943); *Dr. Faustus* by Thomas Mann, translated by H. T. Lowe-Porter © (1948); *Essays and Soliloquies* by Miguel de Unamuno, translated by J. E. Crawford Flitch.

Longman Group Limited, London: *Personal Religion and the Life of Devotion* by William R. Inge © (1924); *Freedom, Love and Truth* by William R. Inge © (1936); *Outspoken Essays* by William R. Inge © (1921); *Things Old and New* by William R. Inge © (1933); *God and the Astronomers* by William R. Inge © (1934); *The Mount of Purification* by Evelyn Underhill © (1946); *The Fruits of the Spirit* by Evelyn Underhill © (1952).

Macmillan Publishing Company: *Letters and Papers from Prison* by Dietrich Bonhoeffer, rev. enlarged ed., Copyright © 1972; Copyright © 1953, 1967, 1971 by SCM Press Ltd.; *Ethics* by Dietrich Bonhoeffer, Copyright 1955 by Macmillan Publishing Company, © SCM Press Ltd., 1955; *Between Man and God* by Martin Buber, Copyright 1947; *Dream and Reality* by Nikolai Berdyaev, Copyright 1950, renewed 1978 by Geoffrey Bles, Ltd.; "The Song of Honour" from *Poems of Ralph Hodg-*

Open Court Publishing Co.: Reprinted from *The Logic of Perfection and Other Essays in Neoclassical Metaphysics* by Charles Hartshorne, by permission of the Open Court Publishing Company, La Salle, Ill. © 1962; reprinted from *The Point of View* by Paul Carus © 1927.

Paulist Press: Reprinted from Abraham Isaac Kook—*The Lights of Penitence, Lights of Holiness, The Moral Principles, Essays, Letters and Poems,* translated by Ben Zion Bokser, Copyright © 1978 by Ben Zion Bokser. Used by permission of Paulist Press.

Penguin Books, Ltd.: *Christianity and the Social Order* by William Temple, Penguin Special, Copyright 1942 by William Temple.

Philosophic Library, Inc.: *Religion of Tomorrow* by John Elof Boodin © 1943; *The Word of God and the Word of Man* by Karl Barth © 1949; *Dogmatics in Outline* by Karl Barth © 1949; *Hasidism* by Martin Buber © 1948; *The Perennial Scope of Philosophy* by Karl Jaspers © 1949; *Words of Faith* by François Mauriac © 1955; *Perplexities and Paradoxes* by Miguel de Unamuno © 1945; *Intellectual Foundation of Faith* by Henry Nelson Wieman © 1961.

Princeton University Press: Diasetz T. Suzuki, *Zen and Japanese Culture,* Bollingen Series 64. Copyright © 1959 by Princeton University Press. Excerpt reprinted by permission of Princeton University Press.

Fleming H. Revell Company: *Christianity and Progress* by Harry Emerson Fosdick © 1922; *Sermons* by George Herbert Morrison © 1929.

Routledge & Kegan Paul Ltd., London: *Two Types of Faith* by Martin Buber © 1951; *Man in the Modern Age* by Karl Jaspers © 1951; *Answer to Job* by Carl Jung © 1954; *Notebooks* by Simone Weil © 1956; *Waiting for God* by Simone Weil © 1951.

Schocken Books, Inc.: *Israel and the World* by Martin Buber, Copyright © 1948 by Schocken Books, Inc.; *On Judaism* by Martin Buber Copyright © 1967 by Schocken Books, Inc.; *Parables* by Franz Kafka, Copyright © 1971 by Schocken Books, Inc.

Charles Scribner's Sons: William Adams Brown, *The Life of Prayer in a World of Science* © 1927; William Adams Brown, *Beliefs That Matter* © 1928; William Adams Brown, *God at Work* © 1933; Emil Brunner, *Our Faith* © 1936; Emil Brunner, *The Theology of Crisis* © 1929; Emil Brunner, *The Word and the World* © 1931; Emil Brunner, *Man in Revolt* © 1939; John Baillie, *The Interpretation of Religion* © 1928; John Baillie, *Our Knowledge of God* © 1939; Martin Buber, *Good and Evil* © 1953; Martin Buber, *I and Thou* © 1958; Nicholas Berdyaev, *The Meaning of History* © 1936; Nicholas Berdyaev, *The Destiny of Man* © 1937; Nicholas Berdyaev, *Freedom and Spirit* © 1935; Nicholas Berdyaev, *Solitude and Society* © 1938; Henry Sloane Coffin, *Joy in Believing* © 1956; Henry Sloane Coffin, *The Meaning of the Cross* © 1931; William R. Inge, *Faith and Its Psychology* © 1910; Jacques Maritain, *The Range of Reason* © 1952; Jacques Maritain, *Freedom in the Modern World* © 1936; Jacques Maritain, *Ransoming the Time* © 1941; Jacques Maritain, *The Degrees of Knowledge* © 1959; Jacques Maritain, *True Humanism* © 1938; Reinhold Niebuhr, *The Nature and Destiny of Man* © 1941; Reinhold Niebuhr, *Discerning the Signs of the Times* © 1946; Reinhold Niebuhr, *Beyond Tragedy* © 1937; James A. Pike, *Beyond Anxiety* © 1953; Josiah Royce, *Sources of Religious Insight* © 1914; George Santayana, *The Life of Reason* © 1922; George Santayana, *Reason in Religion* © 1926; George Santayana, *Soliloquies in England* © 1923; Paul Tillich, *The New Being* © 1955; Paul Tillich, *The Shaking of the Foundations* © 1948; Henry Van Dyke, *The Builders* © 1897.

Seabury Press, Inc.: From *He Who Lets Us Be* by Geddes MacGregor, Copyright © 1975 by

Seabury Press, Inc. Used by permission of the publisher.

Simon & Schuster, Inc.: *Peace of Mind* by Joshua Loth Liebman © 1948.

Stanford University Press: *Exploration into God* by John A. T. Robinson © 1967.

Taplinger Publishing Company, Inc.: From *Reality and Man: An Essay in the Metaphysics of Human Nature* by S. L. Frank, translated by Natalie Duddington (Taplinger Publishing Co., Inc. 1966). Copyright © 1965 by Tatiana Frank. Reprinted by permission.

University of Chicago Press: Reprinted from *Systematic Theology* by Paul Tillich by permission of the University of Chicago Press © 1951; reprinted from *Biblical Religion and the Search for Ultimate Reality* by Paul Tillich by permission of the University of Chicago Press © 1952.

Westminster Press: *The Christian Doctrine of God* by Emil Brunner © 1950; *Truth as Encounter* by Emil Brunner © 1964; *Eternal Hope* by Emil Brunner © 1954; *Revelation and Reason* by Emil Brunner © 1946; *The Divine-Human Encounter* by Emil Brunner © 1943; *Christian Freedom in a Permissive Society* by John A. T. Robinson © 1970.

Yale University Press: *The Meaning of God in Human Experience* by William E. Hocking © 1919; *The Courage to Be* by Paul Tillich © 1952.

YMCA Press: *The Meaning of the Creative Act* by Nicolai Berdyaev, Copyright 1955 by YMCA Press, Paris, France.

Introduction

Long before I became an inveterate collector of enduring sayings, aphorisms, and proverbs, the original meaning of the word *anthology* deeply engrossed me. Derived from the Greek *anthologia,* its etymological roots are *anthos,* which means "flower," and *logia* from the verb "gather." An anthologist in this sense visits many gardens, meadows, and vales throughout the world looking for *les fleurs justes.* The colors, shapes, and fragrance of these flowers have to be beautiful not only in themselves, but ideally blend with the other flowers collected and arranged into the final bouquet.

This anthology is my arrangement of some three thousand flowers which first bloomed in the spiritual gardens of those truly remarkable men and women whom I call, in one encompassing term, the God Seekers. From the dawn of mankind's religious awareness these undaunted souls have been willing to risk the disdain, the apathy, and often the scorn and opprobrium of their contemporaries to explore the meaning of earthly life vis-à-vis God.

I am quite aware that sometimes the bouquet tells a reader more about the anthologist's orientation, his likes and dislikes, and his critical peccadilloes than he realized or wished. However, in this anthology I will spare you the effort of speculating on the religious and philosophic premises that influenced my choice in picking one particular flower over another. By virtue of your taking the effort and interest to peruse this book you are entitled to know why the bouquet before you derives its particular shape and style.

For most of my life I permitted myself a grudging half-search for God without really wanting to come to grips with the awe-striking magnitude of his presence as the absolute core of my existence. The intense, egoistic clamor with which I sought to understand the world and its travails virtually precluded anything more than a *de facto* acknowledgment that I *might* possess a spiritual self.

In the back of my mind I kept telling myself that someday when I had put my materialistic accounts into order—well, yes, I would surely look into my soul, whatever or wherever that might be. I thought I was getting along well enough without trying to find the soul-nourishing peace that possibly lay dormant within me.

Then one evening in 1964, when I had gone to Hamburg to pursue some leads for a series of investigative articles, a young German baroness, Katherina von Kettlholdt, introduced me to the religious poetry of Rainer Maria Rilke. We were having dinner at a venerable rathskeller and somehow the conversation turned to literature in general and subsequently to poets who had influenced us. If I had read Rilke before, it had escaped me; but after that night, during which his extraordinary spiritual sensibility spoke directly to my heart, I began to read everything I could find by and about this exemplary God Seeker.

My theophanic encounter with Rilke's poem, "God Speaks to Everyone Just Before He Makes Him," became the seed that I would plant in fallow soil and nurture into what has become, I hope, a sturdy tree of spiritual awareness. When for the first time I read these lines,

> Do not let yourself be separated from Me
> The place is nearby that they call Life,

I became vividly aware of Rilke's rapport with the Oversoul of the Universe, the Creator whose essence is compassion and love for every single being He has ever created. Even as the poets who composed the immortal Psalms twenty-five hundred years ago, so in our time this poet, Rilke, felt the overwhelming power of God's voice speaking within his heart.

In the spiritual nexus between man's *I* and the eternal *Thou*, which Martin Buber explored so compellingly a few years later, Rilke seemed to urge me to understand one paramount truth: God without man loses *some* of His meaning; man without God is nothing more than a concatenation of fortuitous events transpiring in a random universe.

That night in Hamburg when I discovered Rilke's spiritual journey I also began to see my own "goals" for what they truly were—momentarily satisfying, but always goading me to strive for something bigger or better. More than I realized, I had been yearning to extricate myself from the engulfing materialistic *schema* that had pervaded my life. For no matter what I accomplished, the satisfaction was brief and quickly dissolved. While shivering in the icy shadow of my next goal and the next one, *ad infinitum*, I was always preparing myself to overcome the supposed adversary—life. Then suddenly, in the poet's lines, I saw the key that could unlock a portion of the lasting richness that life, no longer an enemy, could offer.

I asked myself why I had always evaded the day when I would truly acknowledge that I had a God-given soul. Was it perhaps because I could not reconcile a loving God with the totality of human suffering, or a compassionate God with one who could allow the Holocaust? Why, instead of exulting in the illimitable power and magnitude of God, the Ultimate Mystery, had I been running away as fast I could, trying in vain to overtake the shadow of my fear?

And yet even this preliminary intuition couldn't begin until my heart accepted, as Rilke's had, that even though I was only an infinitely minute entity within God's totality, nevertheless I was unique in his consciousness. If there had never been anyone exactly like me in all his created works, as indeed there will never be again after my role on earth has been played, there had to be a reason for my existence. And behind that reason, the cause itself was God's will. I did not tell myself this with hauteur or ego-driven pride, but simply in recognition of the gift of life that God vouchsafed to me. That moment of awareness marked the beginning of my personal search.

I recognize, however, that God may, and probably has, entered into this same unique nexus with every one of his created beings, not only his human children on this Ark adrift in the sea of eternity, but with each and every single being among the 500,000 other species of his creatures with which we share the earth.

If Saint Francis of Assisi could see the Divine Hand in the creation of the birds and beasts, whom he called his brothers and sisters, why could I not carry his understanding to its ultimate step—namely, that everything that God has ever created, in this and the countless other "worlds" in his cosmogony, is equally meaningful and precious to Him?

In Albert Einstein's words, God does not play dice with a universe so vast that it takes more than five million years for a beam of light traveling 186,300 miles a second to traverse even our small group of galaxies. Can we be certain at all that what we call the universe, which scientists hypothesize started some eighteen billion man-reckoned years ago, is anything more than a fragment in a multiverse, itself only an infinitesmal portion of God's magnitude?

In one of the most remarkable theological treatises ever written, "Apology for Raimond Sebond," Michel Eyquem de Montaigne posited an uncomplicated, natural way to approach God. In it he wrote:

Of all human and long-existent beliefs concerning religion, that one seems to me to be most probable and most justifiable which recognizes God as a power incomprehensible, source and preserver of all things; all goodness, all perfection, receiving and accepting in good part the honor and reverence which human beings render him under whatever form, under whatever name, and in whatever manner it may be.

Throughout this book I make reference to God as He or Him, but only because I am compelled to use the limiting, restricting tools of symbolic language when I write about the *Thou* of my existence. Clearly, God is infinitely beyond the genders to which He divided all living entities on this particular planet, and it would be equally futile to describe Him with the pronoun Her or with the even more vacuous nondescription of It.

The ancient Hebrews grappled with this problem, and because theirs, like their contemporary cultures throughout the world, was a male-dominated society, they could do no more than conceive of God as an all-powerful He. The enigma was never better encountered than in the third chapter of the Old Testament book of Exodus.

And Moses said unto God: "Behold, when I come unto the children of Israel, and shall say unto them: 'The God of your fathers hath sent me unto you'; and they shall say to me: 'What is His name?' what shall I say unto them?" And God said unto Moses: "I AM THAT I AM."

The Creator of the Universe is so far beyond the polarity of the male/female dichotomy, so far beyond such pronouns as Who or What, that we, even with the great gift of language, shall never come closer than the biblical description "I am that I am."

I gathered this collection of some three thousand passages, not only from the various holy scriptures of many peoples, races, and cultures, but also from the writings of hundreds of theologians, philosophers, poets, dramatists, and novelists, all men and women of deep religious sensibility, all in some way or another inspired by the preceding God Seekers and the divine *biblia* they had recorded.

It is my central premise that these men and women, whom I have called collectively "The God Seekers," were chosen by the Creator of the Universe to be the ambassadors of his plan for this world, our own small island in his cosmogonic ocean.

This thought was expressed with much eloquence and insight by Theodore Parker, the superb nineteenth-century New England Unitarian clergyman. A voluminous writer, a leading activist in antislavery agitation, a minister whose voice could not be silenced by the promise of material rewards, Parker made this sentient observation in his book, *Lessons in the World of Matter and the World of Men*:

Tell me of Moses, Isaiah, Confucius, Zoroaster, Buddha, Pythagoras, Jesus, Paul, Mohamet, Aquinas, Luther, and Calvin—a whole calendar of saints. I give God thanks for them, and bare my brow, and do them reverence, and sit down at their feet to learn what they have to offer. They are but leaves and fruit on the tree of humanity which still goes on leafing, flowering, fruiting with other Isaiahs and Christs, whereof there is no end.

I, too, thank God for all of the great religionists whom Parker called his "calendar of saints," and not only for them but for the entire array of God Seekers from Ikhnaton of ancient Egypt to Ralph Waldo Emerson and Parker himself a century ago; to such men in our time as Karl Rahner and Hans Küng; Paul Tillich and Emil Brunner; Martin Buber, Leo Baeck, Abraham Isaac Kook, and Abraham Joshua Heschel; to Sarvapelli Radhakrishnan, Rabindranath Tagore, and Kirpal Singh.

I have found life-nourishing inspiration and hope in their perennial quest for God, as well as in the words and deeds of such women throughout history as Julian of Norwich, Madame Guyon, and Glueckel of Hameln; and, in our time, Mary Baker Eddy, Georgia Harkness, Simone Weil, and Mother Theresa of Calcutta, for they all are, in the truest sense, God Seekers.

The quotations I have selected may suggest to some readers that I favor those theologians and religious philosophers who fall into the general classification of *mystics*. True, I have gone often to that deep well of spiritual wisdom, perhaps because it reflects my personal conviction that all striving to find God involves us in the Ultimate Mystery.

Until that day when we may possibly understand why God, whose universe is coexistent with himself, allows evil and suffering to prevail on his earth, we shall be involved in a mystery of unfathomable proportions. Even if we accept the notion that there is a divine reason that places worldly evil and suffering in its proper perspective, the mystery is no less powerful.

But are we not short-sighted if we limit ourselves to agonizing over the mystery of God's rationale for the negative aspects of human existence? As Fyodor Dostoevsky wrote in *A Raw Youth*, "What is mystery? Everything is mystery, dear. In all is God's mystery. In every tree, in every blade of grass that same mystery lies hid. Whether the tiny bird of the air is singing, or the stars in all their multitudes shine at night in heaven, the mystery is one, ever the same."

Meister Eckhart, the greatest of medieval mystics, clearly will appear to be one of my favorite sources. But whether this is because Eckhart's voluminous works give testimony to his extraordinary spiritual rapport with God or simply because for me he gets to the heart of religious truths only begs the question. I often turn to Eckhart and those he influenced, such as Johannes Denck, Johannes Tauler, Jacob Boehme, and Nicholas of Cusa because for me they transcend the narrow bounds of parochialism.

Sören Kierkegaard, on the other hand, did not accept the mystical insights of Eckhart or Boehme, but I have found his spiritual explorations to be so unforgettably cogent that his commentaries appear throughout this anthology. It does not distress me that Kierkegaard is called an existentialist; Pascal, a Jansenist; Emerson, a transcendentalist; or Madame Guyon, a quietist; although it may serve scholastics to put the various God Seekers into conveniently labeled cubby-holes, what I am looking for is their essential sameness.

When Jesus of Nazareth observed, "There are many mansions in my Father's house," was he not telling us that God's essential message is always the same, and that the diverse ways that mankind perceive it are not of ultimate importance?

It makes little difference to me that Eckhart was accused—even as he lay dying—of heresy by the hierarchy of the Roman Catholic Church in 1327, or that two years later the Church condemned much of what he had written. Nor does it matter much today, when the dust of history has settled, that the Orthodox coreligionists of Benedict Spinoza in Amsterdam excommunicated him because of his pantheistic philosophy, just as Eckhart had been excoriated some three hundred years before. The perennial truths which Spinoza and Eckhart each voiced—and which survive as strong as ever today—are all that need concern us about the bitter jurisdictional quarrels of their epochs.

Another master spirit I turn to time and time again is Martin Buber, for in his work

I see the flowering of that true ecumenical understanding drawing all of the great God Seekers together in a common bond. Who but Buber perceived that Meister Eckhart and the Baal Shem Tov, although separated by centuries of time, religious creeds, and traditions, were true brothers in spiritual perceptivity? Who more sensitively than Buber saw the essential kinship of Guatama Buddha, Lao-tse, and Jesus of Nazareth?

Any study of the God Seekers' diverse life stories will reveal that the majority of them did *not* achieve their ultimate serenity and peace without a great deal of conflict, intense self-examination, and, in the most literal sense of the phrase, soul-searching. One has only to read the *Confessions* of Saint Augustine, or to recall the life of Giovanni Francesco Bernardone, or to peruse Izaak Walton's sensitive biography of John Donne, to understand that for some periods of their lives they tried to evade the spiritual imperative welling up within themselves. Walton said of Donne, for example, "But God, who is able to prevail, wrestled with him, as the angel did with Jacob, and marked him for his own."

There is often doubt and vestiges of deep-ingrained guilt in the God Seekers' struggle with themselves. In the well-known autobiographical preface to his complete works, Martin Luther described such feelings with all the honesty and candor that personified his very existence:

For however irreproachably I lived as a monk, I felt myself in the presence of God to be a sinner with a most unquiet conscience, nor could I believe that I pleased him with my satisfactions. I did not love, indeed I hated this just God, if not with open blasphemy, at least with huge murmuring. . . .

God Seekers are often rejected and reviled by the majority of people to whom they wish to convey a message of salvation and self-fulfillment. The prophet Jeremiah was such a man, for the truths he uttered stirred up the guilt of a wayward nation. Like Hosea before him, when Jeremiah personified Israel as a fallen virgin who had faithlessly deserted Yahweh for the gaudy idols of Canaan, he became, in Isaiah's words, "despised, and forsaken of men."

It may well be that Jeremiah was the prototype that Isaiah had in his mind when, in the famous 53rd chapter of his Old Testament book, he described the suffering servant of God—the man of sorrows acquainted with grief. Yet, as Isaiah adds, the true prophet is not deterred by the revilement and calumny of the mob, even though "of the travail of his soul he shall see to the full, even My servant, who by his knowledge did justify the Righteous One to the many, and their iniquities he did bear."

A thorny dilemma presented itself when I encountered certain God Seekers who, in their various works, made some of the most sublime observations on the nature of God, but who were so poisoned with the prejudices of their ages or the narrowness of their creeds that they appear almost hypocritical in their quests. I resolved this when I realized that if I selected quotations for this anthology only from writers who were morally flawless, this would be a thin book indeed. The world has seen few God Seekers with the temperament of a Saint Francis of Assisi, a Benedict Spinoza, a Jalal-ud-din Rumi, not that they felt or claimed moral superiority over their fellow-men.

Thus, it is not for me to judge that Saint John Chrysostom was not a *bona fide* God Seeker because he went even beyond the prejudices of his time in the virulence of his anti-Semitism. This fourth-century founding father of the Greek Orthodox Church was so eloquent that soon after his death he became known as *chrysostomos*, literally "golden-mouthed." But for many centuries the Jews throughout Europe listened to the echo of three words that came from Saint John's golden tongue, "God hates you!"

Yet there are some beautifully perceptive passages in his sermons that showed facets of Chrysostom's spirituality that we cannot disregard and they are included in this volume. Chrysostom was not the first anti-Semite who, any more than Voltaire, could not cope with the reality that Jesus of Nazareth was born, lived, and died a Jew, and Chrysostom certainly will not be the last.

If the disease of anti-Semitism were to exclude a theologian from being represented in this volume, we would also not have any quotations from Saint Bernard of Clairvaux, a priest of no mean dimensions and a profound student of God's ruling ethical plan for the world. To be sure, anti-Semitism was a dominant mode of thought in Bernard's time, and thus he was only reiterating the feelings of the people around him. Yet Bernard's contemporary, Peter Abélard, to his lasting credit fought the prevailing notion of Jewish culpability for all the world's misfortunes. Nor have Christians been loath to attack fellow Christians when their beliefs were not congruent with each other's dogma. Consider such great theologians as Martin Luther, who wrote and preached against the forerunners of the Mennonites; and let us not forget that even the saintly Augustine riled against the Donatists, the Punic-speaking Christians of North Africa who did not want to follow the Latin rite of Rome.

It may be that for certain God Seekers the overwhelming need to establish rapport with God was actually accentuated by their acute awareness of the pettiness and prejudice that was destroying the equanimity of their lives. In the deepest recesses of their hearts, in the cavern of silence where the soul shines with an undimmed light, Chrysostom and Bernard of Clairvaux alike must have known that if they were truly to follow the precepts of Jesus of Nazareth they could not behold the mote in their fellowman's eyes and disregard the beam in their own. But we must recognize that even God Seekers of their considerable powers were still human, very human.

Each of the eight segments of this anthology deals with a major question that God Seekers have wrestled with from the earliest days, while striving to understand God's plan for this world. In selecting what I feel are the most relevant quotations that reinforce these dominant themes, I have tried to show that the God Seekers *collectively* are dealing with these basic questions.

To place this wide spectrum of quotations into a universal perspective, I have written a short essay to precede each of the sections. These essays represent my analysis of the God Seekers' concerted, perennial attempt to address such integral themes as God the Unknowable, God and the prevalence of evil on this earth, and God vis-à-vis the enigma of suffering.

One major thing I have learned in compiling this anthology is that the religious wisdom which has revealed itself during the past four or five thousand years is in the truest sense *ecumenical,* i.e., that it belongs to the whole world. When we examine those forces which threaten to literally destroy this earth—fear, greed, the love of power above any other emotion—we can only ponder whether the teaching of the Creator's plan by the God Seekers from every epoch, race, and creed will eventually prevail. Perhaps it is already too late and we have doomed ourselves as a species because we still persist in bowing down to the corrosive, temporal acquisitions of our short sojourn on this earth.

We, and we alone, must shoulder the blame if some day all that remains in this world are some gigantic atomic mushroom clouds, because we relegated the God Seekers and their messages to a tiny segment of our lives. Why are we so contemptuous of divine wisdom that we have not even given lip service to God's message, delivered through the prophet Micah twenty-five hundred years ago: "And they shall beat their swords into ploughshares, and their spears into pruning-hooks; nation shall not lift up sword against nation, neither shall they learn war any more (Micah 4:3).

It is estimated that in the 1980s the nations of the world will spend the equivalent of nearly two trillion dollars on military defenses, fabricating an ever-increasing number of sophisticated weapons to mete out wholesale death. Nearly half of that enormous sum will be spent by the United States and the Soviet Union alone. Humanity quivers with a fear beyond naming as each of these world powers, like two paranoid giants glowering ominously, seems to be daring the other to knock the nuclear chip off his shoulder.

My reading of the great thoughts of the God Seekers has led me to believe that each person in the world discovers God's presence within his or her heart during some moment of life. It may come only at that last moment before God gathers back our portion of the Oversoul into the Eternal Now; but, if we choose, we can find Him during the active days of our lifetime.

However God alerts us to his presence, whether through a poet such as Rilke, as in my case, or from reading the various divine scriptures in which He has revealed himself to all races, is not a paramount concern. When a starving child in the fetid slums of Calcutta lifts his eyes to the skies and asks "Why?" God is there and will answer that call in his inscrutable way. Even if we choose to obliterate God's dwelling within us by our myopic vision of survival in a transitory world, we cannot escape his presence; the choice was his, not ours.

Harry Emerson Fosdick recalls a story that took place when Helen Keller was a young girl. Phillips Brooks, one of the most eloquent ministers of nineteenth-century America, was enlisted to teach little Helen something about God. With Annie Sullivan interpreting the minister's spirited discourse, Dr. Brooks did his best to describe the inner presence of the unseen Spirit. Suddenly the youngster signaled back that she had always known there was a God, but had not before known his name.

Helen Keller, of course, went on to overcome the virtually insuperable handicaps with which she had been born, and in her many books and lectures she demonstrated the faith in God's will that her entire life exemplified. Whenever I begin to feel sorry for myself because my day or week hasn't gone well, I think of Helen Keller or I go to a nearby V.A. hospital and talk with a quadraplegic patient whose life was shattered on Iwo Jima; and then I am ashamed of complaining, even momentarily, about my petty discomfitures.

Finally, my reading of the God Seekers' discoveries has led me to believe that the Master of the Universe directs himself to each of his human children from the fountainhead of love and compassion that is his essence. And even when we choose to reject that portion of the eternal love and mercy He has placed within us, it still remains in our soul and will return in its pristine form to the Oversoul of all creation.

I presume that when you read this anthology certain of the God Seekers will speak out to you more strongly than others; you may even want to earmark your favorite quotations to buttress your preferences. This would be gratifying to me, for it would mark the beginning of your own personal anthology, one in which you will explore the meaning of *your* life vis-à-vis God. Although it would be patently thrasonical of me to suggest that I have represented every significant religious figure from the dawn of mankind's history, I have endeavored to provide a broad overview of the God Seekers' thoughts.

Even though this volume makes no pretense of being a scholarly tome, since there are neither footnotes nor an annotated bibliography, the quotations *per se* will lead you to many books, since each passage is identified by the volume in which it originally appeared. All but a few of these books are available at public libraries in our larger cities, and certainly at most university libraries.

For example, if you are making your first discovery of Miguel de Unamuno through the passages I have chosen and want to examine this little-known but truly great Spanish moral philosopher more deeply, you will want to read his book *The Tragic Sense of Life* in its entirety. It is not unlikely that you will choose for your personal anthology some portions that I may have overlooked.

The noted English science-fiction writer, Arthur C. Clarke, wrote a short story in 1952 which he called "The Nine Billion Names of God." This ingenious tale involves some computer experts who undertake an assignment in a Tibetan lamasery, a place not unlike Shangri-La. Their task is to verify that all the possible permutations of letters churned out by gigantic computers in the acres of electronic typewritten pages will include all the names of God.

In a larger sense, every human being who has ever lived on this earth in the past three to four million years has sought to define God, the Mystery of Mysteries. And even if we knew all of the nine billion names, or ninety billion, by which mankind has sought to define our Creator we still would not understand a quintillionth of a fraction of God's magnitude.

The miracle of the mystery is that this illimitable Force is also the *Thou* of our lives, and even though his form of love, mercy, and justice far transcends our limited human definitions, these three indispensable attributes can permeate our lives, if we allow them.

This present world has more than its share of those who deny God, who relegate him to the ash heap of man's brief sojourn on this earth, who even would point their laser guns into the heavens and "kill" God if they could. If they prevail, this earth will become a smouldering nuclear wastebin swallowed into some black hole of cosmic history.

But it doesn't have to end like this, for God has sent us a perfect plan for joyous survival. His emissaries, the God Seekers, in concert have brought us his ethical plan for the world. To their glory, they reverently faced the Ultimate Mystery and did not retreat.

In a particularly beautiful passage from his introspective *Journal Intime,* the Swiss philosopher and poet Henri Frédéric Amiel captured the essence of what I've tried to say in these introductory pages, if not indeed in this entire anthology:

Let mystery have its place in you; do not be always turning up your whole ploughshare of self-examination, but leave a little fallow corner in your heart ready for any seed the wind may bring, and reserve a nook of shadow for the passing bird; keep a place in your heart for the unexpected guest, an altar for the unknown God.

I · What Could God Be

That Being, whose will is his deed, whose principle of action is in himself,—that Being, in a word, whatever it may be, that gives motion to all parts of the universe, and governs all things, I call God.

JEAN JACQUES ROUSSEAU

IN THE FIRST SECTION of this collection of the great thoughts of the God Seekers, we consider some of the ways that men and women have tried to define God, attempting with words to encounter the undefinable. God's human children have been granted or endowed with certain ways of seeking him (mainly through the use of language, art, and music) because He willed it thus. Perhaps this is his way of witnessing and becoming involved in the unfolding of that brief moment in the time and place He has allotted us in his universe. For God *is* involved in the existence of every single one of his creations, each of whom inalienably seeks his or her Creator in the unique way He has prescribed. Perhaps for them there could be no contentment unless they, at least, strove to symbolize God in terms compatible with their fragile lives on earth. Yet, as Montaigne so wisely observed, it is for God alone to know himself and to interpret his works. When we say that God is angry with us, individually or collectively, or that God loves us, Montaigne reminds us that these are essentially human passions and emotions that could not possibly dwell in God in the same form as in us.

Paul Tillich reiterates Montaigne's admonition when he tells us that we cannot speak of God as "living" in the same sense that we define life on earth, and that although it is fitting to aspire to a communion with the "living God," as our God Seekers have throughout human history, we must realize that we are always addressing God in symbolic terms. But Tillich kindly adds, "Yet every true symbol participates in the reality it symbolises."

A central theme of the God Seekers is that *everything* that exists (and has ever existed or will in the future exist) is a "thought" of the Creator. Theodore Parker said that whether we study the movements of the solar system, the composition of a grain of phosphorus in the human brain, or the trace of an atom in a drop of ether, we are always studying the "thought" of the Infinite Creator.

As Parker's friend and contemporary Ralph Waldo Emerson put it, "It must be that when God speaketh he should communicate, not one thing, but all things; should fill the world with his voice, should scatter forth light, nature, time, souls. . . ."

In the late Bishop Fulton J. Sheen's analogy of God as the architect of the universe, God possesses the archetypal concept of every "flower, bird, tree, springtime and melody."

Another important leitmotiv in this section concerns God's ubiquity. Martin Luther wrote:

God is not confined to any place, nor is He excluded from any. He is in all places, nay even in the meanest creatures, such as a leaf or a blade of grass, and yet he is nowhere. Nowhere? Understand me, nowhere palpably or within limits. But He is in all places, for He creates, moves and upholds all things.

That God is nearer to us than we can ever realize is another theme explored in this section. Swami Vivekenanda perceived this: "It is the God within your own self that is impelling you to seek Him. . . ." Vivekananda saw that we too often seek God exclusively in shrines, temples, or churches, as if He would only commune with us in sacerdotal surroundings. Yet, in this Indian sage's view, we have merely to commune with our own souls to find that the Creator whom we seek, to whom we weep and pray in mosques, synagogues, and chapels, "is the nearest of the near, in your own Self, the reality of your life, body and soul."

Is this not the same message that God sent through the prophet Jeremiah: "I am a God who is near, and not a God afar off"? Or that Meister Eckhart envisioned when he wrote that to know and seek the nearness of God's kingdom is merely to echo the patriarch Jacob's discovery: "God is in this place and I did not know it"?

The God Seekers have constantly sought to define the one Creator, from the days of Ikhnaton in ancient Egypt to the present time, and surely will continue to do so as long as men and women dwell on this earth. In the depths of our hearts we know that the Creator is the central source of our existence, whether we call him God, Adonai, Jahweh, Brahma, or Allah. We must never lose sight that these are merely human symbols, sacred, to be sure, in the religious traditions of the varied nations and cultures, all seeking to define the undefinable, to name the unnamable. Was He not the same Master of the Universe to the Zoroastrians who called him Ahura Mazda, or the Incas who called him Pachacamak, or the Babylonians who called him Anshar?

Whether He is called Kuloscap by the Algonquin Indians or The Way by the followers of Lao-tse, the Creator is beyond all symbolic attempts to name and define him. Yet God does not renounce whatever name we seek him by, for He alone knows the meaning of the quest and the eventual ending of all humankind's search for him. An unnamed poet in ancient India summarized this search in the Upanishads: "Within the city of Brahman, which is the body, there is the heart, and within the heart there is a little house. This house has the shape of a lotus, and within it dwells that which is to be sought, inquired about, and realized."

· TRYING TO DEFINE GOD ·

He, who is called Brahma or the Most High; who is the Supreme Spirit Who permeates the whole universe; Who is a true personification of Existence, Consciousness, and Bliss; Whose nature, attributes, and characteristics are Holy; Who is Omniscient, Infinite, Just and Merciful; Who is the Author of the universe, sustains and dissolves it; Who awards all souls the fruits of their deeds in strict accordance with the requirements of absolute justice and is possessed of the like attributes—even Him I believe to be the great God.

SWAMI DAYANANDA SARASWATI (1824–1883)
The Light of Truth

Yea, it is a Unity which is the unifying source of all unity and a Super-Essential Essence, a Mind beyond the reach of mind and a Word beyond utterance, eluding Discourse, Intuition, Name, and every kind of being.

DIONYSIUS THE AREOPAGITE (5th century)
The Celestial Hierarchy

God is incorporeal, divine, supreme, infinite, Mind, Spirit, Soul, Principle, Life, Truth, Love.

MARY BAKER EDDY (1821–1910)
Science and Health

Call it Nature, Fate, Fortune; all these are names of the one and selfsame God.

LUCIUS ANNAEUS SENECA (4 B.C.–A.D. 65)
De Beneficiis IV

Who is supreme in heaven? Thou alone art supreme. Who is supreme on earth? Thou alone art supreme. Thy mighty word createth right and ordaineth justice for mankind, and thy powerful ordinance reacheth unto the uttermost parts of heaven and earth.

ANONYMOUS
A Sumerian Prayer to the Moon-God

One God—hidden in all creatures,
Pervading all, Inner Self of all things,
Surveying all deeds, abiding in all creatures,
Witness, thinker, Alone, unqualified.

The Upanishads

I am the father of this world, the mother, the guardian, the father's father; I am the end of knowledge, the purifier, the sacred syllable, the hymn, the chant, the sacred sentence.

I am the way, the supporter, the lord, the witness, the home, the refuge, the beloved; the forthcoming and withdrawing, the place, the treasure, the everlasting seed.

I am equal toward all beings; nor is any hatred or favored of Me; but they who love Me with dear love, they are in Me and I in them.   *The Bhagavad Gita*

God is day and night, winter and summer, war and peace, satiety and hunger; but He takes various shapes, just as fire, when it is mingled with different incenses, is named according to the savour of each.

HERACLITUS (540?–480 B.C.)
Fragments

We conceive God first of all as the perfect totality of act, the plenitude of being itself. It follows from this concept that He is one, that a term opposite to Him cannot be imagined.

GIOVANNI PICO DELLA MIRANDOLA
(1463–1494)
On Being and One

They call Him Indra, Mitra, Varuna and Agni. To what is One, the poets give many a name.   *The Rig-Veda*

But what things dost thou now
Looking Godward, to cry
'I am I, thou are thou,

I am low, thou art high'?
I am thou, whom thou seekest to find him;
    find thou but thyself,
thou art I.
> ALGERNON CHARLES SWINBURNE (1837–1909)
> *Hertha*

He is the first and the last; the Seen and
Hidden; and He knoweth all things!
> *The Koran*

God is himself in no interval nor extension
of place, but in his immutable, pre-eminent
all-possibility is both within everything, because all things are in him, and without
everything because he transcends all things.
> SAINT AUGUSTINE (354–430)
> *On the Trinity*

Our Lord God is an endless being without
changing, almighty without failing, sovereign
wisdom, light, soothness without error or
darkness; sovereign goodness, love, peace,
and sweetness.
> WALTER HILTON (1340–1396)
> *The Song of Angels*

You are the dark blue butterfly,
You are the green parrot with red eyes,
You are the thunder-cloud, the seasons, the
    seas.
You are without beginning,
You pervade all things,
and from you all beings were born.
> *The Upanishads*

The Eternal Spring, whence streaming
    bounty flows;
The Eternal Light! whence every radiance
    glows;
The Eternal Height of indetermin'd space!
The Eternal Depth of condescending grace!
Supreme! and Midst! and Principle! and
    End!
The Eternal Father! and the Eternal Friend!

The Eternal Love! who bounds in ev'ry
    breast;
The Eternal Bliss! whence ev'ry creature's
    bless'd.
> HENRY BROOKE (1703–1783)
> *Universal Beauty*

God is a light that is never darkened, an
unwearied life that cannot die; a fountain always flowing; a garden of life; a seminary of
wisdom; a radical beginning of all goodness.
> FRANCIS QUARLES (1592–1644)
> *Emblems*

I am Alpha and Omega, the beginning and
the end, the first and the last.
> *The New Testament*
> *Revelation 22:13*

See, I am God. See, I am in all things. See,
I do all things. See, I never lift my hands off
my works, nor ever shall, without end. See, I
lead all things to the end that I ordain it to,
from without-beginning, by the same might,
wisdom and love that I made it with. How
should anything be amiss?
> JULIAN OF NORWICH (1343–1416)
> *Revelations of Divine Love*

The seed of all born beings likewise am I,
O Arjuna; there is naught that can be in existence, moving or unmoving, without Me.
> *The Bhagavad Gita*

Since the nature of the One produces all
things, it is none of them. It is not a thing or
quality or quantity or intellect or soul; It is
not in motion or at rest, in place or in time,
but exists in Itself, a unique Form; or rather
It is formless, existing before all form, before
motion, before rest; for these belong to being
and make it multiple.
> PLOTINUS (205–270)
> *Enneads*

All who have any education know that God
has no right hand nor left; that He is not
moved nor at rest, nor in a particular place,

but that He is absolutely infinite and contains in Himself all perfections.

> BENEDICT SPINOZA (1632–1677)
> *Theologico-Political Treatise*

By the nature of God I understand a Substance infinite, independent, all-knowing, all-powerful, and by which I myself and every other thing that exists were created.

> RENÉ DESCARTES (1596–1650)
> *Meditations*

There is underlying all change a Living Power that is changeless, that holds all together. That informing Power or Spirit is God. He alone is. This power is purely benevolent. God is Life, Truth, Light; He is Love. He is the Supreme Good.

> MOHANDAS K. GANDHI (1869–1948)
> *Autobiography*

The Creator took thought and discerned that, out of the things that are by nature visible, no work destitute of reason could be made so fair as that which possessed reason. He also saw that reason could not dwell in anything devoid of Soul. This being his thought he put Spirit in Soul and Soul in Body, that he might be the maker of the fairest and best of works. Hence we shall probably be safe in affirming that the universe is a living creature endowed with Soul and Spirit by the providence of God.

> PLATO (427–347 B.C.)
> *Timaeus*

But what is God? The universal Intelligence. What is God? did I say? All that you see and all that you cannot see. His greatness exceeds the bounds of thought. He is all in all, He is at once within and without His Works. In us the better part is spirit, in Him there is nothing but spirit.

> LUCIUS ANNAEUS SENECA (4 B.C.–A.D. 65)
> *The End of Being*

Immortal! Ages past, yet nothing gone!
Morn without eve! A race without a goal!
Unshorten'd by progression infinite!
Futurity forever future! Life
Beginning still, where computation ends!
'Tis the description of a Deity!

> EDWARD YOUNG (1683–1765)
> *Night Thoughts*

God is mightiest in power, fairest in beauty, immortal in existence, supreme in virtue; therefore, being invisible to every mortal nature, he is seen through his works themselves.

> ARISTOTLE (384–322 B.C.)
> *De Mundo*

The Being who, to me, is the real God is the one who created this majestic universe and rules it. He is the only originator, the only originator of thoughts; thoughts suggested from within, not from without. The originator of colors and all their possible combinations; of forces and the laws that govern them; of forms and shapes of all forms—man has never invented a new one. He is the only originator. He made the materials of all things; he made the laws by which, and by which only, man may combine them into the machines and other things which outside influences suggest to him. He made character—man can portray it but not "create" it, for He is the only creator. He is the perfect artisan, the perfect artist.

> MARK TWAIN (1835–1910)
> *Autobiography*

God is an Unutterable Sigh in the Human Heart, said the old German mystic.

> HAVELOCK ELLIS (1859–1939)
> *Impressions and Comments*

There is but one God. He is all that is.
He is the Creator of all things and He is all-pervasive.
He is without fear and without enmity.
He is timeless, unborn and self-existent.
He is the Enlightener
And can be realised by grace of Himself alone.

He was in the beginning; He was in all ages.
The True One is, was, O Nanak, and shall
  forever be.
                    GURU NANAK (1469–1539)
                    Sikh Morning Prayer

God's deity is no prison in which he can
exist only in and for Himself. It is rather His
freedom to be in and for Himself but also
with and for us, to assert but also to sacrifice
Himself, to be wholly exalted but also completely humble, not only almighty but almighty mercy, not only Lord but servant, not
only judge but also Himself the judged, not
only man's eternal king but also his brother
in time. And all that, without in the slightest
forfeiting his deity!
                    KARL BARTH (1886–1968)
                    The Humanity of God

The world in all its detail, from the mechanical movement of what we call the atom
of matter to the free-movement of thought
in the human-ego is the self-revelation of the
"Great I am."
                    MAHOMED IQBAL (1873–1938)
                    Reconstruction

It is unseen, unrelated, inconceivable, un-
inferable, unimaginable, indescribable. It is
the essence of the one self-cognition common
to all states of consciousness. All phenomena
cease in it. It is peace, it is bliss, it is nondual-
ity.   *The Upanishads*

Than whom there is naught else higher,
than whom there is naught smaller, naught
greater, One stands like a tree established in
heaven; by Him, the Person, is the whole universe filled.   *The Upanishads*

God is not a what but a that.
                    JOHANNES SCOTUS ERIUGENA (815–877)
                    On the Division of Nature

The end of being is to find out God!
And what is God? A vast almighty Power
Great and unlimited, whose potent will

Brings to achievement whatso'er He
  please.
He is all mind. His being infinite—
All that we see and all that we do not see.
                    LUCIUS ANNAEUS SENECA (4 B.C.–A.D. 65)
                    The End of Being

Everything is in thee, and Thou art
  everything.
Thou fillest everything and dost encompass
  it.
When everything was created, Thou wast
  everything,
Before everything was created, Thou wast
  everything.
                    The Unity Hymn (13th century)

I speak of God as of the Fountain-Head
from whence come one after the other,
through an effect of His liberty, the "cur-
rents" or "impulses" each one of which will
form a world.
                    HENRI BERGSON (1859–1941)
                    Letters

There is but one Reality—like a brimming
ocean in which all appearances are dissolved.
It is changeless, formless and absolute. How
can it be divided?   SHANKARA (700–750)
                    Viveka Chudamani

Fire in his head, his eyes the sun and the
moon, his speech the Vedas disclosed, the
wind his breath, his heart the universe; from
his feet came the earth; he is indeed the inner
Self of all things.   *The Upanishads*

The great central fact of the universe is
that spirit of infinite life and power that is
back of it all, that manifests itself in and
through all. This spirit of infinite life and
power that is back of all is what I call God.
                    WILLIAM JAMES (1842–1910)
                    The Varieties of Religious Experience

He is a Being who, though the Highest, yet
in the work of creation, conservation, government, retribution, makes Himself, as it

were, the minister and servant of all; who, though inhabiting eternity, allows Himself to take an interest, and to have sympathy, in the matters of time and space.

JOHN CARDINAL NEWMAN (1801–1890)
Parochial and Plain Sermons

The Supreme is everywhere and yet nowhere. He is everywhere in entirety; He is, at once, that everywhere and everywise; He is not in the everywhere but is the everywhere as well as the giver to the rest of things of their being in that everywhere.

PLOTINUS (204–269)
Free Will and the Will of One

Religion is the faith that God is the ultimate Personal Creator and Sustainer of all values, and that human beings realize the utmost in value when they join him, conscientiously and joyously, in the creation of value.

PETER A. BERTOCCI (1910–)
Introduction to the Philosophy of Religion

God is not a transcendent being living in a distant heaven whence from time to time he intervenes in the affairs of the earth. He is an ever-present spirit guiding all that happens to a wise and holy end.

DAVID HUME (1711–1776)
Dialogues Concerning Natural Religion

Moses conceived the Deity as a Being who has always existed, does exist, and always will exist, and he therefore called him Jehovah, which in Hebrew signifies these three phases.

BENEDICT SPINOZA (1632–1677)
Theologico-Political Treatise

God cannot prove His existence in any other sense than He can swear; He has nothing higher to swear by.

SÖREN KIERKEGAARD (1813–1855)
Journals

This is the great Atman, the Spirit never born, the consciousness of life. He dwells in our own hearts, as ruler of all, master of all,

lord of all. His greatness becomes not greater by good actions nor less great by evil actions. He is the Lord supreme, sovereign and protector of all beings, the bridge that keeps the worlds apart that they fall not into confusion.

The Upanishads

The principle of life is in God; for energy of mind doth constitute life, and God is this energy. His joy is in the exercise of His essential energy. He is eternal and perfect, without parts and passions, indivisible and unchanging.

ARISTOTLE (384–322 B.C.)
Metaphysics

Thou didst create the earth, Thou didst make the sky and the celestial river Hep; Thou didst fashion the great deep and give life to all that therein is. Thou hast knit together the mountains. Thou hast made mankind and the beasts of the field to come into being.

Egyptian Hymn to Ra (1580–1350 B.C.)
The Book of the Dead

That which cannot be expressed by words, but through which all expression cometh, this know thou to be Brahma. That which cannot be thought by the mind, but by which all thinking cometh, this know thou as Brahma. That which cannot be seen by the eye but by which the eye beholdeth, is Brahma.

The Upanishads

God, called the One, is the creator of everything, and he is everything. This name of God signifies the One that is self-existing, requiring no other cause for his existence. And if it be considered that from an arithmetical point of view one is the beginning of all numbers, and that all of them are composed of units, it will be found that this is the One which at the same time is the whole.

RABBI BEN EZRA (1092–1167)
Commentaries

I do dimly perceive that while everything around me is ever-changing, ever-dying, there is underlying all that change a living power that is changeless, that holds together, that creates, dissolves, and re-creates. That informing power or spirit is God. And since nothing else I see merely through my senses can or will persist, He alone is.

MOHANDAS K. GANDHI (1869–1948)
Young India

God is the fact of the fact, the life of the life, the soul of the soul, the incomprehensible, the sum of all contradictions, the unit of diversity. He who knows him, knows him not; he who is without him, is full of him.

God cannot be seen; but by him all seeing comes. He cannot be heard; yet by him all hearing comes. Turn your back upon him, then turn your back upon gravity, upon air, upon light.

He is not a being, yet apart from him there is no being—there is no apart from him.

JOHN BURROUGHS (1837–1921)
Accepting the Universe

I am the Eye with which the universe
Beholds itself and knows itself divine.

PERCY BYSSHE SHELLEY (1792–1822)
Hymn of Apollo

We say that God is a living being, eternal, most good, so that life and duration continuous and eternal belong to God; for this IS God.   ARISTOTLE (384–322 B.C.)
Metaphysics

God is the Eternal Substance, and is known as such; God is also the Eternal Order of things: but God is That Which does whatever Substance is found to do.

WILLIAM ERNEST HOCKING (1873–1966)
The Meaning of God in Human Experience

God is the soul of the cosmos, the spiritual field in which all things move and which suffuses all things and gives order, meaning and beauty to the world so far as it is responsive.

We perceive his genius throughout the levels of patterns in nature—atom, molecule, crystal, cell, plant, animal, man—working with the material of electrons or whatever is the ultimate material, subliming it into more and more spiritual structure.

JOHN ELOF BOODIN (1869–1950)
God: A Cosmic Philosophy of Religion

God is not Existent in any ordinary sense, but in a simple and undefinable manner embraces and anticipates all existence in Himself. Hence He is called "King of the Ages," because in Him and around Him all Being is and subsists, and He neither was, nor will be, nor hath entered the life-process, nor is doing so, nor ever will, or rather He doth not even exist, but is the Essence of existence in things that exist; and not only the things that exist but also their very existence comes from Him that Is before the ages. For He Himself is the Eternity of the ages and subsists before the ages.

DIONYSIUS THE AREOPAGITE (5th century)
On the Divine Names and the Mystical Theology

All that exists, exists only by the communication of God's infinite being. All that has intelligence, has it only by derivation from His sovereign reason; and all that acts, acts only from the impulse of His supreme activity. It is He who does all in all; it is He who, at each instant of our life, is the beating of our heart, the movement of our limbs, the light of our eyes, the intelligence of our spirit, the soul of our soul.

FRANÇOIS FÉNELON (1651–1715)
Maximes des Saints

Our God, if we have a God, must be one that the soul of man can worship and fix his trust upon in time of need, and must be one that will not affront the thought of scientist or philosopher. Such a God must be an indwelling power that is manifest in human life, in physical things, in natural law, in creative energy. Such a God must be something more than a sum of all the universe; for it is the "something more" that makes him God.

GEORGIA HARKNESS (1891–1974)
Conflicts in Religious Thought

God is not a personality, but God is more worthful than any personality could ever be. God is not nature and he is not the universe, but he is the growth of living connections of value in the universe.

HENRY NELSON WIEMAN (1884–1975)
The Growth of Religion

Since everything we see below us shows a progression of power, where is the difficulty in supposing that there is, at the *summit of all things,* a Being in whom an infinity of power unites with the infinity of the will? When this simple idea presents itself to our mind, we have the idea of a perfect Being that man calls God.   THOMAS PAINE (1737–1809)
The Age of Reason

The Hebrew wisdom imperatively asserts an unbeginning creative One, who neither became the world, nor is the world eternally, nor made the world out of himself by emanation, or evolution;—but who willed it, and it was!

SAMUEL TAYLOR COLERIDGE (1772–1834)
On the Prometheus of Aeschylus

God is, and is ours—immanent in each sentient being, the life of all lives, the spirit animating every soul. But this is not all. God is also the transcendent Creator and Law-Giver, the Father who loves and, because He loves, also educates His children.

ALDOUS HUXLEY (1894–1963)
The Perennial Philosophy

He is not eternity or infinity, but eternal and infinite; He is not duration or space, but he endures and is present. He endures forever, and is every where present; and by ex-

isting always and every where, he constitutes duration and space. Since every particle of space is always, and every indivisible moment of duration is every where, certainly the Maker and Lord of all things cannot be never and nowhere.

SIR ISAAC NEWTON (1642–1727)
Principia

God fills all things; He contains but is not contained. To be everywhere and nowhere in His property and His alone. He is nowhere, because He Himself created space and place coincidentally with material things, and it is against all right principle to say that the Maker is contained in anything that He has made. He is everywhere, because He has made His powers extend through earth and water, air and heaven, and left no part of the universe without his presence, and uniting all with all has bound them fast with invisible bonds, that they should never be loosed.   PHILO JUDAEUS (30 B.C.–A.D. 40)
Works

God is the all-fair. Truth, and goodness, and beauty, are but different faces of the same.

RALPH WALDO EMERSON (1803–1882)
Nature

The mind of God is all the mentality that is scattered over space and time, the diffused consciousness that animates the world.

BENEDICT SPINOZA (1632–1677)
Ethics

That is the Great Real Self who, though without hands or feet, is the swiftest of approach; though without eyes or ears, sees and hears everything; though uncomprehended, comprehends everything knowable.

The Upanishads

The latent ego of the invisible Infinite, that is God. God is the invisible made evident.

The world concentrated is God; God expanded is the world.

VICTOR HUGO (1802–1885)
William Shakespeare

The most intensely thoughtful and the most intensively active being in the universe is God. He is never weary of his work.

HENRY WARD BEECHER (1813–1887)
Sermons

The principle of life is in God, for energy of mind constitutes life, and God is this energy. He, the first mover, imparts motion, and pursues the work of creation as something to be loved.

ARISTOTLE (384–322 B.C.)
Metaphysics

God is more than a universal reason, more than a vast, anonymous consciousness, more than a self-thinking thought drawn in upon itself, more than the pure truth of the cosmos or the blind justice of history. God is not a neuter, but a God of men who provokes a decision of faith or unbelief: he is spirit, creative freedom, the primal identity of truth and love, a partner encompassing and establishing all interpersonal relationships.

HANS KÜNG (1928–)
On Being a Christian

Ask what God is? His name is love; He is the good, the perfection, the peace, the joy, the glory, and blessing of every life.

WILLIAM LAW (1686–1761)
The Spirit of Prayer

We know not how to teach that Brahma. It is something else than the *known*, but also something higher than the *unknown*. That which is not spoken in speech, but *by* which speech is spoken, this, know thou, is Brahma. That which does not think by means of the heart, but that by means of which we think, this, know thou, is Brahma.

The Upanishads

"God is love, and he that dwelleth in love dwelleth in God and God in him." (1 John 4:16)

For it is not merely through our values we reach God or that from them we infer Him, but rather that in them we find Him. Love is not merely an outward mark and symbol of His presence, but is His very self in action in our world.

JOHN BAILLIE (1886–1960)
The Interpretation of Religion

There is a Creative Factor in this universe favorable to personality, or else personality never would have arrived. A Cosmic Power is operative here, propitious to enlarging truth, creative beauty, and expanding goodness, or else they would never have existed. If by the term God one means this, then one does most certainly mean something real and efficient in this universe, whereof the picture-thinking of our religious symbolism is only the partial representative.

HARRY EMERSON FOSDICK (1878–1969)
As I See Religion

It is the dominion of a spiritual being which constitutes a God; a true, supreme, or imaginary dominion makes a true, supreme, or imaginary God. And from His true dominion it follows that the true God is a living, intelligent, and powerful Being; and from His other perfections that He is supreme or most perfect. He is eternal and infinite, omnipotent and omniscient; that is, His duration reaches from eternity to eternity, His presence from infinity to infinity.

ISAAC NEWTON (1642–1727)
Principia

God is He who sees with the eyes of love, by whose seeing things are enabled to be themselves, by whose seeing I am enabled to be myself.

ROMANO GUARDINI (1885–1968)
The Living God

That Incomprehensible, which is not a still undigested remnant but the blinding darkness of plenitude, the bottomless abyss that sustains all things, the boundless absolute future, nowhere to be laid hold of and present everywhere, is called God.

KARL RAHNER (1904–)
Servants of the Lord

There is a Spirit that is mind and life, light and truth and vast spaces. He contains all works and desires and all perfumes and all tastes. He enfolds the whole universe, and in silence is loving to all.   *The Upanishads*

· BORN FROM THE LIVING GOD . . . ·

The living God we praise, exalt, adore!
He was, He is, He will be evermore.
No unity like unto His can be;
Eternal, inconceivable is He.

MAIMONIDES (1135–1204)
Yigdal

Life is filled with dreadful contradictions; but it is beautiful, and it is filled with mystical, sacred meaning—filled with the presence of the eternal living God.

MIKHAIL BAKUNIN (1814–1876)
Letters

To seek our divinity merely in books and writings is to seek the living among the dead. We do but in vain seek God many times in these, where his truth too often is not so much enshrined as entombed.

JOHN SMITH (1616–1652)
Discourses

Everything that is born of God is truly no shadowy work, but a true life work. God will not bring forth a dead fruit, a lifeless and powerless work, but a living, new man must be born from the living God.

JOHANN ARNDT (1555–1621)
True Christianity

We have not to do with a God Who is "off there" above the sky, who can deal with us only through "the violation of physical law." We have instead a God "in whom we live and move and are," whose being opens into ours, and ours into His, Who is the very life of our lives, the matrix of our personality; and there is no separation between us unless we make it ourselves.   RUFUS JONES (1863–1948)
A Call to What Is Vital

I forget that it is live things God cares about—live truths, not things set down in a book or in a memory, or embalmed in the joy of knowledge, but things lifting up the heart, things active in an active will.

GEORGE MACDONALD (1824–1905)
Unspoken Sermons

It is an overwhelming experience to fall into the hands of the living God, to be invaded to the depths of one's being by His presence, to be, without warning, wholly uprooted from all earth-born securities and assurances, and to be blown by a tempest of unbelievable power which leaves one's old proud self utterly, utterly defenseless.

THOMAS R. KELLY (1893–1941)
A Testament of Devotion

Take heed, brethren, lest there be in any of you an evil heart of unbelief, in departing from the living God.   *The New Testament*
Hebrews 3:12

The living God, the human God, is reached not by the way of reason but by the way of love and of suffering. It is not possible to know Him in order that afterwards we may love Him; we must begin by loving Him, longing for Him, hungering for Him, before knowing Him.

MIGUEL DE UNAMUNO (1864–1936)
Essays and Soliloquies

In one's own soul Brahman is realized clearly, as if seen in a mirror. In the heaven of Brahma also is Brahman realized clearly, as one distinguishes light from darkness. In the world of the fathers he is beheld as in a dream. In the world of angels he appears as if reflected in water.   *The Upanishads*

The Lord showed me, so that I did see clearly, that he did not dwell in these temples which men had commanded and set up, but in people's hearts.

GEORGE FOX (1624–1691)
Journal

Glorious indeed is the world of God around
    us,
but more glorious the world of God within
    us
There lies the Land of Song; there lies the
    poet's native land.

HENRY WADSWORTH LONGFELLOW
(1807–1882)
Hyperion

Where can God be found? Not in our world of sense anywhere, answers the mystic. Every possible object in our world is a mere finite appearance. It may be as huge as the sun or even the Milky Way, or as minute as the dust speck in the sunbeam; it makes no difference. It is a form of finitude. It is in contrast to the Absolute, an illusion, a thing of unreality. It cannot show God or take you to Him.   RUFUS JONES (1863–1948)
Social Law in the Spiritual World

Yes, write it in the rock, Saint Bernard said,
'Grave it on brass with adamantine pen!
'Tis God himself becomes apparent, when
God's wisdom and God's goodness are
    displayed.

MATTHEW ARNOLD (1822–1888)
The Divinity

God is in all that liberates and lifts;
In all that humbles, sweetens, and consoles.
A mystery of purpose gleaming through the
    secular confusions of the world,
Whose will we darkly accomplish doing ours.

JAMES RUSSELL LOWELL (1819–1891)
The Soul's Horizon

Let us stun and astonish the intruding rabble of men and books and institutions by a simple declaration of the divine fact. Bid the invaders take the shoes from off their feet, for God is here within.

RALPH WALDO EMERSON (1803–1882)
Self-Reliance

God is wholly in every place, included in no place; not bound with bands except those of love; not divided into parts, nor changeable into several shapes; filling heaven and earth with His present power and with His never-absent nature. So that we may imagine God and be as the air and the sea, and we are all enclosed in this circle, wrapped up in the lap of this infinite nature, or as infants in the wombs of their pregnant mothers; and we can no more be removed from the presence of God than from our own being.

JEREMY TAYLOR (1613–1667)
The Rule of Holy Living

· INFINITE SPIRIT ·

In things spiritual there is no partition, no number, no individuals. How sweet is the oneness of the Friend with His friends! Catch the spirit and clasp it to your bosom.

JALAL-UD-DIN RUMI (1207–1273)
The Masnawi

And in the last days it shall be, God declares
that I will pour out my Spirit upon all flesh,
and your sons and your daughters shall
  prophesy,
and your young men shall see visions,
and your old men shall dream dreams.

New Testament
Acts 2:17

As rivers have their source in some far-off fountain, so the human spirit has its sources. To find his fountain of spirit is to learn the secret of heaven and earth.

LAO-TSE (604–531 B.C.)
Tao Te Ching

We see the world piece by piece, as the sun, the moon, the animal, the tree; but the whole, of which these are the shining parts, is the soul. Only by its vision of that Wisdom can the horoscope of the ages be read, and by falling back on our better thoughts, by yielding to the spirit of prophecy which is innate in every man, we can know what it saith.

RALPH WALDO EMERSON (1803–1882)
The Over-Soul

The Body is but the dark lantern, the Soul or Spirit is the Candle of the Lord that burns in it.   JOHN RAY (1627–1705)
Wisdom of God in the Creation

God tells man, " Behold, I am pure, my habitation is pure, my ministering angels are

pure, and the spark of myself deposited with you is pure; take heed that you restore to me that spark in the same state of purity as when it was given to you."   *The Midrash*

If one thinks that his infinite Spirit does the finite work which nature does, he is a man of clouded vision and he does not see the truth.   *The Bhagavad Gita*

What is happiness other than the grace of being permitted to unfold to their fullest bloom all the spiritual powers planted within us.   FRANZ WERFEL (1890–1945)
Between Heaven and Earth

This transforming of the will in love, this simplifying and supernaturalizing of the whole drive and intention of our life, by its immersion in the great movement of the In-finite Life, is itself the work of Creative Spirit. It is only possible because that Spirit already indwells the soul's ground, and there pursues the secret alchemy of love, more and more possessing and transmuting us, with every small movement of acceptance or renuncia-tion in which we yield ourselves to the quiet action of God.

EVELYN UNDERHILL (1875–1941)
The Golden Sequence

Can man ever acquire, in place of the per-sonal and solitary consciousness which he now finds in himself, a general consciousness, which would make him constantly aware that he was a portion of a great spiritual whole?

PETER YAKOVLEVICH CHAADAYEV (1794–1856)
Letters

The eternal spiritual principle, in which is the root of all being, is conscious of itself in our consciousness. Everything comes from God, everything leads to God, everything culminates in God.

NICHOLAS N. STRAKHOV (1828–1896)
Letter to Leo Tolstoy

The love of all things springs from love of
  one;
Wider the soul's horizon hourly grows,
And over it with fuller glory flows
The sky-like spirit of God.

JAMES RUSSELL LOWELL (1819–1891)
Collected Poems

Love designs, thought sketches, action sculptures the works of spirit. Love is divine, conceiving, creating, completing, all things. Love is the Genius of Spirit.

BRONSON ALCOTT (1799–1888)
Orphic Sayings

That which intellectually considered we call Reason, considered in relation to nature, we call Spirit. Spirit is the Creator. Spirit hath life in itself. And man in all ages and countries embodies it in his language as the Father.

RALPH WALDO EMERSON (1803–1882)
Nature

The spiritual life is the flower not of a featureless but a conscious and diversified oneness.   SRI AUROBINDO (1872–1950)
The Human Cycle

When we say God is a spirit, we know what we mean, as well as we do when we say that the pyramids of Egypt are matter. Let us be content, therefore, to believe him to be a spirit, that is, an essence that we know nothing of, in which originally and necessarily reside all energy, all power, all capacity, all activity, all wisdom, all goodness.

JOHN ADAMS (1735–1826)
Letter to Thomas Jefferson

The mystery, and the unexpressed hope of God, lie in their union, in the genuine penetration of the spirit into the world of the soul, in the inter-penetration of both principles, in a hallowing of the one through the other which should bring about a present humanity blessed with blessing from heaven above and from the depths beneath.

THOMAS MANN (1875–1955)
Joseph and His Brothers

The fruit of the spirit is love, joy, peace, long suffering, kindness, goodness, faithfulness, meekness, temperance: against such as these there is no law.   *The New Testament*
Galatians 5:22–24

Material worlds are but play-houses to liberate spirit, and to realize the beauty of spirit. Civilizations are like the snow-castles which the children build for an hour. They arise and perish, and the earth too shall perish with all its beauty. But spirit is eternal; and from the point of view of spirit the chief importance of the cosmic drama is the emergence and salvaging of spirit.

JOHN ELOF BOODIN (1869–1950)
God: A Cosmic Philosophy of Religion

What are these virtues of the spirit? They are faith, which shows us truths entirely elevated above the senses; hope, which makes us aspire to things invisible; charity, which makes us love not of sense, not of nature, not of self-interest, but with a love pure, solid and unchangeable, having its foundation in God.

SAINT FRANCIS OF SALES (1567–1622)
Letters

So sometimes comes to soul and sense
  The feeling which is evidence,
That very near about us lies
  The realm of spiritual mysteries.

JOHN GREENLEAF WHITTIER
(1807–1892)
The Meeting

Wait in the measure of the Spirit of God to guide you up to God, and keep you all in peace and unity.

GEORGE FOX (1624–1691)
Epistles

There is a bridge between time and eternity; and this bridge is Atman, the spirit of man. Neither day nor night cross that bridge, nor old age, nor death, nor sorrow. It is this spirit that we must find and know: man must find his own soul. He who has found and knows his soul has found all the worlds, has achieved all his desires.   *The Upanishads*

When the Bible speaks of man being made in "the image of God," it means that he is a free spirit as well as a creature, and that as spirit he is finally responsible to God.

REINHOLD NIEBUHR (1892–1971)
Does Civilization Need Religion?

An indwelling spirit sustains, and a mind fused throughout the limbs sways the whole mass and mingles with the giant frame.

VERGIL (70–19 B.C.)
Aeneid

Every visible, conscious thing is a revelation of the invisible, spiritual Creator. Matter is a revelation of Mind, the flesh of the Spirit, the world of God. All growth, production, progress, are but stages of the spiritual Being. They denote the Spirit struggling to represent, reveal, shadow forth itself to the sense and reason of man. They are tests of his faith in the infinite, invisible, spiritual life that flows through and quickens all things and beings.

BRONSON ALCOTT (1799–1888)
Journals

Spirit is man's whole creative act. Spirit is freedom, and freedom has its roots in the depths of pre-existential being.

NIKOLAI BERDYAEV (1874–1948)
Spirit and Reality

As the wind, though one, takes on new forms in whatever it enters; the Spirit, though one, takes new forms in whatever that lives.   *The Upanishads*

Because the strength of the soul is spiritual it is generally despised: but if ever you would be Divine, you must admit this principle: That spiritual things are the greatest, and that spiritual strength is the most excellent, useful, and delightful.

THOMAS TRAHERNE (1637–1674)
Centuries of Meditation

There is much mystery wrapped up in this junction of spirit and matter in ourselves. We do not know how the chasm is bridged. We have no way of explaining how spirit can move matter nor how matter can report itself to spirit. There never was and never will be a greater mystery.

RUFUS JONES (1886–1948)
Religious Foundations

Let every Brahman with fixed attention consider all nature, both visible and invisible, as existing in the divine spirit; for, when he contemplates the boundless universe existing in the divine spirit, he cannot give his heart to iniquity.   *The Laws of Manu*

This spirit of ours does not belong to this world, nor to temporal objects; it was created for God alone, and therefore capable of enjoying true fellowship with him. It may, and it ought to be, the temple and sacred residence of the Deity. Its occupation is to contemplate, love, and enjoy this beneficent Being, and to repose in him; for this end it was created; for this it possesses capacity. God, as a Spirit, is near our spirits, and can alone be sought and found there.

GERHARD TERSTEEGEN (1697–1769)
On Inward Prayer

The soul of God touches the soul of man. God and man are united by the intersphering of soul-life. God's ever-watchful soul broods tenderly over every human being by day and by night.

HENRY WARD BEECHER (1813–1887)
Sermons

From that great deep, before our world
  begins,
Whereon the spirit of God moves as he will.

ALFRED LORD TENNYSON (1809–1892)
De Profundis

Spirit is not a mysterious substance; it is not a part of God. It is God himself; but not God as the creative ground of all things and not God directing history and manifesting himself in its central event, but God as present in communities and personalities, grasping them, inspiring them, and transforming them.

PAUL TILLICH (1886–1965)
The Eternal Now

If one does not strain his spiritual powers in their spirituality simply by choosing the inward direction, he discovers nothing at all, or he does not discover in the deeper sense that God is.

SÖREN KIERKEGAARD (1813–1855)
Concluding Unscientific Postscript

God is a spirit whom thou shouldst adore in spirit! What does he urge more than that? and what tenet is mightier than this in binding all species of religion together?

GOTTHOLD EPHRAIM LESSING (1729–1781)
Education of the Human Race

There is a spirit in man: and the inspiration of the Almighty giveth them understanding.

The Old Testament
Job 32:8

"The spirit of man is the candle of the Lord."

The Old Testament
Proverbs 20:27

This phrase is a spiritual fragment of human experience of a deeper level than most of the words of the Book in which it is found. It is like a piece of floating star-dust, caught and preserved in the amber of this Book of practical sayings. Only the profoundest of prophetic souls could have discovered the truth and have uttered it with such extraordinary simplicity. It means that there is something in man's inmost being that can be kindled and struck into flame by God, and as we feed the flame with our lives we can become revealing places for God, a flame of God's life.

RUFUS JONES (1863–1968)
The Luminous Trail

God hath not created in the earth or in the lofty heaven anything more occult than the spirit of Man. He hath revealed the mystery of all things, moist and dry, but He hath sealed the mystery of the spirit: "it is of the Word of my Lord."

JALAL-UD-DIN RUMI (1207–1273)
The Masnawi

God is perpetually pouring his soul through time and space though but few know it. Not one man in a thousand ever understands a great nature in his own age. We see this on the human plane; and how much more should we expect to see it in the divine sphere!

HENRY WARD BEECHER (1813–1887)
Sermons

God is spirit, and the physical must become spiritualized before it can reach him. All the power, life, and goodness which he put into the world returns to him in proportion to the spiritual thanks offered by men. So, too, the will he placed in creation returns only insofar as it is fulfilled by men. The life and abundance of God consist in the return of his spirit from the world in the spirit of human beings. And whatever does not so return in

the spirit of men is lost, imprisoned in crea-
tureliness.
ALBERT SCHWEITZER (1875–1965)
Reverence for Life

There is only a spiritual world; what we call
the physical world is the evil in the spiritual
one, and what we call evil is only a necessary
moment in our endless development.
FRANZ KAFKA (1883–1924)
The Great Wall of China

God is a Spirit; and they that worship him
must worship him in spirit and in truth.
The New Testament
John 4:24

The written code kills, but the Spirit gives
life.   *The New Testament*
2 Corinthians 3:6

The Spirit of the Lord is upon me, because
he has annointed me to preach good news to
the poor. He has sent me to proclaim release
to the captives and recovering of sight to the
blind, to set at liberty those who are oppressed, to proclaim the acceptable year of
the Lord.   *The New Testament*
Luke 4:16–21

What, but God?
Inspiring God! who boundless Spirit all,
And unremitting Energy, pervades,
Adjusts, sustains and agitates the whole.
JAMES THOMSON (1700–1748)
The Seasons

And if tonight my soul may find her peace
in sleep, and sink in good oblivion,
and in the morning wake like a new-opened
   flower
then I have been dipped again in God, and
   new-created.
D. H. LAWRENCE (1885–1930)
Shadows

· WHEN GOD MAKES HIS PRESENCE FELT ·

How impossible is it, that the world should
exist from Eternity, without a Mind.
JONATHAN EDWARDS (1703–1758)
Notes on the Mind

At times the Universe and its fullness are
insufficient to contain the glory of God's Divinity; at other times He speaks with man between the hairs of his head.   *The Talmud*

Men esteem truth remote, in the outskirts
of the system, behind the farthest star, before
Adam and after the last man. In eternity
there is indeed something true and sublime.
But all these times and places and occasions
are now and here. God himself culminates in
the present moment, and will never be more
divine in the lapse of all the ages.
HENRY DAVID THOREAU (1817–1862)
Walden

In the Bible God's name is named, not as
philosophers do it, as the name of a timeless
Being, surpassing the world, alien and supreme, but as the name of the living, acting,
working Subject who makes Himself known.
KARL BARTH (1886–1968)
Dogmatics in Outline

So shalt thou see and hear
The lovely shapes and sounds
   intelligible

Of that eternal language, which thy God
Utters, who from eternity doth teach
Himself in all, and all things in himself.
SAMUEL TAYLOR COLERIDGE
(1772–1834)
Frost at Midnight

In divine things there is no prudence
which is not bold. It must live and work in
the dark as briskly as in the light. It must be
gay, playing blithely with difficulties; for difficulties are the stones out of which all God's
houses are built.
FREDERICK WILLIAM FABER (1814–1863)
Spiritual Conferences

When God makes His presence felt
through us, we are like the burning bush:
Moses never took any heed what sort of bush
it was—he only saw the brightness of the
Lord.   GEORGE ELIOT (1819–1880)
Adam Bede

God vouchsafes to speak to us one by one,
to manifest Himself to us one by one, to lead
us forward one by one; He gives us something to rely upon which others do not experience, which we cannot convey to others,
which we can but use for ourselves.
JOHN CARDINAL NEWMAN (1801–1890)
Sermons

The speech of created beings is with
sounds. The word of God is silence. God's
secret world of love can be nothing else but
silence.   SIMONE WEIL (1909–1943)
Waiting for God

All history becomes the unfolding of the
purpose of the immanent God who is working in the race toward the commonwealth of
spiritual liberty and righteousness. History is
the sacred workshop of God.
WALTER RAUSCHENBUSCH (1861–1918)
Christianizing the Social Order

God is present in a silent way always. A
certain hidden element or hiding element
there is in the divine mind. God's blessings
steal into life noiselessly. They are neither
self-proclaiming nor even self-announcing.
HENRY WARD BEECHER (1813–1887)
Sermons

And do you say God is invisible? Speak not
so. Who is more manifest than God? For this
very purpose has He made all things, that
through all things you may see Him. This is
God's goodness, that He manifests Himself
through all things.
Corpus Hermeticum (1st century)

The Spirit of God is around you in the air
that you breathe—His glory in the light that
you see; and in the fruitfulness of the earth,
and the joy of its creatures, He has written
for you, day by day, His revelation, as He has
granted you, day by day, your daily bread.
JOHN RUSKIN (1819–1900)
Deucalion

God is especially present in the hearts of
his people, by his Holy Spirit: and indeed the
hearts of holy men are temples in the truth
of things, and in type and shadow, they are
heaven itself. For God reigns in the hearts of
his servants: there is his kingdom.
JEREMY TAYLOR (1613–1667)
The Rule of Holy Living

As God plays with the time of this outward
world, so likewise the inward, Divine man
should play with the outward in the manifested wonders of God in this world, and
open the Divine wisdom in all creatures, each
according to his nature.
JACOB BOEHME (1575–1624)
Mysterium Magnum

We say that God fears, that God is wroth,
that God loves—these are all passions and
emotions which can not dwell in God in the
same form as in us; nor can we imagine the

form in him. It is for God alone to know himself and to interpret his works.

MICHEL EYQUEM DE MONTAIGNE (1533–1592)
Apology for Raimond Sebond

God is Lord of history. He is leading it towards a mysterious goal. Just where that lies we cannot tell. Some say at the height of human achievement, others at the depth of human decline, still others think it will be reached when all possibilities of human accomplishment have been exhausted.

ROMANO GUARDINI (1885–1968)
The Faith and Modern Man

How can you expect God to speak in that gentle and inward voice which melts the soul, when you are making so much noise with your rapid reflections? Be silent and God will speak again.

FRANÇOIS FÉNELON (1651–1715)
Spiritual Letters

The Infinite Brahman is manifesting Itself through so many human forms, Human bodies are like pillow-cases of different shapes and various colors, but the cotton wool of the internal Spirit is one.

SRI RAMAKRISHNA (1834–1886)
Gospel

God has no need of natural or logical witnesses, but speaks himself within the heart, being indeed that ineffable attraction which dwells in whatever is good and beautiful, and that persuasive visitation of the soul by the eternal and incorruptible by which she feels herself purified, rescued from mortality, and given an inheritance in the truth.

GEORGE SANTAYANA (1863–1952)
Reason in Religion

We must not brood over things of divine nature, but recognize them only in their works; for these are the signs of the Master who lives in heaven. As the house is the sign of its master and confirms him to be a carpenter, as the pot is the sign of the potter, so the works are signs of their Master and bear witness that He is God Himself.

PARACELSUS (1493–1541)
Works

The world is the book where the eternal Wisdom wrote its own concepts, and the living temple where, depicting its deeds and own example, it adorned the depth and the height with statues; that every spirit here, lest it become impious, may learn and contemplate art and law, and can say: I fulfill the universe, by contemplating God in all things.

TOMMASO CAMPANELLA (1568–1639)
Italian Writings

The world is God's seed-bed. He has planted deep and multitudinously, and many things there which have not yet come up.

HENRY WARD BEECHER (1813–1887)
Sermons

The world is not divine sport, it is divine destiny. There is divine meaning in the life of the world, of man, of human persons, of you and me.   MARTIN BUBER (1878–1965)
I and Thou

God took seeds from different worlds and sowed them on this earth, and His garden grew up and everything came up that could come up, but what grows lives and is alive only through the feeling of its contact with other mysterious worlds. If that feeling grows weak or is destroyed in you, the heavenly growth will die away in you.

FYODOR DOSTOEVSKY (1821–1881)
The Brothers Karamazov

The Lord thy God in the midst of thee is mighty; he will save, he will rejoice over thee with joy; he will rest in his love, he will joy over thee with singing.   *The Old Testament*
Zephaniah 3:17

As a spider sends forth and draws in, as herbs grow on the earth, as the hair on the head and the body of a living person, so from the Imperishable arises here the universe.

The Upanishads

What were a God who only wrought
    externally,
And turned the all in a circle on his finger?
It becomes him to move the world in its
    interior,
To cherish nature in himself and himself in
    nature;
So that whatsoever lives and weaves and is in
    him
Never lacks his presence and his Spirit.

JOHANN WOLFGANG VON GOETHE (1749–1832)
God, Soul, World

When God spoke to Moses, all the people saw the voice. The voice of man is audible, but the voice of God is visible in truth. What God speaks is not his word, but his works, which eyes and not ears perceive.

PHILO JUDAEUS (30 B.C.–A.D. 40)
Quis Rerum Diviniarum Haeres

Luther's main axiom is: "God works through means." This is to say that we should not look for Him in that which is exceptional or in the vulgar sense a "miracle," but that we should learn to appreciate the everyday course of events as being God's dispensation.

RUDOLF OTTO (1869–1937)
Religious Essays

To one in all, to all in one—
    Since love the work began

Life's everwidening circles run
    Revealing God to man.

JOHN BANNISTER TABB
(1845–1909)
Communion

"Ye heard the voice of words but ye saw no form" (Deuteronomy 4:12). The voice speaks in the guise of all world events; it speaks to the men of all generations, makes demands upon them, and summons them to accept their responsibility.

MARTIN BUBER (1878–1965)
Israel and the World

The Sacred Rights of Mankind are not to be rummaged for among old parchments or musty records. They are written, as with a sunbeam, in the whole volume of human nature, by the Hand of Divinity itself.

ALEXANDER HAMILTON (1755–1804)
Reply to "Westchester Farmer"

If it is possible to say that the death of God in the Nietzschean sense preceded and made possible the agony of man which we are now witnessing, it is legitimate in a certain sense to say that it is from the ashes of man that God can and must rise again.

GABRIEL MARCEL (1889–1973)
Homo Viator

The sun, the moon, the stars, the seas, the
    hills and the plains—
Are not these, O Soul, the vision of Him
    who reigns?

ALFRED LORD TENNYSON (1809–1892)
The Higher Pantheism

· GOD, POET AND SYMPHONIST OF THE UNIVERSE ·

When we ask poets and artists to tell us what they have found in God, they answer with one voice, "We have found him in beauty. Only it is a beauty that never was on land or sea, a beauty that in its transcendent excellence makes our best handiwork seem tawdry."

WILLIAM ADAMS BROWN (1865–1943)
God at Work

God reveals Himself—the Creator of the world—an author!

JOHAN GEORG HAMANN (1730–1788)
Journal

Today, as always, art must make Transcendence perceptible, doing so at all times in the form which arouses contemporary faith. It may well be that the moment draws near when art will again tell man what his God is and what he himself is.

KARL JASPERS (1883–1969)
Man in the Modern Age

I say God is a God of emotion, and if he observes mathematics, it is mathematics set to music, and his figures are written, not in white chalk on blackboards, but by a finger of sunlight on walls of jasmine and trumpet-creeper.

THOMAS DE WITT TALMAGE (1832–1902)
Sermons

God creates Art by man having for a tool the human intellect. The great Workman has made this tool for himself; he has no other.

VICTOR HUGO (1802–1885)
William Shakespeare

Music and art and poetry attune the soul to God because they induce a kind of contact with the Creator and Ruler of the Universe.

THOMAS MERTON (1915–1968)
No Man Is an Island

Good art is nothing but a replica of the perfection of God and a reflection of His art.

MICHELANGELO BUONARROTI (1475–1564)
Dialogues

The world is God's journal wherein he writes his thoughts and traces his tastes.

HENRY WARD BEECHER (1813–1887)
Sermons

We speak of the Volume of Nature: and truly a Volume it is—whose Author and Writer is God. To read it! Dost thou, does man, so much as well know the Alphabet thereof? With its Words, Sentences, and grand descriptive Pages, poetical and philosophical, spread out through Solar Systems, and Thousands of Years, we shall not try thee. It is a Volume written in celestial hieroglyphs, in the true Sacred-writing; of which even Prophets are happy that they can read here a line and there a line.

THOMAS CARLYLE (1795–1881)
Sartor Resartus

I raised my eyes aloft, and I beheld the scattered chapters of the Universe gathered and bound into a single book by the austere and tender hand of God.

DANTE (1265–1321)
The Divine Comedy

For every sentence, clause, and word,
That's not inlaid with Thee, (my Lord,)
Forgive me, God, and blot each line
Out of my book, that is not Thine.

ROBERT HERRICK (1591–1674)
Prayer for Absolution

The Bible is a page torn out of the great volume of human life; only, torn by the hand of God, and annotated by his Spirit.

JOSEPH PARKER (1830–1902)
Sermons

The greatest work of art has for its material humanity itself, and the Deity directly fashions it. For this work the sense must soon awake in many, for at present, He is working with bold and effective art. And you will be the temple servants when the new forms are set up in the temple of time. Expound the Artist then with force and spirit; explain the earlier works from the later. Let the past, the present, and the future surround us with an endless gallery of the sublimest works of art, eternally multiplied by a thousand brilliant mirrors.

FRIEDRICH SCHLEIERMACHER (1768–1835)
On Religion

Art imitates nature as well as it can, as a pupil follows his master; thus it is a sort of grandchild of God.   DANTE (1265–1321)
Inferno

Act first, this earth, a stage so gloom'd with
    woe
    You all but sicken at the shifting scenes.
And yet be patient, Our Playwright may
    show
    In some fifth Act what this wild drama
    means.
        ALFRED LORD TENNYSON (1809–1892)
The Play

What the poet writes, filled with the holy spirit and with God, is very good.
        DEMOCRITUS (4th century B.C.)
Fragments

God is the perfect poet,
Who in his person acts his own creations.
        ROBERT BROWNING (1812–1889)
Paracelsus

He who in any way, shows us better than we knew before that a lily of the fields is beautiful, does he not show it us as an effluence of the Fountain of all Beauty; as the *Handwriting*, made visible there, of the great Maker of the Universe?
        THOMAS CARLYLE (1795–1881)
On Heroes and Hero-Worship

A poet is a man who keeps no secrets from God in his heart, and who, in singing his griefs, his fears, his hopes, and his memories, purifies and purges them from all falsehood. His songs are your songs, are my songs.
        MIGUEL DE UNAMUNO (1864–1936)
Essays and Soliloquies

Poetry is God in the holy dreams of earth.
        V. A. ZHUKOVSKY (1783–1852)
Camoens

To me it seems as if when God conceived the world, that was poetry; He formed it, and that was sculpture; He colored it, and that was painting; He peopled it with living things, and that was the grand, divine eternal Drama.   DAVID BELASCO (1854–1931)
Forty Years a Theatrical Producer

Whenever a masterpiece appears, a distribution of God is taking place. The masterpiece is a variety of the miracle.
        VICTOR HUGO (1802–1885)
William Shakespeare

If the poet remains content with his gift, if he persists in worshipping the beauty in art and nature without going on to make himself capable, through selflessness, of apprehending Beauty as it is in the divine Ground, then he is only an idolater.
        ALDOUS HUXLEY (1894–1963)
The Perennial Philosophy

God on His throne is
    Eldest of poets;
Unto His measures
    Moveth the Whole.
        WILLIAM WATSON (1858–1935)
England My Mother

As it is dislocation and detachment from the life of God that makes things ugly, the poet, who re-attaches things to nature and the Whole—re-attaching even artificial things and violations of nature, to nature, by a deeper insight—disposes very easily of the most disagreeable facts.
        RALPH WALDO EMERSON (1803–1882)
The Poet

I sometimes think that the analogy of a poet and his work—say Shakespeare and his plays—is the most helpful in forming an idea of the relation of God to the world.
        WILLIAM RALPH INGE (1860–1954)
God and the Astronomers

Good poetry could not have been otherwise written than it is. The first time you hear it, it sounds rather as if copied out of some invisible tablet in the Eternal mind, than as if arbitrarily composed by the poet.

RALPH WALDO EMERSON (1803–1882)
Art

· WHERE GOD DWELLS . . . ·

I had rather be a doorkeeper in the house of my God than to dwell in the tents of wickedness.   *The Old Testament*
Psalms 84:10

The eternal God is your dwelling place, and underneath are the everlasting arms.
The Old Testament
Deuteronomy 33:27

God says to man, "If you come to my house, I will come to your house."
Babylonian Talmud
Sukkah

And Jacob awaked out of his sleep, and he said: Surely the Lord is in this place; and I knew it not. And he was afraid, and said: How full of awe is this place; this is none other than the house of God, and this is the gate of heaven.   *Old Testament*
Genesis 28: 16–17

It is God who made the earth for you as an abode and the heaven for a building. He fashioned you: comely did he fashion you and with good things did he provide you.
The Koran

Lord, who shall sojourn in Thy tabernacle? Who shall dwell upon Thy holy mountain? He that walketh uprightly, and worketh righteousness, and speaketh truth in his heart.
Old Testament
Psalms 15: 1–2

Millions in our arms we gather,
To the world our kiss is sent!
Past the starry firmament,
Brothers, a loving Father lives.
FRIEDRICH SCHILLER
(1759–1805)
Ode to Joy

"Where is the dwelling of God?"
This was the question with which Rabbi Mendel of Kotzk surprised a number of learned men who were visiting him. They laughed at him: "What a thing to ask! Is not the whole world full of his glory!"
Then he answered his own question: "God dwells wherever man lets him in."
RABBI MENDEL OF KOTZK (died 1859)
Hasidic Accounts

Science and Art, compeers in glory,
Boast each a haunt divine.
"My place is in God's laboratory."
"And in His garden mine."
SIR WILLIAM WATSON (1858–1935)
The Guests of Heaven

But will God indeed dwell on earth? Behold, heaven and the highest heaven cannot contain thee; how much less this house which I have built!   *The Old Testament*
1 Kings 8:27

Slowly, through all the universe, that temple of God is being built. Wherever, in any world, a soul, by free-willed obedience, catches the fire of God's likeness, it is set into the growing walls, a living stone.

PHILLIPS BROOKS (1835–1893)
Sermons

In what strange quarries and stone-yards the stones for the celestial wall are being hewn! Out of the hillsides of humiliated pride; deep in the darkness of crushed despair; in the fretting and dusty atmosphere of little cares; in the hard cruel contacts that man has with man; wherever souls are being tried and ripened, in whatever commonplace and homely ways—there God is hewing out the pillars for his temple.

PHILLIPS BROOKS (1835–1893)
Sermons

A mountain of God is the mountain of
   Bashan;
A mountain of peaks is the mountain of
   Bashan.
Why look ye askance, ye mountains of
   peaks,
At the mountain which God hath desired for
   His abode?
Yea, the Lord will dwell therein for ever.

The Old Testament
Psalms 68:16–18

Except the Lord built the house, they labour in vain that build it: except the Lord keep the city, the watchman waketh but in vain.

The Old Testament
Psalms 127:1–2

In whatever we may set our foot we are always, Lord, within Thy resort. In whatever place or corner we may entrench ourselves, we are always near to Thee. Perhaps, we say, there is a path which leads elsewhere, and yet, let our pathway be whatever it will, it invariably leads to Thee.

JALAL-UD-DIN RUMI (1207–1273)
The Diwan

The soul is a temple; and God is silently building it, by night and by day. Precious thoughts are building it; disinterested love is building it; all-penetrating faith is building it.

HENRY WARD BEECHER (1813–1887)
Sermons

The red upon the hill
Taketh away my will;
If anybody sneer,
Take care, for God is here,
That's all.

EMILY DICKINSON (1830–1886)
Mysteries

The abode of God, is it not wherever there is earth and sea and air, and sky, and virtue? Why further do we seek the Gods of heaven? Whatever thou dost behold and whatever thou dost touch, that is Jupiter.

LUCAN (39–65)
Pharsalia

Know that the Prophet built an external
   Kaaba
Of clay and water,
And an inner Kaaba in life and heart.
The outer Kaaba was built by Abraham, the
   Holy;
The inner is sanctified by the glory of God
   Himself.

SHEIKH 'ABDULLAH ANSARI (1005–1090)
Invocations

Slowly, through all the universe, that temple of God is being built wherever, in any world, a soul, by free-willed obedience, catches the fire of God's likeness. When, in your hard fight, in your tiresome drudgery, or in your terrible temptation, you catch the purpose of your being, and give yourself to God, and so give him the chance to give himself to you, your life, a living stone, is taken up and set into the growing wall.

PHILLIPS BROOKS (1835–1893)
Sermons

The whole world will be a Temple, every spot holy ground, every bush burning with the Infinite; all time the Lord's day, and every moral act worship and a sacrament.

THEODORE PARKER (1810–1860)
Theism, Atheism, and the Popular Theology

The world's Thy book: there I can read
Thy power, wisdom, and Thy love.

RICHARD BAXTER (1615–1691)
The Resolution

A good man finds every place he treads upon holy ground; to him the world is God's temple; he is ready to say with Jacob, "This is none other but the house of God, and this is the gate of heaven." (Genesis 28:17)

JOHN SMITH (1616–1652)
Discourses

There is a river, the streams whereof shall make glad the city of God, the holy place of the tabernacles of the most High. God is in the midst of her; she shall not be moved: God shall help her, and that right early.

The Old Testament
Psalms 46:4–5

For we are labourers together with God: ye are God's husbandry, ye are God's building.

The New Testament
1 Corinthians 3:9

We are men, each containing within himself the ontological mystery of personality and freedom; in each of us the abyss of holiness of the Supreme Being is present with His universal presence, and He asks us to dwell there as in His temple, by manner of a gift of Himself to us.

JACQUES MARITAIN (1882–1973)
Ransoming the Time

The stars are mansions built by Nature's hand,
And, haply, there the spirits of the blest

Dwell, clothed in radiance, their immortal vest.

WILLIAM WORDSWORTH (1770–1850)
Sonnets

In the house of God there is never-ending festival; the angel choir makes eternal holiday; the presence of God's face gives joy that never fails. And from that everlasting, perpetual festivity there sounds in the ears of the heart a strain, mysterious, melodious, sweet —provided the world does not drown it.

SAINT AUGUSTINE (354–430)
Patrologia Latina

Shall man confine his Maker's sway
To Gothic domes of mouldering stone?
Thy temple is the face of day;
Earth, Ocean, Heaven, thy boundless
  throne.

GEORGE GORDON, LORD BYRON
(1788–1824)
The Prayer of Nature

The Lord desires thee for His dwelling place
Eternally and blest is he whom God has
  chosen for the grace
Within thy courts to rest.

JUDAH HALEVI (C. 1085–C. 1140)
Ode to Zion

In my Father's house are many mansions.

The New Testament
John 14:2

We win the presence of God when most we flee. We have no other dwelling-place but the single unity of the divine consciousness. In the light of the eternal we are manifest, and even this very passing instant pulsates with a life that all the worlds are needed to express. In vain would we wander in the darkness; we are eternally at home in God.

JOSIAH ROYCE (1855–1916)
The World and the Individual

I have poured forth my soul above myself. No longer is there any being for me to touch except my God. The "house of my god" is there; there, above my soul, is His dwelling. From there he governs me and provides for me. From there He lures me and calls me and directs me, leads me in the way and to the end of my way.

SAINT AUGUSTINE (354–430)
On Psalm 41

Watch your step when you go to the house of God, for it is better to understand than to offer sacrifice like the fools, who do not even know how to do evil! Do not hasten to speak, nor let yourself be rushed into uttering words before God, for God is in heaven and you are on earth—therefore, let your words be few.

The Old Testament
Ecclesiastes 5:1–2

The hidden room in man's house where
   God sits all the year,
The secret window whence the world looks
   small and very dear.

G. K. CHESTERTON (1874–1936)
Lepanto

Thou liest in Abraham's bosom all the year;
And worship'st at the Temple's inner shrine,
God being with thee when we know it not.

WILLIAM WORDSWORTH (1770–1850)
It Is a Beauteous Evening

Thus says the high and lofty One who inhabits eternity, whose name is Holy: "I dwell in the high and holy place, and also with him who is of a contrite and humble spirit, to revive the spirit of the humble, and to revive the heart of the contrite."

The Old Testament
Isaiah 57:15

Some proclaim His Existence
To be far, desperately far, from us;
Others sing of Him
As here and there a Presence
Meeting us face to face.

GURU NANAK (1469–1539)
The Adi Granth

God may not be where one would like to see Him, and He may be where one refuses to see Him. The presence of God in the world is mysterious, and not susceptible to precise definition.

NIKOLAI BERDYAEV (1874–1948)
The Divine and the Human

See that you seek God where He is to be sought, in the temple and dwelling-place of the Divine glory, which is your heart and your soul.   JOHANNES DENCK (1495–1527)
Works

To be with God, there is no need to be in church. We may make an oratory of our heart wherein to retire from time to time to converse with Him in meekness, humility, and love. Every one is capable of such familiar conversation with God, some more, some less.   BROTHER LAWRENCE (1605–1691)
The Practice of the Presence of God

God has written his religion in the heart, for growing wisdom to read perfectly, and time to make triumphant.

LEIGH HUNT (1784–1859)
The Religion of the Heart

You men of thought, ask your minds the question: what was the forest from which the tree was cut to build up the earth and heaven? And what is the place, standing on which the Lord holds the world?

The Rig-Veda

Within the lotus of the heart He dwells, where the nerves meet like the spokes of a wheel. Meditate upon him as OM, and you may easily cross the ocean of darkness. In the effulgent lotus of the heart dwells Brahman, passionless and indivisible.

The Upanishads

God dwells in the heart of all beings, Arjuna: thy God dwells in thy heart. And at his power of wonder moves all things—puppets in a play of shadows—whirling them onwards on the stream of time.

The Bhagavad Gita

It was opened in me that God, who made the world, did not dwell in temples made with hands. This, at the first, seemed a strange world because both priests and people used to call their temples or churches, dreadful places, and holy ground, and the temples of God. But the Lord showed me, so that I could see clearly, that He did not dwell in these temples which men had commanded and set up, but in people's hearts.

GEORGE FOX (1624–1691)
Journal

God is in all that liberates and lifts,
In all that humbles, sweetens, and consoles.

JAMES RUSSELL LOWELL (1819–1891)
Complete Poems

If we cannot find God in your house or in mine, upon the roadside or the margin of the sea; in the bursting seed or opening flower; in the day duty or the night musing; in the general laugh or the secret grief; in the procession of life, ever entering afresh, and solemnly passing by and dropping off; I do not think we should discern Him any more on the grass of Eden, or beneath the moonlight of Gethsemane.

JAMES MARTINEAU (1805–1900)
Rationale of Religious Inquiry

In seas, on earth, this God is seen:
All that exist, upon him lean;
He lives in all, and never stray'd
A moment from the works he made.

PHILIP FRENEAU (1752–1832)
*On the Universality and Other
Attributes of the God of Nature*

What causes you to perform a given action, which I call virtuous, rather than another? I reply, that I cannot know which method, out of the infinite methods at His disposal, God employs to determine you to the said action. It may be, that God has impressed you with a clear idea of Himself so that you forget the world for love of Him, and love your fellow-men as yourself; it is plain that such a disposition is at variance with those dispositions which are called bad, and, therefore, could not co-exist with them in the same man.

BENEDICT SPINOZA (1632–1677)
Letters

As fragrance dwells in a flower,
And reflection in a mirror;
So does God dwell in every soul.
Seek Him therefore in thy self.

GURU NANAK (1469–1539)
The Adi Granth

He who is bewildered is bewildered because he sees not the creator, the holy Lord, abiding within himself.   *The Upanishads*

Whate'er we leave to God, God does
And blesses us.

HENRY DAVID THOREAU (1817–1862)
Inspiration

God is in all things, but so far as God is Divine and so far as he is rational, God is nowhere so properly as in the soul—in the innermost of the soul.

MEISTER ECKHART (1260–1327)
Works

I know not where His islands lift
Their fronded palms in air;
I only know I cannot drift
Beyond His love and care.

JOHN GREENLEAF WHITTIER
(1807–1892)
The Eternal Goodness

It is the God within your own self that is impelling you to seek Him, to realize Him. After long searches here and there, in tem-

ples and churches, on earth and in heaven, at last you come back to your own soul, completing the cycle from where you started, and find that He whom you have been seeking all over the world, for whom you have been weeping and praying in churches and temples, on whom you were looking as the mystery of all mysteries, shrouded in the clouds, is the nearest of the near, is your own Self, the reality of your life, body, and soul.   SWAMI VIVEKANANDA (1863–1902)
Jnana-Yoga

Who has not found the heaven below
    Will fail of it above.
God's residence is next to mine—
    His furniture is love.
            EMILY DICKINSON (1830–1886)
God's Residence

The Infinite Dwelling of the Infinite Being is everywhere: in earth, water, sky, and air.
            KABIR (1454–1518)
The Adi Granth

To me remains nor place nor time;
My country is in every clime;
I can be calm and free from care
On any shore, since God is there.
            MADAME GUYON (1648–1717)
Hymns

It is within yourself that you carry him, and do you not observe that you profane him by impure thought and unclean actions. If the mere external image of God were present, would you dare to act as you do, and when God himself is within you, and hears and sees all, are you not ashamed to act thus—insensible of your own nature, and at enmity with God?   EPICTETUS (1st century)
Discourses

It is true that when reason, and especially the heart, are unclouded by passion, man's flesh and his very bones feel a power over them which transcends them. Call it what you will, but Hobbes felt it and so did Spinoza; and if you are not a monster, O Man, then you must sense your Father, for He is everywhere. He lives in you, and your very sensibility is a gift from the All-Loving.
            ALEXANDER RADISCHEV (1749–1802)
Man's Mortality and Immortality

And therefore God works in us from within outwards; but all creatures work from without inwards. And thus it is that grace, and all the gifts of God, and the Voice of God, come from within, in the unity of our spirit; and not from without, into the imagination, by means of sensible images.
            JAN VAN RUYSBROECK (1293–1381)
The Sparkling Stone

And I heard a great voice out of heaven saying, Behold the tabernacle of God is with men, and he shall dwell with them, and they shall be his people, and God himself shall be with them, and be their God.
            The New Testament
            Revelation 21:3

God, in all that is most living and incarnate in him, is not far away from us, altogether apart from the world we see, touch, hear, smell and taste about us. Rather he awaits us instant in our action, in the work of the moment.
            PIERRE TEILHARD DE CHARDIN (1881–1955)
The Divine Milieu

Vast heavenly, unthinkable its form,
More subtle than the subtle, forth it shines:
More distant than the distant, it is yet here,
    right near;
For those who see, it is always here, hidden
    in a secret place.
            The Upanishads

Ibn Umar reports that the Prophet was once asked as to where God is found either on earth or in heaven. "He is in the hearts of his faithful servants," replied the Prophet.

ABU-HAMID MUHAMMAD AL-GHAZZALI
(1058–1111)
The Renovation of the Science of Religion

I am a God who is near, and not a God afar off. Shall a man do anything in secret, and I not see him? Do not I fill the heavens and the earth? saith the Lord.   *The Old Testament*
Jeremiah 23:23–24

For the kingdom of God is not in word, but in power.   *The New Testament*
1 Corinthians 4:20

Once when some pilgrims journeyed to Kaaba, they found themselves in a fruitless vale beholding a lofty house of stone. They sought with zeal to find God, but found him not. Long had they the house of stone encircled with their march, when from within a voice was heard saying, "Why stand ye here to worship stone? Go and adore in God's true house—the house of truth, home of the heart!"   JALAL-UD-DIN RUMI (1207–1273)
The Diwan

In eternity there is indeed something true and sublime. But all these times and places and occasions are now and here. God Himself culminates in the present moment, and will never be more divine in the lapse of all the ages. And we are enabled to apprehend at all what is sublime and noble only by the perpetual instilling and drenching of the reality that surrounds us.

HENRY DAVID THOREAU (1817–1862)
Walden

"I shall place the candle in the holder, and a beam of knowledge will shine into all eyes that see it from afar."

Who shall be the holder and who the candle?

And the Lord said: "I am the light, and the holder is your heart."

MECHTILD OF MAGDEBURG (1207–1294)
Letters

All the attempts of philosophic thought to find God in the world are completely vain. The world is not like God; it contains nothing divine. Therefore, it much more readily conceals God than reveals him.

VICTOR I. NESMELOV (1863–1920)
The Science of Man

God is wholly present in every point of being, not substantially, i.e., as the substance of concrete things, but in His creative reason, idea, power, and grace.

ARCHIMANDRATE NIKONOR (1827–1890)
Works

In the highest golden sheath there is the Brahman without passions and without parts. That is pure, that is the light of lights, that is it which they know who know the Self.

The Upanishads

He is the innermost Self in all beings. He who knows him hidden in the shrine of his heart cuts the knot of ignorance even in his life. Self-luminous, ever present in the hearts of all, is the great Being.   *The Upanishads*

According to the Apostle, "you are God's planting, God's building" (1 Corinthians 3:9), a planting in the good soil and a building on the rock, therefore as God's building let us stand unshaken before the wintry storm, and as God's planting let us not think about the Evil One or about the tribulation or persecution that happens on account of the world or about the care of this age, or about the deceit of wealth or about the pleasures of life.

ORIGEN (185–254)
An Exhortation to Martyrdom

The world is the photograph of the spirit; the world is the mirror, the reflection of God.
ABBA HILLEL SILVER (1893–1963)
Sermons

Thus saith the Lord, The Heaven is my throne and the earth is my footstool; where is the house that ye build unto me? and where is the place of my rest?
The Old Testament
Isaiah 66:1

Manifest, near, moving in the cave of the heart is the great Being. In it everything is centered which ye know as moving, breathing, as being and not-being, as the best, that is beyond the understanding of creatures.
The Upanishads

The seed of God is in us. If it was cultivated by a good, wise and industrious laborer, it would thrive all the more and would grow up to God, whose seed it is, and the fruit would be like the Divine nature. The seed of a pear tree grows into a pear tree, a hazel seed into a hazel tree, a seed of God into God.
MEISTER ECKHART (1260–1327)
Sermons

Thy lovingkindness, O Lord, is in the
  heavens;
Thy faithfulness reacheth unto the skies.
Thy righteousness is like the mountains of
  God;
Thy judgments are a great deep.
O Lord, thou preservest man and beast.
How precious is thy lovingkindness, O God!
The Old Testament
Psalms 36:5–7

None knoweth whence creation has arisen,
And whether He has or has not produced it;
He who surveys it in the highest heaven,
He only knows, or haply he may know not.
The Rig-Veda

First there is the *Power,* and in the power is the Tone or *Tune,* which rises up in the spirit, into the Head, into the *Mind,* as in Man in the Brain; and into the Mind it *has its open doors or gates:* but in the *Heart* it has its *Seat,* Residence and Original, where it exists out of all Powers.
JACOB BOEHME (1575–1624)
Aurora

Neither shall they say, Lo here! or, lo there! for, behold, the kingdom of God is within you.
The New Testament
Luke 17:20

God sleeps in a stone, dreams in a flower, moves in an animal, and wakes in man.
IRENAEUS (130–200)
Sermons

Everywhere I find the signature, the autograph of God, and he will never deny his own handwriting. God hath set his tabernacle in the dewdrop as surely as in the sun. No man can any more create the smallest flower than he could create the greatest world.
JOSEPH PARKER (1830–1902)
Sermons

Not only is God in the place where you are, but He is, in a most particular manner, in your heart and in the very center of your spirit.
SAINT FRANCIS OF SALES (1567–1622)
Treatise

In two ways God dwells in the human heart, to wit, through knowledge and through love; yet the dwelling is one, since every one who knows Him, loves, and no one can love without knowing.
HUGH OF SAINT VICTOR (1096–1141)
De Vanitate Mundi

He dwells in all,
From life's minute beginnings, up at last
To man—the consummation of this
  scheme

Of being—the completion of this sphere
Of life.

ROBERT BROWNING (1812–1889)
Paracelsus

There is a breath of God in every man, a
force lying deeper than the stratum of will,
which may be stirred to become an aspiration
strong enough to give direction and even to
run counter to all winds.

ABRAHAM JOSHUA HESCHEL (1907–1972)
The Wisdom of Heschel

High understanding it is, inwardly to see
and know that God, which is our Maker,
dwelleth in our soul; and a higher understanding it is, inwardly to see and know that
our soul, that is made, dwelleth in God's substance: of which Substance, God, we are that
we are.   JULIAN OF NORWICH (1343–1416)
Revelations of Divine Love

Adopting the path of love leading to God,
Praying for his great grace if you ask:
Where does he dwell, I say: Here, in the
    hearts of people like me.

KARAIKKALAMMAIYAR (6th century)
Poem of the Admirable

Men talk of "finding God," but no wonder
it is difficult; He is hidden in that darkest of
hiding places, your own heart.

CHRISTOPHER MORLEY (1890–1957)
Religio Journalistici

To love another better than one's self is to
begin heaven here. The great lesson of all is
that the Father's mansions are within one's
own breast. Heaven is here; the world of
hope, anticipation, feeling, is all here. We
have it here first, if we have it all.

FRANÇOIS FÉNELON (1651–1715)
Maximes des Saints

Of all teachings that which presents a far
distant God is the nearest to absurdity. Either
there is none, or He is nearer to every one of
us than our nearest consciousness of self.

GEORGE MACDONALD (1824–1905)
Unspoken Sermons

As I behold creation, I am amazed and astonished. God is contained in the hearts of
men. In my heart I hold God, Who filleth
every place.   GURU NANAK (1469–1539)
Hymns

The inaccessible and illimitable God dwelleth in man's heart. The body is the palace,
the temple, the house of God. Into it He put-
teth His eternal light.

GURU NANAK (1469–1539)
Hymns

God's Throne is His omnipresence, and
that is infinite, who dwelleth in Himself, or
in that Light, which is inaccessible.

THOMAS TRAHERNE (1637–1674)
Centuries of Meditations

To God belong the East and the West;
whichever way you turn the Face of God is
there.   *The Koran*

God is to be found and seen, not through
an illimitable vacancy between Himself and
the Spirit of man, but in and through all
things that stir men to love. He is to be seen
in the light of a cottage window as well as in
the sun or the stars.

ARTHUR CLUTTON-BROCK (1868–1924)
Studies in Christianity

He is in thy world,
But thy world knows him not.
He is the mighty Heart
From which life's varied pulses part.
Clouded and shrouded there doth sit.
The Infinite. . . .

RALPH WALDO EMERSON (1803–1882)
Gnothi Seuton

All ye inhabitants of the world, and dwellers on the earth, see ye, when he lifteth up an ensign on the mountains; and when he bloweth a trumpet, hear ye. For so the Lord said unto me, I will take my rest, and I will consider in my dwelling place like a clear heat upon herbs, and like a cloud of dew in the heat of harvest.
The Old Testament
Isaiah 18:4–5

The spirit of man is the lamp of the Lord, searching all the inward parts.
The Old Testament
Proverbs 20:27

Well said Saint Chrysostom, with his lips of gold, "the true Shekinah is Man"; where else is the God's Presence manifested not to our eyes only, but to your hearts, as in fellowman?
THOMAS CARLYLE (1795–1881)
Sartor Resartus

He that dwelleth in the secret place of the Most High shall abide under the shadow of the Almighty.
The Old Testament
Psalms 91:1

· IN GOD'S WIDE GRASP ·

In God's wide grasp, and comprehensive
    eye,
Immediate worlds on worlds unnumbered
    lie:
Systems enclos'd in his perception roll,
Whose all-informing mind directs the whole:
Lodg'd in his grasp, their certain ways they
    know;
Plac'd in that sight from whence can nothing
    go.
SAMUEL BOYSE (1708–1749)
The Deity

When I consider how many and how great mysteries men have understood, discovered, and contrived, I very plainly know and understand the mind of man to be one of the works of God, yea, one of the most excellent.
GALILEO (1564–1642)
Dialogue on the Great World Systems

Tumult and peace, the darkness and the
    light
Were all like workings of one mind, the
    features
Of the same face, blossoms upon one tree;

Characters of the great Apocalypse,
The types and symbols of Eternity,
Of first, and last, and midst, and without
    end.
WILLIAM WORDSWORTH (1770–1850)
The Prelude

The basis of all health, sinlessness, and immortality is the great fact that God is the only Mind; and this Mind must be not merely believed, but it must be understood.
MARY BAKER EDDY (1821–1910)
Science and Health

Thus it must be, one served a God whose nature was not repose and abiding comfort, but a God of designs for the future, in whose will inscrutable, great, far-reaching things were in process of becoming, who, with His brooding will and His world-planning, was Himself only in process of becoming, and thus was a God of unrest, a God of cares, who must be sought for, for whom one must at all times keep oneself free, mobile and in readiness.
THOMAS MANN (1875–1955)
Joseph and His Brothers

Everywhere on earth, at this moment, in the new spiritual atmosphere created by the idea of evolution, there float, in a state of extreme mutual sensitivity, love of God and faith in the world: the two essential components of the Ultra-Human.

PIERRE TEILHARD DE CHARDIN (1881–1955)
Let Me Explain

In your excessive self-love you are like a molecule closed in upon itself and incapable of entering easily into any new combination. God looks to you to be more open and more pliant. If you are to enter into him you need to be freer and more eager. Have done,

then, with your egoism and your fear of suffering.

PIERRE TEILHARD DE CHARDIN (1881–1955)
Let Me Explain

No God behind us in the empty Vast,
No God enthroned on yonder
  heights above,
But God emerging, and evolved at
  last
Out of the inmost heart of human
  Love.

ROBERT WILLIAMS BUCHANAN
(1841–1901)
God Evolving

· THE MUSIC OF GOD ·

Yes, music is the Prophet's art;
Among the gifts that God hath
  sent,
One of the most magnificent!
It calms the agitated heart;
Temptations, evil thoughts, and all
The passions that disturb the soul,
Are quelled by its divine control,
As the evil spirit fled from Saul,
And his distemper was allayed,
When David took his harp and
  played.

HENRY WADSWORTH LONGFELLOW
(1807–1882)
Martin Luther

The first string that the musician usually touches is the bass, when he intends to put all in tune. God also plays upon this string first, when he sets the soul in tune for itself.

JOHN BUNYAN (1628–1688)
The Pilgrim's Progress

In the presence of all Israel, Judith struck up this hymn of praise and thanksgiving, in which all the people joined lustily:

"Strike up a song to my God with
  tambourines;
sing to the Lord with cymbals;
raise a psalm of praise to him."

The Old Testament Apocrypha
Judith 16:2

The noise of the moment scoffs at the music of the Eternal.

RABINDRANATH TAGORE (1861–1941)
Stray Birds

For every fiery prophet in old time,
And all the sacred madness of the bard,
When God made music through him
Could but make his music by the framework
  and the chord.

ALFRED LORD TENNYSON (1809–1892)
Holy Grail

Sorrow is hard to bear, and doubt is slow to
  clear,
  Each sufferer says his say, his scheme of
    the weal and woe:
But God has a few of us whom he whispers
  in the ear;

The rest may reason and welcome: 'tis
we musicians know.
ROBERT BROWNING (1812–1889)
Abt Vogler

The human soul is a silent harp in God's
choir, whose strings need only to be swept by
the divine breath to chime in with the harmonies of creation.
HENRY DAVID THOREAU (1817–1862)
Journals

God's music will not finish with one tune.
SIR EDWIN ARNOLD (1832–1904)
With Sadi in the Garden

I will sing with knowledge, and all my singing will be to the glory of God, and the lyre
and my harp for his perfect holiness. And I
will raise the flute of my lips in the chord of
his judgment.   *The Dead Sea Scrolls*

It is a good thing to give thanks unto the
     Lord,
And to sing praises unto Thy name, O Most
     High;
To declare Thy lovingkindness in the
     morning,
And thy faithfulness in the night seasons,
With an instrument of ten strings, and with
     the psaltery;
With a solemn sound upon the harp.
The Old Testament
Psalms 92:2–4

What is to reach the heart must come from
above. If it does not come thence it will be
nothing but notes—body without spirit.
LUDWIG VAN BEETHOVEN (1770–1827)
Letter to J. A. Stumpff

The high that proved too high, the heroic
     for earth too hard,
The passion that left the ground to lose
     itself in the sky,

Are music sent by God to the lover and the
     bard;
Enough that He heard it once: we shall hear
     it by and by.
ROBERT BROWNING (1812–1889)
Abt Vogler

O Mind! The knowledge of the science and
art of music bestows on a person the bliss of
oneness with the Supreme Being. Music such
as is accompanied by the blissful oceanlike
stories of the Lord which are the essence of
love and all the other sentiments blesses a
person with oneness with the Lord.
TYAGARAJA (1767–1847)
Sangitajnanamu

Music religious heat inspires,
It wakes the soul, and lifts it high,
And wings it with sublime desires,
And fits it to bespeak the Deity.
JOSEPH ADDISON (1672–1719)
Song for Saint Cecilia's Day

Tune me, O Lord, into one harmony
     With Thee, one full responsive vibrant
          chord;
Unto thy praise, all love and melody,
Tune me, O Lord.
CHRISTINA ROSSETTI (1830–1894)
Collected Poems

The Lord was ready to save me; therefore
we will sing my songs to the stringed instruments all the days of our life in the house of
the Lord.   *The Old Testament*
Isaiah 38:20

Such music (as 'tis said)
Before was never made,
     But when of old the sons of morning
          sung,
While the Creator great
His constellations set,
     And the well-balanced world on hinges
          hung,

And cast the dark foundations deep,
And bid the welt'ring waves their oozy
  channel keep.

JOHN MILTON (1608–1674)
The Hymn

Learn to dance the festive measure
    Which the Lord
God invented in his leisure;
    Imitate with knowing pleasure
Heaven's chord.

JOOST VAN DEN VONDEL
(1587–1679)
Adam in Ballingschap

Music strikes in me a deep fit of devotion,
and a profound contemplation of the First
Composer. There is something in it of Divinity more than the ear discovers.

SIR THOMAS BROWNE (1605–1682)
Religio Medici

We are all strings in the concert of His joy;
the spirit from His mouth strikes the note
and tune of our strings.

JACOB BOEHME (1575–1624)
Threefold Life of Man

From harmony, from heavenly harmony
This universal frame began:
From harmony to harmony
Through all the compass of the notes it ran,
The diapason closing full in Man.

JOHN DRYDEN (1631–1700)
Song for Saint Cecilia's Day

Glorious the northern lights astream;
Glorious the song, when God's the theme;
Glorious the thunder's roar.

CHRISTOPHER SMART (1722–1771)
Song to David

What is that gate, what is that mansion
where thou, O God, sittest and watchest over
all things? How many various and countless
instruments are played! How many musicians, how many musical measures with their
consorts, and how many singers sing Thee!

GURU NANAK (1469–1539)
The Japji

Music is an agreeable harmony for the
honor of God and the permissible delights of
the soul.

JOHANN SEBASTIAN BACH (1685–1750)
Letters

When I think upon my God, my heart is so
full of joy that the notes dance and leap from
my pen; and since God has given me a cheerful heart, it will be pardoned me that I serve
Him with a cheerful spirit.

FRANZ JOSEPH HAYDN (1732–1809)
Letters

Music is one of the greatest gifts that God
has given us: it is divine and therefore Satan
is its enemy. For with its aid many dire temptations are overcome; the devil does not stay
where music is.

MARTIN LUTHER (1483–1546)
In Praise of Music

Music is a manifestation of the highest energy . . . almost the definition of God.

THOMAS MANN (1875–1955)
Dr. Faustus

Of all God's prerogatives, song is the fairest.   THEOCRITUS (3rd century B.C.)
Idylls

Not without design does God write the
music of our lives. Be it ours to learn the
time, and not be discouraged at the Rests. If
we say sadly to ourselves, "There is no music
in a rest," let us not forget "there is the making of music in it." The making of music is
often a slow and painful process in this life.
How patiently God works to teach us! How
long He waits for us to learn the lesson.

JOHN RUSKIN (1819–1900)
Works

Among the first things created was the bird. Why? Because God wanted the world to have music at the start. And this infant world, wrapped in swaddling clothes of light, so beautifully serenaded at the start is to die amid the ringing blast of the archangel's trumpet; so that as the world had music at the start, it is going to have music at the last.

THOMAS DE WITT TALMAGE (1832–1902)
Sermons

As a choir of singers encircling the leader may for a time have their attention drawn from him and so sing out of tune, yet when they turn to him they sing in perfect harmony; so do we encircle God. But near as He is to us, we often do not look towards Him.

When we do turn to Him, our utmost wish is crowned, our souls have rest, our song is no longer a discord but a hymn divine.

PLOTINUS (205–270)
Enneads

Every genuine strain of music is a serene prayer, or bold, inspired demand, to be united with all, at the Heart of things.

JOHN SULLIVAN DWIGHT (1813–1893)
Aesthetic Papers

When you sing, O soul, remember that you are as truly communicating with the holy and omnipresent God as when you are praying.

GERHARD TERSTEEGEN (1697–1769)
Discourse

· HE WILLED THE INFINITE CREATION ·

Unless we believe that God renews the work of creation every day, our prayers and obeying of the commandments grow old and accustomed, and tedious. As it is written in the psalm: "Cast me not off in the time of old age"—that is to say, do not let my world grow cold.   BAAL SHEM TOV (1700–1760)
Sayings

The age of the world, as it deepens, does but prolong its testimony to God, and make it worthier of his eternity: its scale, as it expands, does but place us in a temple more august, and nearer to his Infinity.

JAMES MARTINEAU (1805–1900)
Faith and Progressive Knowledge

God was, alone in unity. He willed
The infinite creation; and it was.

PHILIP JAMES BAILEY (1816–1902)
The Mystic

Brahma is the great Creator,
        Life a mystic drama;

Heaven, and Earth, and living Nature
        Are but masks of Brahma.

JOHN STUART BLACKIE (1809–1895)
Trimurti

The Lord did not create the world a void; He created it to be dwelt in.

The Old Testament
Isaiah 45:18

Creation in itself, without reference to the Almighty Spirit from which it sprung, is formless and without order—a mass of chaotic objects, of whose uses we are ignorant and whose destiny we cannot imagine. It is only when its visible glory leads our minds to its unseen Author, and we regard it as a manifestation of Divine Wisdom, that we can truly comprehend its character and designs.

GEORGE RIPLEY (1802–1880)
Discourses on the Philosophy of Religion

The earth which, like our own bodies, though dust in its degradation, is full of

splendour when God's hand gathers its atoms.   JOHN RUSKIN (1819–1900)
The Stones of Venice

God established the world as "a will to existence, to consciousness, to spirit." He established it, not as complete, but as becoming. He does not build it as a house, but plants it, like a flower, in the seed, that it may grow, that it may struggle upwards stage by stage to fuller existence, aspiring with toil and endeavor towards the height where, in the image of the Creator, as a free and reasonable spirit capable of personality, it may realize the aim of its being.
RUDOLF OTTO (1869–1937)
Naturalism and Religion

As the shell, the pith, and the kernel of a fruit are all produced from one parent seed of the tree, so from the one Lord is produced the whole of creation, animate and inanimate, spiritual and material.
SRI RAMAKRISHNA (1833–1886)
Sayings

Everything is a thought of Infinite God. And in studying the movements of the solar system, or the composition of an ultimate cell arrested in a crystal, developed in a plant; in tracing the grains of phosphorus in the brain of man; or in the powers, and action thereof —I am studying the thought of the Infinite God.   THEODORE PARKER (1810–1860)
Theism, Atheism, and the Popular Theology

To make God a momentary Creator, who once and for all finished His work, would be cold and barren, and we must differ from profane men especially in that we see the presence of divine power shining as much in the continuing state of the universe as in its inception.
JOHN CALVIN (1509–1564)
Institutes of the Christian Religion

Eternal God! Thy word is not finished; thy thought, the thought of the world, is not yet revealed. It still creates, and will continue to create, for long ages beyond all human calculation. The ages that have run their course have revealed to us only a few fragments.
GIUSEPPE MAZZINI (1805–1872)
The Duties of Man

The "world" is the immeasurable totality of energies and forms, a tissue of relations extending into ever-increasing enormity and withdrawing into ever-decreasing minuteness. All this was thought, willed, and realized by God. Nothing was supplied for Him, neither models nor matter. And all these forms and arrangements, so full of truth, which science strives unceasingly to penetrate, only to see again and again that they continue into the vast unknown; this profusion of value and meaning which ever and ever again impinges upon the human mind yet can never be fathomed—God has made them.
ROMANO GUARDINI (1885–1968)
The Wisdom of the Psalms

God created many worlds and destroyed many worlds before he created this one of heaven and earth.   *The Midrash*

Let me tell you then why the Creator made this world of generation. He was good, and the good can never have any jealousy of anything. And being free from jealousy, he desired that all things should be as like himself as they could be. This is in the truest sense the origin of creation and of the world, as we shall do well in believing on the testimony of wise men: God desired that all things should be good and nothing bad, so far as this was attainable.   PLATO (427–347 B.C.)
Timaeus

The primary Imagination I hold to be the living Power and prime Agent of all human

Perception, and as a repetition in the finite mind of the eternal act of creation in the Infinite I Am.

SAMUEL TAYLOR COLERIDGE (1772–1834)
Biographia Literaria

Verily, in the creation of the Heavens and of the earth, and in the succession of the night and of the day, are signs for men of understanding; who, standing and sitting and reclining, bear God in mind and reflect on the creation of the Heavens and of the earth, and say: "Oh, our Lord! Thou has not created this in vain."   *The Koran*

My heart is awed within me when I
    think
Of the great miracle that still goes on,
In silence, round me—the perpetual work
Of thy creation, finished, yet renewed
Forever. Written on thy works I read
The lesson of thy own eternity.

WILLIAM CULLEN BRYANT (1794–1878)
A Forest Hymn

How endless is that volume which God hath written of the world! wherein every creature is a letter, every day a new page.

JOSEPH HALL (1574–1656)
The Pleasure of Study

What is there more natural, and yet more magnificent, what is easier to conceive and more in accord with human reason, than the Creator descending into the primordial night to make light with a word?

FRANÇOIS RENÉ DE CHATEAUBRIAND
(1768–1848)
Genius of Christianity

The miracle of Creation, however it may teem with images, is best described with little diffusion of language: He spake the word, and they were made.

DR. SAMUEL JOHNSON (1709–1784)
The Lives of the English Poets

The beginning! but where is the beginning? You know that the beginning is God.

EDGAR ALLAN POE (1809–1849)
Mesmeric Revelation

The creation of the world consists metaphysically in God's having posited his own divine world not as eternally subsisting but as becoming. In this sense He fused it organically with nothingness, immersing it in becoming.

SERGEI BULGAKOV (1871–1944)
The Lamb of God

Creation: good broken up into pieces and scattered throughout evil.

SIMONE WEIL (1909–1943)
Gravity and Grace

It is very clear that everything that is produced in time must necessarily have a proximate cause which has produced it. In its turn, that cause has a cause and so forth till finally one comes to the First Cause of all things, I mean God's will and free choice.

MAIMONIDES (1135–1204)
Guide for the Perplexed

The world is a mirror of infinite beauty, yet no man sees it. It is a Temple of Majesty, yet no man regards it. It is a region of Light and Peace, did not men disquiet it. It is the Paradise of God.

THOMAS TRAHERNE (1634–1704)
Centuries of Meditations

The divine in the creation is only adequately represented when the whole of the time-process is gathered up into its final meaning and purpose, when, in fact, the mode of becoming is united with the mode of being. This I conceive to be the eternal world—not a world of immobility in contrast with a world of change, but a world in which the antinomy of becoming and being, of motion and rest, is transcended.

WILLIAM RALPH INGE (1860–1954)
Faith and Its Psychology

The ultimate Author of all our volitions is the Creator of the world, who first bestowed motion on this immense machine, and placed all beings in that particular position, whence every subsequent event, by an inevitable necessity, must result.

DAVID HUME (1711–1776)
An Enquiry Concerning Human Understanding

God creates out of nothing—wonderful, you say: yes, to be sure, but he does what is still more wonderful: he makes saints out of sinners.

SÖREN KIERKEGAARD (1813–1855)
Journals

"My Lord, my Master," I said, "was it not you, and you alone, who in the beginning spoke the Word that formed the world? O Lord, at the beginning you spoke the Word." *The Old Testament Apocrypha*
2 Esdras 9:6

All this cosmos is pervaded by Me in form
   Unmanifest;
In Me all beings must subsist although in
   them I never rest.

The Bhagavad Gita

He who first by the mind filled the blessed
   spaces with light,
He created Righteousness by his will,
By which he upholds Best Mind.
Thou hast, O Wise One, increased it by thy
   Spirit
Which is even now with thee, O Lord!
Through the mind, O Wise One, have I
   known thee as the first and the last,
As the Father of Good Mind.

ZOROASTER (6th century B.C.)
The Gathas

Search into days gone by, long before your time, beginning at the day when God created man on earth; search from one end of

heaven to the other, and ask if any deed as mighty as this has been seen or heard.

The Old Testament
Deuteronomy 4:32

Ever fresh, the broad creation,
A divine improvisation,
From the heart of God proceeds
A single will, a million deeds.
Once slept the world, an egg of stone,
And pulse and sound and light were
   none,
And God said "throb," and there was
   motion,
And the vast mass became vast ocean.

RALPH WALDO EMERSON (1803–1882)
Wood Notes

God set the soul in the center of the body and drew it through the whole framework, yea, and wrapped the whole body with a covering of soul, and made it a sphere revolving in a circle, one only Universe in lonely splendor, but able by reason of its excellence to be its own companion, and needing none other, being sufficient unto itself for acquaintance and friend.

PLATO (427–347 B.C.)
Timaeus

At the time when the Holy One created the world and wanted to reveal deep matters from their hidden recesses, and light from within darkness, they were intertwined with one another. Because of this, that out of darkness came light and from out of the hidden recesses were revealed deep matters, that one came from the other, it also is the other way round: out of the good emerges evil, and out of love emerges strict justice, since they are intertwined. *The Zohar*

When we examine a process like evolution, which brought about such prodigies as human intelligence and conscience, we should never take the rapidity or slowness of the event into consideration. . . . To an imaginary being, with a life span of ten thousand million years, evolution would seem very rapid. To God, whom we cannot even conceive in relation to time, it may well have been "instantaneous."

PIERRE LECOMTE DU NOUY (1883–1947)
Human Destiny

When the radiant morn of creation broke,
And the world in the smile of God awoke,
And the empty realms of darkness and
    death
Were moved through their depths by his
    mighty breath . . .

WILLIAM CULLEN BRYANT (1794–1878)
The Song of the Stars

The world is just the materializing of God's thoughts, for the world is a thought in God's eye. He made it first from a thought that came from His own mighty mind, and everything in the majestic temple He has made has a meaning.

CHARLES HADDON SPURGEON (1834–1892)
Harvest Time

Only That which made us, meant us to be
    mightier by and by,
Set the sphere of all the boundless Heavens
    within the human eye,
Sent the shadow of Himself, the boundless,
    thro' the human soul;
Boundless inward, in the atom, boundless
    outward, in the whole.

ALFRED LORD TENNYSON (1809–1892)
Locksley Hall Sixty Years After

May not this universe of yours, of which You are the eternal and infinite Consciousness be a dream? May it not be a dream of yours? May it perhaps be that You are dreaming us? And if such is the case, what will become of the universe, what will become of us, what will become of me, when You, God of my life, awake?

MIGUEL DE UNAMUNO (1864–1936)
The Life of Don Quixote and Sancho

Hindu wisdom, long ago, regarded the world as the dream of Brahma. Must we hold with Fichte that it is the individual dream of each individual ego? Every fool would then be a cosmogonic poet producing the firework of the universe under the dome of the infinite.   HENRI FRÉDÉRIC AMIEL (1821–1881)
Journal Intime

There seems to be a necessity in spirit to manifest itself in material forms; and day and night, river and storm, beast and bird, acid and alkali, preexist in necessary Ideas in the mind of God, and are what they are by virtue of preceding affections in the world of spirit.

RALPH WALDO EMERSON (1803–1882)
Nature

God, having determined to found a mighty state, first of all conceived its form in His mind, according to which form He made a world perceptible only by the intellect, and then completed one visible to the external senses, using the first one as a model.

PHILO JUDAEUS (30 B.C.–A.D. 40)
On the Creation of the World

The world—the clustering spheres He
    made,
The glorious light, the soothing shade,
    Dale, champaign, grove, and hill;
The multitudinous abyss,
Where Secrecy remains in bliss,
    And Wisdom hides her skill.

CHRISTOPHER SMART (1722–1770)
A Song to David

In addition to the world or aggregate of finite things there is some unique Being who governs, not only like the soul in me, or rather like the Ego itself in my body, but in a

much higher relation. For one Being domi-
nating the universe not only rules the world
but he creates and fashions it, is superior to
the world, and, so to speak, extra mundane,
and by this very fact is the ultimate reason of
things.   GOTTFRIED WILHELM VON LEIBNIZ
(1646–1716)
Theodicy

Io dwelt within the breathing-space of
    immensity.
The Universe was in darkness, with water
    everywhere.
There was no glimmer of dawn, no
    clearness, no light.
And he began by saying these words—
    "Darkness, become a light-possessing
        darkness."
And at once light appeared.
                              Maori Folklore
                              Creation Poem

At the beginning all things were in the
mind of Wakonda. All creatures, including
man, were spirits. They moved about in
space between the earth and the stars. They
were seeking a place where they could come
into a bodily existence. They ascended to the
sun, but the sun was not fitted for their
abode. They moved on to the moon and
found it was not good for their home. Then
they descended to the earth.
                        Omaha Indian Folklore
                        The Creation

God, how I understand your hour, when you
put your voice before you that it might be
round in space; nothingness was like a
wound to you, so you cooled it with the
world.   RAINER MARIA RILKE (1875–1926)
                              Book of Hours

How then dost Thou create things other
than Thyself—for Thou wouldst seem to create Thyself? Yet this is no real difficulty, since

with Thee creation and existence are the
same. And creating and being created are
naught else than the sharing of Thy Being
among all, that Thou mayest be All in all, and
yet mayest abide freed from all.
                  NICHOLAS OF CUSA (1401–1464)
                        The Vision of God

The divine and creative Word was not uttered once for all, but it receives perpetual
utterance in the radiation of light, in the
movements of the stars, in the development
of life, in the reason and conscience of man.
              WILLIAM TEMPLE (1881–1944)
                        Daily Readings

Creation is the language of God, Time is
His song, and things of space the consonants
in the song. To sanctify time is to sing the
vowels in unison with Him.
        ABRAHAM JOSHUA HESCHEL (1907–1973)
                              The Sabbath

The highest Father, God the master-
builder, by the laws of his secret wisdom, fab-
ricated this house, this world which we see, a
very superb temple of divinity.
        GIOVANNI PICO DELLA MIRANDOLA
                        (1463–1494)
                        On the Dignity of Man

The Lord by wisdom hath founded the
earth; by understanding hath he established
the heavens. By his knowledge the depths are
broken up, and the clouds drop down the
dew.   *The Old Testament*
                        Proverbs 3:19–20

We believe that God hath made all things
out of nothing: because, even although the
world hath been made of some material, that
very same material hath been made out of
nothing.   SAINT AUGUSTINE (354–430)
                  Of the Faith and the Creed

The creation is the Bible of the Deist.
He there reads, in the handwriting of the

Creator Himself, the certainty of His existence, and the immutability of His power, and all other Bibles and Testaments are to him forgeries.

THOMAS PAINE (1737–1809)
The Age of Reason

What was the basis, what the beginning, how was it—that from which Visvakarman, the all-seeing, generated the earth and unfolded the heavens in their greatness?

The Rig-Veda

I always see the Garden, and God there,
A-making man's wife—and, my lesson learned,

The value and significance of flesh,
I can't unlearn ten minutes afterwards.

ROBERT BROWNING (1812–1889)
Fra Lippo Lippi

In the very beginning, when this great universe lay in the mind of God, like unborn forests in the acorn-cup; long ere the echoes waked the solitudes, before the mountains were brought forth, and long ere the light flashed through the sky, God loved his chosen creatures.

CHARLES HADDON SPURGEON (1834–1892)
Sermons

God has made all atoms in space mirrors, and fronts each one with his perfect face.

Persian Saying

· GOD'S OMNIPRESENCE ·

He that dwelleth in the secret place of the Most High shall abide under the shadow of the Almighty.   *The Old Testament*
Psalms 91:1

The Divine and Eternal are ever near us. God does not dwell in some far-off point of space; he is not more present anywhere else than on this earth of ours, nor could any local transition or physical transformation bring him nearer.

JOHN CAIRD (1820–1898)
Sermons

Thus saith the Lord, The Heaven is my throne and the earth is my footstool; where is the house that ye build unto me? and where is the place of my rest?

The Old Testament
Isaiah 66:1

Manifest, near, moving in the cave of the heart is the great Being. In it everything is centered which ye know as moving, breath-

ing, as being and not-being, as the best, that is beyond the understanding of creatures.

The Upanishads

According to the Apostle, "you are God's planting, God's building" (1 Corinthians 3:9), a planting in the good soil and a building on the rock, therefore as God's building let us stand unshaken before the wintry storm, and as God's planting let us not think about the Evil One or about the tribulation or persecution that happens on account of the world or about the care of this age, or about the deceit of wealth or about the pleasures of life.

ORIGEN (185–254)
An Exhortation to Martyrdom

Thus says the high and lofty One who inhabits eternity, whose name is Holy: "I dwell in the high and holy place, and also with him who is of a contrite and humble spirit, to revive the spirit of the humble, and to revive the heart of the contrite.

The Old Testament
Isaiah 57:15

But will God in very deed dwell with men on the earth? Behold, heaven and the heaven of heavens cannot contain thee; how much less this house which I have built!

The Old Testament
2 Chronicles 6:18

If we maintain holy intercourse with the little world entrusted to us, if we help the holy spiritual substance to accomplish itself in that section of Creation in which we are living, then we are establishing, in this our place, a dwelling for the Divine Presence.

MARTIN BUBER (1878–1965)
I and Thou

To love another better than one's self is to begin heaven here. The great lesson of all is that the Father's mansions are within one's own breast. Heaven is here; the world of hope, anticipation, feeling, is all here. We have it here first, if we have it at all.

FRANÇOIS FÉNELON (1651–1715)
Maximes des Saints

In the highest golden sheath there is the Brahman without passions and without parts. That is pure, that is the light of lights, that is it which they know who know the Self.

The Upanishads

He is the innermost Self in all beings. He who knows him hidden in the shrine of his heart cuts the knot of ignorance even in his life. Self-luminous, ever present in the hearts of all, is the great Being.

The Upanishads

THE INDEFINABLE, MYSTERIOUS POWER
THAT PERVADES EVERYTHING

God is not external to anyone, but is present with all things, though they are ignorant that He is so.

PLOTINUS (205–270)
Enneads

There is an indefinable, mysterious power that pervades everything. I feel it though I do not see it. It is this Unseen Power which makes itself felt and yet defies all proof because it is so unlike all that I perceive through my senses.

MOHANDAS K. GANDHI (1869–1948)
Young India

God as being-itself transcends nonbeing absolutely. On the other hand, God as creative life includes the finite and, with it, nonbeing, although nonbeing is eternally conquered and the finite is eternally reunited within the infinity of the divine life. The certainty of God's directing creativity is based on the certainty of God as the ground of being and meaning. The confidence of every creature, its courage to be, is rooted in faith in God as its creative ground.

PAUL TILLICH (1886–1965)
Systematic Theology

The true doctrine of omnipresence is that God reappears with all his parts in every moss and cobweb. The value of the universe contrives to throw itself into every part.

RALPH WALDO EMERSON (1803–1882)
Compensation

"God came down to see [the Tower of Babel]" (Genesis 11:5). But did He need to come down? Is not all patent and revealed to Him who "knoweth what is in the darkness, and with whom light dwells" (Daniel 2:22)? The answer is that God did this to teach to mankind not to pass sentence, yea, not even to utter a single word, on hearsay, but to look with their own eyes.   *The Midrash*

We are actors in a great historical drama. It rests upon us to decide if a new era is to dawn in the transformation of the world into the kingdom of God, or if Western civilization is to descend to the graveyard of dead civilizations and God will have to try once more.

WALTER RAUSCHENBUSCH (1861–1918)
Christianity and the Social Crisis

It is God's world still. It has been given to man not absolutely, but in trust, that man may work out in it the will of God; given— may we not say?—just as a father gives a child a corner of his great garden, and says, "There, that is yours; now cultivate it."

PHILLIPS BROOKS (1835–1893)
Visions and Tasks

The world is a great stage on which God displays His many wonders.

SAINT FRANCIS OF SALES (1567–1622)
Introduction to the Devout Life

The expression "God's world," may sound sentimental to some ears. For me it did not have this character at all. To "God's world" belonged everything superhuman—dazzling light, the darkness of the abyss, the cold impassivity of infinite space and time, and the uncanny grotesqueness of the irrational world of chance.

CARL JUNG (1875–1961)
Memories, Dreams, Reflections

Slowly the Bible of the race is writ,
And not on paper leaves nor leaves of stone;
Each age, each kindred, adds a verse to it,
Texts of despair or hope, of joy or moan.

JAMES RUSSELL LOWELL (1819–1891)
Bibliolatres

This visible World is wonderfully to be delighted in, and highly to be esteemed, because it is the theater of God's righteous Kingdom.

THOMAS TRAHERNE (1636–1674)
Centuries of Meditations

Creation is not an instantaneous act, but is an eternal process. The immanence of God which follows from this hypothesis is the pledge that evil and error, ugliness and imperfection are not ultimate. Evil has reference to the distance which good has to traverse. Error is the stage on the pathway to truth.

SARVEPALLI RADHAKRISHNAN (1888–1975)
Addresses

The longer I live, the more clearly I see how all souls are in His hand—the mean and the great. Fallen on the earth in their baseness, or fading as the mist of morning in their goodness—still in the hand of the potter as the clay, and in the temple of their master as the cloud.   JOHN RUSKIN (1819–1900)
Modern Painters

It is written (Lamentations 3:23): "They are new every morning: great is thy faith." A man should believe that each day the world is re-created, and that he is reborn each morning. His faith will then be increased, and he will take a fresh interest daily in his service to the Lord.

BAAL SHEM TOV (1700–1760)
Sayings

Place yourself in the middle of the stream of power and wisdom which flows into you as life, place yourself in the full center of that flood, then you are without effort impelled to truth, to right, and a perfect contentment.

RALPH WALDO EMERSON (1803–1882)
Journal

The Spirit is the master-builder. Flesh is but the instrument, and matter the material by which and in which the divine design is elaborated and shaped to the senses—whether sensual or intellectual—of man.

BRONSON ALCOTT (1799–1888)
Psyche

Let us study the visible creation as we will; take the anatomy of the smallest animal; look at the smallest grain of corn that is planted in the earth, and the manner in which its germ produces and multiplies; observe attentively the rose-bud, how carefully it opens to the sun, and closes at its setting; and we shall see more skill and design than in all the works of man.

FRANÇOIS FÉNELON (1651–1715)
On the Existence of God

Let each man think himself an act of God,
His mind a thought, his life a breath of God.

PHILIP JAMES BAILEY (1816–1902)
Festus

I am not too certain who put me on this earth. I have been told that it was God; and if it wasn't He, who could it be?

ANDRÉ GIDE (1869–1951)
On Joy and Progress

Only the creative thoughts of God are truly objective, have actuality in their outward expression, and stand forth existent and living in the products of creative power. Man can only give names to these creations, arrange and link them together.

JOHANN GOTTFRIED HERDER (1744–1803)
The Spirit of Hebrew Poetry

The first thing which God created was a pen, and he said to it, "Write." It said, "What shall I write?" And God said, "Write down the quantity of every separate thing to be created." And it wrote all that was and all that will be to eternity.   *The Sunan*

Creative force, like a musical composer, goes on unweariedly repeating a simple air or theme, now high, now low, in solo, in chorus, ten thousand times reverberated, till it fills earth and heaven with the chant.

RALPH WALDO EMERSON (1803–1882)
Representative Men

In all parts of Nature's spacious sphere,
Of art ten thousand miracles appear;
And will you not the Author's skill adore
Because you think He might discover more?

RICHARD BLACKMORE (1825–1900)
The Creation

Creativity is the basic attribute of God, identical with His uniqueness.

HERMANN COHEN (1842–1918)
Rational Religion

One with the flower of a day, one with the
  withered moon,
One with the granite mountains that melt
  into the noon,
One with the dream that triumphs beyond
  the light of the spheres,
We come from the Loom of the Weaver that
  weaves the Web of Years.

ALFRED NOYES (1880–1958)
Collected Poems

That memorable Hour of wond'rous Birth,
When the dread Sire, on Emanation bent,
And big with Nature, rising in his might,
Call'd forth Creation.

EDWARD YOUNG (1683–1765)
Night Thoughts

For America, and for today, just the same as any day, the supreme and final science is the science of God—what we call science being only its minister—as Democracy is, or shall be also. And a poet of America must fill himself with such thoughts, and chant his best out of them.

WALT WHITMAN (1819–1892)
Preface to "As a Strong Bird"

Therefore Agathon rightly says: "Of this alone even God is deprived, the power of making things that are past never to have been.   ARISTOTLE (384–322 B.C.)
Ethics

God made all the creatures, and gave them
  our love and our fear,
To give sign, we and they are his children,
  one family here.
          ROBERT BROWNING (1812–1889)
Saul

Body and spirit are twins: God only knows which is which.
ALGERNON CHARLES SWINBURNE (1837–1909)
The Higher Pantheism in a Nutshell

In the creative vision of God the individual is present as a whole in his essential being and inner teleos and at the same time in the infinity of the special moments of his life process. Of course this is said symbolically, since we are unable to have a perception of or even an imagination of that which belongs to the divine life. The mystery of being beyond essence and existence is hidden in the mystery of the creativity of the divine life.
          PAUL TILLICH (1886–1965)
Systematic Theology

I believe that our Heavenly Father invented man because He was disappointed in the monkey.   MARK TWAIN (1835–1910)
Letters

We indeed created man; and We know what his soul whispers within him, and We are nearer to him than the jugular vein.
The Koran

The Lord created me at the beginning of his way, the first of his acts of old. Ages ago I was set up, at the first, before the beginning of the earth. When he established the heavens, I was there, when he drew a circle on the face of the deep, when he marked out the foundations of the earth, then was I beside him, like a master workman.
The Old Testament
Proverbs 8:22–23

The whole Creation is a mystery and particularly that of man. At the blast of His mouth were the rest of the creatures made; and at His bare Word they started out of nothing: but in the frame of men (as the text describes it) he played the sensible operator, and seemed not so much to create as make him.   SIR THOMAS BROWNE (1605–1682)
Religio Medici

All created things are but the crumbs which fall from the table of God.
          SAINT JOHN OF THE CROSS (1542–1591)
Ascent of Mount Carmel

It is so impossible for the world to exist without God that if God should *forget* it, it would immediately cease to be.
          SÖREN KIERKEGAARD (1813–1855)
Journals

I can know myself as a person only where I feel my existence grounded in responsibility, and that means where I know myself to be created by and in the Word of God.
          EMIL BRUNNER (1889–1966)
The Word and the World

Creation—happens to us, burns into us, changes us, we tremble and swoon, we submit. Creation—we participate in it, we encounter the creator, offer ourselves to him, helpers and companions.
          MARTIN BUBER (1878–1965)
I and Thou

From all eternity God knew that he could make a great number of creatures past all counting, endowed with different perfections, different characteristics, to which he could give himself. Realizing that he could give himself in no better fashion than by uniting himself with a created nature—in such a way as to engraft the creature into the godhead, so as to form one person—his infinite goodness, naturally self-sharing, decided on that method.

SAINT FRANCES OF SALES (1567–1622)
The Love of God

God the Creator becomes the molder of man's heart and spirit. "He that fashioneth the hearts of them all" (Psalms 33:15), and He "who stretched forth the heavens, and laid the foundation of the earth, and formed the spirit of man within him" (Zechariah 12:1). As the calling-into-being of heaven and earth is a special act of creation, so is the forming of man's spirit within him.

HERMANN COHEN (1842–1918)
Jewish Writings

Imagine yourself alone in the world, a musing, wondering, reflecting spirit, lost in thought, and imagine thereafter the creation of man!—man made in the image of God!

HENRY DAVID THOREAU (1817–1862)
Journals

If I were the author of my being, I should doubt of nothing, I should desire nothing, and, in fine, no perfection would be awanting me; for I should have bestowed upon myself every perfection of which I possess the idea, and I should thus be God.

RENÉ DESCARTES (1596–1650)
Principles of Philosophy

As God Himself planted this seed and pressed it in and begat it, it can quite well be covered and hidden and yet never destroyed nor extinguished in itself. It glows and sparkles and burns and turns without intermission to God.   ORIGEN (185–254)
Homiliae in Genesim

O rich and various man! thou palace of sight and sound, carrying in thy senses the morning and the night, and the unfathomable galaxy; in thy brain, the geometry of the city of God; in thy heart, the power of love and the realms of right and wrong. An individual man is a fruit which it cost all the foregoing ages to form and ripen.

RALPH WALDO EMERSON (1803–1882)
Collected Essays

The greatness of God is infinite; for while with one die man impresses many coins and all are exactly alike, the King of Kings, the Holy One—blessed be He!—with one die impresses the same image on all men, and yet not one of them is like his neighbor. So that every one ought to say, "For myself is the world created."   *The Talmud*

· GOD FULFILLS HIMSELF IN MANY WAYS ·

In no single act or passion can salvation stand; far hence, beyond Orion and Andromeda, the cosmic process works and shall work forever through unbegotten souls.

FREDERIC WILLIAM HENRY MYERS (1843–1901)
Human Personality

When God wanted sponges and oysters, He made them, and put one on a rock, and the other in the mud. When He made man, He did not make him to be a sponge, or an oyster; He made him with feet and hands, and head and heart, and vital blood, and a place to use them, and said to him, "Go, work!"

HENRY WARD BEECHER (1813–1887)
Royal Truths

What has been, already exists, and what is still to be, has already been, and God always seeks to repeat the past.

The Old Testament
Ecclesiastes 3:15

Ancient of Days! except thou deign
  Upon the finished task to smile,
The workman's hand hath toiled in vain,
  To hew the rock and rear the pile.

WILLIAM CULLEN BRYANT (1794–1878)
Except the Lord Build the House

The old order changeth, yielding place to new,
And God fulfills Himself in many ways,
Lest one good custom should corrupt the world.

ALFRED LORD TENNYSON (1809–1892)
Morte d'Arthur

All of God's works are signs and expressions of his attributes; and thus it seems that all of physical nature is an expression and image of the spiritual world. All finite creatures are able to perceive truth and the nature of things only in images.

JOHANN GEORG HAMANN (1730–1786)
Schriften

God offers to every mind its choice between truth and repose.

RALPH WALDO EMERSON (1803–1882)
Essays

The ways of God are as the number of the souls of the sons of men. *Persian Proverb*

There is no vein by which life and being flows into us, derived from any source other than Thy workmanship, O Lord, for Thou art life and being in the highest degree.

SAINT AUGUSTINE (354–430)
Confessions

As there is an infinity of possible universes in the ideas of God, and as only one of them can exist, there must be a sufficient reason for the choice of God, which determines him for one rather than for another.

GOTTFRIED WILHELM VON LEIBNIZ
(1646–1716)
Philosophical Works

The works of God are but a kind of voice or language of God to instruct intelligent beings in things pertaining to Himself.

JONATHAN EDWARDS (1703–1758)
Images

Revelation is God's word, Creation his work, the Spirit sole seer and interpreter of both. BRONSON ALCOTT (1799–1888)
Journals

All God's great works are silent. They are not done amid rattle of drums and flare of trumpets. Light as it travels makes no noise, utters no sound to the ear. Creation is a silent process; nature rose under the Almighty hand without clang or clamor, or noises that distract and disturb.

ANDREW MARTIN FAIRBAIRN (1838–1912)
Sermons

The universality of law means that God works everywhere and in all things by constant and unchangeable method. This is observed not only in the wide things, in the vast movements of solar systems, but in the tiniest details of nature, so that all the intricacies of the wing of a butterfly are as much the result in each detail of the universal law or method by which God works in all things as the vastest cosmic movement.

CHARLES GORE (1853–1932)
Sermons

Man is in process of becoming the perfected being whom God is seeking to create. However, this is not taking place—it is important to add—by a natural and inevitable evolution, but through a hazardous adventure in individual freedom.

JOHN HICK (1922–)
Evil and the God of Love

Blind to the working of that secret power
That balances the wings of every hour,
The busy trifler dreams himself alone,
Frames many a purpose, and God works his
  own.

WILLIAM COWPER (1731–1800)
Expostulation

That anything may be found to be an infinite treasure, its place must be found in Eternity and in God's esteem. For as there is a time, so there is a place for all things. Everything in its place is admirable, deep, and glorious: out of its place like a wandering bird, is desolate and good for nothing. How therefore it relateth to God and all creatures must be seen before it can be enjoyed.

THOMAS TRAHERNE (1637–1674)
Centuries of Meditations

The Almighty does nothing without reason, though the frail mind of man cannot explain the reason.

SAINT AUGUSTINE (354–430)
The City of God

Today, even now, Thy work doth abide in that Thou hewest a pathway for the rivers. The hills bow down before Thee as were they friends; the wide spaces of the universe are knit together by Thee.   *The Rig-Veda*

It will not do for any of us to make up his mind that he cannot be any good and noble thing, until first he has asked himself whether it is as impossible in God's sight as in his.   PHILLIPS BROOKS (1835–1893)
Perennials

It is very fit and becoming of God, who is infinitely wise, so to order things that there should be a voice of His in His works, instructing those that behold them and painting forth and showing divine mysteries and things more immediately appertaining to Himself and His spiritual kingdom.

JONATHAN EDWARDS (1703–1758)
Images

The first author of "speech" was God Himself, that instructed Adam how to name such creatures as He presented to his sight.

THOMAS HOBBES (1588–1679)
Leviathan

· GOD IS MADE ONE WITH NATURE ·

Know that, by nature, every creature seeks to become like God. Nature's intent is neither food nor drink nor clothing, nor comfort, nor anything else in which God is left out. Whether you like it or not, whether you know it or not, secretly nature seeks, hunts, tries to ferret out the track on which God may be found.

MEISTER ECKHART (1260–1327)
Works

All that we see, about, abroad,
What is it all, but nature's God?
In meaner works discover'd here
No less than in the starry sphere.

> PHILIP FRENEAU (1752–1832)
> *On the Universality and Other*
> *Attributes of the God of Nature*

The world around us is the mighty volume wherein God hath declared himself. Human languages and characters are different in different nations. And those of one nation are not understood by the rest. But the book of nature is written in an universal character, which every man may read in his own language.

> JOHN WESLEY (1703–1791)
> *Letters*

Look at this vigorous plant that lifts its head
  from the meadow,
See how its leaves are turned to the north, as
  true as the magnet;
This is the compass-flower, that the finger of
  God has planted
Here in the houseless wild, to direct the
  traveller's journey.

> HENRY WADSWORTH LONGFELLOW
> (1807–1882)
> *Evangeline*

Take a view of the works of nature, listen to voice within, and then tell me what God hath omitted to say to your sight, your conscience, your understanding?

> JEAN JACQUES ROUSSEAU (1712–1778)
> *Emile*

I do not count the hours I spend
  In wandering by the sea;
The forest is my loyal friend,
  Like God it useth me.

> RALPH WALDO EMERSON
> (1803–1882)
> *Collected Verse*

All the energies of nature are activities of a cosmic mind—the mind that our value experiences reveal to be the eternal God. Every law of nature is a law of God, every energy of nature a deed of God.

> EDGAR S. BRIGHTMAN (1884–1953)
> *Nature and Values*

God loves an idle rainbow,
No less than labouring seas.

> RALPH HODGSON (1871–1962)
> *A Wood Song*

Laws of Nature are God's thoughts thinking themselves out in the orbits and the tides.

> CHARLES H. PARKHURST (1842–1933)
> *Sermons*

The course of nature God seldom alters or perverts; but, like an excellent artist, hath so contrived His work that, with the self-same instrument, without a new creation, He may effect His obscurest designs.

> SIR THOMAS BROWNE (1605–1682)
> *Religio Medici*

Thou glorious mirror, where the Almighty's
  form
Glasses itself in tempests.

> GEORGE GORDON, LORD BYRON (1788–1824)
> *Childe Harold*

A little Madness in the Spring
Is wholesome even for the King,
But God be with the Clown—
Who ponders this tremendous scene—
This whole Experiment of Green—
As if it were his own!

> EMILY DICKINSON (1830–1886)
> *Collected Verse*

The question before the human race is whether the God of nature shall govern the world by His own laws, or whether priests and kings shall rule it by fictitious miracles.

> THOMAS JEFFERSON (1743–1826)
> *Letter to John Adams*

Slave to no sect, who takes no private road,
But looks through nature up to nature's
  God.

ALEXANDER POPE (1688–1744)
Essay on Man

Nature herself has imprinted on the minds
of all the idea of God.

MARCUS TULLIUS CICERO (106–43 B.C.)
De Natura Deorem

Nature, this world, is an existence which
contradicts my wishes, my feelings. Here it is
not as it ought to be; this world passes away;
but God is existence as it ought to be.

LUDWIG FEUERBACH (1804–1872)
The Essence of Christianity

Truly, One alone of all these was the greatest, inspiring to all minds, the great white
Rock, standing as high as the heavens, en-
wrapped in mist, verily as high as the heavens.   *Omaha Indian Hymn*

And what if all of animated nature
Be but organic Harps diversely fram'd
That tremble into thought, as o'er them
          sweeps
Plastic and vast, one intellectual breeze,
At once the Soul of each, and God of all?

SAMUEL TAYLOR COLERIDGE (1772–1834)
Poetical Works

To the eye of the seer every leaf of the tree
is a page of the holy book that contains divine
revelation, and he is inspired every moment
of his life by constantly reading and understanding the holy script of nature.

HAZRAT INAYAT KHAN (died 1927)
The Sufi Message

Let man learn the revelation of all nature
and thought to his heart: that the Highest
dwells within him, that the sources of nature
are in his own mind.

RALPH WALDO EMERSON (1803–1882)
The Over-Soul

All nature's wonders serve to excite and
perfect this idea of their Author. 'Tis here he
suffers us to see, and even converse with him,
in a manner suitable to our frailty; how glorious is it to contemplate him, in this noblest
of his works apparent to us, the system of the
bigger world.

LORD SHAFTSBURY (1671–1713)
Works

Go out into a garden and examine a seed;
examine the same plant in the bud and in the
fruit, and you must confess the whole process
a miracle, a perpetual miracle. Take it at any
period, make yourself as familiar with all the
facts as you can at each period, and in each
explanation there will be some step or appearance to be referred directly to the Great
Creator; something not the effect of the sow-
er's deposit nor of the waterer's hope. It is
not the loam, nor the gravel, it is not the fur-
row of the ploughshare, nor the glare of the
sun that calls greenness from the dust, it is
the present power of Him who said "Seed-
time and harvest shall not fail." Needs there,
my brethren, any other book than this returning summer that reminds us of the first
creation, to suggest the presence of God?

RALPH WALDO EMERSON (1803–1882)
Sermons

Learn, O student, the true wisdom! See
yon bush aflame with roses, like the burning-
bush of Moses! Listen, and thou shalt hear if
thy soul be not deaf, how from out it, soft
and clear, speaks to thee the Lord Almighty!

HAFIZ (14th century)
The Diwan

The kingdom of man over nature, which
cometh not with observation—a dominion
such as now is beyond his dream of God—he
shall enter without more wonder than the
blind man feels who is gradually restored to
perfect sight.

RALPH WALDO EMERSON (1803–1882)
Nature

If I trust myself in the woods or in a boat upon the pond, nature makes a Brahmin of me presently: eternal necessity, eternal compensation, unfathomable power, unbroken silence,—this is her creed.

RALPH WALDO EMERSON (1803–1882)
Letters

Nature is the word of God—"He spake and it was done"; science is the commentary on this revelation.

CHARLES EDWARD GARMAN (1850–1907)
Lectures

It is possible that God says every morning, "Do it again" to the sun; and every evening, "Do it again" to the moon. It may not be automatic necessity that makes all daisies alike; it may be that God makes every daisy separately, but has never got tired of making them. It may be that He has the eternal appetite of infancy; for we have sinned and grown old, and our Father is younger than we.

G. K. CHESTERTON (1874–1936)
Orthodoxy

The order and arrangement of nature, the curious adjustment of final causes, the plain use and intention of every part and organ— all these bespeak in the clearest language an intelligent cause or author. The heavens and the earth join in the same testimony: The whole chorus of nature raises one hymn to the praises of its Creator.

DAVID HUME (1711–1766)
Dialogues Concerning Natural Religion

What God would outwardly alone control,
And on His finger whirl the mighty Whole?
He loves the inner world to move, to view
Nature in Him, Himself in nature too,
So that which in Him works, and is, and
    lives,

The measure of His strength, His spirit
    gives.

JOHANN WOLFGANG VON GOETHE (1749–1832)
Works

Our greatest ideas about the Godhead reach us through reason alone. Observe Nature. Listen to the voice within. Has not God told us everything through our eyes, our conscience, our judgment? What more will men say to us?

JEAN JACQUES ROUSSEAU (1712–1778)
Emile

It is but the outer hem of God's great mantle that our poor stars do gem.

JOHN RUSKIN (1819–1900)
Praeterita

The characters of nature which everywhere meet the eye are not a common but a sacred writing—they are the hieroglyphics of God.

RICHARD CHENEVIX TRENCH (1807–1886)
Sermons

Nature is school-mistress, the soul the pupil; and whatever one has taught or other learned has come from God—the Teacher of the teacher.   TERTULLIAN (160–230)
De Testimonio Animae

All Nature is a display and a play of God, power and action and self-creation of the one spiritual being.

SRI AUROBINDO (1872–1950)
The Supramental Manifestation

Oh, mystical secrets of Nature, great
    Universe undefined,
Ye are part of the infinite work of a mighty
    ineffable Mind.

SIR LEWIS MORRIS (1833–1907)
A New Orphic Hymn

The voice of God is heard in the rushings of the wind and the whisperings of the breeze, in the roar of the thunder and the fall of the rain; his hand is visible in the glories of the midnight sky and the splendor of the opening morn, in the fierce majesty and might of winter, and in the greenness and beauty of the returning spring; every object is an image of the goodness of God; every sound, a call for his adoration; every spot a hallowed temple for his praise.

GEORGE RIPLEY (1802–1880)
Discourses on the Philosophy of Religion

While we may not see God in each natural event, we must yet look through nature to God and his mind in each natural event.

WILLIAM RITCHIE SORLEY (1855–1935)
Moral Values and the Idea of God

What unnumbered cathedrals has God reared in the forest shades, vast and grand, full of curious carvings, and haunted evermore by tremulous music!

HENRY WARD BEECHER (1813–1887)
Sermons

In the woods is perpetual youth. Within these plantations of God, a decorum and sanctity reign, a perennial festival is dressed, and the quest sees not how he should tire of them in a thousand years. In the woods, we return to reason and faith.

RALPH WALDO EMERSON (1803–1882)
Nature

Nature, the totality of created things, is the work of God. And yet God is not there; but within the individual man there is a potentiality (man is potentially spirit) which is awakened in inwardness to become a God-relationship, and then it becomes possible to see God everywhere.

SÖREN KIERKEGAARD (1813–1855)
Point of View

That delicate forest flower
With scented breath and look so like a smile,
Seems, as it issues from the shapeless mold,

An emanation of the indwelling Life,
A visible token of the upholding Love,
That are the soul of this wide universe.

WILLIAM CULLEN BRYANT (1794–1878)
A Forest Hymn

Touched by a light that hath no name,
  A glory never sung,
Aloft on sky and mountain wall
  Are God's great pictures hung.

JOHN GREENLEAF WHITTIER
(1807–1892)
Sunset on the Bearcamp

Nature which is the time-vesture of God, and reveals Him to the wise, hides Him from the foolish.

THOMAS CARLYLE (1795–1881)
Sartor Resartus

The best thing is to go from nature's God down to nature; and if you once get to nature's God, and believe him, and love him, it is surprising how easy it is to hear music in the waves, and songs in the wild whisperings of the winds; to see God everywhere in the stones, in the rocks, in the rippling brooks, and hear him everywhere, in the lowing of cattle, in the rolling of thunder, and in the fury of tempests.

CHARLES HADDON SPURGEON (1834–1892)
Sermons

Nature would be scarcely worth a puff of the empty wind if it were not that all Nature is but a temple, of which God is the brightness and the glory.

HENRY WARD BEECHER (1813–1887)
Sermons

What is Nature? Ha, why do I not name thee God? Art not thou the "Living Garment of God"? O Heavens, is it, in very deed, He, then, that ever speaks through thee; that lives and loves in thee, that lives and loves in me?

THOMAS CARLYLE (1795–1881)
Sartor Resartus

He who reads the inscrutable Book of Nature as if it were a Merchant's Ledger, is justly suspected of having never seen that Book, but only some school Synopsis thereof; from which, if taken for the real Book, more error than insight is derived.

THOMAS CARLYLE (1795–1881)
On History

When the sky is clear, and the wind hums in the fir-trees, 'tis the heart of a God who reveals himself.

Shinto Proverb

One walks in holiness across the fields, and the soft songs of all herbs, while they voice to God, enter into the song of our soul.

MARTIN BUBER (1878–1965)
Hasidism

The Lord said to the bee: "Choose your habitation in the hills and build your hives in the trees; eat of every fruit and walk in the path of the Lord." And the bees out of their body produce honey which is a cure for men. Verily, these are signs for men to reflect upon. *The Koran*

He is the Lord, by whom the world is made budding, the world is made green, By whom the water and earth have been fixed; blessed is the Creator. *The Adi Granth*

Certainly, every religious man finds God present in nature; but that is only because he has already found Him present in his own soul. JOHN BAILLIE (1886–1960)
The Interpretation of Religion

Nothing in nature is exhausted in its first use. When a thing has served an end to the uttermost, it is wholly new for an ulterior service. In God, every end is converted into a new means.

RALPH WALDO EMERSON (1803–1882)
Nature

Oh! this wonder of divine power that can build a habitation for God in an apple blossom, and tune a bee's voice until it is fit for the eternal orchestra, and can say to a firefly, "Let there be light," and from holding an ocean in the hollow of his hand, goes forth to find heights and depths and lengths and breadths of omnipotency in a dew-drop.

THOMAS DE WITT TALMAGE (1832–1902)
Sermons

Are God and Nature then at strife,
  That Nature lends such evil dreams?
  So careful of the type she seems,
So careless of the single life.

ALFRED LORD TENNYSON (1809–1892)
In Memoriam

These motions everywhere in nature must surely be the circulations of God. The flowing sail, the running stream, the waving tree, the roving wind—whence else their infinite health and freedom? I can see nothing so proper and holy as unrelaxed play and frolic in this bower God has built for us.

HENRY DAVID THOREAU (1817–1862)
Journals

The spirit of the worm beneath the sod,
In love and worship, blends itself with God.

PERCY BYSSHE SHELLEY (1792–1822)
Epipsychidion

Nature's self, which is the breath of God,
Or His pure Word by miracle revealed.

WILLIAM WORDSWORTH (1770–1850)
The Prelude

Nor doubt but He to whom yon Pine-trees
  nod
Their heads in sign of worship,
Nature's God,
These humbler adorations will receive.

WILLIAM WORDSWORTH (1770–1850)
Oxford

My words are tied in one, with the great mountains, with the great rocks, with the great trees; in one with my body and my heart. Do you all help me with supernatural power; all of you see me one with this world.

Yokuts Indian Chant

The Amen! of Nature is always a flower.

OLIVER WENDELL HOLMES (1809–1894)
The Autocrat of the Breakfast-Table

I hold that to be rightly materialistic—to understand and to take nature as she is—is to get on the true divine highroad. That we should attain to a healthy humanity, is surely the most pleasant thing in God's sight.

GEORGE MEREDITH (1828–1909)
Letters

There is no grass without its own guardian star in the firmament which strikes it and says to it, Grow!　　　　*The Talmud*

Every impression of nature in man is not only a reminder but a pledge of the basic truth—who the Lord is. Every reaction of man toward the creature is a letter and seal of our participation in the divine nature, and that we are of his race.

JOHANN GEORG HAMANN (1730–1788)
Works

The heavens and the earth alike speak of God, and the great natural world is but another Bible, which clasps and binds the written one; for nature and grace are one—grace the heart of the flower, and nature its surrounding petals.

HENRY WARD BEECHER (1813–1887)
Sermons

Oh, Adam was a gardner, and God who
　　made him sees
That half a proper gardener's work is done
　　upon his knees.
So when your work is finished, you can wash
　　your hands and pray

For the Glory of the Garden that it may not
　　pass away!
And the glory of the Garden it shall never
　　pass away!

RUDYARD KIPLING (1865–1936)
The Glory of the Garden

Go thou and seek the House of Prayer!
I to the woodlands wend, and there,
In lovely Nature see the God of Love.

ROBERT SOUTHEY (1774–1843)
Written on Sunday Morning

The groves were God's first temples.

WILLIAM CULLEN BRYANT (1794–1878)
A Forest Hymn

The Infinite has written its name on the heavens in shining stars, and on the earth in tender flowers.

JEAN PAUL RICHTER (1763–1825)
Hesperus

Nature with open volume stands,
　　To spread her Maker's praise abroad;
And every labour of His hands
　　Shows something worthy of a God.

ISAAC WATTS (1674–1748)
Hymns

How does the meadow-flower its bloom
　　unfold?
Because the lovely little flower is free
Down to its root, and, in that freedom, bold.

WILLIAM WORDSWORTH (1770–1850)
A Poet! He Hath Put His Heart to School

Nature is not at variance with art, nor art with nature, they being servants of His providence; nature hath made one world, and art another. In brief, all things are artificial; for nature is the art of God.

SIR THOMAS BROWNE (1605–1682)
Religio Medici

Nature is the art of God eternal.

DANTE (1265–1321)
De Monarchia

God Himself does not speak prose, but communicates with us by hints, omens, inference, and dark resemblances in objects lying all around us.

RALPH WALDO EMERSON (1803–1882)
Poetry and Imagination

Nature has some perfections, to show that she is the image of God; and some defects, to show that she is only His image.

BLAISE PASCAL (1623–1662)
Pensées

Nature tells me I am the image of God, as well as Scripture. He that understands not this much hath not his introduction or first lesson, and is yet to begin the alphabet of man.   SIR THOMAS BROWNE (1605–1682)
Religio Medici

The heavens declare the glory of God, and the firmament sheweth his handiwork.

The Old Testament
Psalms 19:1

Go thou and seek the House of Prayer!
I to the woodlands wend, and there,
In lovely Nature see the God of Love.

ROBERT SOUTHEY (1774–1843)
Written on Sunday Morning

One impulse from a vernal wood
May teach you more of man,
Of moral evil and of good,
Than all the sages can.

WILLIAM WORDSWORTH
(1770–1850)
Poetical Works

The course of nature is the art of God.
The miracles thou call'st for, this attest;
For say, could nature nature's course
   control?
But, miracles apart, who sees Him not?

EDWARD YOUNG (1683–1765)
Night Thoughts

God the first garden made, and the first city Cain.

ABRAHAM COWLEY (1618–1667)
The Garden

And through the garden of the world I
   rove,
Enamoured of its leaves in measure solely
As God the Gardener nurtures them above.

DANTE (1265–1321)
Paradiso

God made the rivers to flow. They feel no weariness, they cease not from flowing. They fly swiftly like birds in the air. May the stream of my life flow into the river of righteousness; let not the thread of my song be cut while I sing; and let not my work end before its fulfilment.   *The Rig-Veda*

Nature, so far as in her lies,
Imitates God.

ALFRED LORD TENNYSON
(1809–1892)
On a Mourner

Know then that nature is art, and the great Lord the maker; the whole world is filled with what are his members. If a man discerned him, who being one only, rules over every cause, in whom all this comes together and comes asunder again, who is the Lord, the bestower of blessing, the adorable god, then he passes for ever into that peace.

The Upanishads

God has two revelations, as Nature and Spirit. Both these divine formations are temples of God that He fills by His presence.

GEORG WILHELM FRIEDRICH HEGEL
(1770–1831)
Philosophy of Nature

The Infinite has sowed his name in the heavens in glowing stars, but on the earth he has sowed his name in tender flowers.

JEAN PAUL F. RICHTER (1763–1825)
Hesperus

The day is full of the singing of birds, the night is full of stars—Nature has become all kindness, and it is a kindness clothed upon with splendor. I felt myself in the temple of the infinite, in the presence of the worlds, God's guest in this vast nature.

> HENRI FRÉDÉRIC AMIEL (1821–1881)
> *Journal Intime*

These are thy wonders, Lord of love,
To make us see we are but flowers that
    glide:
  Which when we once can find and
      prove,
Thou hast a garden for us, where to hide.

> GEORGE HERBERT (1593–1633)
> *The Flower*

Would that Nature might be pleased, some day, to lay open her bosom to us and make us see, as they are, the modes and guidance of her movements, and there to prepare our eyes! O God! what deceptions, what errors, we should find in our paltry learning!

> MICHEL EYQUEM DE MONTAIGNE (1533–1592)
> *Apology for Raimond Sebond*

God's great power is in the gentle breeze, not in the storm.

> RABINDRANATH TAGORE (1861–1941)
> *Stray Birds*

The course of Nature's phases, on this little fraction of a Planet, is partially known to us: but who knows what deeper courses these depend on; what infinitely larger Cycle (of causes) our little Epicycle revolves on?

> THOMAS CARLYLE (1795–1881)
> *Sartor Resartus*

And Nature, the old Nurse, took
    The child upon her knee,
Saying, "Here is a story book
    Thy Father has written for thee.
Come, wander with me," she said,
    "Into regions yet untrod,

And read what is yet unread
  In the manuscripts of God."

> HENRY WADSWORTH LONGFELLOW
> (1807–1882)
> *On the Fiftieth Birthday of Agassiz*

Everything takes place by the power of God. Nature herself is the power of God under another name, and our ignorance of the power of God is co-extensive with our ignorance of Nature. It is absolutely folly, therefore, to ascribe an event to the power of God when we know not its natural cause, which is the power of God.

> BENEDICT SPINOZA (1632–1677)
> *Theologico-Political Treatise*

God Almighty first planted a garden; and, indeed, it is the purest of human pleasures.

> FRANCIS BACON (1561–1626)
> *Of Gardens*

God is in every blade of grass, in every grain of sand, and in every atom that floats in the sunshine.

> GIORDANO BRUNO (1548–1600)
> *A Philosophy of the Infinite Universe*

Nature is but a name for an effect,
Whose cause is God.

> WILLIAM COWPER (1731–1800)
> *The Winter Walks at Noon*

O! Thou God of Nature!—In vain do we attempt to scan thy immensity, or to comprehend thy various modes of existence, when a single particle of light issued from thyself, and kindled into intelligence in the bosom of man, thus dazzles and confounds our understandings.

> BENJAMIN RUSH (1745–1813)
> *Influence of Physical Causes*

I believe a leaf of grass is no less than the
    journey-work of the stars,
And the pismire is equally perfect, and a
    grain of sand, and the egg of the wren,

And the tree toad is a chef-d'oeuvre for the
highest,
And the running blackberry would adorn
the parlors of heaven.
WALT WHITMAN (1819–1872)
Song of Myself

God is seen God
In the star, in the stone, in the flesh, in the
soul and the clod.
ROBERT BROWNING (1812–1889)
Saul

Flower in the crannied wall,
I pluck you out of the crannies,

I hold you here, root and all, in my hand,
Little flower—but if I could understand
What you are, root and all, and all in all,
I should know what God and man is.
ALFRED LORD TENNYSON (1809–1892)
Flower in the Crannied Wall

My profession is to be always on the alert
to find God in nature, to know his lurking-
places, to attend all the oratorios, the operas,
in nature.
HENRY DAVID THOREAU (1817–1862)
Journals

· NOTHING WITH GOD CAN BE ACCIDENTAL ·

Lord! who thy thousand years dost wait
    To work the thousandth part
Of thy vast plan, for us create
    With zeal a patient heart.
JOHN CARDINAL NEWMAN (1801–1890)
Verses on Various Occasions

Know well, my soul, God's hand controls
    Whate'er thou fearest;
Round Him in calmest music rolls
    Whate'er thou hearest.
JOHN GREENLEAF WHITTIER (1807–1892)
Complete Verse

Thou who mad'st the mighty clock
    Of the great world go;
Mad'st its pendulum swing and rock,
    Ceaseless to and fro;
Thou whose will doth push and draw
    Every orb in heaven,
Help me move by higher law
    In my spirit graven.
GEORGE MACDONALD (1824–1905)
Collected Verse

The Ruler of the universe has ordered all
things with a view to the excellence and pres-
ervation of the whole, and each part, as far

as may be, does and suffers what is proper to
it. And one of the these portions of the universe is thine own, unhappy man, which, infinitesimal though it be, is ever striving
towards the whole; and you do not seem to
be aware that this and every other creation is
in order that the life of the whole may be
blessed; and that you are created for the sake
of the whole, and not the whole for the sake
of you.
PLATO (427–347 B.C.)
Laws

We do not understand, but somehow we
are part of a creative destiny, reaching backward and forward to infinity—a destiny that
reveals itself, though dimly, in our striving,
in our love, our thought, our appreciation.
We are the fruition of a process that stretches
back to star-dust. We are material in the
hands of the Genius of the universe for a still
larger destiny that we cannot see in the everlasting rhythm of worlds. We fail and fall
by the way, yet redeeming grace fashions
us anew and eliminates our failures in the
larger pattern.
JOHN ELOF BOODIN (1869–1950)
Cosmic Evolution

How confused is the course of the world,
yet it is the working out of a moral system,
and is overruled in every point by God's Will!
JOHN CARDINAL NEWMAN (1801–1890)
Discussions and Arguments

Above, below, in sky and sod
In leaf and spar, in star and man,
Well might the wise Athenian scan
The geometric signs of God,
The measured order of his plan.
JOHN GREENLEAF WHITTIER
(1807–1892)
The Over-Heart

Thy will is done, O God!
The star hath ridden high
Through many a tempest, but she rode
Beneath thy burning eye
EDGAR ALLAN POE (1809–1849)
Al Aaraaf

At first laying down, as a fact fundamental,
That nothing with God can be accidental.
HENRY WADSWORTH LONGFELLOW
(1807–1882)
The Golden Legend

Of the building of life, God is the architect
and man is the contractor. God has one plan
and man has another. Is it strange that there
are clashings and collisions?
HENRY WARD BEECHER (1813–1887)
Sermons

God, doubtless, is pursuing some design
and carrying on some scheme in the various
changes and revolutions which from age to
age come to pass in the world. It is most reasonable to suppose that all revolutions, from
the beginning of the world to the end of it,
are but the various parts of the same scheme,
all conspiring to bring to pass that great event
which the great Creator and Governor of the
world has ultimately in view.
JONATHAN EDWARDS (1703–1758)
A History of the Work of Redemption

And God gives to every man
The virtue, temper, understanding, taste,
That lifts him into life, and lets him fall
Just in the niche he was ordain'd to fill.
WILLIAM COWPER (1731–1800)
The Task

We have not created the Heavens and the
earth and whatever is between them in sport:
We have not created them but for a serious
end: but the greater part of them understand
it not.
The Koran

In spite of all appearances to the contrary,
God still has a plan for this bankrupt world.
He still has something in store for it. This
dark, satanic earth, drowned in blood and
tears, this earth of ours, He still wants as a
theater for His grace and glorious direction.
HELMUT THIELICKE (1908–)
The Silence of God

Just as Plato says in the Timaeus that God
gave to each what is best for it and for the
whole, in the same way we must think of the
whole human race. For the whole human
race is like a single body composed of different members also with different functions,
yet ordered to the common advantages of the
human race.
PIETRO POMPOMAZZI (1462–1525)
De immortalitate animae

Whatsoever states of being there are be
they of the nature of goodness, passion, or
darkness, know that all of them come from
Me alone. *The Bhagavad Gita*

The greatest part of morality is of a fixed
eternal nature, and will endure when faith
shall fail. JOSEPH ADDISON (1672–1719)
The Spectator

The kingdom of God is the community to
come in which all who hunger and thirst for
righteousness will be satisfied; it will come

not by divine grace alone but only out of the collaboration of divine grace with the human will and the mysterious union of the two.

MARTIN BUBER (1878–1965)
On Judaism

Had Allah pleased, He could have made you one nation: but it is His wish to prove you by that which He has bestowed upon you. Vie with each other in good works, for to Allah you shall return and He will declare to you what you have disagreed about.

The Koran

Let us not suppose that God, the most wise, heeds the great things, but neglects the little things. All things have been ordered by God who has the world in his care to the salvation and virtue of the whole. That which happens to thee is best for the whole and for thee, so far as the common creation permits.

PLATO (427–347 B.C.)
Laws

Thus yesterday, to-day, to-morrow come,
They hustle one another and they pass;
But all our hustling morrows only make
The smooth to-day of God.

MATTHEW ARNOLD (1822–1888)
Lucretius

God, so great an artificer in great things, is not less great in small things.

SAINT AUGUSTINE (354–430)
The City of God

The World is God's book, which he set man at first to read; and every Creature is a Letter, or Syllable, or Word, or Sentence, more or less, declaring the name and will of God.

RICHARD BAXTER (1615–1691)
Christian Directory

Some people assume that the Universe was created solely for the sake of man's existence, that he might serve God. On examining this opinion, as intelligent persons ought to examine all different opinions, we will discover that it is erroneous. Those who maintain it may be asked whether God could have created man without previous creations, or whether man could only have come into existence after the creation of all other things. If they answer in the affirmative, insisting that man could have been created even if, for example, the heavens did not exist, then they must be asked what is the object of all those other things, since they do not exist for their own sake, but for the sake of something that could exist without them? Even if the Universe existed for man's sake and man existed for the purpose of serving God, one must still ask: What is the end of serving God? He does not become more perfect if all His creatures serve Him. Nor would He lose anything if nothing existed beside Him.

It might perhaps be replied that the service of God is not intended for God's perfection, but for our own. Then, however, the question arises: What is the object of our being perfect?

Pressing the inquiry as to the purpose of the Creation, we must at last arrive at the answer: it was the will of God. Logic as well as tradition prove clearly that the Universe does not exist for man's sake, but that all things in it exist each for its own sake.

MAIMONIDES (1135–1204)
Guide for the Perplexed

Everything is in the hands of merciful God: the present, the past, the future. All our misfortune comes only because, looking at the present, we remark something sad and mournful, in the past something simply foul; if it is not made as we would wish, we give it up as lost and stare at the future. That is why God does not give us prescience; that is why all the future is in suspense for us.

NIKOLAI GOGOL (1809–1852)
Letters

Nothing endures: the wind moans,
   saying so;

We moan in acquiescence: there's life's pact,
    Perhaps probation—do I know?
God does: endure his act!

ROBERT BROWNING (1812–1889)
James Lee's Wife

O, Life, that ever lives in the sky,
That throbs in the star, that flows in the sea,
That still lives on when all things die,
Power, Love, or God, live, live in me,
Like music or fragrance or morning light.

WATHEN MARK WILKS CALL (1817–1890)
Golden Histories

God's foreknowledge of what He will do
doth not necessitate Him to do.

STEPHEN CHARNOCK (1628–1680)
Sermons

When the Most High parcelled out the
    nations,
When he dispersed all mankind,
He laid down the boundaries of every
        people,
    according to the number of the sons of
        God.

The Old Testament
Deuteronomy 32:8

The rich and the poor meet together:
The Lord is the maker of them all.

The Old Testament
Proverbs 22:2

For you, O lord, the most just ruler of the
universe can so act by Your secret influence
upon both those who consult and those who
are consulted—neither of them knowing
what they do—that when a man consults he
hears what it behooves him to hear, given the
hidden merits of souls, from the abyss of
Your last judgment. Let no man say to You:
What is this? or Why is this? He must not say
it, he must not say it. For he is a man.

SAINT AUGUSTINE (354–430)
Confessions

God's permitting sin was as high an exercise of holiness as any we can think of.

SAMUEL HOPKINS (1721–1803)
Sin Through Divine Interposition

The world's a stage, where God's omnipo-
    tence,
His justice, knowledge, love, and providence
Do act the parts.

GUILLAUME DE SALLUSTE, SEIGNEUR DU BARTAS
(1544–1590)
The Week

Whatever is, is right. Though purblind man
Sees but a part o' the chain, the nearest link:
His eyes not carrying to the equal beam,
That poises all above.

JOHN DRYDEN (1631–1700)
Collected Poems

Holiness is the architectural plan upon
which God buildeth up His living temple.

CHARLES HADDON SPURGEON (1834–1892)
Holiness

I know the concern which God has given
men to be afflicted with. Everything He has
made proper in its due time, and He has also
placed the love of the world in men's hearts,
except that they may not discover the work
God has done from beginning to end.

The Old Testament
Ecclesiastes 3:10–11

We are all working together to a single
end, some consciously and with understanding, some without knowledge, as Heraclitus,
I think, says that even "sleepers are workers
and fellow workers in what comes to pass in
the world." One helps in one way, one in another, and even he who finds fault and tries
to resist or destroy what is coming to pass;
for the Universe has need even for such a
one. Therefore, see with which you take your
post, for in any event he who controls the
Whole will employ you aright and will accept

you as one part of the fellow laborers and fellow workers.

> MARCUS AURELIUS (121–180)
> *Meditations*

O world, as God has made it! All is beauty:
And knowing this, is love, and love is duty.
  What further may be sought for or
    declared?

> ROBERT BROWNING (1812–1889)
> *The Guardian Angel*

All is concentered in a life intense,
Where not a beam, nor air, nor leaf is lost,
But hath a part of being, and a sense
Of that which is of all Creator and defense.

> GEORGE GORDON, LORD BYRON
> (1788–1824)
> *Childe Harold*

Blind unbelief is sure to err,
And scan his work in vain;
God is his own interpreter,
And he will make it plain.

> WILLIAM COWPER (1731–1800)
> *Light Shining Out of Darkness*

The Immanent Will that stirs and urges everything.

> THOMAS HARDY (1840–1928)
> *The Convergence of the Twain*

From God derived to God by nature joined,
We act the dictates of His mighty mind;
And tho' the priests are mute, and temples
    still,
God never wants a voice to speak His will.

> LUCAN (A.D. 39–65)
> *De Bello Civili*

Ten thousand suns blaze forth, with each its
    train
Of worlds dependent, all beneath the eye,
And equal rule of one eternal Lord.

> DAVID MALLET (1705–1765)
> *The Excursion*

Whate'er we leave to God, God does
And blesses us.

> HENRY DAVID THOREAU (1817–1862)
> *Inspiration*

I know not where His islands lift
Their fronded palms in air;
I only know I cannot drift
Beyond His love and care.

> JOHN GREENLEAF WHITTIER
> (1807–1892)
> *The Eternal Goodness*

· A COAL FROM GOD'S ALTAR ·

He set the world aflame,
And laid me on the same;
A hundred tongues of fire
Lapped round my pyre.
And when the blazing tide
Engulfed me, and I sighed,
Upon my mouth in haste
His hand He placed.

> JALAL-UD-DIN RUMI (1207–1273)
> *The Masnawi*

Be kindled, child; become God's candle
    light;
The brighter thou, the darker Belial's night.

> ANGELUS SILESIUS (1624–1677)
> *Spiritual Maxims*

That measureless love which is God Himself, dwells in the pure deeps of our spirit, like a burning brazier of coals. And it throws forth brilliant and fiery sparks which stir

and enkindle heart and senses, will and desire, and all the powers of the soul, with a
fire of love.

JAN VAN RUYSBROECK (1293–1381)
The Book of Supreme Truth

As from a blazing fire sparks of like substance fly forth a thousandfold, so from
the Imperishable, beings manifold are produced, and return thither also.

The Upanishads

It is a coal from God's altar that must kindle our fire; and without fire, true fire, no
acceptable sacrifice.

WILLIAM PENN (1644–1718)
Works

If Thou hast formed us out of dust
Through ages long—in Thee we trust;

O grant us in our souls to see
The living flame that comes from Thee.

HENRY VAN DYKE (1852–1933)
The Burning Bush

God is the fire of this world, its vital principle, a warm pervading presence everywhere. What thing of outward nature can so
picture to us the mysterious, the subtle, the
quick, live, productive and destructive
thought, which has always lifted men's hearts
and solemnized their faces when they have
said the word *God,* as this strange thing—
so heavenly, so unearthly, so terrible, and
yet so gracious; so full of creativeness, and
yet so quick and fierce to sweep whatever opposes it out of its path—this marvel, this
beauty and glory and mystery of fire?

PHILLIPS BROOKS (1835–1893)
Sermons

I I · God the Unknowable

Instead of complaining that God has hidden
Himself, you should give Him thanks for
having revealed so much of Himself.

BLAISE PASCAL

I N THIS SECTION the God Seekers grapple with one of the most difficult of all religious questions: can anyone truly believe he or she "knows" God? Or, as John Ruskin notes, since the infinity of God is unfathomable how do we even begin to seek our Creator? Such a quandary can lead us to consider that if God is, in the ultimate analysis, unknowable, why should we even try to define or know him? Even the most devout and dedicated of God Seekers at times voice despair in their quest to actualize God. Pascal, for example, approached agnosticism in his otherwise God-affirming *Pensées:* "If there is a God, He is infinitely incomprehensible, since having neither parts nor limits, He has no affinity to us. We are then incapable of knowing either what He is or if He is. This being so, who will dare to undertake the decision of the question? Not we, who have no affinity to Him."

Essentially, the God Seekers agree that at best God can be intuited and that He must be accepted with a pervasive faith that supersedes cold, rational understanding. As the Zohar puts it, God conceals himself from man's mind but reveals himself to his heart.

Would we actually be more content if we *could* "know" God, or even thought we had conceptualized him completely? Harry Emerson Fosdick said he would rather live in a world where his life was surrounded by mystery than in a world that was so small his mind could comprehend it. And what mystery could be more profound, indeed more miraculous, than our unique place in the universe?

Throughout human history there have been vast numbers who have doubted the existence of God, either in the agnostic sense of saying that they truly *did not know* and therefore, in their heart of hearts could not affirm him, or who actively proclaimed that there is no God and thereby promulgated their atheistic philosophy. Perhaps they began with the dilemma of not being able to accept a force they could not rationally analyze, and their subsequent frustration led them to agnostic despair.

We have been living for the past century in a world where for many serious and sincere thinkers God is on trial. Has modern man reversed the role of the ancients, who (C. S. Lewis points out) always approached God or the gods as accused persons would approach a judge? Today we have become the judge and put God in the dock. We may be a kindly, compassionate judge, and, Lewis adds, "if God should have a reasonable defense for being the god who permits war, poverty and disease" we are ready to listen.

In the end, we, the judge and the jury, may even acquit God of the charges against him. How, indeed, Lewis asks us to consider, did we get the temerity to elevate ourselves to the bench and put God on trial?

One thing seems certain—and that is that God did not make any of his creations without flaws and without natural enemies or antagonists, although why He willed it thus is known only to him. Each of the so-called lower animals has been subdued by man, the temporary "king of the hill" in God's evolutionary plan on this minute speck among the billions of the manifestations of his universe. Although the forces of nature can and often do play havoc with man's plans, they are not his greatest antagonist. Man's greatest enemy is himself, but again why God created us with this flaw is known only to him.

The most intuitive God Seekers are those with a strong amalgam of patience and faith, which enables them to believe that their Creator has a purpose in every act that occurs throughout the universe. Thus their inability to know why God wills any specific action in their individual lives, or in the collective life of his world or universe, is less a matter of rage and frustration than of reverent awe at the magnitude of the unknowable mystery. As Mary Baker Eddy aptly stated: "The everlasting I AM is not bounded nor compressed within the narrow limits of physical humanity, nor can He be understood aright through mortal concepts."

The wisest of the God Seekers knew with Shakespeare's Hamlet that there are more things under heaven and earth than ever dreamed of in the most profound of philosophies. Many contemporary scientists who profess not to believe in God do not hesitate for a moment to deal with electrons, which although no one has ever seen one is "known" through its effects. Taking faith in their theories and hypotheses they never doubt that an electron possesses a negative electric charge of approximately 1.602×10 to the minus 19 coulumbs. But the God they have never seen is another matter!

Although the God Seekers inevitably affirm the unknowable God this does not mean that they are loth to try to understand his ways. In a poignantly dramatic section of his *Confessions,* Saint Augustine pondered the first line of the book of Genesis in the Old Testament. Addressing himself to God, Augustine prayed to understand how "in the beginning You made heaven and earth." If the "author" of Genesis, Moses, were still alive, Augustine averred, he would approach him and ask him to please explain the true meaning of earth's creation: "I would catch hold of him, and I would ask him, and through You I would beseech him to make these things plain to me."

Saint Anselm reiterated this quest in a passage from his *Proslogion:* "I ask not, Lord to attain Thy height, with which my understanding is not compatible, but I desire in some measure to understand Thy truth, which my heart believes and loves."

Philo Judaeus, on the other hand, virtually chides those who wish to pry into God's secrets. How can we speculate on the essence of God, he asks, when, for the most part, we are ignorant of the essence of our own souls. So how dare we presume to have an accurate knowledge of the soul of the universe, which is God?

The God Seekers are often perplexed as they contemplate the plight of the world. The Book of Job may be the supreme articulation of this quandary, but many other great religious thinkers have echoed the questions it raises. Sometimes the anguish becomes so profound that they question whether God has *any* plan for the world or whether He has forgotten or forsaken it.

This bitterness seldom has been expressed more trenchantly than by the Victorian novelist and poet Thomas Hardy, in his poem "Nature's Understanding," where he asks whether God is impotent to tend the world He has created, whether God has "framed us in jest, and left us now to hazardry," or even worse, whether God is dead, but we are the live remains of "Godhead dying downwards, brain and eye now gone." Yet, having visualized the worst of all possible scenarios, Hardy ends his distraught soliloquy on a Job-like affirmation, a glimmer of hope that there is "some high Plan betides as yet not understood, of evil stormed by Good" and that we may just be "the Forlorn Hope over which Achievement strides."

Doubt of God's relationship to his earthly creatures, even as bitterly expressed as Hardy's, does not necessarily signify the negation of faith. Rather, as Paul Tillich said, it may be an element that has always been concomitant within the act of faith. To Tillich, "existential doubt and faith are poles of the same reality, the state of ultimate concern."

In the last part of this section we examine the stance of those who deny that there is any God. Phillips Brooks points out that atheism is not necessarily skeptical or even blasphemous; it is simply "to live as if there were no God—no God to help us, no God to be responsible to, no God for us to trust and love." Jean-Paul Sartre put it essentially the same way in opting for atheism. Sartre accepts Dostoevsky's maxim "If God did not exist, everything would be permitted" as the starting point for existentialism. True, everything is permitted if God does not exist—the senseless killing of fellow humans from Cain's slaying Abel to the brutality of a Buchenwald or Babi Yar. But in a world where there is no God to be responsible to or turn to for help and love, this self-declared "freedom" brings no great happiness. As Sartre admits, man is forlorn "for he cannot find anything to depend upon either within or outside himself."

Perhaps the greatest force leading men and women to atheism is their frustration in reconciling the evil aspect of the world with a compassionate, beneficent Creator. Albert Camus wrote: "If evil is essential to divine creation, then creation is unacceptable." In *The Myth of Sisyphus,* Camus recalls the enigma that has brought so many atheists to their belief: "You know the alternative: either we are not free and God the all powerful is responsible for evil. Or we are free and responsible but God is not all powerful. All the scholastic subtleties have neither added anything to nor subtracted anything from the acuteness of this paradox."

We have seen in the post-World War II years a movement loosely called The Death of God. To what ends can our ego drive itself to decide that *our* words could "kill" the Master of the Universe? The horror of the Holocaust may have challenged our faith to the very edge of the breaking piont, as was Job's before us, but many who believe they have repudiated or "killed" God may only be acting out their despair in contemplating this material world. Maybe, as Franz Kafka once mused, there is only a *spiritual* world and what we call the physical world is the evil part of the spiritual one. What we call evil may only be a stage in spiritual evolution. These are matters we shall examine in depth in subsequent sections of this anthology.

In that great storehouse of law, ethics, metaphysical speculations, and folklore known as the Talmud, the story is told about the Roman emperor Hadrian, who one day demanded of Rabbi Joshua Ben Hananiah, "I want to see your God." When the rabbi answered, "You cannot see Him," the emperor insisted that his order be followed. Whereupon the rabbi had him face the sun during its height and said to Hadrian, "Look up at it."

"I cannot," answered the emperor.

"If you cannot even look at the sun, which is just one of God's attendants," said Rabbi Joshua, "how do you presume to be able to look at the divine presence?"

· FATHOMING THE UNKNOWABLE ·

In many forms we try
To utter God's infinity,
But the boundless has no form,
And the Universal Friend
Doth as far transcend
An angel as a worm.
It leaves the learned in the lurch;
No art, nor power, nor toil can find
The measure of the Eternal Mind
Nor hymn, nor prayer, nor church.

RALPH WALDO EMERSON
(1803–1882)
The Bohemian Hymn

Canst thou find the Almighty to perfection? No, not only because the power and wisdom He has manifested in the structure of the Creation that I behold is to me incomprehensible, but because even this manifestation, great as it is, is probably but a small display of the immensity of power and wisdom, by which millions of other worlds, to me invisible by their distance, were created and continue to exist.

THOMAS PAINE (1737–1809)
The Age of Reason

By continually seeking to know and being continually thrown back with a deepened conviction of the impossibility of knowing, we may keep alive the consciousness that is alike our highest wisdom and our highest duty to regard that through which all things exist as The Unknowable.

HERBERT SPENCER (1820–1903)
First Principles of a New System of Philosophy

Compared to the vast oceanic volume of the unknown spiritual facts, what is all our own material knowledge before the immensity of that which is to come, the spiritual, the unknown, the immensity of being and facts around us of which we cannot possibly take any cognizance.

WALT WHITMAN (1819–1892)
Notebooks

God hath not made a Creature that can comprehend Him; 'tis a privilege of His own nature. I AM THAT I AM, was His own definition unto Moses; and 'twas a short one, to confound mortality, that durst question God, or ask Him what He was.

SIR THOMAS BROWNE (1605–1682)
Religio Medici

The secret things belong unto the Lord our God: but those things which are revealed belong to us and to our children for ever, that we may do all the words of this law.

*The Old Testament
Deuteronomy 29:29*

God whom I praise: how could I praise
If such as I might understand,
Make out, and reckon on His ways
And bargain for His love?

ROBERT BROWNING (1812–1889)
Johannes Agricola in Meditation

The "Name" which cannot be defined is turned into a definition. The meaning of the Sacred Name is precisely this: I am the Mysterious One, and I will remain so; I AM THAT I AM the Incomparable, therefore I cannot be defined nor named.

EMIL BRUNNER (1889–1966)
The Christian Doctrine of God

O Lord, none but Thyself can fathom Thee,
Yet every mosque and church doth harbor
    Thee;
I know the seekers and what 'tis they seek—

Seekers and sought are all comprised in
  Thee.
                NUR-UD-DIN 'ABN-ALRAHMAN JAMI
                      (1414–1492)
                      Haft Aurang

We cannot speak of God, He is beyond
  compare,
And so we can adore Him best with silent
  prayer.
                ANGELUS SILESIUS (1624–1677)
                The Cherubic Wanderer

God cannot be inferred in anything—in
nature, say, as its author, or in history as its
master, or in the subject as the self that is
thought in it. Something else is not "given"
and God then elicited from it; but God is the
Being that is directly, most nearly, and last-
ingly, over against us, that may properly only
be addressed, not expressed.
                MARTIN BUBER (1878–1965)
                      I and Thou

As no man knows the place of the soul, so
no man knows the place of God. So let the
soul, of which no man knows the place, praise
God, who is exalted above His world, and
whose "place" no man knows.
                      The Midrash

Can anyone praise him as he truly is?
We have seen but a small part of his works,
and there remain many mysteries greater
  still.
The Lord has made everything
and has given wisdom to the godly.
                The Old Testament Apocrypha
                Ecclesiasticus 43:31–33

What is the last end? It is the mystery of
the darkness of the eternal Godhead which is
unknown and never shall be known. Therein
God abides to Himself unknown.
                MEISTER ECKHART (1260–1327)
                      Sermons

Our powers are so far from conceiving the
divine height that, of the works of our creator, those best bear his stamp, and are most
his, which we understand least.
        MICHEL EYQUEM DE MONTAIGNE (1533–1592)
                Apology for Raimond Sebond

He who is the self of all beings and the
  salvation of all beings,
About whose path even the heavenly powers
  are in confusion,
Seeking the track of the trackless,
As one cannot find the path of the birds in
  the air.
                      The Upanishads

For what man knows the counsel of God?
Or who shall conceive what the Lord wills?
For the thoughts of mortals are timorous,
And our purposes are prone to fail.
And with difficulty do we divine the things
  of the earth
And the things close at hand do we discern
  with labor;
But the things in heaven who can trace out?
                The Old Testament Apocrypha
                The Wisdom of Solomon 9:13–16

No organism corresponds completely to
the Idea that lies at its root; behind everyone
the higher Idea is hidden. That is my God,
that is the God we all seek after and hope to
find, but we can only feel Him, we cannot see
Him.
        JOHANN WOLFGANG VON GOETHE (1749–1832)
                      Faust

If thou seek Him in the spaceless, He
  beckoneth to Space:
When thou seekest Him in Space, He fleeth
  to the spaceless.
His Name will flee, the while thou mouldest
  thy lips for speech:
Thou may'st not even say, Such a one will
  flee:
He will flee from thee, so that if thou paint
  His picture,

The picture will flee from the tablet, and His features from thy soul.

JALAL-UD-DIN RUMI (1207–1273)
The Masnawi

The Lord of heaven and earth, the God of Gods
Without Him nothing is. Yet what he is we know not!
When we strive to comprehend, our feeble guesses leave the most concealed.

LUCIUS ANNAEUS SENECA (4 B.C.–A.D. 65)
Epistolae morales ad Lucilium

O world invisible, we view thee,
O world intangible, we touch thee,
O world unknowable, we know thee,
Inapprehensible, we clutch thee!

FRANCIS THOMPSON (1859–1907)
The Kingdom of God

God now appears as He wishes, not as He is. No wise man, no saint, no prophet, is able to see Him as He is, nor has been able in this mortal body.

SAINT BERNARD OF CLAIRVAUX (1091–1153)
Sermons on the Canticles

God represents the Central Point, Cause of all things, which remains hidden from all the worlds, which is unknown and which will remain eternally unknown; this is the supreme mystery of the Infinite. From this mysterious point there issues a slender ray of light, which, although likewise hidden and invisible, contains all lights. This slender ray of light receives the vibrations of Him who does not vibrate, of the mysterious Point, and reflects the light of Him who sheds no light, the mysterious Point.   *The Zohar*

That mind is perfect which, through true faith, in supreme ignorance supremely knows the supremely Unknowable; and which, in gazing upon the universe of His handiwork, has received from God comprehensive knowledge of His providence and judgment.

SAINT MAXIMUS THE CONFESSOR (580–662)
Centuries on Charity

We look at it and do not see it;
Its name is The Invisible.
We listen to it and do not hear it;
Its name is The Inaudible.
We touch it and do not find it;
Its name is The Subtle.
These three cannot be further inquired into,
And hence merge into one.
Going up high it is not bright, and coming down low, it is not dark,
Infinite and boundless, it cannot be given any name;
It reverts to nothingness.

Tao Te Ching

You cannot plumb the depths of the human heart nor find out what a man is thinking; how do you expect to search out God who made all things, and find out his mind or comprehend his thoughts?

The Old Testament Apocrypha
Judith 8:14

That which cannot be expressed by speech but that by which speech is expressed: know that this indeed, not what is adored here, is the true Brahman.   *The Upanishads*

All speculation concerning the mysteries of God is a very dangerous thing by which the willing spirit can be trapped. As long as the willing spirit follows the Spirit of God, it has strengths in its resigned humility to see all the wonders of God.

JACOB BOEHME (1575–1624)
The Way to Christ

Although we may affirm or deny the things below Him, we can neither affirm nor deny Him, inasmuch as the all-perfect and unique Cause of all things transcends all affirmation, and the simple pre-eminence of His absolute nature is outside of every negation—free from every limitation and beyond them all.

DIONYSIUS THE AREOPAGITE (5th century)
Celestial Hierarchy

What is too wonderful for thee, do not seek,
And what is hidden from thee, do not
search,
Understand that which is permitted thee,
And have no concern with mysteries.

The Old Testament
Ecclesiastes 3:20

As there is a foolish wisdom, so there is a wise ignorance; in not prying into God's ark, not inquiring into things not revealed. I would fain know all that I need, and all that I may: I leave God's secrets to Himself. It is happy for me that God makes me of His court though not of His council.

JOSEPH HALL (1574–1656)
Sermons

When the soul that loves God searches into the nature of the Existent, it enters into an invisible search, from which the chief benefit which accrues to it is to comprehend that God is incomprehensible and to know that he is invisible.

PHILO JUDAEUS (30 B.C.–A.D. 40)
Works

I wish to speak of that of God which is unknown and invisible in vessels of material of little worth.

SAINT BERNARD OF CLAIRVAUX (1091–1153)
Canticle of Canticles

God is best known in not knowing Him.

SAINT AUGUSTINE (354–430)
De Ordine

God, singly and alone, abideth in His Own Place which is Holy above space and time, mention and utterance, sign, description and definition, height and depth.

BAHA'U'LLAH (1817–1892)
The Hidden Words

Thou known Unknown, dark, radiant sea
In whom we live, in whom we move,
My spirit must lose itself in Thee,
Crying a name—Life, Light, or Love.

EDWARD DOWDEN (1843–1913)
Complete Poems

Verily thou art a God that hidest thyself.

Old Testament
Isaiah 45:15

Canst thou by searching find out God?
Canst thou find out the Almighty unto
perfection?

Old Testament
Job 11:7

The One cannot be enumerated along with anything, nor even with uniqueness nor with ought else. The One cannot be enumerated in any way because It is measure without itself being measured.

PLOTINUS (205–270)
Enneads

Hail unto Thee, O Tranquil Soul!
Yea, hail to Thee, most hidden One!
Unthinkable, unlimited, beginningless and
endless too!

The Upanishads

What is true of the relation between two men is not true of the relation of man to God: that the longer they live together and the better they get to know each other, the closer do they come to one another. The very opposite is true in relation to God: the longer one lives with Him, the more infinite He becomes—and the smaller one becomes oneself. Alas, as a child it seemed as though God and man could play together. Alas, in youth one dreamed that if one really tried with all the passion of a man in love the relationship might yet be brought into being. Alas, as a man one discovers how infinite God is, and the infinite distance.

SÖREN KIERKEGAARD (1813–1855)
Journals

God, who confronts all human disquiet with an unconditional command, "Halt!" and all human rest with an equally unconditional command, "Advance!" is for our thinking also the Yes in our No and the No in our Yes, the First and the Last, and consequently the Unknown.   KARL BARTH (1886–1968)
The Epistle to the Romans

Like some wild-flaming, wild-thundering train of Heaven's Artillery, does this mysterious Mankind thunder and flame, in long-drawn, quick-succeeding grandeur through the unknown Deep. But whence?—O Heaven whither? Sense knows not; Faith knows not; only that it is through Mystery to Mystery, from God and to God.
THOMAS CARLYLE (1795–1881)
Sartor Resartus

The father and maker of this Universe is beyond discovering, and even if we did find him, to tell of him to all men would be impossible.   PLATO (427–347 B.C.)
Theaetetus

I believe in the incomprehensibility of God.   HONORÉ DE BALZAC (1799–1850)
Letter to Madame de Hanska

The chess-board is the world, the pieces are the phenomena of the universe, the rules of the game are what we call the laws of Nature. The player on the other side is hidden from us. We know that his play is always fair, just, and patient. But also we know, to our cost, that he never overlooks a mistake, or makes the smallest allowance for ignorance.
THOMAS HENRY HUXLEY (1825–1895)
A Liberal Education

We demand "proof" of God, forgetting that if we could prove God He would be within the compass of our rationalities, and then our logical mind would be our own grotesque God.
GEORGE ARTHUR BUTTRICK (1892–1979)
Christ and History

The less theorizing you do about God, the more receptive you are to his inpouring.
MEISTER ECKHART (1260–1327)
Works

One thought, and one law, and one awful
and infinite power;
In atom and world; in the bursting of fruit
and of flower;
The laughter of children, and the roar of
the lion untamed;
And the stars in their courses—one name
that can never be named.
RICHARD WATSON GILDER (1844–1909)
Collected Poems

All that which we call the attributes of God are only so many human ways of our conceiving that abyss. All which can neither be spoken nor conceived by us.
WILLIAM LAW (1686–1761)
Works

There is in God's infinite plenitude or creation and providence, such an infinite display, or reason, that the most exalted finite rational beings, fall infinitely short of the comprehension thereof.
ETHAN ALLEN (1738–1789)
Reason, the Only Oracle of Man

The Psalmist's word, "He that sitteth in the heavens shall laugh," must have been written for men who believe that human knowledge can completely compass the infinite. We cannot reach the end; but as long as we live and use sound method, we may grow endlessly.
EDGAR S. BRIGHTMAN (1884–1953)
A Philosophy of Religion

We ought to beware lest, in our presumption, we imagine that the ends which God proposed to Himself in the creation of the world are understood by us.
RENÉ DESCARTES (1596–1650)
Principles of Philosophy

He cannot be sculptured in stone. He cannot be seen. Service cannot be rendered to

Him. Gifts cannot be presented to Him. He is not to be approached in the sanctuaries. Where He is is now known. He is not to be found in inscribed shrines. No habitation can contain Him.   *Anonymous Egyptian Scribe*

The great Idea baffles wit,
Language falters under it,
It leaves the learned in the lurch;
No art, nor power, nor toil can find
The measure of the eternal Mind,
Nor hymn, nor prayer, nor church.
RALPH WALDO EMERSON (1803–1882)
The Bohemian Hymn

I know there is a God. But who will show me what that God is? The more I reflect the more convinced I am, that it is not possible for any or all of the creatures to take off the veil which is on my heart, that I might discern this unknown God; to draw the curtain back which now hangs between, that I may see Him which is invisible.

JOHN WESLEY (1703–1791)
A Further Appeal to Men of Reason and Religion

We cannot bring God nigh to us, that we should see him with our eyes; nor can we lay hold on him with our hands—the two highways by which faith enters into the heart of man. For he is not provided with a human head upon his limbs: two branches do not spring from his shoulders: he has no feet, no swift knees: he is only a sacred and unutterable mind shooting with swift thoughts through all the world.

EMPEDOCLES (490–430 B.C.)
Fragments

The mystery of mystery is that something exists; and if the one underived or uncaused existent be God, the creator of all things else, God is "the last irrationality," and creation is the next to last inexplicability.

F. R. TENNANT (1866–1957)
Philosophical Theology

Onward the chariot of the Untarrying
  moves;
Nor day divulges him nor night conceals;
Thou hear'st the echo of unreturning
  hooves
And thunder of irrevocable wheels.
WILLIAM WATSON (1858–1935)
Epigrams

Thy hand unseen sustains the poles
On which the huge creation rolls:
The starry arch proclaims thy pow'r,
Thy pencil glows in every flow'r:
. . . There's not a spot or deep or high,
Where the Creator has not trod,
And left the footstep of a God.
ISAAC WATTS (1674–1748)
Poetical Works

The One is an Absolute transcending all thought and is even beyond Being.
PLOTINUS (205–270)
Enneads

The simple eye beholds, in the divine light with simple gaze and look, whatever God is. The intellectual eye follows the gaze, desiring to explore and have experience in the same light; but at the sight of God, reason, with all that is distinct, succumbs and fails. It sees something, but what? It cannot tell; for the faculty of understanding is lifted up in a kind of knowledge without mode or form of any kind.   JAN VAN RUYSBROECK (1293–1381)
The Sparkling Stone

He cannot be graven in marble as an image bearing the double crown. He cannot be beheld; He hath neither ministrant nor offerings; He is not to be approached in sanctuaries; His abode is not known; He is not to be found in shrines with painted figures. No habitation can contain Him. Unknown is His name in heaven; He doth not manifest His forms!   *Hymn to Hapi, the God of the Nile*
(16th century B.C.)

Thou heir of Everlastingness, self-begotten and self-born, Mighty Being, One, though of myriad forms and aspects, Lord of Eternity, Thou art unknowable, and no tongue can describe Thy similitude.

Egyptian Hymn to Ra (1580–1350 B.C.)
The Book of the Dead

He whom no man knoweth, refulgent are His forms, His glory is a veil of light. Mystery of mysteries! Mystery unknown!

Egyptian Hymn of Praise (1500 B.C.)

Since the world was created, God Himself has made plain His invisible nature, everlasting power and divine being.

The New Testament
Romans 1:19–20

How small a portion of His mighty work is entrusted to us! But He who directs them all, who established and laid the foundations of the world, who has clothed Himself with creation, and is the greater and better part of His work, He is hidden from our eyes. He can be perceived only by thought.

LUCIUS ANNAEUS SENECA (4 B.C.–A.D. 65)
Questiones Naturales

God is immaterial. He is therefore beyond conception. As He is invisible, He cannot have a form; but from the manifestation of His works we must conclude that He is eternal, omnipotent and omnipresent. Whatever is free from desire and greed, is the Mighty One.

LUDWIG VAN BEETHOVEN (1770–1827)
Notebook (1816)

When we say anything is infinite, we signify only that we are not able to conceive the ends and bounds of the things named; having no conception of the thing, but of our own inability. And therefore the name of God is used, not to make us conceive Him, for He is incomprehensible, and His greatness and power are unconceivable; but that we may honor Him.

THOMAS HOBBES (1588–1679)
Leviathan

I know nothing of his having created matter, bodies, spirits, or the world. The idea of creation confounds me and surpasses my conception, though I believe as much of it as I am able to conceive. But I know that God hath formed the universe and all that exists, in the most consummate order. He is doubtless eternal, but I am incapacitated to conceive an idea of eternity. All that I can conceive is, that he existed before all things, that he exists with them, and will exist after them, if they should ever have an end.

JEAN JACQUES ROUSSEAU (1712–1778)
Emile

Ordinarily, God hides himself and discloses himself rarely to those whom he wishes to engage in his service. All things cover up some mystery; all things are the veils that cover God.   BLAISE PASCAL (1623–1662)
Letters

The Word of God is not a sounding but a piercing Word, not pronounceable by the tongue but efficacious in the mind, not sensible to the ear but fascinating to the affection. His face is not an object possessing beauty of form but rather it is the source of all beauty and all form. It is not visible to the bodily eyes, but rejoices the eyes of the heart. And it is pleasing not because of the harmony of its color but by reason of the ardor of the love it excites.

SAINT BERNARD OF CLAIRVAUX (1091–1153)
Sermons on the Canticles

So perfect and comprehensive is His creation that no mind nor heart, however keen or pure, can ever grasp the nature of the most insignificant of His creatures; much less fathom the mystery of Him Who is the Day

Star of Truth, Who is the invisible and unknowable Essence.

BAHA' U'LLAH (1817–1892)
The Great Announcement

O Thou—as represented here to me
In such conception as my soul allows—
Under Thy measureless, my atom width!—
Man's mind, what is it but a convex glass
Wherein are gathered all the scattered
  points
Picked out of the immensity of the sky,
To reunite there, be our heaven for earth,
Our known unknown, our God revealed to
  man?

ROBERT BROWNING (1812–1889)
The Ring and the Book

The mystic mazes of thy will,
The shadows of celestial light,
Are past the power of human skill—
But what th' Eternal acts is right.

THOMAS CHATTERTON (1752–1770)
The Resignation

God dwells beyond all our knowledge. Before our ignorance begins, however, "your
God" gives Himself to you, to your call, to
your preparedness.

FRANZ ROSENZWEIG (1886–1929)
Anmerkungen zu Jehuda Halevi

God has made thee to love Him, and not to
understand Him.   VOLTAIRE (1694–1778)
La Henriade

In vain our haughty reason swells,
  For nothing's found in Thee
But boundless inconceivables
  And vast eternity.

ISAAC WATTS (1674–1748)
The Infinite

Thou Eye among the blind,
That deaf and silent, read'st the eternal
  deep
Haunted forever by the eternal mind.

WILLIAM WORDSWORTH (1770–1850)
Intimations of Immortality

That deeply emotional conviction of the
presence of a superior reasoning power,
which is revealed in the incomprehensible
universe, forms my idea of God.

ALBERT EINSTEIN (1879–1955)
On Zionism, the Land of Israel and the Arabs

Thine are the secrets that no mind or
thought can encompass, and the life over
which decay has no rule, and the throne that
is higher than all height, and the habitation
that is hidden at the pinnacle of mystery.

SOLOMON IBN GABIROL (1021–1058)
The Crown of the Kingdom

Are not those men then simple who speculate on the essence of God? For how can
they who are ignorant of the nature of the
essence of their own soul, have any accurate
knowledge of the soul of the universe? For
the soul of the universe is God.

PHILO JUDAEUS (30 B.C.–A.D. 40)
Works

God's knowledge is something so utterly
unlike our own that it is more like willing
than knowing. But perhaps the wisest way is
to say that we do not know how God's
thought is performed and that it's simply
vain to attempt it. We cannot so much as
frame any notion of what the phrase "the
performance of God's mind" means. Not the
faintest! The question is gabble.

CHARLES PEIRCE (1839–1914)
Collected Papers

Unmeet to be profaned by praise
  Is he whose coils the world enfold;
The God on whom I ever gaze,
  The God I never once behold:
Above the cloud, beneath the clod:
  The Unknown God, the Unknown
  God.

SIR WILLIAM WATSON (1858–1935)
The Unknown God

In all religion there is this presentiment of the hidden, the far off; in the faith in the One God this becomes a peculiar feeling of the divine secrecy, a consciousness of God's infinitude.   LEO BAECK (1873–1956)
The Essence of Judaism

For the rest, let that vain struggle to read the mystery of the Infinite cease to harass us. It is a mystery which, through all ages, we shall only read here a line of, there another line of. Do we not already know that the name of the Infinite is Good, is God?
THOMAS CARLYLE (1795–1881)
Characteristics

Of lower states—of acts of routine and sense, we can tell somewhat, but the masterpieces of God, the total growths and universal movements of the soul, he hideth; they are incalculable.

RALPH WALDO EMERSON (1803–1882)
Circles

The electron is materially inconceivable and yet, it is more perfectly known through its effects than a simple piece of wood. If we could really conceive God we could no longer believe in Him because our representation, being human, would inspire us with doubts.
PIERRE LECOMTE DU NOUY (1883–1947)
Human Destiny

And God the Maker doth my heart grow
    bold
  To praise for wintry works not
    understood,
Who all the worlds and ages doth behold,
  Evil and good as one, and all as good.
ROBERT BRIDGES (1844–1930)
January

The world, as a work of God, may be contemplated by us as a divine publication of the designs of his will. In this however it is frequently for us a shut book; but it is always this when to conclude from it, though an ob-

ject of experience, even the final end of God (which is always moral), is aimed at.
IMMANUEL KANT (1724–1804)
On the Failure of All Philosophical Essays in Theodicy

When we wish to speak about God, since we do not know Him, lacking a concept, words also are lacking by which we could say something in the proper way concerning His indescribable majesty.

COLUCCIO SALUTATI (14th century)
Novati

The mystery of mysteries is that something exists; and if the one underived or uncaused existent be God, the creator of all things else, God is "the last irrationality," and creation is next to the last inexplicability.

F. R. TENNANT (1866–1957)
Philosophical Theology

I have seen the task that God has given to the sons of men; He has made all things beautiful in its time, but he has also implanted in the hearts of men the mystery, so that man cannot find out what God has done from the beginning to the end.

*The Old Testament
Ecclesiastes 3:10–11*

There is one truth which must always become clearer to us—the truth that there exists an Unattainable Existence manifesting itself everywhere, which we cannot find nor can we either think of its beginning or end. Amidst the secrets which thus become more mysterious the more we think about them, there will remain "only one absolute certainty: that we are continually face to face with an Infinite and Eternal Energy from which all things come."

THOMAS MASARYK (1850–1937)
Modern Man and Religion

Of that ineffable essence which we call Spirit, he that thinks most, will say least. We can foresee God in the coarse, and as it were, distant phenomena of matter; but when we try to define and describe himself, both language and thought desert us, and we are helpless as fools and savages.

RALPH WALDO EMERSON (1803–1882)
Nature

The knowledge of the supreme cause of all, which is God, is most remote, and the most difficult thing reason can have to do with. That there is a God, blear-eyed reason can see; but what that God is, is infinitely beyond all the fathoms of reason. If anything, therefore, be attainable in this kind it must be by revelation, and that must be from Himself; for none can reveal but he that comprehends, and none doth or can comprehend God but himself.

WILLIAM LAUD (1573–1645)
Treatises

Not above, not across, nor in the middle has one grasped Him. There is no likeness of Him whose name is Great Glory.

The Upanishads

What man can think of himself as called out and separated from nothing, of his being made a conscious, a reasonable, and a happy creature; in short, in being taken in as a sharer of existence, and a kind of partner in eternity, without being swallowed up in wonder, in praise, in adoration! It is indeed a thought too big for the mind of man, and rather to be entertained in the secrecy of devotion, and in the silence of his soul, than to be expressed by words.

JOSEPH ADDISON (1672–1719)
The Spectator

Veil after veil will lift—but there must be
    Veil upon veil behind.

SIR EDWIN ARNOLD (1832–1904)
The Light of Asia

There exists for man one mystery of complete and enduring incomprehensibility: God. It is precisely within this illuminating and sheltering mystery of God's incomprehensibility that man, through faith and hope and love, entrusts himself to become free and happy.

KARL RAHNER (1904–)
Meditations on the Sacraments

I suppose that even the sounds in nature that are discordant and repulsive make harmony in God's ear. You know you can come so near to an orchestra that the sounds are painful instead of pleasurable, and I think we stand so near the devastating storm and frightful whirlwind we cannot hear that which makes to God's ear a music as complete as it is tremendous.

THOMAS DE WITT TALMAGE (1832–1902)
Sermons

There is a mystery before which we pause because our knowledge has acquired depth. God is Mystery, and the knowledge of God denotes a participation in a mystery which, in consequence of such participation, becomes even more mysterious.

NIKOLAI BERDYAEV (1874–1948)
Dream and Reality

Our minds do and always will emotionally speculate on the Unknowable, on what lies behind Nature, the Mysterious and Miraculous Adjustment conditioning all things. We shall never know, never find out, and this it is which constitutes the "glory and poetry of God," just as the poetry and glory of our lives is that we do not know from moment to moment what is coming.

JOHN GALSWORTHY (1867–1933)
Letters

Thy glory baffles wisdom. All the tracks
Of science making toward Thy Perfectness
Are blinding desert sand; we scarce can
    speak
The Alif of Thine alphabet of love.

ALFRED LORD TENNYSON (1809–1892)
Akbar's Dream

Have you learned the alphabet of heaven and can count three? Do you know the number of God's family? Can you put mysteries into words? Do you presume to fable of the ineffable? Pray, what geographer are you, that speaks of heaven's topography? Whose friend are you that speak of God's personality?   HENRY DAVID THOREAU (1817–1862)
A Week on the Concord and Merrimack Rivers

Sacred ignorance has taught us that God is ineffable, because He is infinitely greater than anything that words can express.
NICHOLAS OF CUSA (1400–1464)
On Learned Ignorance

We have seen but a small part of His works, and there remain many mysterious greater still.   *The Old Testament Apocrypha*
Ecclesiasticus 43:22

Our soundest knowledge is to know that we know Him not as indeed He is, neither can know Him; and our safest eloquence concerning Him is our silence, when we confess without confession that His glory is inexplicable, His greatness above our capacity and reach.   RICHARD HOOKER (1554–1600)
The Laws of Ecclesiastical Polity

A voice in the wind I do not know;
A meaning on the face of the high hills
Whose utterance I cannot comprehend.
A something is behind them: that is God.
GEORGE MACDONALD (1824–1905)
Within and Without

There are millions and millions of worlds below and above ours. Man's mind is tired of this great search, for it cannot reach the end of His vastness. How can the infinite be reduced to the finite?
GURU NANAK (1469–1539)
The Adi Granth

Is there any man that can take the reed of his understanding and lay it along the line of God's latitude and longitude, as if it were as measurable as a city?
HENRY WARD BEECHER (1813–1887)
Sermons

We sit in a boundless Phantasmagoria and Dream-grotto; boundless, for the faintest star, the remotest century, lies not even nearer the verge thereof: sounds and many-coloured visions flit around our sense; but Him, the Unslumbering, whose work both Dream and Dreamer are, we see not; except in rare half-waking moments, suspect not.
THOMAS CARLYLE (1795–1881)
Sartor Resartus

I beheld all the work of God, that man cannot find out the work that is done under the sun: because however much a man labor to seek it out, yet he shall not find it.
The Old Testament
Ecclesiastes 8:17

We cannot talk to one we cannot comprehend—and we cannot comprehend God; we can only believe in Him.
IMMANUEL KANT (1724–1804)
Lectures

If there were no obscurity, man would not be sensible of his corruption; if there were no light, man would not hope for a remedy. Thus it is not only fair, but advantageous to us, that God be partly hidden and partly revealed; since it is equally dangerous to man to know God without knowing his own wretchedness, and to know his own wretchedness without knowing God.
BLAISE PASCAL (1623–1662)
Pensées

God Almighty, to reserve to Himself the sole right of instructing us, and to prevent our solving the difficulties of our own being, has hid the knot so high, or, to speak more properly, so low, that we cannot reach it.
BLAISE PASCAL (1623–1662)
Pensées

All creatures desire to bespeak God in their works; they all bespeak him as well as they can, but they cannot really pronounce him.
MEISTER ECKHART (1260–1327)
Works

Men live on the brink of mysteries and harmonies into which they never enter, and with their hand on the door-latch they die outside.
RALPH WALDO EMERSON (1803–1882)
Letter to Thomas Carlyle

Though we cannot fully comprehend the Deity nor exhaust the infiniteness of its perfection, yet may we have an idea or conception of a Being absolutely perfect, "agreeable and proportionate to our measure and scantling," as we may approach near to a mountain and touch it with our hands, though we cannot encompass it all around and enclasp it within our arms.
RALPH CUDWORTH (1617–1688)
The True Intellectual System of the Universe

If we knew the predestination of Heaven, we should also know the fate of man. Only God knows his predestination, that is to say, his end.
PARACELSUS (1493–1541)
Works

To find the Father and Maker of this Universe is a hard task, and when you have found Him, it is impossible to speak of Him before all people.
PLATO (427–347 B.C.)
Timaeus

For life is a blindfold game, and the Voice
from view is hid.
I face him as best I can, still groping, here
and there,
For the hand that has touched me lightly,
the lips that have said "Declare!"
EDWARD ROWLAND SILL (1841–1887)
Blindfold

God is infinite and incomprehensible, and all that is incomprehensible about Him is His infinity and incomprehensibility.
SAINT JOHN OF DAMASCUS (675–749)
On the Orthodox Faith

O Thou, who are beyond what others have
said and
whatever we have studied or heard;
The meeting is now over, this life is at the
end, but
We are still at the beginning of defining you.
SAADI (died 1291)
Gulistan

For the drift of the Maker is dark, an Isis
hid by the veil.
Who knows the ways of the world, how God
will bring them about?
ALFRED LORD TENNYSON (1809–1892)
Maud

Who fathoms the Eternal Thought?
Who talks of scheme and plan?
The Lord is God! He needeth not
The poor device of man.
JOHN GREENLEAF WHITTIER (1807–1892)
The Eternal Goodness

How can the human mind measure off the measureless essence of God according to its own little measure, a mind as yet unable to establish for certain the nature of the sun's body, though man's eyes daily gaze upon it.
JOHN CALVIN (1509–1564)
Institutes of the Christian Religion

What God thinks of us, what He wants to give and to do to deliver us from sin and death and to save us—which is the particular and the true knowledge of God—this men do not know. Thus it can happen that someone's face may be familiar to me but I do not really know him, because I do not know what he has in mind. Men know naturally that there is a God, but they do not know what He wants and what He does not want.

MARTIN LUTHER (1483–1546)
Lectures on Galatians

And Man's spirit that spends and is spent in
  mystical questionings,
Oh, the depths of the fathomless deep, oh,
  the riddle and secret of things,
And the voice through the darkness heard,
  and the rush of winnowing wings!

SIR LEWIS MORRIS (1833–1907)
A New Orphic Hymn

If you do not know what there is on earth, do you expect to know what there is in heaven?   *The Talmud*

We should believe that God has dealt more bountifully with the sons of men, than to give them a strong desire for that knowledge which he has placed quite out of their reach.

GEORGE BERKELEY (1685–1753)
Principles of Human Knowledge

If we are to speak of God at all, we must either mean something or be totally silent. If we think the divine essence to be truly and wholly incomprehensible and deem those frivolous who inquire about it, we ought not to say God, but should speak only of "The Incomprehensible which it is frivolous to try to comprehend."

EDGAR S. BRIGHTMAN (1884–1953)
A Philosophy of Religion

Many of the strongest feelings and movements of our nature we cannot comprehend on earth. Let not that be a stumbling block, and think not that it may serve as a justification to you for anything. For the Eternal Judge asks of you what you can comprehend and not what you cannot.

FYODOR DOSTOEVSKY (1821–1881)
The Brothers Karamazov

I am persuaded that God is greater than logic, although not contrary to logic, and our

mere inability to catch Him in the little net of human reason is no proof of His non-existence, but only of our need that our little reason shall be supplemented by His tender visitations, and that He may lead and guide us to the end of the road in ways superior to any that our intellects can plan.

THOMAS R. KELLY (1893–1941)
Reality of the Spiritual World

As a blind man has no idea of colors, so have we no idea of the manner by which the all-wise God perceives and understands all things.   SIR ISAAC NEWTON (1642–1727)
Principia

God is to us, and to every creature, incomprehensible. If thou couldst fathom or measure Him, and know His greatness by a comprehensive knowledge, He were not God. A creature can comprehend nothing but a creature. You may know God, but can comprehend Him; as your foot treadeth on the earth, but doth not cover all the earth.

RICHARD BAXTER (1615–1691)
Call to the Unconverted

God cannot be found by thought; He can only be known through His own manifestation of Himself, and in this He shows Himself to be the absolute Mystery, who can be understood only through His own self-revelation.   EMIL BRUNNER (1889–1966)
Revelation and Reason

I give Thee thanks, my God, because Thou makest plain to me that there is no other way of approaching Thee than that which to all men, even the most learned philosophers, seems utterly inaccessible and impossible. For Thou hast shown me that Thou canst not be seen elsewhere than where impossibility meets and faces me.

NICHOLAS OF CUSA (1401–1464)
The Vision of God

The question is not concerning the *being* but the *nature* of God. This, I affirm, from the infirmities of human understanding to be altogether incomprehensible and unknown to us. The essence of that supreme mind, his attributes, the manner of his existence, these are mysterious to man.

DAVID HUME (1711–1776)
Dialogues Concerning Natural Religion

When I reject a doctrine as inconsistent with God's nature it is not as being inconsistent with what God is in himself, but with what he is as manifested to us.

JOHN STUART MILL (1806–1873)
An Examination of Sir William Hamilton's Philosophy

The infinity of God is not mysterious, it is only unfathomable—not concealed, but incomprehensible. It is a clear infinity—the darkness of the pure, unsearchable sea.

JOHN RUSKIN (1819–1900)
Sesame and Lillies

The great chain of causes, which links one to another, even to the throne of God himself, can never be unravelled by any industry of ours. When we go but one step beyond the immediate sensible qualities of things, we go out of our depth. All we do after is but a faint struggle that shows we are in an element which does not belong to us.

EDMUND BURKE (1729–1797)
On the Sublime and Beautiful

Our anthropomorphism reaches its most dangerous form in our inward imaginations of God's character. . . . Man has read his vanities into God, until he has supposed that singing anthems to God's praise might flatter him as it would flatter us. . . . Man has read his racial pride into God; nations have thought themselves his chosen people above all his other children because they seemed so to themselves. The centuries are sick with a god made in man's image, and all the time the real God has been saying, "Thou thoughtest that I was altogether such a one as thyself."

HARRY EMERSON FOSDICK (1878–1969)
Christianity and Progress

Our safest eloquence concerning him is our silence, when we confess without confession that his glory is inexplicable, his greatness above our capacity and reach. He is above, and we upon earth; therefore it behoveth our words to be wary and few.

THOMAS HOOKER (1586–1647)
Sermons

He has devised this wondrous play and
    Himself remained concealed.
He has thrown the curtain of Maya across
    the doorway, so that none may perceive
    Him.
Planting desire in the soul, He has set it
    a-wandering.
All have passed away crying, O Beloved,
    Beloved; but He has not disclosed
    Himself.

DADU (1554–1603)
The Bani

If God is really Organizing Mind, Source and Goal of ideals, Cosmic Companion and Poet of the Universe, he is a God whose wisdom, goodness, sustaining care, and creativity transcend our power to think. Before such a deity we may bow in reverence, or rise in action, but so great is he that we shall never encompass his meaning to confine it within our grasp.

GEORGIA HARKNESS (1891–1974)
The Recovery of Ideals

The whole is linked together and through it His energising Spirit runs. On any hypothesis it must be to the Lord that we pray—to the highest we know or can conceive; but the answer shall come in ways we do not know, and there must always be a far Higher than ever we can conceive.

SIR OLIVER LODGE (1851–1940)
Man and the Universe

Incomprehensible? But because you cannot understand a thing, it does not cease to exist.   BLAISE PASCAL (1623–1662)
Pensées

Shall we think that with our tiny brains we can unravel the mysteries of Him who made the whole vast cosmos? He who Causes to Be must smile in great pity when He hears men talking about some day finding out, of their own selves, the secrets of matter, and of life, and of death, and of Him.

BERNARD IDDINGS BELL (1886–1958)
Beyond Agnosticism

No one but God could be a true theologian, as none but He can reach the full knowledge of the infinite greatness of the divine perfections.

SAINT FRANCIS OF SALES (1567–1622)
Treatise

The way of the Most High has been formed without measure, how, then, should it be possible for a mortal in a corruptible world to understand the ways of the Incorruptible?   *The Old Testament Apocrypha*
Ezra 4: 11

We cannot comprehend the secret counsels of God and yet we are frequently obliged to attempt an explanation of them. What? Are we to attempt an explanation of things which we are unable to understand? We can render explanations, human explanations, to be sure, though we may still be unable to comprehend God's own explanations.

BISHOP OTTO OF FREISING (1114–1158)
The Two Cities

The theist does not know how God punishes, how he protects, how he forgives; for he is not rash enough to flatter himself that he knows how God acts; but he knows that God does act and that he is just.

VOLTAIRE (1694–1778)
Philosophical Dictionary

The first and most important thing we know about God is that we know nothing about him except what he himself makes known.   EMIL BRUNNER (1889–1966)
On Faith

The names that are applied to God are taken from the creatures, since in Himself he is inexpressible and exalted above all that can be named or spoken of.

NICHOLAS OF CUSA (1401–1464)
Uber den Frieden im Glauben

God is none of the things you can name; he is more than wise, more than essential, more than good, for none of the terms applied to him can describe how infinitely far he stands above them, nor can human understanding, however deep it is, ever come within reach of him.

JOHANNES TAULER (1300–1361)
Sermons

Fortune, Minerva, Muse, Holy Ghost— these are quaint names, too narrow to cover this unbounded substance. The baffled intellect must still kneel before the cause, which refuses to be named—ineffable cause, which every genius has essayed to represent by some emphatic symbol, as Thales by water, Anaximenes by air, Anaxagoras by thought, Zoroaster by fire, Jesus and the moderns by love; and the metaphor of each has become a national religion.

RALPH WALDO EMERSON (1803–1882)
Works

O God, what mysteries I find in thee!
How vast the number of thy purposes!
I try to count them—they are more than the
   sand;
I wake from my dream, and I am still lost in
   thee.

The Old Testament
Psalms 139:23

I have no knowledge to take up the Lord in all His strange ways, and passages of deep and unsearchable providences. For the Lord is before me, and I am so bemisted that I cannot follow Him; He is behind me and following at my heels, and I am not aware of Him; He is above me, but His glory so dazzles my twilight of short knowledge that I cannot look up to Him.

SAMUEL RUTHERFORD (1600–1661)
Sermons

In the moment when God reveals to Job the immeasurable distance between creature and creator, between the Eternal and the ephemeral human being, when Job, who till then has seen these things only with human eyes, can now see them, so to speak, from God's point of view—in that wondrous moment Job recognizes again *his* God.

MARGARETE SUSMAN (1874–1966)
God the Creator

I have seen the work that God has given the sons of men to be busy with. He has made everything beautiful in its time; also he has set the world in their heart, so that no man can find out the work that God has done from beginning to end.

The Old Testament
Ecclesiastes 3:9–11

How, then, are we to speak of the One? How can we speak of it at all, when we do not grasp it as itself? The answer is that though the One escapes our knowledge, it does not entirely escape us. We have possession of it in such a way that we speak of it, but not in such a way that we can express it. We are like men inspired and possessed who know only that they have in themselves something greater than themselves—something they know not what—and who therefore have some perception of that which has moved them, and are driven to speak of it because they are not wholly one with that which moves them.   PLOTINUS (205–270)
Enneads

Who has ascended up to heaven, or descended? who has gathered the wind in his fists? who has bound the waters in a garment? who has established all the ends of the earth? what is his name, and what is his son's name, if you can tell?   *The Old Testament*
Proverbs 30:4

A sheer conundrum is not mysterious, nor is a blank wall; but forests are mysterious, in which at first you observe but little, yet in which, with time, you see more and more, although never the whole; and the starry heavens are thus mysterious, and the spirit of man, and, above all, God, our origin and home.

FRIEDRICH VON HÜGEL (1852–1925)
Religion and Agnosticism

The thoughts of God are so deep, who can know the mysterious way in which He moves?

RABBI BEN EZRA (1092–1167)
Book of the Upright

The everlasting I AM is not bounded nor compressed within the narrow limits of physical humanity, nor can He be understood aright through mortal concepts. The precise form of God must be of small importance in comparison with the sublime question, What is infinite Mind or divine Love?

MARY BAKER EDDY (1821–1910)
Science and Health

You are real,
but hearing and seeing cannot reach you,
how and why and where have nothing to do
    with you,
You are real, but to Yourself, and no one
    takes part,
You are real; before all time you were and
    dwelt without place,
You are real, Your secret hidden, and who
    can catch it.
Deep, deep. Who can find it?

SOLOMON IBN GABIROL (1021–1058)
The Crown of the Kingdom

O the depths of the riches and wisdom and knowledge of God! How unsearchable are his judgments and how inscrutable his ways! For who has known the mind of the Lord, or who has been his counselor? Or who has given a gift to him that he might be repaid?

The New Testament
Romans 11:33–36

If I cannot understand my own intelligence, if I cannot know by what I am animated, how can I have any acquaintance with that ineffable intelligence which visibly presides over the universe?

VOLTAIRE (1694–1778)
The Ignorant Philosopher

No reason can be given for the nature of God, because that nature is the ground of rationality.

ALFRED NORTH WHITEHEAD (1861–1947)
Science and the Modern World

Lord of the worlds, You who are One beyond all numbers; You are the highest of the highest, most hidden of the undisclosed. No thought scheme can grasp you.

The Zohar

· IS GOD ON TRIAL? ·

And yet who is there that has never
  doubted?
And doubting and believing, has not said,
"Lord, I believe; help thou my unbelief"?

HENRY WADSWORTH LONGFELLOW
(1807–1882)
The New England Tragedies

It seems to me that when believers in God save his goodness by saying that he is not really omnipotent, they are taking the best course open to them, since both the personality and the goodness of God present much fewer difficulties if he is not conceived as omnipotent. But then they must accept the consequences of their choice, and realize that the efforts of a non-omnipotent God in favor of a good may be doomed to almost total defeat. It is not a very cheerful creed, unless it can be supplemented by some other dogmas which can assure us of God's eventual victory. But it is less depressing and less revolting than the belief that the destinies of the universe are at the mercy of a being who, with the resources of omnipotence at his disposal,

decided to make a universe no better than this.   JOHN M. E. M'TAGGART (1866–1925)
Some Dogmas of Religion

My atheism, like that of Spinoza, is true piety towards the universe, and denies only gods fashioned by men in their own image, to be servants of their human interests.

GEORGE SANTAYANA (1863–1952)
Soliloquies in England

On the ground that God is unknowable, man excuses himself to what is yet remaining of his religious conscience for his forgetfulness of God, his absorption in the world: he denies God practically by his conduct—the world has possession of all his thoughts and inclinations—but he does not deny him theoretically, he does not attack his existence; he lets that rest.

LUDWIG FEUERBACH (1804–1872)
The Essence of Christianity

When faith overflows my mind, God's
  providence all-embracing

Banishes griefs: but when doubt whispers,
 "Ah, but to know!"
No clue through the tangle I find of fate
 and of life for my tracing:
There is ever a change and many a change,
And the mutable fortune of men evermore
 sways to and fro
Over limitless range.

> EURIPIDES (485–407 B.C.)
> *Hippolytus*

It is the fool that saith in his heart there is
no God. But what shall we call the man who
tells us that with this sort of a world God bids
us be content?

> HENRY GEORGE (1839–1897)
> *Social Problems*

Complaint against God is far nearer to God
than indifference about Him.

> GEORGE MACDONALD (1824–1905)
> *Unspoken Sermons*

Whence are we born? Whereby do we live
and whither do we go? O ye who know
Brahma, tell us whose command we abide
here, whether in pain or pleasure. Should
time, or nature or necessity, or chance or the
elements be considered as the cause, or He
who is called Purusha, that is, the Supreme
Spirit?

> *The Upanishads*

Keep not Thou Silent, O God!
Sit no longer blind, Lord God, deaf to our
 prayer
And dumb to our dumb suffering. Surely
 Thou,
Too, are not white, O Lord, a pale,
 bloodless,
Heartless thing.

> W. E. B. DUBOIS (1868–1963)
> *Dark Water*

Surely God helps when the world becomes
so desolate and savage! Who should not
rightly groan because he lives in this
darkened world? Everything works so absurdly against everything, and of nothing are
we so sure than that we do not know. For the
first time I experience and understand that
the world is not only dark but darkness itself,
as John 1:3 says, and that the Devil is its god
and prince. When we read through the
chronicles and perceive there the work of
God, we discover nothing else than that the
world is God's carnival, a fable in his eyes.

> SEBASTIAN FRANCK (1449–1542)
> *Chronicles*

Can it be fancied that Deity ever vindictively
Made in his image a mannikin merely to
 madden it?

> EDGAR ALLAN POE (1809–1849)
> *The Rationale of Verse*

Careless seems the great Avenger; history's
 pages but record
One death-grapple in the darkness 'twixt old
 systems and the Word;
Truth forever on the scaffold, Wrong
 forever on the throne—
Yet that scaffold sways the Future, and,
 behind the dim unknown,
Standeth God within the shadow, keeping
                                    watch above his own.

> JAMES RUSSELL LOWELL (1819–1891)
> *Sea Weed*

If there be only one religion in the world
that can prevent our suffering eternal dam-
nation, and there be on any part of the earth
a single mortal who is sincere, and is not convinced by its evidence, the God of that religion must be the most iniquitous and cruel of
tyrants.

> JEAN JACQUES ROUSSEAU (1712–1778)
> *Emile*

A clerical friend of the author's impressed
him very much in early youth by the words:
God likes to have us doubt his existence, if
we do so sincerely and earnestly. . . . Surely,
if God exists, he knows as much about philosophy as any of us do; he has at least as much

appreciation for a philosophic problem as we can have. And if his own existence presents a fine philosophic problem, he delights therein as much as we do.

JOSIAH ROYCE (1855–1916)
Religious Aspects of Philosophy

Man stands as in the centre of Nature; his fracton of Time encircled by Eternity, his handbreath of Space encircled by Infinitude: how shall he forbear asking himself, What am I; and Whence; and Whither?

THOMAS CARLYLE (1795–1881)
Characteristics

Agnosticism should have its ritual no less than faith. It has sown its martyrs, it should reap its saints, and praise God daily for having hidden Himself from man.

OSCAR WILDE (1854–1900)
De Profundis

But what is the philosophy of this generation? Not God is dead, that period was passed long ago. Perhaps it should be stated that death is God. This generation thinks—and this is its thought of thoughts—that nothing faithful, vulnerable, fragile, can be durable or have any true power. Death waits for these things as a cement floor waits for a dropping light bulb.

SAUL BELLOW (1915–)
Herzog

In the eyes of the rebel, what is missing from the misery of the world, as well as from its moments of happiness, is some principle by which they can be explained.

ALBERT CAMUS (1913–1960)
The Rebel

The question of God can be asked because there is an unconditional element in the very act of asking any question. The question of God must be asked because the thread of non-being, which man experiences as anxi-ety, drives him to the question of being conquering non-being and of courage conquering anxiety.

PAUL TILLICH (1886–1965)
Systematic Theology

Has some vast Imbecility
    Mighty to build and blend,
    But impotent to tend,
Framed us in jest, and left us now to
    hazardry?

Or come we of an Automaton
    Unconscious of our pains?
    Or are we live remains
Of Godhead dying downwards, brain and
    eye now gone?

Or is it that some high Plan betides
    As yet not understood,
    Of evil stormed by Good,
We the Forlorn Hope over which
    Achievement strides?

THOMAS HARDY (1840–1928)
Nature's Questioning

The Last Judgment, which so tortured the Middle Ages and which our day has forgotten so absolutely, is no mere invention of selfish and uneducated monks. The Last Judgment is the supreme reality. The Last Judgment decides whether there shall be freedom of will, immortality of the soul, or not—whether there shall be a soul, or not. And, maybe, even the existence of God is still undecided. Even God waits, like every living soul, on the Last Judgment.

LEV SHESTOV (1866–1938)
In Job's Balances

If God permits an Action to be done, it is because he wants either Power or Inclination to hinder it; in saying he wants Power, we deny Him to be almighty; and if we say He wants Inclination or Will, it must be, either because He is not Good, or the Action is not evil (for all Evil is contrary to the Essence of infinite Goodness).

BENJAMIN FRANKLIN (1706–1790)
A Dissertation on Liberty and Necessity, Pleasure and Pain

God, as I seek here to interpret human experience, is not the foundation of human experience: he is the pillar of cloud by day and the pillar of fire by night that lead men onward in their journey toward the Promised Land. . . . If the universe, as the physicists now suppose, has taken some three billion years to come forth out of chaos and old night, God is the faint glimmer of a design still fully to emerge, a rationality still to be achieved, a justice still to be established, a love still to be fulfilled.

LEWIS MUMFORD (1895–)
The Conduct of Life

As flies to wanton boys are we to the gods;
They kill us for their sport.

WILLIAM SHAKESPEARE (1564–1616)
King Lear

If God is the negation of everything finite, then logically the finite is also the negation of God.   LUDWIG FEUERBACH (1804–1872)
The Essence of Christianity

Belief in a personal God has released an enormous amount of energy directed towards good ends; but it has probably released an equal amount of energy directed towards ends that were silly, or mad, or downright evil.   ALDOUS HUXLEY (1894–1963)
Ends and Means

The metaphysical proofs of God are so remote from the reasoning of men, and so complicated, that they make but little impression; and even were this to serve some persons, it would be only during the instant of their seeing the demonstration, and an hour afterwards they would fear they had been deceived.   BLAISE PASCAL (1623–1662)
Pensées

Let the Father tomorrow cover the heavens with a dark cloud or with pure sunshine; he can not render vain the past, or destroy what the fleeting hour has borne away.

HORACE (65–8 B.C.)
Odes

Through all the thick mists of the dim doubts in my mind, divine intuitions now and then shoot, enkindling my fog with a heavenly ray. And for this I thank God; for all have doubts; many deny; but doubts or denials, few along with them, have intuitions. Doubts of all things earthly, and intuitions of some things heavenly; this combination makes neither believer nor infidel, but makes a man who regards them both with equal eye.

HERMAN MELVILLE (1819–1891)
Moby Dick

Since man was so desirous to match himself with God, he would have done better, Cicero says, to have given to himself the divine properties and to have drawn them down here below, than to send there on high his corruption and his wretchedness; but, truly apprehended, he has in different ways done both the one and the other with equal pride of opinion.

MICHEL EYQUEM DE MONTAIGNE (1533–1592)
Apology for Raimond Sebond

There lives more faith in honest doubt,
Believe me, than in half the creeds.

ALFRED LORD TENNYSON (1809–1892)
In Memoriam

God who is all-positivity, an infinite being and infinitely being, is blinded by his omnipotence: He perceives the creature only insofar as it is a positivity. In order for the divine understanding to conceive the negative, it would, to a certain degree, have to be affected with negativity. Thus, the nothingness which is secreted by the creature is a veil that hides it from the sight of the Almighty,

like the ink in which the cuttlefish envelops itself.   JEAN-PAUL SARTRE (1905–1980)
Saint Genet

When I consider the short duration of my life, swallowed up in the eternity before and after, the little space which I fill, and even can see, engulfed in the infinite immensity of spaces of which I am ignorant, and which knows me not, I am frightened, and am astonished at being here rather than there; for there is no reason why here rather than there, why now rather than then. Who has put me here? By whose order and direction have this place and time been allotted to me?
BLAISE PASCAL (1623–1662)
Pensées

The content of absolute faith is the "God above God." Absolute faith and its consequences, the courage that takes the radical doubt, the doubt about God, into itself, transcends the theistic idea of God.
PAUL TILLICH (1886–1965)
The Courage to Be

Much contemporary religion bears the moral mark of an illegitimate surrender. It has abandoned at the behest of science immortality, since for science there is no other world than this world, and mind and body are inseparable; then freedom, since science under the name of psychology takes over all of human nature into the natural system of causes and effects; and finally God as anything more than a name for our highest values. It was at first inclined to hand these three notions over to metaphysics; it has ended by abandoning metaphysics itself as a house built too near the crater of Vesuvius.
WILLIAM E. HOCKING (1873–1966)
Science and the Idea of God

If God is not omnipotent, the fact that God exists and is good gives us no guarantee that the universe is more good than bad, or even that it is not very bad. If God exists and is good, the universe will of course be as good as he can make it. But, if there are some things that he cannot do, how can we tell that among these impossibilities may not be the impossibility of preventing it from being very bad?
JOHN M. E. M'TAGGART (1866–1925)
Some Dogmas of Religion

If God be all-pervading, all-in-all, it is impossible to conceive anything coming into being alien to Himself, within Himself. If He created spirits able to choose evil, He must have created the evil for them to choose, for a man could not choose what did not exist; if man can defy God, God must have given him the thought of defiance, for no thought can enter the mind of man not permitted by God.
ARTHUR CHRISTOPHER BENSON (1865–1922)
The Altar Fire

Whence could arise the solitary and strange conceit that the Almighty, who had millions of worlds equally dependent on his perfections, should quit the universe and come to die in our world because they say one man and one woman had eaten an apple?
THOMAS PAINE (1737–1809)
The Age of Reason

To maintain that God is Good now and then, and present and operative here and there, or that order rules the universe at times and in certain spots, while elsewhere contingencies are rampant and particulars run amok—all this seems to me as foolish as to say that 2 × 2 is 4 now and then on certain days and in certain places.
SIR HENRY JONES (1852–1922)
A Faith That Enquires

Is there no God, then; but at best an absentee God, sitting idle, ever since the first Sabbath, at the outside of his Universe, and seeing it go?
THOMAS CARLYLE (1795–1881)
Sartor Resartus

If the maker of the world can do all that he will, he wills misery, and there is no escape from the conclusion.

JOHN STUART MILL (1806–1873)
Three Essays on Religion

The capacity of the strenuous mood lies so deep down among our natural human possibilities that even if there were no metaphysical or traditional grounds for believing in a God, men would postulate one simply as a pretext for living hard, and getting out of the game of existence its keenest possibilities of zest.   WILLIAM JAMES (1842–1910)
The Moral Philosopher and the Moral Life

Many visible proofs, the verification of numberless predictions, a multitude of wonderful works have compelled all nations to believe, either that God, or that some evil power whose name was unknown, presided over the affairs of the world.

JOHN MILTON (1608–1674)
De Doctrina

And the stars that watch blind earth in the
  deep night swim
Laugh, saying, "What God is your God, that
  ye call on him?
What is man, that the God who is guide of
  our way should care
If day for a man be golden, or night be
  grim?"

ALGERNON CHARLES SWINBURNE (1837–1909)
A Nympholept

We incline to think that God cannot explain His own secrets, and that He would like a little information upon certain points Himself. We mortals astonish Him as much as He us.

HERMAN MELVILLE (1819–1891)
Letter to Nathaniel Hawthorne

I don't know whether this world has a meaning that transcends it. But I know that I do not know that meaning and that it is impossible for me just now to know it. What can a meaning outside my condition mean to me? I can understand only in human terms. What I touch, what resists me—that is what I understand. And these two certainties—my appetite for the absolute and for unity and the impossibility of reducing this world to a rational and reasonable principle—I also know that I cannot reconcile them.

ALBERT CAMUS (1913–1960)
The Myth of Sisyphus

O me! for why is all around us here
As if some lesser God had made the world,
But had not force to shape it as he would?

ALFRED LORD TENNYSON (1809–1892)
Morte d'Arthur

Ah! must—
Designer infinite!—
Ah! must Thou char the wood ere Thou
  canst limn with it?

FRANCIS THOMPSON (1859–1907)
The Hound of Heaven

If God be good, how came he to create—or, if he did not create, how comes he to permit—the devil? The evil facts must be explained as seeming: the devil must be whitewashed, the universe must be disinfected, if neither God's goodness nor his unity and power are to remain impugned.

WILLIAM JAMES (1842–1910)
The Dilemma of Determinism

We owe it to the Eternal to be virtuous; but we have the right to add to this tribute our irony as a sort of personal reprisal. In this way we return to the right quarter jest for jest; we play the trick that has been played on us. Saint Augustine's phrase: Lord, if we are deceived, it is by Thee! remains a fine one, well suited to our modern feeling. Only we wish the Eternal to know that if we accept the fraud, we accept it knowingly and willingly. We are resigned in advance to losing the interest on our investments of virtue, but we wish not to appear ridiculous by having counted on them too securely.

ERNEST RENAN (1823–1892)
Feuilles detachées

When God sleeps even the angels become insolent.   *Russian Proverb*

One sticks one's finger into the soil to tell by the smell in what land one is: I stick my finger into existence—it smells of nothing. Where am I? Who am I? How came I here? What is this thing called the world? What does this world mean? Who is it that has lured me into this thing and now leaves me there? How did I come into this world? Why was I not consulted, but thrust into the ranks as though I had been bought of a kidnapper, a dealer in souls? How did I obtain an interest in this big enterprise they call reality? Why should I have an interest in it? Is it not a voluntary concern? And if I am compelled to take part in it, where is the director? Whither shall I turn with my complaint?

SÖREN KIERKEGAARD (1813–1855)
Works

We have a sort of family history of our God—so have the Tahitians of theirs—and some old poet's grand imagination is imposed on us as adamantine everlasting truth, and God's own word. Pythagoras says, truly enough, "A true assertion respecting God is an assertion of God."

HENRY DAVID THOREAU (1817–1862)
A Week on the Concord and Merrimack Rivers

To every man come times when he is oppressed with his own Lilliputian insignificance—one among such swarming myriads of his kind, an ephemeral being whose span of life is a mere wink in the duration of our ancient planet, a dweller upon one of the meaner bodies in a system of innumerable stars, a walking chemical factory driven by instincts of hunger and sex.

HENRY SLOANE COFFIN (1877–1954)
The Meaning of the Cross

In my most extreme fluctuations I have never been an atheist in the sense of denying the existence of a God. I think that generally (and more and more as I grow older), but not always, an agnostic would be the more correct description of my state of mind.

CHARLES DARWIN (1809–1882)
Autobiography

· DENYING GOD ·

I knew an atheist novelist who used to say his prayers every night. That didn't alter anything. How he gave it to God in his books! What a dressing down, as one might say. A militant freethinker to whom I spoke of this raised his hands—with no evil intention, I assure you—to heaven: "You're telling me nothing new," that apostle of free thought sighed, "they're all like that." According to him, 80 percent of our writers, if only they could avoid putting their names to it, would write and hail the name of God.

ALBERT CAMUS (1913–1960)
The Fall

I have made my peace with my Maker, much to the dismay of my enlightened friends, who reproach me for this backsliding into the old "superstition," as they like to call my homecoming to God. The entire high clergy of atheism has pronounced its anathema over me, and there are fanatic priestlings of unbelief who would like to span me on the rack that I might revoke my heresies.

HEINRICH HEINE (1797–1856)
Works

He only is a true atheist to whom the predicates of the Divine Being—for example, love, wisdom and justice—are nothing.

LUDWIG FEUERBACH (1804–1872)
The Essence of Christianity

Until recently, man had managed to have various escapes outside of himself, but the plunge into the unconscious self is the last and final flight from God. The new psychology offers man an escape from the responsibility of being guilty, almost an escape from the responsibility of being human. In the Garden of Paradise, man hid from God in the garden; now man hides within himself. In this state he regards it as bad taste to speak of God.

FULTON J. SHEEN (1895–1979)
The Electronic Christian

Have you not heard of that madman who lit a lantern in the bright morning hours, ran to the marketplace, and cried incessantly, "I seek God! I seek God!" Since many of those who did not believe in God were standing around just then, he provoked much laughter.

"Why, did he get lost?" said one. "Or is he hiding? Is he afraid of us? Has he gone on a voyage? Or emigrated?" Thus they yelled and laughed.

The madman jumped into their midst and pierced them with his glances. "Whither is God," he cried. "I shall tell you. *We have killed him*—you and I. All of us are his murderers."

FRIEDRICH NIETZSCHE (1844–1900)
The Gay Science

The fool hath said in his heart, There is no God.

The Old Testament
Psalms 14:1

Having a form of godliness, but denying the power thereof; from such turn away. . . . Ever learning, and never able to come to the knowledge of truth.

The New Testament
2 Timothy 3:5, 7

What is it: is man only a blunder of God, or God only a blunder of man?

FRIEDRICH NIETZSCHE (1844–1900)
The Twilight of the Idols

It is true, we adore God like ignorant slaves, who tremble under a master whom they know not; we foolishly pray to him, although he is represented to us as immutable; although, in truth, this God is nothing more than nature acting by necessary laws necessarily personified, or destiny, to which the name of God is given.

BARON PAUL D'HOLBACH (1723–1789)
The System of Nature

No one is so much alone in the universe as a denier of God. With an orphaned heart, which has lost the greatest of fathers, he stands mourning by the immeasurable corpse of the universe.

JEAN PAUL RICHTER (1763–1825)
Flower, Fruit and Thorn Pieces

If there is no God, and everything, therefore, is permitted, the first thing permitted is despair.

FRANÇOIS MAURIAC (1885–1907)
Words of Faith

Even where man revolts against God in titanic rebellion, and with great daring and insolence "gets rid" of Him, or deifies himself, even there, behind the human perversion, the Divine image itself looks forth. Man could not be godless without God; he could not curse God if he were not first of all loved by God.

EMIL BRUNNER (1889–1966)
Man in Revolt

It is easier to suppose that the universe has existed from all eternity than to conceive a Being beyond its limits capable of creating it.
PERCY BYSSHE SHELLEY (1792–1822)
Queen Mab

The atheistic philosopher must be seen as a man who says to anyone who believes in God or who in any way affirms God's reality: "I put myself in your place, that is, I am in some degree able to reconstitute what you call your experience. But in addition I have the capacity, which you do not seem to possess, of correctly interpreting whether this is a real or merely an illusory experience."
GABRIEL MARCEL (1889–1973)
Tragic Wisdom and Beyond

After Buddha was dead, his shadow was still shown for centuries in a cave—a tremendous, gruesome shadow. God is dead: but given the way men are, there may still be caves for thousands of years in which his shadow will still be shown.
FRIEDRICH NIETZSCHE (1844–1900)
The Gay Science

When man, by denying the existence of God, denies his own, the spiritual powers which are dissociated by his denial keep their primitive reality, but disunited and detached they can no longer do anything but drive the beings of flesh and soul back against each other in a despairing conflict—those beings which, had their union been safeguarded and preserved, would have gone forward towards eternal life.
GABRIEL MARCEL (1889–1973)
Homo Viator

If by renouncing the reality of God one has arrived at a reality of the world which is by intention independent of the divine—in substance, it can never be so—then there is no way back to the reality of God. For God is either the beginning or he does not exist.
PAUL TILLICH (1886–1965)
What Is Religion?

God himself is nothing else than undisturbed, uninterruted feeling, feeling for which there exists no limits, no opposite. If God were a being distinct from thy feeling, he would be known to thee in some other way than simply in feeling; but just because thou perceivest him only by feeling, he exists only in feeling—he is himself only feeling.
LUDWIG FEUERBACH (1804–1872)
The Essence of Christianity

The great Creator
We see not—He conceals himself within
His own eternal laws. The skeptic sees
Their operation, but beholds not Him,
"Wherefore a God!" he cries, "the world itself
Suffices for itself!"
FRIEDRICH SCHILLER (1759–1805)
Works

Having given up God so as to be self-sufficient, man has lost track of his soul. He looks in vain for himself; he turns the universe upside down trying to find himself, he finds masks, and behind the masks, death.
JACQUES MARITAIN (1882–1973)
The Range of Reason

Atheism can only mean the attempt to remove any ultimate concern—to remain unconcerned about the meaning of one's existence. Indifference toward the ultimate question is the only imaginable form of atheism. Whether it is possible is a problem which must remain unsolved at this point. In any case, he who denies God as a matter of ultimate concern affirms God, because he affirms ultimacy in his concern.
PAUL TILLICH (1886–1965)
Dynamics of Faith

Supposing all the great points of atheism were formed into a kind of creed, I would fain ask whether it would not require an infinitely greater measure of faith than any set of articles which they so violently oppose.

JOSEPH ADDISON (1672–1719)
The Spectator

It would indeed be very nice if there were a God, who was both creator of the world and a benevolent providence, if there were a moral world order and a future life. But at the same time it is very odd that this is all just as we should wish it ourselves. And it would be still odder if our poor, ignorant, enslaved ancestors had succeeded in solving these difficult riddles of the universe.

SIGMUND FREUD (1856–1939)
The Future of an Illusion

By denying the existence, or providence of God, men may shake off their ease, but not their yoke.   THOMAS HOBBES (1588–1679)
Leviathan

Atheism is rather in the lip than in the heart of man.

FRANCIS BACON (1561–1626)
Of Atheism

Evolution has been an incredible spendthrift of life. Highly organized creatures have been developed again and again only to be pushed up blind alleys and left there to die. If there is a God whose method has been Evolution, his slogan must have been, "We'll fight it out along this line if it takes a millennium!" But, unlike Grant, he always surrendered.   MAX OTTO (1876–1968)
The Human Enterprise

"The wicked man has said in his heart: There is no God." And there is truth in this.

For it is possible for a righteous man to say in his head: God does not exist. But only the wicked can say it in his heart.

MIGUEL DE UNAMUNO (1864–1936)
Essays and Soliloquies

The absolute death of the word "God," including even the eradication of its past, would be the signal, no longer heard by anyone, that man himself had died.

KARL RAHNER (1904–)
Foundations of Christian Faith

Men are frightened at the absence of God from the world, they feel that they can no longer realize the Divine, they are terrified at God's silence, at his withdrawal into his own inaccessibility.

PAUL TILLICH (1886–1965)
Word and Truth

When the throne of God is overthrown, the rebel realizes that it is now his own responsibility to create the justice, order, and unity that he sought in vain within his own condition and, in this way, to justify the fall of God. Then begins the desperate effort to create, at the price of sin if necessary, the dominion of man.

ALBERT CAMUS (1913–1960)
The Rebel

Today He is a Master of a universe made up of myriads upon myriads of gigantic suns, and among them in that limitless sea of light, floats that atom. His earth, which once seemed so good and satisfactory and cost so many days of patient labor to build, is a mere cork adrift in the waters of a shoreless Atlantic.   MARK TWAIN (1835–1910)
Europe and Elsewhere

III · SEEKING GOD

There is one approach to an infinite realm
where God might be. There is one door that
opens to the holy of holies. The search must
begin in your own bosom.

RUFUS JONES

T HIS PORTION of our anthology explores the germinal thoughts of a wide spectrum of religious leaders, theologians, philosophers, and poets on the *ways* they have sought God. Certain underlying themes have been reiterated throughout the centuries, for when we strip away what appear to be the differences among the religions we find that, essentially, these God Seekers are expressing the same things. It is as if some central core of universal truths has emerged from the collective religious wisdom of humankind, and these truths stand forth whether they were first voiced in the deserts of Arabia from the mystic vision of an eleventh-century Sufi or eight hundred years later in a small New England town from the pen of an Emerson, Thoreau, or Alcott.

Is it so strange to think a Divine Purpose determined that five of the most remarkable God Seekers of all time should be living during the same century more than 2500 years ago? For it is a fact that the Hebrew prophet, Jeremiah, Zoroaster in Persia, Guatama Buddha in India, not to mention Confucius and Lao-tse in China were all living at the same time.

A dominant theme in this section is that whether we know it or not, consciously or unconsciously, *every* human being is seeking a unique relationship with God. If, in his endless, eternal workings, God has created each single being with characteristics that never before existed and never again will exist in the same confluence, each of us who seeks him must enter into a singular relationship with God.

Yet how often, constricted by the fetters of our limited understanding, we fail even to consider the idea that God might have unrestricted, illimitable powers of communion with us. Why should it be beyond our belief to consider that God cares about every one of his creatures? Only when we dare to equate our intelligence to God's, and only if we limit his powers to our minuscule perceptions, need we scoff at the thought that He has established a covenant with each of his creations.

The authors in this anthology may or may not be theologians or in any way formal religionists, and some of them led relatively obscure lives. A superb example of a man whose work touched few during his lifetime yet whose insights into the God-person relationship were, by any measure, extraordinary is Henri Frédéric Amiel, the Swiss writer quoted in the Introduction. Born in Geneva in 1821, he was frustrated in his wish to achieve widespread recognition as a poet and only attained the post of teacher of aesthetics at the academy in Geneva. But Amiel expressed his creative energy in a remarkable diary that he kept from 1847 until his death thirty-four years later. When parts of the nearly seventeen thousand pages of his journal were published a few years after his death, the book gained something of a reputation in Europe and eventually was translated into German, Russian, English, and other languages.

Here is a portion of Amiel's *Journal Intime* to show how a rather unknown God Seeker touched on an imperishable truth and articulated it:

I have traversed the universe from the deepest depths of the empyrean to the peristaltic movements of the atoms in the elementary cell. And on all sides stretched mysteries, marvels, and prodigies without limit, without number, and without end. I felt the unfathomable thought, of which the Universe is the symbol, live and burn within me; I touched, proved, tasted, embraced my nothingness and my immensity; I kissed the hem of the garments of God, and gave Him thanks for being Spirit and for being Life.

The God Seekers stress that God is very near to us, indeed as the medieval German mystic Hans Denck proclaimed, "Oh, who will give me a voice that I may cry aloud to the whole world that God, the all-highest, is in the deepest abyss within us and is waiting for us to return to Him." Is God sought less sincerely in the words of an African child's prayer that addresses Him, "O thou Great Chief, light a candle in my heart that I may see what is therein and sweep the rubbish from thy dwelling place"?

An underlying concept throughout this section is that we have the right to approach God by any way that is true to our deepest selves. The noted American preacher Henry Ward Beecher put it most succinctly this way: "If you can think it out, that is your privilege; if you can feel it out, that is your privilege. Wherever you have seen God pass, mark it, and go and sit in that window again."

To explore and find one's deepest self is a laborious and often painful endeavor. As John Baillie perceived, if the formation of our own idea of God is rooted in sloth and selfishness, we shall not find God corresponding to our expectation of him. Because we are unable to look for any other God than the one our ego-driven desires can summon, we invariably fail to find the God who is really there.

If we believe with Ralph Waldo Emerson that "God enters by a private door into every individual," we are able to take the first, all-important step in achieving a spiritual union with the Eternal Source. We need no letter of introduction when we travel to the Celestial City is the way Henry David Thoreau put it in his droll, aphoristic way, and "when you knock, ask to see God,—none of the servants."

We cannot be afraid that our search for God will carry us beyond our understanding. It will, of course, but as Phillips Brooks urged, although the thought of approaching God seems mystical and cloudy, "nevertheless, enter into the cloud without a fear."

Another important theme in this section is that God is constantly seeking *us*, even when we attempt to evade him, even when we do our utmost to entomb ourselves within our human shell, even when we live as if God were not here at all. As John Baillie also noted, "God is not really found until we find not merely One whom we have long sought and could not find, but One who has all the time been seeking us and whom we have all the time been attempting to elude."

Why are we reluctant to listen when God speaks to us? Archbishop Fénelon thought that the noise of the world around us and the "tumult of our passions within" confuse and bewilder us and prevent us from listening to the true yearnings of our lives. Meister Eckhart believed that no one has ever wanted anything as much as God wishes to make our souls aware of him. If, in truth, God enters a soul through its core, then, Eckhart says, "nothing may touch that core except God Himself."

From religion's earliest times a universal way for mankind to seek God has been through prayer, and in this section of our anthology we find some of the deepest introspections of the God Seekers. The seriousness with which prayer must be approached if it is to be anything more than wishful thinking is essential, for to expect God to answer our prayers when we disregard the conditions He has set is not very plausible. How many of us pray for knowledge but are not willing to study, or for an amelioration of our character but are not willing to accept the price of growth, or as William Adams Brown pointed out, pray to be forgiven "even while we harbor enmity against our brother."

In every true prayer, said Paul Tillich, God is both He to whom we pray and He who prays through us, for "it is the divine Spirit who creates the right prayer."

To those who hold that prayer is little more than a self-serving plea, and in effect an unprofitable act, since a person's prayer cannot really change the Unchangeable, the great Danish theologian Kierkegaard had an answer. If every prayer were answered, might not we regret that we had "changed" God? Only our willful insecurity would lead us to think that prayer can change God, but its true efficacy is that it "changes him who prays." In its highest form, therefore, prayer, as Emerson viewed it, is the "soliloquy of a beholding and jubilant soul; it is the spirit of God pronouncing his works good."

Each of us, perhaps, seeks God to the extent of our capabilities, if that is our will. The prophets and kindred great religious figures are able to express their yearning for the Creator in words that have been tested by time and not found wanting, but the expressions of us ordinary human beings are equally dear to Him. The story is told of a fourteenth-century woman who went about the streets of Strasbourg with a pail of water in one hand and a blazing torch in the other. When asked by bystanders to explain this strange behavior, she answered, "I am going to put out hellfire with this pail of water, and with this torch I am going to burn up Heaven, so that men will stop pretending to love God because of their fear of Hell or of their desire for the joys of Heaven."

She understood what Harry Emerson Fosdick also observed, that "God is not a cosmic bell-boy for whom we can press a button to get things."

We shall find throughout this portion that there are no shortcuts or secret formulas in looking for God, let alone finding him. There is no magical "somewhere" that we need to discover him; we need only to contemplate, to see, and to feel the inner limits of ourselves. Sometimes our deepest prayers are directed to God for the sheer joy of trying to reach him. At such times, said the Baal Shem Tov, whose joy in contemplating God had no bounds, our prayers unite with God's abundance, a gift for which He is always seeking a channel.

Finally, let us look at a passage from the *Testament of Devotion,* a short work by yet another relatively unknown God Seeker, an American Quaker named Thomas R. Kelly. Influenced by Rufus Jones while an undergraduate student at Haverford College, Kelly, who unfortunately died before he was fifty, realized a high degree of mystic intuition. "Count on God knocking on the doors of time. God is the Seeker, and not we alone; He is anxious to swell out our time-nows into an Eternal Now by filling them with a sense of Presence."

This, in essence, is one of the most important lessons that we can learn from the collective wisdom and spirituality of the God Seekers in this anthology. The world in which we live is completely framed in a time continuum. Why did our Creator, who is beyond all vestiges of space or time, will it thus? If, as Kelly believed, we can count on God to seek *us,* even as we seek him, and to assure us that our temporal binds are only one phase in the journey to an Eternal Now, then we can be filled with a sense of his presence and begin to see our time-bound lives in their real perspective.

· In Quest of God ·

Not only around our infancy
Doth heaven with all its splendors lie;
Daily, with souls that cringe and plot,
We Sinais climb and know it not.
> JAMES RUSSELL LOWELL (1819–1891)
> *The Vision of Sir Launfal*

Ah! for a vision of God! for a mighty grasp
   of the real,
Feet firm based on granite in place of
   crumbling sand!
> RODEN NOEL (1834–1894)
> *Poems*

Why are you cast down, O my soul,
And why are you disquieted within me?
Hope in God; for I shall again praise Him,
My help and my God.
> *The Old Testament*
> *Psalms 42:12*

And though thy soul sail leagues and
   leagues beyond—
Still, leagues beyond those leagues, there is
   more sea.
> DANTE GABRIEL ROSSETTI (1828–1882)
> *The House of Life*

What I cry out for, like every being, with
my whole life and earthly passion, is something very different from an equal to cherish:
it is a God to adore. To adore: that means to
lose oneself in the unfathomable, to plunge
into the inexhaustible, to find peace in the
incorruptible, to be absorbed in immensity,
to offer oneself to the fire and the transparency.
> PIERRE TEILHARD DE CHARDIN (1881–1955)
> *The Divine Way*

And climb the Mount of Blessing, whence, if
   thou

Look higher, then perchance thou mayest—
   beyond
A hundred ever-rising mountain lines,
And past the range of Night and Shadow—
   see
The high heaven dawn of more than mortal
   day.
> ALFRED LORD TENNYSON (1809–1892)
> *Tiresias*

Look thou within: within thee is the fountain of all good, whose waters shall never
cease to spring, so thou dig deep enough. No
soul is willingly bereaved of Truth, nor of
those natural inclinations to justice and equanimity and kindness that are the fruit of her
knowledge.   MARCUS AURELIUS (121–180)
> *Meditations*

Must God be "found"? Is He not always
near? Must we "seek" Him in San Francisco,
only to hear that He has gone to the Gobi
Desert; or in one decade in history, only to
learn that such an era is not His visiting
hours?
> GEORGE ARTHUR BUTTRICK (1892–1979)
> *Sermons Preached in a University Church*

There is no short cut, no patent tramroad
to wisdom; after all the centuries of invention, the soul's path lies through the thorny
wilderness which must be still trodden in solitude, with bleeding feet, with sobs for help,
as it was trodden by them of old time.
> GEORGE ELIOT (1819–1880)
> *The Lifted Veil*

It is quite natural, and inevitable that, if we
spend sixteen hours daily of our waking lives
in thinking about the affairs of the world and
five minutes in thinking about God and our
souls, this world will seem two hundred times
more real to us than God or our souls.

Things we do not think about always seem unreal to us. Do not then argue that God is unreal because he seems unreal to you. Ask yourself whether you have given him a chance; or, rather, yourself, a fair chance.

WILLIAM RALPH INGE (1860–1954)
Sermons

I see nothing arrogant in the notion that God might permit a man to discern Him. Nothing, it seems to me, is plainer than that if He exists He does not permit all, perhaps not even many, to achieve this discernment, nor does He permit any, even a Moses, to achieve it completely.

GEDDES MACGREGOR (1909–)
God Beyond Doubt

Religion is the vision of something which stands beyond, behind, and within, the passing flux of immediate things. The worship of God is not a rule of safety—it is an adventure of the spirit, a flight after the unattainable.

ALFRED NORTH WHITEHEAD (1861–1947)
Science and the Modern World

I asked the earth and it answered me: 'I am not it' and all things whatsoever in it made the same confession. I asked the sea and the deeps and the creeping things and they answered me: 'We are not thy God; seek beyond us.' I asked the heavens, the sun and moon and stars 'nor,' say they, 'are we the God thou seekest.'

SAINT AUGUSTINE (354–430)
Confessions

My God, my God, let me for once look on
thee
As though nought else existed, we alone!
And as creation crumbles, my soul's spark
Expands till I can say—Even for myself
I need thee and I feel thee and I love thee.

ROBERT BROWNING (1812–1889)
Collected Poems

I askt the seas and all the deeps below
My God to know

I askt the reptiles, and whatever is in the
abyss
Even from the shrimps to the leviathan
Enquiry ran;
But in those deserts that no line can sound
The God I sought for was not to be found.

THOMAS HEYWOOD (1574–1641)
Searching After God

The consummation of man is twofold, in the Self and in Selflessness. By great retrogression back to the source of darkness in me, the Self, deep in the senses, I arrive at the Original, Creative Infinite. By projection forth from myself, by the elimination of my absolute sensual self, I arrive at the Ultimate Infinite, Oneness in the Spirit. They are two Infinites, twofold approach to God. And man must know both.

D. H. LAWRENCE (1885–1930)
Twilight in Italy

In the life to be, there is neither envy nor hatred, nor contention, but the righteous rejoice in the light of God's countenance.

The Talmud

O Lord, I, a beggar, ask of Thee
More than what a thousand kings may ask of
Thee;
Each one has something he needs to ask of
Thee,
I have come to ask Thee to give Thyself.

SHEIKH 'ABDULLAH ANSARI (1005–1090)
Invocations

You want to seek God by this or that opinion: one is of the Pope's opinion, the other of Luther's opinion, the third of Calvin's, and so forth. There is no end to opinions; all this is nothing but intellectual contention. You will not find rebirth and the precious stone in strife or any great wisdom. You must relinquish everything in this world, be it as high-sounding as it is, and must go into yourself.

JACOB BOEHME (1575–1624)
Works

Lord, where shall I find Thee?
High and hidden is Thy place!
And where shall I not find Thee?
The world is full of Thy glory!

> JUDAH HALEVI (C. 1085–C. 1140)

What is the better part? It is God, and
consequently everything, but it is called the
better part because it must be chosen; one
does not receive everything as everything,
that is not how one begins: one begins by
choosing the better part, which is, nevertheless, everything.

> SÖREN KIERKEGAARD (1813–1855)
> *Journals*

Let a certain holy ambition invade our
souls, so that, not content with the mediocre,
we shall pant after the highest, and—since
we may if we wish—toil with all our strength
to obtain it. Let us disdain earthly things, despise heavenly things, and finally esteeming
less whatever is of the world, hasten to that
which is beyond the world and nearest to the
Godhead.

> GIOVANNI PICO DELLA MIRANDOLA
> (1463–1494)
> *Oration on the Dignity of Man*

Search me, O God, and know my heart;
try me, and know my thoughts. And see if
there be any wicked way in me, and lead
me in the way everlasting.

> *The Old Testament*
> *Psalms 139:23–24*

You may turn to the east to the Prophet
but all four winds are God's.   *Suni Proverb*

As the hart panteth after the water brooks,
so panteth my soul after Thee, O God.

> *The Old Testament*
> *Psalms 42:1*

O you, in quest of God, you seek him
    everywhere,
You verily are the God, not apart from Him!

Already in the midst of the boundless ocean,
Your quest resembles the search of a drop
    for the ocean!

> DARA SHIKOH (1615–1659)
> *Hasanat ul-'Arifin*

The best that you can seek from Him is
that which He seeks from you.

> IBN 'ATA'ILLAH (died 1309)
> *Kitab Al-Hakim*

My God, how near You are to me, and how
far I am from you!

> IBN 'ATA'ILLAH (died 1309)
> *Kitab Al-Hakim*

Come now, little man, put aside your business for a while, take refuge for a little from
your tumultuous thoughts; cast off your
cares, and let your burdensome distractions
wait. Take some leisure for God; rest awhile
in Him. Enter into the chambers of your
mind; put out everything except God and
whatever helps you to see Him; close the
door and seek Him.

> SAINT ANSELM (1033–1109)
> *Proslogion*

Art thou looking for God, seeking God
with a view to thy personal good, thy personal profit? Then in truth thou art not seeking God.

> MEISTER ECKHART (1260–1327)
> *Sermons*

Eternity is not beyond the stars—
Some far Hereafter—it is Here, and Now!
The Kingdom of Heaven is within, so
    near
We do not see it save by spirit-sight.
We shut our eyes in prayer, and we are
    There
In thought, and Thoughts are spirit-
    things—
Realities upon the other side.

> GERALD MASSEY (1828–1907)
> *My Lyrical Life*

My only task is to be what I am, a man seeking God in silence and solitude, with respect for the demands and realities of his own vocation, and fully aware that others too are seeking the truth in their own way.

THOMAS MERTON (1915–1968)
Contemplation in a World of Action

The sin for God's sake is greater than the fulfilling of a commandment not for God's sake. *The Midrash*

If you seek God, O my mind, go forth out of yourself and seek for him. But if you remain in the substance of the body, or in the vain opinions of the mind, you are then without any real wish to search into divine things, even if you do put on the appearance and pretence of seeking them.

PHILO JUDAEUS (30 B.C.–A.D. 40)
Works

We search for that which the eye has never seen, that which the ear has never heard, that which has not come into the thought of any man. They say, "God will enlighten them interiorly, and He will be all things in all." This which I expect, the plenitude we await from God, will be nothing else but God Himself.

SAINT BERNARD OF CLAIRVAUX (1091–1153)
Canticle of Canticles

Speak to Him, then, for He hears, and Spirit
with Spirit can meet—
Closer is He than breathing, and nearer
than hands and feet.

ALFRED LORD TENNYSON (1809–1892)
In Memoriam

In the spiritual life there is the city of Light and many roads lead to it, and everyone can reach it. But if one starts to change roads, even on the advice of an experienced man, he might very well never reach that city.

THEOPHANE THE RECLUSE (1815–1894)
Way of Salvation

I can see no hope for our unhappy world save that which lies in the renewal of the moral and spiritual estates which our common ideal of faith has created—in our strengthening hold upon those possessions and in our turning to them with hearts full of faith, in fear of God, in love for him, and in love for his creation—Man.

SHOLEM ASCH (1880–1957)
One Destiny

What does this mean, O Lord my God? Ah yes, how sublime you are in the heights and profound in the abysses! You never withdraw from us, and yet how hard it is to reach you!

SAINT AUGUSTINE (354–430)
Confessions

We are condemned to fumble in these times, for the mist is too thick to see far down the road. But in all our uncertainty we can have Cromwell's hope. "To be a Seeker is to be of the best sect next to a Finder, and such a one shall ever faithful, humble Seeker be at the end." JOHN BUCHAN (1875–1940)
Pilgrim's Way

The mind of the God-seeker must not only be sufficiently open to take whatever truth gives; it must also be sufficiently generous to give whatever truth takes.

RALPH W. SOCKMAN (1889–1970)
Men of the Mysteries

Only one who has been hard and implacable with himself and goes on to spin and weave from his entrails a thread for the exploration of the void, only one who has beaten his soul into metal sheets and rolled it into spindles in the search for his wherefore, for the Soul of the Universe, only he can fearlessly hurl himself into the abyss of the future's deepest darkness.

MIGUEL DE UNAMUNO (1864–1936)
Essays on Faith

'Tis a hazardous thing to plunge into the fathomless sea of the divine mysteries, and hard, hard it is to essay the discovery of the Lights Supernal that are beyond the Veil.

ABU-HAMID MUHAMMAD AL-GHAZZALI
(1058–1111)
Mishkat-al-Anwar

O my heart, if you wish to arrive at the beginning of understanding, walk carefully. To each atom there is a different door, and for each atom there is a different way which leads to the mysterious Being of whom I speak.

FARID-UD-DIN ATTAR (12th century)
The Conference of the Birds

The intellect searches out the absolute order of things as they stand in the mind of God and without the colors of affection.

RALPH WALDO EMERSON (1803–1882)
Nature

This is the life of gods and of god-like and blessed men—liberation from the alien that besets us here, a life taking no pleasure in the things of earth—a flight of the alone to the Alone.　　　　　PLOTINUS (205–270)
Enneads

As a boy holding to a post or pillar whirls about it with headlong speed without fear of falling, so perform thy worldly duties fixing thy hold firmly upon God, and thou shalt be free from danger.

SRI RAMAKRISHNA (1834–1886)
Sayings

He alone escapes from the web of illusion, in this world (even like the lord of beasts from the trip which holds him fast,) who, with all acts, all pleasures, attuned to the Supreme Aim, puts forth strong personal effort in that behalf.　　　　　*The Upanishads*

And Thou, O Lord! by whom are seen
　　Thy creatures as they be,
Forgive me if too close I lean
　　My human heart on Thee!

JOHN GREENLEAF WHITTIER (1807–1892)
The Eternal Goodness

I was early convinced in my mind that true religion consisted in an inward life, wherein the heart does love and reverence God the Creator, and learns to exercise true justice and goodness, not only toward all men, but also toward the brute creatures; that, as the mind was moved by an inward principle to love God as an invisible, incomprehensible Being, so, by the same principle, it was moved to love him in all his manifestations in the visible world.

JOHN WOOLMAN (1720–1772)
Journal

It is not God's will that all He has created for the benefit of man and has given him as his own should remain hidden. And even if He did conceal some things, He left nothing unmarked, but provided all things with outward, visible marks, with special traits—just as a man who has buried a treasure marks the spot in order that he may find it again.

PARACELSUS (1493–1541)
Works

Indeed, the chief natural way whereby we can climb up to the understanding of the Deity is by a contemplation of our own souls. We cannot think of him but according to the measure and model of our own intellect, or frame any other idea of him than what the impressions of our own souls permit us. And therefore the best philosophers have always taught us to inquire for God within ourselves.

JOHN SMITH (1616–1652)
Discourses

I shall be asked, "What is your religion?" and I shall answer that my religion is to seek truth in life and life in truth, conscious that I shall not find them while I live; my religion is to struggle tirelessly and incessantly with the unknown; my religion is to struggle with God as they say Jacob did from earliest dawn until nightfall.

MIGUEL DE UNAMUNO (1864–1936)
Perplexities and Paradoxes

No offering of my own I have,
Nor works my faith to prove;
I can but give the gifts He gave,
And plead His love for love.
JOHN GREENLEAF WHITTIER (1807–1892)
The Eternal Goodness

Strive for your best, that there you may find your most distinctive life. We cannot dream of what interest the world will have when every being in its human multitude shall shine with his own light and color, and be the child of God which it is possible for him to be—which he has ever been in the true homeland of his Father's thought.
PHILLIPS BROOKS (1835–1893)
Sermons

No, when the fight begins within himself,
A man's worth something. God stoops o'er his head,
Satan looks up between his feet—both tug—
He's left, himself, in the middle: the soul wakes
And grows.
ROBERT BROWNING (1812–1889)
Bishop Blougram's Apology

Know thou the God of thy father, serve him with a whole heart, and with a willing mind; for the Lord searcheth the hearts and understandeth all the imaginings of the thoughts; if thou seek him he will be found by thee.   *The Old Testament*
1 Chronicles 28:9

I have not spoken in secret, in a dark place of the earth: I said not unto the seed of Jacob, Seek ye me in vain: I the Lord speak righteousness, I declare things that are right.
The Old Testament
Isaiah 45:19

God blesses the seeking, not the finding.
German Proverb

God is in the heart, yet thou searchest for Him in the wilderness.
GURU NANAK (1469–1539)
The Adi Granth

Those who roam to other lands in pilgrimage to find the God that dwells within them are like a shepherd who searches his own flock for the sheep he has under his arm.
Telugu Proverb

Unlovely, nay frightful, is the solitude of the soul which is without God in the world—this chill, houseless, fatherless, aimless Cain, the man who hears only the sound of his own footsteps in God's resplendent creation.
RALPH WALDO EMERSON (1803–1882)
Sermons

If the eye were not sun-like, how could we ever see light? And if God's own power did not dwell within us, how could we delight in things divine?
JOHANN WOLFGANG VON GOETHE (1749–1832)
Works

This truly is the vision of God: never to be satisfied in the desire to see him. But one must always, by looking at what he can see, rekindle his desire to see more.
SAINT GREGORY OF NYSSA (335–395)
The Life of Moses

We have in common a terrible loneliness. Day after day a question goes up desperately in our minds: Are we alone in the wilderness of the self, alone in the silent universe, of which we are a part, and in which we feel at the same time like strangers? It is such a situation that makes us ready to search for a voice of God in the world of man: the taste of utter loneliness; the discovery that unless God has a voice, the life of the spirit is a freak; that the world without God is a torso; that a soul without faith is a stump.
ABRAHAM JOSHUA HESCHEL (1907–1972)
God in Search of Man

All men, Socrates, who have any degree of right feeling, at the beginning of every enterprise, whether small or great, always call upon God.   PLATO (427–347 B.C.)
Timaeus

No created being is unconnected with Him. But that connection is indescribable, because in the spirit there is no separating and uniting. Pursue that which is without separation and union by aid of spiritual guide, but the pursuit will not allay your thirst.   JALAL-UD-DIN RUMI (1207–1273)
The Masnawi

The real truth is not that man at last concludes that his values imply the reality of God, but rather that from the beginning he finds God in his values.

JOHN BAILLIE (1886–1960)
The Roots of Religion in the Human Soul

And anxious hearts have pondered here
    The mystery of life,
And prayed the eternal Light to clear
    Their doubts, and aid their strife.
RALPH WALDO EMERSON (1803–1882)
Hymn

In these days of despair, the most important thing that anyone can do is to refuse to be desperate and to help others to find power in God, who is our refuge and our strength. To comfort those that mourn, to give them beauty for ashes, the oil of joy for mourning, the garment of praise for the spirit of heaviness—who has a greater task?

GEORGIA HARKNESS (1891–1974)
The Dark Night of the Soul

Curiosity, or the love of knowledge of causes, draws a man from the consideration of the effect, to seek the cause; and again, the cause of that cause; till of necessity he must come to this thought at last, that there is some

cause whereof there is no former cause, but is eternal; which is it men call God.

THOMAS HOBBES (1588–1679)
Leviathan

Do we want to contemplate His power? We see it in the immensity of the Creation. Do we want to contemplate His wisdom? We see it in the unchangeable order by which the incomprehensible whole is governed. Do we want to contemplate His munificence? We see it in the abundance with which He fills the earth. Do we want to contemplate His mercy? We see it in His not withholding that abundance even from the unthankful. In fine, do we want to know what God is?

THOMAS PAINE (1737–1809)
The Age of Reason

All the true religions of the world are forms of the prayer: Search me, and know my heart; prove me, and examine my thoughts; and see if there be any wicked way in me, and lead me in the way everlasting.

JOHN RUSKIN (1819–1900)
Fors Clavigera

To seek our Divinity merely in books and writings is to seek the living among the dead. We do but in vain seek God many times in these, where His Truth too often is not so much enshrined as entombed. No, seek for God within thine own soul.

JOHN SMITH (1618–1652)
Discourses

Some seek God as if He were far removed from us, and surrounded by many walls. Had they been wise, however, they would have known that "no space is free of Him." They can find Him in everything and everywhere, and they should understand that "one who attaches himself to any part of God is as if he were attached to the All in All."

BAAL SHEM TOV (1700–1760)
Sayings

If by patience, if by watching, I can secure one new ray of light, can feel myself elevated for an instant upon Pisgah, the world which was dead prose to me become living and divine, shall I not watch ever? shall I not be a watchman henceforth? If by watching a whole year on the city's walls I may obtain a communication from heaven, shall I not do well to shut up my shop and turn a watchman?

HENRY DAVID THOREAU (1817–1862)
Journals

Into this Dark beyond all light, we pray to come and, unseeing and unknowing, to see and know Him that is beyond seeing and beyond knowing precisely by not seeing, by not knowing. *The Upanishads*

Speak now, my whole heart! speak now to God, saying, I seek thy face, Lord, will I seek (Psalms 27:8). And come thou now, O Lord my God, teach my heart where and how it may seek thee, where and how it may find thee. SAINT ANSELM (1033–1109)
Proslogion

And now here is my secret, a very simple secret: it is only with the heart that one can see rightly; what is essential is invisible to the eye.

ANTOINE DE SAINT-EXUPÉRY (1900–1944)
The Little Prince

Through ways unlooked for, and through many lands,
Far from the rich folds built with human hands,
The gracious footprints of His love I trace.
JAMES RUSSELL LOWELL (1819–1891)
Bibliolatres

To men we use rhetoric, eloquence, because they are influenced by it. To God we use the simplest, shortest words we can find because eloquence is only air and noise to Him.
FREDERICK WILLIAM ROBERTSON (1816–1853)
Sermons

I seek Thee in my dreams,
And lo, Thy glory seems
To pass before me, as of old, the cloud
Descended in his sight, who heard
The music of Thy spoken word.
Then from my couch I spring, and cry aloud,
"Blest be the glory of Thy Name, O Lord!"
JUDAH HALEVI (c. 1085–c. 1140)
The Diwan

God will have all, or none; serve him, or fall
Down before Baal, Bel, or Belial:
Either be hot or cold: God doth despise,
Abhor, and spew out all neutralities.
ROBERT HERRICK (1591–1674)
Hesperides

If thou intend not nor seek nothing else but the pleasing of God and the profit of thy neighbor thou shalt have inward liberty.
THOMAS À KEMPIS (1380–1471)
Imitation of Christ

Let us search and try our ways, and turn again to the Lord.
Let us lift up our hearts with our hands unto God in the heavens.
*The Old Testament
Lamentations 3:40–41*

What a folly then to be so often perplexed about the way to God? For nothing is the way to God, but our heart; God is nowhere else to be found, and the heart itself cannot find Him or be helped by anything else to find Him but by its own love of Him, faith in Him, dependence upon Him, resignation to Him, and expectation of all from Him.
WILLIAM LAW (1686–1761)
A Serious Call to a Devout and Holy Life

The Lord is true, plainly known, his loving kindness infinite;

To those who crave and seek he gives, gives
  with full abandon.
At deathless dawn give Sat Nam thought
  and glory,
Put on the garb of deeds—and salvation's
  way is open!

GURU NANAK (1469–1539)
The Japji

God is silent, that I am not able to deny—
everything within me demands God, that I
am not able to forget.

JEAN-PAUL SARTRE (1905–1980)
Situations

Late have I loved Thee! For behold thou
wert within me, and I outside, and I sought
Thee outside.

SAINT AUGUSTINE (354–430)
Confessions

God cannot be found—cannot even be
sought—on the path of external experience
and rational thought which lead us to dispas-
sionate recognition or, as it were, a cold and
sober registration of "objects": God may and
must be sought only on paths that lead to
actual living meeting with *reality*.

SIMON L. FRANK (1877–1950)
Reality and Man

With my soul have I desired thee in the
night; yea, with my spirit within me will I
seek thee early: for when thy judgments are
in the earth, the inhabitants of the world will
learn righteousness.   *The Old Testament*
Isaiah 25:9

Oh, my dear friends, do not let your religion satisfy itself with anything less than God.
Insist on having your soul get at Him and
hear His voice. Never, because of the mystery, the awe, perhaps the perplexity and
doubt which come with the great experiences, let yourself take refuge in the superficial things of faith.

PHILLIPS BROOKS (1835–1893)
Selected Sermons

If we seek God for our own good and
profit, we are not seeking God.

MEISTER ECKHART (1260–1327)
Works

Canst thou by searching thyself find out
God? Yes, because in the first place, I know I
did not make myself, and yet I have existence; and by searching into the nature of
other things, I find that no other thing could
make itself; and yet millions of other things
exist; therefore it is, that I know, by positive
conclusion resulting from this search, that
there is a power superior to all those things,
and that power is God.

THOMAS PAINE (1737–1809)
The Age of Reason

The great religious conceptions which
haunt the imaginations of civilized mankind
are scenes of solitariness: Prometheus
chained to his rock, Mahomet brooding in
the desert, the meditations of the Buddha,
the solitary Man on the Cross. It belongs to
the depth of the religious spirit to have felt
forsaken, even by God.

ALFRED NORTH WHITEHEAD (1861–1947)
Religion in the Making

Nothing is more wretched than the man
who goes round and round everything, and,
as Pindar says, "searches the bowels of the
earth," and seeks by conjecture to sound the
minds of his neighbors, but fails to perceive
that it is enough to abide with the Divinity
that is within himself and to do Him genuine
service. That service is to keep Him unsullied
by passion, trifling, and discontent with what
comes from God or men.

MARCUS AURELIUS (121–180)
Meditations

I took a day to search for God.
And found Him not. But as I trod
By rocky ledge, through woods untamed,

Just where one scarlet lily flamed,
I saw His footprint in the sod.

BLISS CARMAN (1861–1929)
Vestigia

Doubtless metaphysical anguish, the great anguish of Augustine and Pascal, will always play its part in the human search for God. Yet it seems that in the present situation of mankind it is rather through the practical effort to rediscover man, through the actual experience of the basic conditions for personality, justice, freedom, respect and love for our fellow men, that ordinarily we shall be led to the rediscovery of God.

JACQUES MARITAIN (1882–1973)
The Range of Reason

The world is not a "prison house" but a kind of spiritual kindergarten where millions of bewildered infants are trying to spell God with the wrong blocks.

EDWARD ARLINGTON ROBINSON (1869–1935)
Letters

"The fool said in his heart: There is no God." Sometimes this is a sign of the end and of death. Sometimes of the beginning and of life. As soon as man feels that God is not, he suddenly comprehends the frightful horror and the wild folly of human temporal existence, and when he has comprehended this he awakes, perhaps not to the ultimate knowledge, but to the penultimate. Was it not so with Nietzsche, Spinoza, Pascal, Luther, Augustine, even with St. Paul?

LEV SHESTOV (1866–1938)
In Job's Balances

My longing is not to be submerged in the vast All, in an infinite and eternal Matter or Energy, or in God; not to be possessed by God, but to possess Him, to become myself God, yet without ceasing to be I myself. Tricks of monism avail us nothing; we crave the substance and not the shadow of immortality.

MIGUEL DE UNAMUNO (1864–1936)
The Tragic Sense of Life

As St. Paul says, "The letter killeth (that is, all formal practices), but the spirit maketh alive (that is, inner experience of truth)." Realize this clearly, that whatever leads you closest to this inner truth you are to follow in all you do. Let your spirit be uplifted and now downcast, burning and yet pure, silent and quiet. You need not say to God what you need or desire, for he knows it all beforehand.

MEISTER ECKHART (1260–1327)
Sermons

At the dawn I seek Thee, Refuge, Rock
  sublime,
Set my prayers before Thee in the morning
And my prayer at eventime.
I, before Thy greatness, stand and am
  afraid.
All my secret thoughts Thine eye beholdeth,
Deep within my bosom laid.

SOLOMON IBN GABIROL (1021–1058)
Sources of Life

Man can only know himself taken up, accepted in God insofar as God is to him not a strange being, his relation to whom is merely outward, but insofar as he knows that in God his own being as spirit, as freedom, as subjectivity, is affirmed.

GEORG WILHELM FRIEDRICH HEGEL
(1770–1831)
Philosophy of Religion

This is my philosophy. Am I wrong? I would say to the philosophers, "Drive the ultimates upwards and downwards around the circle till they meet in God."

THEODORE PARKER (1810–1860)
Collected Sermons

How then do I seek Thee, O Lord? For when I seek Thee, I seek a happy life. I will seek Thee that my soul may live. For my body liveth by my soul, and my soul by Thee.

SAINT AUGUSTINE (354–430)
Confessions

If thy heart be straight with God, then every creature shall be to thee a mirror of life and a book of holy doctrine, for there is no creature so little nor so vile but that it showeth and representeth the goodness of God.

THOMAS À KEMPIS (1380–1471)
Imitation of Christ

Whenever any human being comes to Thee, of whatever age, at whatever time of the day, in whatever state: if he comes in sincerity he always finds Thy love equally warm, like the spring's unchanged coolness, O Thou who art unchangeable!

SÖREN KIERKEGAARD (1813–1855)
The Unchangeableness of God

My soul thirsteth for God, for the living
　God:
When shall I come and appear before God?
The Old Testament
Psalms 42:2

Though I was quite convinced of the impossibility of proving the existence of a Deity as Kant had shown, I yet sought for God and hoped that I should find Him. "He exists," said I, and at once life rose within me, and I felt the possibility and joy of being. I returned to the belief in that will which produced me and desires something of me. I returned to the belief that the chief and only aim of my life is to be better, i.e., to live in accord with that Will.

LEO TOLSTOY (1828–1910)
My Confession

O Great God, Lord of all truth, to Thee I came to contemplate thy blessedness. I have known thee; I have always spoken the truth. Take away my faults.

Ancient Egyptian Prayer

Lalande, or whoever it was, who searched the heavens with his telescope and could find no God, would not have found the human mind if he had searched the brain with a microscope.

GEORGE SANTAYANA (1863–1952)
The Life of Reason

Man cannot live without an enduring trust in something indestructible in himself. Yet while doing that he may all his life be unaware of that indestructible thing and of his trust in it. FRANZ KAFKA (1883–1924)
Parables

To search for God and to find the Devil—that is what happened to me.

AUGUST STRINDBERG (1849–1912)
Inferno

That which is the true ultimate transcends the realm of finite reality infinitely. Religiously speaking, God transcends his own name. This is why the use of his name easily becomes an abuse or a blasphemy. Whatever we say about that which concerns us ultimately, whether or not we call it God, has a symbolic meaning. It points beyond itself while participating in that to which it points. In no other way can faith express itself adequately. The language of faith is the language of symbols.

PAUL TILLICH (1886–1965)
Dynamics of Faith

If we here speak and write, it is but as guides to those that long to see: we send them to the Place Itself, bidding them from words to the Vision. The teaching is of the path and the place: seeing is the work of each soul for itself. PLOTINUS (205–270)
Enneads

I am in the world of the roads.
　The night comes. Open thy gate, thou
　　world of the home.
RABINDRANATH TAGORE (1861–1941)
Stray Birds

If ye turn unto Him with all your heart, and
    with all your soul do truth before Him,
Then will He, too, turn unto you, and will
    not hide His face from you.
The Old Testament Apocrypha
Tobit 13:6

The search for God is a search for the purpose of life and for an unfailing source of eternal value.
EDGAR S. BRIGHTMAN (1884–1953)
Religious Values

Do not distract yourself over various things in order to reach Him, for He is unity itself. Halt the movement, unite the multiplicity, and immediately you will reach God, who has long since reached you wholly.
MARSILIO FICINO (1433–1499)
Theologia Platonica

Nothing is better than to search for the true God, even if the discovery of Him eludes human capacity, since the very wish to learn, if earnestly entertained, produces untold joys and pleasures.
PHILO JUDAEUS (30 B.C.–A.D. 40)
Special Laws

A mean searching for God ceases to look to the Beyond, asking "Why?" and, only saying "Because God is," looks to the Present and finds peace.
LEO TOLSTOY (1828–1910)
Emblems

Behind our restlessness and nervous breakdown is a fear we dare not face—the fear that there *is* no Home, and that we are driven fugitives of time and dust: the fear that will vex us until we find God.
GEORGE ARTHUR BUTTRICK (1892–1979)
Prayer

If we had attained the full vision of Truth, we would no longer be mere seekers, would have become one with God, for Truth is God.

But being only seekers we prosecute our quest and are conscious of our imperfection.
MOHANDAS K. GANDHI (1869–1948)
Yervada Mandir

Everything is within oneself, nothing outside oneself,
He who seeketh the Lord outside Himself is lost in doubt.
GURU ARJAN (1563–1606)
Hymns

Consider the immeasurable distance from us of what we know as God's dwelling-place, the heavens; yet how near he is to us when we call upon him.   *The Midrash*

With the foot of search thou dost travel to
    that place;
And thence thou dost fly with the wing of
    the love of God.
SAADI (1184–1291)
Bustan

Whosoever seeketh God through another than himself will never attain unto God.
AL-ALAWI (1869–1934)
Aphorisms

Spirit who sweepest the wild harp of
    time!
It is most hard, with an untroubled ear
Thy dark inwoven harmonies to hear.
SAMUEL TAYLOR COLERIDGE (1772–1834)
Ode to the Departing Year

If we want to know where God stands, we must find out where the best men stand, then draw a line through that point and prolong it to infinity and it will point in the direction of God.
WALTER RAUSCHENBUSCH (1861–1918)
Ethical versus Forensic Conceptions of Salvation

I stretch lame hands of faith, and grope
    And gather dust and chaff, and call
      To what I feel is Lord of all,
    And faintly trust the larger hope.
ALFRED LORD TENNYSON (1809–1892)
In Memoriam

But if from thence thou shalt seek the Lord thy God, thou shalt find HIM, if thou seek with all thy heart and with all thy soul.

The Old Testament
Deuteronomy 4:29

God hath made this life a Bridge to Heaven. It is but a giddy, and a vertiginous thing to stand long gazing upon so narrow a bridge, and over so deep and roaring waters, and desperate whirlpools, as this world abounds with.   JOHN DONNE (1572–1631)
Sermons

There are innumerable definitions of God because his manifestations are innumerable. They overwhelm me with wonder and awe and for a moment stun me. But I worship God as Truth only. I have not found Him, but I am seeking after Him. I am prepared to sacrifice the things dearest to me in pursuit of this quest.

MOHANDAS K. GANDHI (1869–1948)
My Experiment with Truth

Call unto me, and I will answer thee, and shew thee great and mighty things, which thou knowest not.   *The Old Testament*
Jeremiah 33:3

Search yourself and you will find God.
Kurdish Proverb

To say that our intellect naturally desires to see God is to say that it naturally desires a knowledge of which nature itself is incapable.

JACQUES MARITAIN (1882–1973)
Approach to God

He alone is God who can never be sought in vain: not even when He cannot be found.

SAINT BERNARD OF CLAIRVAUX (1091–1153)
De Consideratione

We are not forced to take wings to find Him, but have only to seek solitude and to look within ourselves. You need not be overwhelmed with confusion before so kind a Guest, but with utter humility, talk to Him as

to your Father: ask for what you want as from a father: tell Him your sorrows and beg Him for relief.

SAINT TERESA (1515–1582)
The Way of Perfection

The worship of God is not a rule of safety; it is an adventure of the spirit, a flight after the unattainable.

ALFRED NORTH WHITEHEAD (1861–1947)
Science and the Modern World

O my brave soul!
O farther, farther sail!
O daring joy, but safe! Are they not all the
   seas of God?
O farther, farther, farther sail!

WALT WHITMAN (1819–1892)
Passage to India

No one who seeks Brahman ever comes to an evil end.   *The Bhagavad Gita*

That we may arrive at an understanding of the First Principle, which is most spiritual and eternal and above us, we ought to proceed through the traces which are corporeal and outside us; and this is to be led into the way of God. We ought next to enter into our minds, which are the eternal image of God, spiritual and internal; and this is to walk in the truth of God. We ought finally to pass over into that which is eternal, most spiritual, and above us, looking to the First Principle; and this is to rejoice in the knowledge of God and in the reverence of His majesty.

SAINT BONAVENTURE (1221–1274)
The Mind's Road to God

Oh, who will give me a voice that I may cry aloud to the whole world that God, the all-highest, is in the deepest abyss within us and is waiting for us to return to Him.

JOHANNES DENCK (1495–1527)
On the Law of God

He who seeks God under settled forms lays hold of the form while missing the God con-

cealed in it. But he who seeks God in no special guise lays hold of him as he is in himself,
and such a one "lives with the Son" and is the
life itself.   MEISTER ECKHART (1260–1327)
Sermons

The remarkable thing about the way in
which people talk about God, or about their
relations to God, is that it seems to escape
them completely that God hears what they
are saying.
               SÖREN KIERKEGAARD (1813–1855)
Journals

However imperfect, however childish a religion may be, it always places the human soul
in the presence of God; and however imperfect and childish the conception of God may
be, it always represents the highest ideal of
perfection which the human soul, for the
time being, can reach and grasp.
                     MAX MÜLLER (1823–1900)
Introduction to the Science of Religion

It is the unhappy creatures, who have
passed through the depths of doubt, who
have nowhere left to turn, it is they who are
engaged in what Karl Jaspers calls "the im-
passioned struggle with God for God."
        SARVEPALLI RADHAKRISHNAN (1888–1975)
Recovery of Faith

This human life is not merely animal and
passionate. The best and keenest part of it
consists in that very gift of creation and government which, together with all the transcendental functions of his own mind, man
has significantly attributed to God as to his
highest ideal.
                  GEORGE SANTAYANA (1863–1952)
Poetry and Religion

Men esteem truth remote, in the outskirts
of the system, behind the farthest star, before
Adam and after the last man. In eternity
there is indeed something true and sublime.
But all these times and places and occasions

are now and here. God Himself culminates
in the present moment, and will never be
more divine in the lapse of all the ages.
              HENRY DAVID THOREAU (1817–1862)
Walden

For thus saith the Lord to the house of
  Israel:
Seek ye me, and you shall live.
                            The Old Testament
Amos 5:4

Spiritual knowledge cannot be communicated from one intellect to another, but must
be sought for in the spirit of God.
                     JACOB BOEHME (1575–1624)
Works

Nations are moved by a force whose origin
is unknown and inexplicable. This is what
philosophers call the aesthetic or moral principle; I call it simply the quest for God.
                FYODOR DOSTOEVSKY (1821–1881)
The Devils

To get at the core of God at his greatest,
one must first get into the core of himself at
the least, for no one can know God who has
not first known himself. Go to the depths of
the soul, the secret place of the Most High, to
the roots, to the heights; for all that God can
do is focused there.
              MEISTER ECKHART (1260–1327)
Works

I believe that the greatest need of the modern world is not for a multitude of machines
but for a new and higher conception of God.
                  ELLEN GLASGOW (1874–1945)
I Believe

Canst thou by searching find out God?
canst thou find out the limit of the Almighty?
It is as high as heaven; what canst thou do?
deeper than hell; what canst thou know?
                            The Old Testament
Job 11:7–8

The trivial round, the common task,
Would furnish all we ought to ask;
Room to deny ourselves, a road
To bring us, daily, nearer God.
JOHN KEBLE (1792–1866)
The Christian Year

Ah, fondest, blindest, weakest,
I am He Whom thou seekest!
Thou dravest love from thee, who dravest
Me.
FRANCIS THOMPSON (1859–1907)
The Hound of Heaven

We have to remain quite still and unite
ourselves with that which we desire yet do not
approach.
We unite ourselves to God in this way: We
cannot approach him.
Distance is the soul of the beautiful.
SIMONE WEIL (1909–1943)
First and Last Notebooks

I do not murmur against God, and I bear
no ill will toward men. I search here below,
but I penetrate above. He who knows me is
God.   CONFUCIUS (551–479 B.C.)
Analects

Let a man learn to look for the permanent
in the mutable and fleeting; let him learn to
bear the disappearance of things he was wont
to reverence without losing his reverence; let
him learn that he is here, not to work but to
be worked upon; and that, though abyss
open under abyss, and opinion displace opinion, all are at last contained in the Eternal
Cause.
RALPH WALDO EMERSON (1803–1882)
Representative Men

He who thinks to look God full in the face
and question Him about His existence, blinds
himself thereby, and cannot see God. He sees
something, but what he sees is not God but
himself.   PHILLIPS BROOKS (1835–1893)
Sermons

When someone says "Oh, I can worship
God anywhere," the answer is, "Do you?"
JAMES A. PIKE (1913–1969)
Beyond Anxiety

To realize God, first control the outgoing
senses and harness the mind. Then meditate
upon the light in the heart of the fire—meditate, that is, upon pure consciousness as distinct from the ordinary consciousness of the
intellect. Thus the Self, the Inner Reality,
may be seen behind physical appearances.
The Upanishads

Whether we approach God with devout
words of intimacy, or whether we wish to approach God by pure thought, whether the
idea or the personal tries to express itself the
more forcefully, is essentially the same, if
only we make as our very own that on which
all turns, that for *us* He is the One, that He is
our Lord.   LEO BAECK (1873–1956)
The Essence of Judaism

O eternal and most gracious God, the God
of security, and the enemy of security too,
who wouldst have us always sure of thy love,
and yet wouldst have us always doing something for it, let me always so apprehend thee,
as present with me, and yet to follow after
thee, as though I had not apprehended thee.
JOHN DONNE (1572–1631)
Devotions upon Emergent Occasions

He who seeks God under settled form lays
hold of the form, while missing the God concealed in it.
MEISTER ECKHART (1260–1327)
Works

We may not ever come to know God's essence, but His attributes of activity—namely,
the universal laws of social, mental, and
moral health—these we can possess.
JOSHUA LOTH LIEBMAN (1907–1948)
Peace of Mind

I do thank Thee, O Lord;
    for my face Thou enlightens for Thy
      covenant's sake.
Yea, from evening until morning do I seek
    Thee;
    and as the sure dawn for perfect
      illumination hast Thou appeared to me.
                    The Dead Sea Scrolls

We long for the Absolute only in so far as
in us the Absolute also longs, and seeks,
through our very temporal striving, the
peace that is nowhere in Time, but only, and
yet, Absolutely, in Eternity.
             JOSIAH ROYCE (1855–1916)
        The World and the Individual

The worship of God is not a rule of safety
—it is an adventure of the spirit, a flight after
the unattainable. The death of religion
comes with the repression of the high hope
of adventure.
     ALFRED NORTH WHITEHEAD (1861–1947)
           Religion in the Making

This life, this Kingdom of God, this simplicity of absolute existence, is hard to enter.
How hard? As hard as the Master of salvation
could find words to express the hardness.
        GEORGE MACDONALD (1824–1905)
              Unspoken Sermons

To say, Look to God, is not helpful without
instruction as to what this looking imports.
One can look and still sacrifice no pleasure,
still be the slave of impulse, repeating the
word God but held in the grip of every passion and making no effort to master any. Virtue linked with thought, occupying a Soul,
makes God manifest: God on the lips without
good conduct of life is only a word.
              PLOTINUS (205–270)
                  Enneads

There is a Sanskrit verse which says that
the thoughtless man dives into deep lakes,
penetrates into jungles, ascends steep hills in
search of flowers for the worship of God
while the one lotus which he can offer is his
own mind.
     SARVEPALLI RADHAKRISHNAN (1888–1978)
              My Search for Truth

When we feel within ourselves that we desire God, then God has touched the main-
spring of power, and through this touch it
swings beyond itself and towards God.
             Theologia Germanica

To mount to God is to enter into oneself.
For he who so mounts and enters and goes
above and beyond himself, he truly mounts
up to God. The mind must then raise itself
above itself and say, "He who above all I need
is above all I know."
     SAINT ALBERTUS MAGNUS (1206–1280)
             De Adhaerendo Dei

O Supreme and Unapproachable Light! O
Whole and Blessed Truth, how far thou art
from me, who am so near to thee! How far
art thou removed from my vision, though I
am so near to thine! Everywhere thou art
wholly present, and I see thee not. In thee I
move, and in thee I have my being, and cannot come to thee; thou art within me, and
about me, and I feel thee not.
         SAINT ANSELM (1033–1109)
               Proslogion

God-longing, to find the positive pole,
must go hand in hand with the longing for
the God-virtues, with love for the entire creation.   SHOLEM ASCH (1880–1957)
               What I Believe

He alone is God who never can be sought
in vain, even when He cannot be found.
    SAINT BERNARD OF CLAIRVAUX (1091–1153)
            De Consideratione

As soon as we believe that we know God
well enough, we no longer know him.
        MAURICE BLONDEL (1861–1949)
                L'Action

Since man cannot help seeking the infinite, he now seeks the meaning of his life in an infinity of things.

EMIL BRUNNER (1889–1966)
The Divine Imperative

Now at last the Alpha and Omega of all known things, the human figure, has taken hold of me and I of it, and I say, "Lord, I will not let thee go unless thou bless me, though I should wrestle myself lame."

JOHANN WOLFGANG VON GOETHE (1749–1832)
Travels in Italy

Direct your efforts to the multiplying of those times in which you are with God or endeavoring to approach Him and to decreasing those times in which you are with other than He and in which you make no efforts to approach Him.

MAIMONIDES (1135–1204)
Guide for the Perplexed

The prophet David says "To you have I lifted up my eyes, you who dwell in heaven" (Psalms 123:1) and "To you, O God, have I lifted up my soul" (Psalms 25:1). For the eyes of the mind are lifted up from their preoccupation with earthly things and from their being filled with the impression of material things. And they are so exalted that they peer beyond the created order and arrive at the sheer contemplation of God and at conversing with Him reverently and suitably as He listens.

ORIGEN (185–254)
On Prayer

The way we lost God in the Past is not revealed to us. What we are told is what we do need to know, the way we may return to Him.

PLOTINUS (205–270)
Enneads

What can we mortals possibly mean by having any idea of God at all? The Creator and Sustainer of this universe is not to be caught under the butterfly nets of our understanding.

HARRY EMERSON FOSDICK (1878–1969)
In Search of God and Immortality

How dare we create our gods in our own image? What *can* bridge the difference that divides the Everlasting God from the passing show we call man? And yet, when the religious consciousness is at its noblest height, and is most worthy of man and most true in its testimony, it makes man share the divine life.

SIR HENRY JONES (1852–1922)
A Faith That Enquires

I have never been really greedy.
The Divine Name is the only thing I really
hanker for.
Kabir says: My inner self is happy,
And when this is so, then I recognize God!

KABIR (1398–1515)
The Adi Granth

Countless are the pearls lying hidden in the sea. If a single dive yields you none, do not conclude that the sea is without pearls. Similarly, if after practising spiritual disciplines for a little while you fail to have the vision of God, do not lose heart. Continue to practise the disciplines with patience, and at the proper time you are sure to obtain grace.

SRI RAMAKRISHNA (1834–1886)
Precepts

I pray for faith, I long to trust;
    I listen with my heart, and hear
A Voice without a sound: "Be just,
    Be true, be merciful, revere
The Word within thee: God is near!"

JOHN GREENLEAF WHITTIER (1807–1892)
Collected Poems

Give me each day new devotion, each day a
    new Name by which to call Thee;
Give me each day new love.

DADU (1554–1603)
The Bani

If thou seekest aught of thine thou shalt never find God, for thou are not seeking God merely. Thou art seeking something with God, making a candle of God, as it were, with which to find something, and then, having found it, throwing the candle away.

MEISTER ECKHART (1260–1327)
Sermons

Unless we are to assume that God is an observable object, we need not look for Him with the instruments and methods of any empirical science, though all sciences present clues which point toward the great Reality. The God we should "find" by that sort of search would be a finite god—a god in space and time—not an eternal Being.

RUFUS JONES (1863–1948)
The Testimony of the Soul

Some there are that for all their effort have not attained the Vision; the soul in them has come to no sense of the splendor there. It has not taken warmth; it has not felt burning within itself the flame of love for what is there to know.   PLOTINUS (205–270)
Enneads

Even as the needle, that directs the hour,
Touched with the loadstone, by the secret
    power
Of hidden nature, points unto the Pole;
Even so the wavering powers of my soul,
Touched by the virtue of Thy Spirit, flee
From what is earth, and point alone to
    Thee.
FRANCIS QUARLES (1592–1644)
Dependence on God

Meditate on God either in an obscure corner, or in the solitude of forests, or within the silent sanctuary of your own heart.

SRI RAMAKRISHNA (1833–1886)
Sayings

He has hidden Himself inside the atom, this Ancient One who resides in the inmost recess of every human heart. The sages realized Him through the power of introspections and went beyond joy and misery, beyond what we call virtue and vice, beyond good and bad deeds, beyond being and nonbeing. He who has seen Him has seen Reality.

SWAMI VIVEKANANDA (1863–1902)
Jnana-Yoga

If we labor in thy works with the sweat of our brows thou wilt make us partakers of thy vision and thy Sabbath.

FRANCIS BACON (1561–1626)
Novum Organum

If it has taken the race several hundred thousand years to learn a smattering of the science of humanity since it acquired self-consciousness, so it may take it millions of years to acquire a smattering of the science of God after its acquisition of cosmic consciousness.

RICHARD M. BUCKE (1837–1902)
Cosmic Consciousness

Appreciate that whoever knows the name of God has the spirit of God, the holy spirit within him. That holy influence, descending by virtue of divine grace, will bestir, move and incline a man to strive to attain the knowledge of God so as to sanctify Him and declare His name to all the earth.

ABRAHAM ABULAFIA (13th century)
Sefer-ha-Ot

What shall I do, that I may find my God? "The invisible things of God being understood by the things made" (Romans 1:20) I will consider the earth, and its great beauty; I marvel at the greatness of the sea; I look up and behold the heavens, and gaze upon the beauty of the stars; I wonder at the splendor of the sun and the moon. Yet, although I praise these things—for Him who made them, I thirst.

SAINT AUGUSTINE (354–430)
Sermons

In the hour of God cleanse thy soul of all self-deceit and hypocrisy and vain self-flattering that thou mayest look straight into thy spirit and hear that which summons it.

SRI AUROBINDO (1872–1950)
The Hour of God

When a man seeks the words of the living God, they will be fixed firmly in his soul for ever. His light will break through as the dawn, to fill his soul with tangible satisfaction, to increase the divine light with great expansiveness and with an everlasting root and foundation. Then shall he be as a tree planted by the waters with all the evil winds in the world unable to move him. And this is sufficient for him who understands.

DOV BAER (1773–1827)
Tract on Ecstasy

A man should orient his will and all his works to God and having only God in view go forward unafraid, not thinking, am I right or am I wrong?

MEISTER ECKHART (1260–1327)
Works

They say to us: "Look to God." But it is useless merely to affirm this unless they can tell us how we are to look to Him. And it might be asked, what is to prevent us from looking to God, while at the same time freely satisfying our sensual appetites and not restraining our angry passions. Virtue perfected, enlightened, and deeply rooted in the soul will reveal God to us, but without it He will be but an empty name.

PLOTINUS (205–270)
Enneads

If the feeling for God were not in man, we could not implant it any more than we could squeeze blood from a stone.

SARVEPALLI RADHAKRISHNAN (1888–1975)
Eastern Religions and Western Thought

And only when we found in earth and air,
    In heaven or hell, that such might
        nowhere be—
That we could not flee from Thee
    anywhere,
        We fled to Thee.

RICHARD CHENEVIX TRENCH (1807–1886)
If There Had Anywhere

Who seeks for heaven alone to save his soul,
May keep the path, but will not reach the
    goal;
While he who walks in love may wander far,
But God will bring him where the Blessed
    are.

HENRY VAN DYKE (1852–1933)
The Way

We cannot in this life know what God is, but we can know what he is not; and in this consists the perfection of our knowledge as wayfarers in this world.

SAINT THOMAS AQUINAS (1225–1274)
De Caritate

Anyone who is moved by proofs to have faith in God's *reality* can be certain that he has comprehended nothing of the reality of God; and whoever thinks to proclaim something of God's reality by means of evidences of God is debating about a mirage. For every "talking about" presupposes a standpoint apart from that which is being talked about. But there can be no standpoint apart from God, and for that reason God does not permit himself to be spoken of in general propositions, universal truths which are true without reference to the concrete existential situation of the one who is talking.

RUDOLF BULTMANN (1884–1976)
What Sense Is There to Speak of God?

The spiritual sense, the instinct for the real, is not satisfied with anything less than the absolute and the eternal. It shows an incurable dissatisfaction with the finiteness of the finite, the transiency of the transient.

Such integral intuitions are our authority for religion. They reveal a Being who makes himself known to us through them and produces revolt and discontent with anything short of the eternal.

SARVEPĀLLI RADHAKRISHNAN (1888–1978)
An Idealist View of Life

In wonder workings, or some bush aflame,
Men look for God and fancy him concealed;
But in earth's common things he stands
    revealed,
While grass and flowers and stars spell out
    his name.

MINOT JUDSON SAVAGE (1841–1918)
Seek Not Afar for Beauty

Consider the variety of forms in which every single kind of fellowship with the Universe has already appeared. Do not be scared either by mysterious darkness or by wonderful dazzling traits. Do not admit the delusion that it may all be imagination and romance. Dig ever deeper where your magic rod has once pointed, and without fail you will bring forth the heavenly stream to the light of day.

FRIEDRICH SCHLEIERMACHER (1768–1835)
On Religion

The slipperiness or elusiveness of the truth or reality, or, shall I say, God, when one tries to get hold of it or him by means of concepts or intellection, is like trying to catch a catfish with a gourd. D. T. SUZUKI (1870–1966)
Zen and Japanese Culture

The thirst after, the longing for, the reaching out and the crying aloud for God, for the Reality which underlies, environs, protects, and perfects all the lesser realities and all our apprehensions of them—this will have to impel and sustain our long search after a more explicit grasp of what we already dimly hold, of what, in strictness, already holds us from without and from within.

FRIEDRICH VON HÜGEL (1852–1925)
The Reality of God

Infinitude is too wide for a man to take in. He is therefore permitted to take in portions and spread his vision over the wide circumference by little and little; and in these portions doth the Infinite shadow forth itself, God in all and all in God.

BRONSON ALCOTT (1799–1888)
Journals

Hide not thy face from us, we beseech Thee, O Lord. Enlarge thou the narrowness of our souls, that Thou mayest enter in. Repair the ruinous mansions, that thou mayest dwell there. SAINT AUGUSTINE (354–430)
Sermons

We are no more bankrupt in our capacity for finding God than in our capacity for finding harmony, or beauty, or moral goodness, or truth. We shall not find all there is of any of these values, but all we do find is real, and is good to live by. So also with our findings of God, they do not exhaust His being. They do not carry us to the full height of all that He is. But what we have proves to be solid building material for life-purposes, and every spiritual gain that is achieved makes the next one more possible and more sure.

RUFUS JONES (1863–1948)
Pathways to the Reality of God

Surely whoever truly loves his Creator will not neglect serving Him for any reason in the world, unless he is physically prevented from doing so. He will not need to be coaxed or enticed into serving Him. On the contrary, unless prevented by some great obstacle, his heart itself will lift him.

MOSES LUZZATTO (1707–1747)
Way of the Upright

When I look into the blue sky, it seems so deep, so peaceful, so full of a mysterious tenderness, that I could lie for centuries and wait for the dawning of the face of God out of the awful loving-kindness.

GEORGE MACDONALD (1824–1905)
Unspoken Sermons

God grants to every creature to live by its own nature. How can I bind my nature's wings? I must speed to my God before all things. My God, by His nature my Father above, my brother in humanity, my Bridegroom in his ardent love, and I his from eternity.

MECHTILD OF MAGDEBURG (1217–1282)
The Book of the Flowing Light of the Godhead

I have a great deal of sympathy with those who call themselves atheists. For the God they are tilting against, the God they honestly feel that cannot believe in, is so often an image of God instead of God, a way of conceiving him which has become an idol. Paul had the perception to see that behind the idols of the Athenians there was an unknown, an unacknowledged God, whom dimly they sensed and felt after. And to help men through to the conviction about ultimate Reality that alone matters we may have to discard every image of God—whether of the "one above," the one "out there," or any other.   JOHN A. T. ROBINSON (1919–)
Honest to God

God is a tranquil Being, and abides in a tranquil eternity. So must thy spirit become a tranquil and clear little pool, wherein the serene light of God can be mirrored.

GERHARD TERSTEEGEN (1697–1769)
Sermons

The Psalmist's word, "He that sitteth in the heavens shall laugh," must have been written for men who believe that human knowledge can completely compass the infinite. We cannot reach the end; but as long as we live and use sound method, we may grow endlessly.

EDGAR S. BRIGHTMAN (1884–1953)
A Philosophy of Religion

People who are far from God think they are very near to him, when they begin to take a few steps to approach him. The most polite and most enlightened people have the same stupidity about this as a peasant who thinks he is really at court, because he has seen the king.   FRANÇOIS FÉNELON (1651–1715)
Sermons

We have no definition of God; we have only a roadway that leads out toward God. We are convinced beyond peradventure that he who travels merely the path of electrons, atoms, molecules toward a vision of the Ultimate misses it, and that he who travels the road of spiritual values—goodness, truth, beauty—finds it. The eternal and creative Power cannot be adequately approached through the metrical world alone; the innermost nature of the Ultimate is revealed also in the personal world of spiritual values.

HARRY EMERSON FOSDICK (1878–1969)
As I See Religion

Had man always dwelt in the dread mysterious presence of oracles and miracles, had there been no ominous silence, no moral darkness that might be felt; men had never dreamed of that firmament of thought wherein arise and shine the truths of the eternal. They would still be looking for God in the heavens above, or in the earth beneath; they would not easily find Him in the still small voice, in that holy of holies in our hearts.

CHARLES EDWARD GARMAN (1850–1907)
Lectures

Let us not confine ourselves to falling prostrate beneath the tree of creation and contemplating its vast ramification full of stars. We have a duty to perform, to cultivate the human soul, to adore the incomprehensible and reject the absurd; to purify faith and obliterate superstition from the face of reli-

gion, to remove the vermin from the garden of God.   VICTOR HUGO (1802–1885)
Les Misérables

There is no expeditious road
To pack and label men for God
And save them by the barrel-load.
          FRANCIS THOMPSON (1859–1907)
A Judgment in Heaven

With my soul have I desired thee in the night; yea, with my spirit within me will I seek thee early: for when thy judgments are in the earth the inhabitants of the world will learn righteousness.   *The Old Testament*
Isaiah 26:9

God is a highest conception, not to be explained in terms of other things, but explainable only by exploring more and more profoundly the conception itself.
          SÖREN KIERKEGAARD (1813–1855)
Concluding Unscientific Postscript

· BRIDGING THE GULF ·

God of His great love keeps hold of man; just as, when a nestling falls from the nest, the mother bird flutters above, and if perchance a serpent gapes for it, flitting around with cries, the mother mourns for her offspring.

Now God is a Father, and seeks His creature. He remedies the falling away, drives off the reptile, restores the nestling to strength again, and urges it to fly back to the nest.
          CLEMENT OF ALEXANDRIA (150–215)
Eclogae propheticae

God always demands of us the impossible, and it is in this that the chief difference between God and men consists. Or perhaps, on the contrary, the resemblance: is it not said that God created man in His image? It is only when man wishes the impossible that he remembers God. To obtain that which is possible he turns to fellow men.
          LEV SHESTOV (1866–1938)
Athens and Jerusalem

Throw on God (He loves the burden)
God's task to make the heavenly period
     perfect the earthen.
          ROBERT BROWNING (1812–1889)
Grammarian

O God, Thou art looking down on me, Thou knowest, Thou canst see into my inmost being. Thou knowest that the love of humanity and the desire to do good ever actuate me.
          LUDWIG VAN BEETHOVEN (1770–1827)
Heiligenstadt Testament

Expecting Him, my door was open wide;
     Then I looked round
If any lack of service might be found,
And saw Him at my side:
How entered, by what secret stair,
I know not, knowing only He was there.
          THOMAS EDWARD BROWN (1830–1897)
Praesto

The gulf between man and God is bridged, not by man's achievement, but by God's humiliation.   WILLIAM TEMPLE (1881–1944)
Daily Readings

If man is to deal with God and receive anything from Him, it must happen in this wise, not that man begin and lay the first stone, but that God alone, without any entreaty or desire of man, must first come and give him a promise. This word of God is the beginning, the foundation, the rock, upon which afterward all works, words and thoughts of man must build.

MARTIN LUTHER (1483–1546)
Treatise on the New Testament

The inward stirring and touching of God makes us hungry and yearning; for the Spirit of God hunts our spirit: and the more it touches it, the greater our hunger and craving.   JAN VAN RUYSBROECK (1293–1381)
The Mirror of Eternal Salvation

The Lord desires thee for his dwelling-place
    eternally,
And blessed is he whom God has chosen for
    the grace
Within thy courts to rest.

JUDAH HALEVI (c. 1085–c. 1140)
Ode to Zion

God does not demand the end when only the beginning is possible, does not scorn the dawn because it is not noon. He welcomes the first movement of man's spirit toward him, not for the fruit which yet is unmatured, but for the seed which still is in the germ.

HARRY EMERSON FOSDICK (1878–1969)
The Meaning of Service

We are always completely, and therefore equally, known to God. That is our destiny, whether we like it or not. But though this knowledge never varies, the quality of our being known can.

C. S. LEWIS (1898–1963)
Letters to Malcolm

God looked upon me in my conscience, and now it is impossible for me to forget that he sees me. And because God looked upon me I had and have to look towards God.

SÖREN KIERKEGAARD (1813–1855)
Journals

For let a man go away or come back: God never leaves. He is always at hand and if he cannot get into your life, still he is never farther away than the door.

MEISTER ECKHART (1260–1327)
Works

When He says to your disturbed, distracted, restless soul, or mine, "Come unto me," He is saying, come out of the strife and doubt and struggle of what is at the moment where you stand, into that which was and is and is to be—the eternal, the essential, the absolute.   PHILLIPS BROOKS (1835–1893)
Sermons

For the eyes of the Lord run to and fro throughout the whole earth, to show himself strong in the behalf of them whose heart is perfect toward him.   *The Old Testament*
2 Chronicles 16:9

Want in God is treasure to us. For had there been no need He would not have created the World, nor made us, nor manifested His wisdom, nor exercised His power, nor beautified Eternity, nor prepared the Joys of Heaven. But He wanted Angels and Men, Images, Companions: And these He had from all Eternity.

THOMAS TRAHERNE (1637–1674)
Centuries of Meditations

A wise old proverb says, "God comes to see us without bell:" that is, as there is no screen or ceiling between our heads and the infinite heavens, so is there no bar or wall in the soul, where man, the effect, ceases, and God, the cause, begins. The walls are taken away.

RALPH WALDO EMERSON (1803–1882)
The Over-Soul

The door is locked to the access of people
That they may not spread out my faults.
What profiteth a closed door? The
    Omniscient
Knows what I conceal or reveal.

SAADI (1184–1291)
Gulistan

He who stoops down to the level of us all, both believers and unbelievers, is the real God alone, in His grace and mercy. And it is only by the fact that he knows this that the believing man is distinguished from the unbeliever. Faith consists precisely in this—in the life which is lived in consequence of God's coming down to our level.

KARL BARTH (1886–1968)
Church Dogmatics

God never ceases to speak to us; but the noise of the world without, and the tumult of our passions within, bewilder us, and prevent us from listening to him.

FRANÇOIS FÉNELON (1651–1715)
The Spirit of God Teaches Within

I will betroth you to me in righteousness and in justice, in steadfast love, and in mercy. I will betroth you to me in faithfulness; and you shall know the Lord.

The Old Testament
Hosea 2:19–20

But God, who is able to prevail, wrestled with him, as the Angel did with Jacob, and marked him; marked him for his own.

IZAAK WALTON (1593–1683)
Life of Donne

God wants to come to his world, but he wants to come to it through man. This is the mystery of our existence, the superhuman chance of mankind.

MARTIN BUBER (1878–1965)
I and Thou

For the Lord seeth not as a man seeth; for man looketh on the outward appearance, but the Lord looketh on the heart.

The Old Testament
1 Samuel 16:7

No man ever wanted anything so much as God wants to make the soul aware of him. God is ever ready, but we are so unready.

God is in, we are out; God is at home, we are strangers.

MEISTER ECKHART (1260–1327)
Sermons

When He appoints to meet thee, go thou
forth—
    It matters not
If south or north,
    Bleak waste or sunny plot.
Nor think, if haply He thou seek'st be late,
    He does thee wrong.

THOMAS EDWARD BROWN (1830–1897)
Specula

God might reveal Himself to us in all His effulgent majesty; and, at the sight of Him, we would prostrate ourselves and worship Him. And that would satisfy us, but it could not satisfy God. For God does not desire His glorification but ours. God will do anything to win us to His love—anything but coerce us.   SÖREN KIERKEGAARD (1813–1855)
The Divine Incognito

Listen, and grasp the idea once and for all: if you are wondering whether God is attracting you, pray that he does so.

SAINT AUGUSTINE (354–430)
Confessions

O God, that at all times you may find me as you desire me and where you would have me be, that you may lay hold on me fully, both by the Within and the Without of myself, grant that I may never break this double thread of my life.

PIERRE TEILHARD DE CHARDIN (1881–1955)
The Divine Milieu

I the Lord search the heart, I try the reins, even to give every man according to his ways, and according to the fruit of his doings.

The Old Testament
Jeremiah 17:10

Seek God and you shall find him and all good with him. To the man who cleaves to God, God cleaves and adds virtue. Thus, what you have sought before, now seeks you; what once you pursued, now pursues you; what once you fled, now flees you. Everything comes to him who truly comes to God, bringing all divinity with it, while all that is strange and alien flies away.

MEISTER ECKHART (1260–1327)
Works

The will, perverted in its exercise by sin, hurries towards what can satisfy it, vanity fools itself, iniquity lies to itself. But God is there who seeks us, who precedes us.

SAINT BERNARD OF CLAIRVAUX (1091–1153)
On the Love of God

If a man is conscious of the fact that God has created him by calling him forth, so that he is one who is addressed by God; if he regards the various situations of his life as modes of this call, and his own action as the answers that he gives, then the core of his person becomes more and more solid, secure and free; his nature becomes ever richer and more receptive of eternity.

ROMANO GUARDINI (1885–1968)
The Wisdom of the Psalms

God's call is a call to man's own. He makes the start, makes it in love and in changeless fidelity to his own plan. But this very plan is man's freedom, man's history, what man himself has done and hazarded and won in battle, what he has undergone, his own. God does not take us from ourselves; he gives us to ourselves.   KARL RAHNER (1904–)
Servants of the Lord

If we need something to buttress us in the inevitable struggles of life, there is nothing than can help us more than the conviction that each one of us is sought by Him who made the Pleiades and Orion, that each of us is truly known as no finite men can ever know us, and that, in spite of our feebleness and sin, we can become channels of God's universal love.   D. ELTON TRUEBLOOD (1900–)
Declaration of Freedom

I am sought of them that asked not for me; I am found of them that sought me not.

The Old Testament
Isaiah 65:1

Behind every "O Lord" of thine are a thousand "Here am I's."

JALAL-UD-DIN RUMI (1207–1273)
The Masnawi

God does desire love from us, because his wisdom very well knows, that without love the world would be in vain, and the end of the Creation frustrated: his goodness is diffusive and infinitely desires to communicate itself, which it cannot do, unless it be beloved.

THOMAS TRAHERNE (1637–1674)
Christian Ethics

Many of our troubles are God dragging us, and they would end if we would stand upon our feet and go whither he would have us.

HENRY WARD BEECHER (1813–1887)
Sermons

Our heart oft times wakes when we sleep, and God can speak to that, either by words, by proverbs, by signs and similitudes, as well as if one was awake.

JOHN BUNYAN (1628–1688)
The Pilgrim's Progress

It is further from us to God than from God to us.   *Russian Proverb*

God is closer to the soul than the soul is to itself and therefore God is in the soul's core —God and all the Godhead.

MEISTER ECKHART (1260–1327)
Sermons

God is not really found until we find not merely One whom we have long sought and could not find, but One who has all the time been seeking us and whom we have all the time been attempting to elude.

JOHN BAILLIE (1886–1960)
Invitation to Pilgrimage

Not one of us has been left alone by God. Not one of us has been allowed to live a purely human life with complete peace of mind. It is, indeed, our common sin and shame that we do our best to ignore God's gracious approach, shutting ourselves up within our human finitude, living unto ourselves alone, as if God were not there at all.

JOHN BAILLIE (1886–1960)
Our Knowledge of God

Think not it is with God as with a human carpenter, who works or works not as he chooses, who can do or leave undone at his good pleasure. It is not thus with God; but finding thee ready he is obliged to act, to overflow into thee; just as the sun must needs burst forth when the air is bright and clear, and is unable to contain itself. He loved us before we were, and also when we were hostile to him. So necessary is our friendship to God that He approaches us and asks us to be his friends.

MEISTER ECKHART (1260–1327)
Works

We do not need to go "somewhere" to find God, any more than the fish needs to soar to find the ocean or the eagle to plunge to find the air. We only need to be prepared to see and feel what fringes the inner margins of ourselves.

RUFUS JONES (1863–1948)
Religious Foundations

The inward stirring and touching of God makes us hungry and yearning; for the Spirit of God hunts our spirit: and the more it touches it, the greater our hunger and our craving.

JAN VAN RUYSBROEK (1293–1381)
The Mirror of Eternal Salvation

God's abundance fills the world at all times, since there is no time above us; and it always seeks a channel through which it may descend unto men. If our words of prayer or learning are concentrated upon God, they unite with His abundance and form the channel through which it descends upon the world.

BAAL SHEM TOV (1700–1760)
Sayings

He plucks the world out of our hearts, loosening the chains of attachment. And He hurls the world into our hearts, where we and He together carry it in infinitely tender love.

THOMAS R. KELLY (1893–1941)
A Testament of Devotion

We do not seek God—God seeks us. There is a spirit pervading time and space who seeks the souls of men. At last the seeking becomes reciprocal—the divine presence is felt afar, and the soul begins to turn toward it. Then when we begin to seek God, we become conscious that God is seeking us.

FREDERICK WILLIAM ROBERTSON (1816–1853)
Sermons

The Lord seeks us ourselves, and not what is ours. He stands in no need of our wealth who bestows all things. For it is he to whom it is said, "My goods are nothing unto thee."

PETER ABÉLARD (1079–1142)
The Resurrection of Lazarus

The human soul is God's treasury, out of which he coins unspeakable riches. Thoughts and feelings, desires and yearnings, faith and hope—these are the most precious things which God finds in us.

HENRY WARD BEECHER (1813–1887)
Sermons

· A CALL TO PRAYER ·

Forget me not, but come, O King,
And find me softly slumbering
　In dark and troubled dreams of Thee,
Then, with one waft of Thy bright wing,
　Awaken me!
　　　　　ROBERT WILLIAMS BUCHANAN
　　　　　　　　　(1841–1901)
　　　　　　　　　Poems

Welcome, O life! I go to encounter for the millionth time the reality of experience and to forge in the smithy of my soul the un-created conscience of my race. Old father, old artificer, stand me now and ever in good stead.
　　　　　JAMES JOYCE (1882–1941)
　　A Portrait of the Artist as a Young Man

O God of Courage grave,
O Master of this night of Spring!
Make firm in me a heart too brave
To ask Thee anything.
　　　　　JOHN GALSWORTHY (1867–1933)
　　　　　　　　The Prayer

A child is born through the rending of the
　womb;
A man is born through the rending of the
　world.
The call to prayer signalizes both kinds of
　birth,
The first is uttered by the lips, the second of
　the very soul.
　　　　　MAHOMED IQBAL (1873–1938)
　　　　　　　　Javid Nama

The Lord bless thee, and keep thee:
The Lord make his face shine upon thee,
　and be gracious unto thee:
The Lord lift up his countenance upon thee,
　and give thee peace.
　　　　　　　　Old Testament
　　　　　　　　Numbers 6:24

Wa-kon-da dhe dhu-Wapa-dhin-a-ton-he
Father, a needy one stands before Thee.
I that sing am he.
　　　　　Omaha Indian Tribal Prayer

The only way truly to pray is to approach alone the One who is Alone. To contemplate that One, we must withdraw into the inner soul, as into a temple, and be still.
　　　　　PLOTINUS (205–270)
　　　　　　　Enneads

He prayeth best who loveth best
All things both great and small;
For the dear God who loveth us,
He made and loveth all.
SAMUEL TAYLOR COLERIDGE (1772–1834)
　　The Rime of the Ancient Mariner

The heavens are wide, exceedingly wide.
The earth is wide, very, very wide.
From time immemorial the God of old bids
　us all
Abide by his injunctions.
Then shall we get whatever we want, be it
　white or red.
It is God, the Creator, the Gracious One.
Good morning to you, God, good morning.
I am learning; let me succeed.
　　　　　　　African Prayer
　　　　　　　Akan of Ghana

Prayer is the burden of a sigh,
The falling of a tear;
The upward glancing of an eye
When none but God is near.
　　　　　JAMES MONTGOMERY
　　　　　　　(1771–1854)
　　　　　　What Is Prayer?

Great God, I ask thee for no meaner pelf
Than that I may not disappoint myself,

That in my action I may soar as high,
As I can now discern with this clear eye.

HENRY DAVID THOREAU (1817–1862)
Collected Poems

God Almighty Creator,
God Mbunwa Mukungu a Kinyima
Created trees, created people, created all the
   countries.
Created the land where the sun rises,
Created the fish at Msengye,
Created the eatable and uneatable ants.
God, thou art the Lord,
Who cometh in the roar of the whirlwind,
Out of your dwelling place from where the
   sun rises.

African Prayer
Milembwe of Zaire

O Thou who are unchangeable, whom
nothing changes! Thou who art unchangeable in love, precisely for our welfare not submitting to any change: may we too will our
welfare, submitting ourselves to the discipline of Thy unchangeableness, so that we
may, in unconditional obedience, find our
rest and remain at rest in Thy unchangeableness.

SÖREN KIERKEGAARD (1813–1855)
Journals

O God of heaven, O God of earth,
I pray thee uphold my hand.
My ancestors and ancestresses,
Lean upon earth and succour me
That I may not quickly come to you.

African Prayer
Nigerian Yoruba Chant

Father of Light! great God of Heaven!
Hear'st thou the accents of despair?
Can guilt like man's be e'er forgiven?
Can vice atone for crimes by prayer?

GEORGE GORDON, LORD BYRON (1788–1824)
The Prayer of Nature

As down in the sunless retreats of
   the Ocean,

Sweet flowers are springing no
   mortal can see,
So, deep in my soul the still prayer
   of devotion
Unheard by the world, rises
   silent to Thee.

THOMAS MOORE (1779–1852)
As Down in the Sunless Retreats

Prayer is the world in tune,
   A spirit-voice, And vocal joys,
Whose echo is heaven's bliss.

HENRY VAUGHAN (1622–1695)
The Morning Watch

He who rises from prayer a better man, his
prayer is answered.   *The Talmud*

When thou prayest, rather let thy heart be
without words, than thy words without heart.

JOHN BUNYAN (1628–1688)
Sermons

Prayer is the turning of the mind and heart
to God. To pray is to stand in awareness before God, to see him constantly and to talk
with him in hope and fear.

SAINT DEMETRIUS OF ROSTOV
(1651–1709)
Sermons

Guide us to that topmost height of mystic
love where the simple absolute and unchangeable mysteries of heavenly truth lie
hidden in the dazzling obscurity of the Secret
Silence.

DIONYSIUS THE AREOPAGITE (5th century)
The Celestial Hierarchy

Then repeat the words of Jesus (God bless
and preserve both our Prophet and him): "O
God, I here this morning am unable to repel
what I loathe and to gain what I hope for; by
Thy hand has this morning come, not by the
hand of any other; I this morning am obliged
to do my work, and no needy man is in
greater need than I am of Thee, while no

rich man is less in need than Thou art of me. O God, let not my enemy rejoice over me, and let not my friend think evil of me; May I not come into misfortune in my religion. May this world not be the greatest of my cares nor the sum of my knowledge. Let not him who has no mercy for me prevail over me by my sin."

ABU-HAMID MUHAMMAD AL-GHAZZALI
(1058–1111)
The Beginning of Guidance

To lift up the hands in prayer gives God glory, but a man with a dung-fork in his hand, a woman with a sloppail, give him glory, too. He is so great that all things give him glory if you mean they should.

GERARD MANLEY HOPKINS (1844–1889)
Letters

Two things have I asked of Thee;
deny me then not before I die:
Remove far from me falsehood and lies;
Give me neither poverty nor riches;
Feed me with mine alloted bread;
Lest I be full, and deny, and say:
            "Who is the Lord?"
Or lest I be poor and steal
And profane the name of my God.

The Old Testament
Proverbs 30:8–9

For this each pious one will pray to thee
    when Thou art near,
"May the flood of great waters not reach me.
Thou art my shelter and wilt guard me from
    the foe,
with songs of deliverance Thou wilt
    surround me."

The Old Testament
Psalms 32:6

Prayer is the soul's breathing itself into the bosom of its heavenly Father.

THOMAS WATSON (died 1686)
Sermons

O Lord, support us all the day long, until the shadows lengthen and the evening comes, and the busy world is hushed, and the fever of life is over, and our work is done. Then in thy mercy grant us a safe lodging, and a holy rest, and peace at last.

The Book of Common Prayer
Prayer at Night

Lord God of Hosts, be with us yet,
Lest we forget, lest we forget.

RUDYARD KIPLING (1865–1936)
Recessional

Hallowed be thy name, then,
Thou who art nameless—
All things that turn to thee
have their kingdom, their power, and their
    glory.
And I, a naked man, calling
calling to thee for my manna,
my kingdom, my power, and my glory.

D. H. LAWRENCE (1885–1930)
Lord's Prayer

My God, you who are my father who begot
    me, lift up my face.
How long will you neglect me, leave me
    unprotected?
How long will you leave me unguided?

Anonymous
Sumerian (2000 B.C.)

From the ingrained fashion
Of this earthly nature
That mars thy creature;
From grief that is but passion,
From mirth that is but feigning,
From tears that bring no healing,
From wild and weak complaining,
    Thine old strength revealing,
        Save, oh! save.

MATTHEW ARNOLD (1822–1888)
Stagirius

Be not forgetful of prayer. Every time you pray, if your prayer is sincere, there will be new feeling and new meaning in it, which will give you fresh courage, and you will understand that prayer is an education.

FYODOR DOSTOEVSKY (1821–1881)
The Brothers Karamazov

Sweet Mercy! to the gates of heaven
This minstrel lead, his sins forgiven;
The rueful conflict, the heart riven
With vain endeavor,
And memory of Earth's bitter leaven
Effaced forever.

WILLIAM WORDSWORTH (1770–1850)
Thoughts Suggested on the Banks of the Nith

How sweet it was in years far hied
To start the wheels of day with trustful
   prayer,
To lie down liegely at the eventide
And feel a blessed assurance He was there!

THOMAS HARDY (1840–1928)
God's Funeral

Cause us to lie down, O Lord our God, in peace; and cause us to rise, O our King, to life. And spread over us the tabernacle of Thy peace; and guide us by Thy good counsel. Deliver us for Thy Name's sake, and be a shield about us. Keep us from every enemy —pestilence and sword, hunger, and grief; drive away the evil one from before us and behind us. Shelter us under the shadow of Thy wings, for Thou, O God, art our Guardian and Deliverer; for Thou, O God, art a gracious and merciful King.

Hebrew Prayer
Haskibenu

O Lord, who dost inhabit eternity, to whom the sky and the highest heavens belong; whose throne is beyond imagining, and whose glory is past conceiving; who art attended by the host of angels trembling as they turn themselves into wind and fire at thy bidding; whose word is true and constant; whose commands are mighty and terrible; whose anger melts the mountains, and whose

truth stands for ever: hear thy servant's prayer, O Lord, listen to my petition, for thou hast fashioned me, and consider my words.   *The Old Testament Apocrypha*
2 Esdras 8:20–24

Hear, thou King of the intellectual fire, Titan of the golden reins; O thou Prince, who hast the key of the life-sustaining Fountain. From the world above thou dost direct a rich stream of harmony to the worlds of sense.

Grant me, O Lord, if thou please, the secure wealth of gladsome piety, for thou art able to accomplish all things willingly; thou possessest mighty and boundless strength. But if any mischief befalls us from the spindles of Fate as they make their revolutions to the star-driven threads, do thou restrain this for us by thy potent sway.

PROCLUS (410–485)
Hymn to the Sun

One of the deep constructive energies of life is prayer. It is a way of life that is as old as the human race is, and it is as difficult to "explain" as is our joy over love and beauty. Like all other great springs of life, it has sometimes been turned over to cheap ends and brought down to low levels, but on the whole it has been a pretty steady uplifting power in the long story of human progress. The only way we could completely understand it would be to understand the eternal nature of God and man. Then we should no doubt comprehend why He and we seek one another and why we are unsatisfied until we mutually find one another.

RUFUS JONES (1863–1948)
Pathways to the Reality of God

Prayer without devotion is no prayer at all. What then is devotion? One must free his heart from all other thoughts and regard himself as standing in the presence of God. Therefore, before engaging in prayer, a man ought to go aside for a little in order to bring himself into a devotional attitude, and then he should pray quietly and with feeling, not like one who carries a weight and goes away. Then after prayer the worshipper ought to sit quietly for a little and then depart.

MAIMONIDES (1135–1204)
Mishneh Torah

When the last sea is sailed, when the last
   shallow charted,
When the last field is reaped, and the last
   harvest stored,
When the last fire is out and the last quest
   departed,
Grant the last prayer that I shall pray, Be
   good to me, O Lord!

And in the dim green quiet place far out of
   sight and hearing,
Grant I may hear at whiles the wash and
   thresh of the sea-foam
About the fine keen bows of the stately
   clippers steering
Towards the lone northern star and the fair
   ports of home.

JOHN MASEFIELD (1878–1967)
D'Avalos' Prayer

"Why has God established prayer?" asks Pascal. And Pascal's first answer to his own great question is this. God has established prayer in the moral world in order "to communicate to His creatures the dignity of causality." That is to say, to give us a touch and a taste of what it is to be a Creator.

ALEXANDER WHYTE (1836–1921)
The Magnificence of Prayer

He offered a prayer so deeply devout that he seemed kneeling and praying at the bottom of the sea.

HERMAN MELVILLE (1819–1891)
Moby Dick

Prayer is the soul's sincere desire,
   Uttered or unexpressed,

The motion of a hidden fire
   That trembles in the breast.

JAMES MONTGOMERY (1771–1854)
What Is Prayer?

For what are men better than sheep or goats
That nourish a blind life within the brain,
If, knowing God, they lift not hands of
   prayer
Both for themselves and those who call them
   friend?
For so the whole round earth is every way
Bound by gold chains about the feet of God.

ALFRED LORD TENNYSON (1809–1892)
Morte d'Arthur

In every true prayer God is both he to whom we pray and he who prays through us. For it is the divine Spirit who creates the right prayer. God stands in the divine-human reciprocity, but only as he who transcends it and comprises both sides of the reciprocity. He reacts, but he reacts to that which is his own act working through our finite freedom.

PAUL TILLICH (1886–1965)
Being and Love

Father, in Thy mysterious Presence
   kneeling,
   Fain would our souls feel all Thy
      kindling love;
For we are weak, and need some deep
   revealing
   Of trust and strength and calmness
      from above.

REV. SAMUEL JOHNSON (1696–1772)
Father, in Thy Presence Kneeling

The archimedean point outside the world is the little chamber where a true suppliant prays in all sincerity—where he lifts the world off its hinges.

SÖREN KIERKEGAARD (1813–1855)
Either/Or

Dear Lord and Father of mankind,
   Forgive our foolish ways!
Reclothe us in our rightful mind,

In purer lives Thy service find,
In deeper reverence, praise.
JOHN GREENLEAF WHITTIER (1807–1892)
The Brewing of Soma

A single grateful thought toward Heaven is the most perfect prayer.
GOTTHOLD EPHRAIM LESSING (1729–1781)
Minna von Barnhelm

The Lord's prayer is the prayer above all prayers. It is a prayer which the most high Master taught us, wherein are comprehended all spiritual and temporal blessings, and the strongest comforts in all trials, temptations, and troubles, even in the hour of death.
MARTIN LUTHER (1483–1546)
Table-Talk

Prayer, though it accomplishes nothing material, constitutes something spiritual. It will not bring rain, but until rain comes it may cultivate hope and resignation and may prepare the heart for any issue.
GEORGE SANTAYANA (1863–1952)
The Life of Reason

Prayer is not just the informing of God of our needs, for He already knows them. God does not show Himself equally to all creatures. This does not mean that he has favorites, that He decides to help some and to abandon others, but the difference occurs because it is impossible for Him to manifest Himself to certain hearts under the conditions they set up. The sunlight plays no favorites, but its reflection is very different on a lake and on a swamp.
FULTON J. SHEEN (1895–1979)
The Electronic Christian

He who labors as he prays lifts his heart to God with his hands.
SAINT BERNARD OF CLAIRVAUX (1091–1153)
Ad Sorerum

It is in moments of our being faced with the mystery of living and dying, of knowing and not knowing, of love and the inability to love—that we pray, that we address ourselves to Him who is beyond the mystery.
ABRAHAM JOSHUA HESCHEL (1907–1972)
The Wisdom of Heschel

If I am right, thy grace impart
Still in the right to stay;
If I am wrong, oh teach my heart
To find that better way!
ALEXANDER POPE (1688–1744)
Universal Prayer

Let the words of my mouth, and the meditation of my heart, be acceptable in thy sight, O Lord, my strength and my redeemer.
The Old Testament
Psalms 19:14

Prayer is the little implement
Through which Men reach
Where Presence—is denied them.
They fling their Speech

By means of it—in God's Ear—
If then He hear—
This sums the Apparatus
Comprised in Prayer.
EMILY DICKINSON (1830–1886)
Prayer is the Little Implement

Save me, O God;
For the waters are come in even unto the soul.
I am sunk in deep mire, where there is no standing;
I am come into deep waters, and the flood overwhelmeth me.
The Old Testament
Psalms 69:2–4

Prayer is not asking; it is the longing of the soul.
MOHANDAS K. GANDHI (1869–1948)
Young India

What discord should we bring into the universe if our prayers were all answered! Then *we* should govern the world and not God.

And do you think we should govern it better?
It gives me only pain when I hear the long,
wearisome petitions of men asking for they
know not what.

HENRY WADSWORTH LONGFELLOW
(1807–1882)
Journals

If your hands are stained by dishonesty,
your prayers will be polluted and impure,
and an offense to Him to whom you direct
them. Do not pray at all before you have your
hands purified from every dishonest act.

The Midrash

Prayer is the soul's sincerest desire,
Uttered or unexpressed,
The notion of a hidden fire
That trembles in the breast.

JAMES MONTGOMERY (1771–1854)
What Is Prayer?

O God! drive me not in contempt from Thy
    door;
For no other door appears to me.

SAADI (1184–1291)
Bustan

Prayer from a living source within the will,
And beating up thro' all the bitter world
Like fountains of sweet waters in the sea,
Kept him a living soul.

ALFRED LORD TENNYSON (1809–1892)
Enoch Arden

Kindle Thy light within me, O God, that I
may be guarded against self-deception and
the vanity that creeps into my spirit where a
shadow is cast between me and Thy scrutiny.

HOWARD THURMAN (1899–1982)
Meditations of the Heart

To pray is to expose oneself to the prompt-
ings of God; and, by the same token, to become less suggestible to the low persuasions
of the world.

GEORGE ARTHUR BUTTRICK (1892–1979)
Prayer

Only a theoretical deity is left to any man
who has ceased to commune with God, and a
theoretical deity saves no man from sin and
disheartenment.

HARRY EMERSON FOSDICK (1878–1969)
The Meaning of Prayer

We cannot bridge the gap between God
and ourselves even through the most inten-
sive and frequent prayers; the gap between
God and ourselves can only be bridged by
God.   PAUL TILLICH (1886–1965)

The New Being

Prayer is the world in tune.

HENRY VAUGHAN (1622–1695)
The Morning Watch

If we labor in thy works with the sweat of
our brows thou wilt make us partakers of thy
wisdom and thy Sabbath. Humbly we pray
that this mind may be steadfast in us, and
that through these our hands, and the hands
of others to whom thou shalt give the same
spirit, thou wilt vouchsafe to endow the
human family with new mercies.

FRANCIS BACON (1561–1626)
Novum Organum

Holy, holy, holy, Lord God Almighty!
Early in the morning our song shall rise to
    thee.

REGINALD HEBER (1783–1826)
Hymn

I have a creed, none better and none
shorter. It is told in two words—the first of
the Paternoster. And when I say these words
I mean them.

OLIVER WENDELL HOLMES (1809–1894)
The Autocrat of the Breakfast-Table

A hasty kind of reasoning may hold that
praying is an unprofitable act, because a
man's prayer does not really change the Unchangeable; but even if this in the process
of time were desired, might not changeable
man come easily to regret that he had

changed God? The true kind of reasoning is therefore the only desirable kind as well; prayer does not change God, but changes him who prays.

SÖREN KIERKEGAARD (1813–1855)
Works of Love

May He support us all the day long, till the shades lengthen, and the evening comes, and the busy world is hushed, and the fever of life is over, and our work is done! Then, in His mercy may He give us a safe lodging, and a holy rest, and peace at the last.

JOHN CARDINAL NEWMAN (1801–1890)
Wisdom and Innocence

And the Lord said unto Moses, "Wherefore criest thou unto me?" (Exodus 14:15). Rabbi Eliezer said: God said to Moses, "My children are in trouble; the sea shuts them off on one side, the enemy pursues them on the other, and you stand and make long prayers." And God said, "There is a time to lengthen prayer, and a time to shorten it."

The Talmud

Prayer is conversation with the Existent One who is exalted above the world cycle, above the falsity and wrongness in which the world is submerged.

NIKOLAI BERDYAEV (1874–1948)
The Divine and the Human

Prayer is not a vain attempt to change God's will: it is a filial desire to learn God's will and share it. Prayer is not a substitute for work: it is the secret spring and indispensable ally of all true work—the clarifying of work's goal, the purifying of its motives, and the renewing of its zeal.

GEORGE ARTHUR BUTTRICK (1892–1979)
The Christian Fact and Modern Doubt

Great Spirit, give to me
A heaven not so large as yours
But large enough for me.

EMILY DICKINSON (1830–1886)
Complete Poems

The prayer that reforms the sinner and heals the sick is an absolute faith that all things are possible to God—a spiritual understanding of Him, an unselfish love.

MARY BAKER EDDY (1821–1910)
Science and Understanding

Is not prayer also a study of truth—a sally of the soul into the unfound infinite? No man ever prayed heartily without learning something. But when a faithful thinker, resolute to detach every object from personal relations and see it in the light of thought, shall at the same time kindle science with the fire of the holiest affections, then will God go forth anew into the creation.

RALPH WALDO EMERSON (1803–1882)
Collected Works

The unreflective person thinks and imagines that when he prays, the important thing, the thing he must concentrate upon, is that God should hear what he is praying for. And yet in the true, eternal sense it is just the reverse; the true relation in prayer is not when God hears what is prayed for, but when the person continues to pray until he is the one who hears, who hears what God wills.

SÖREN KIERKEGAARD (1813–1855)
Journals

Pray to Him in any way you like. He is there to hear you, for he can hear even the footfall of an ant.

SRI RAMAKRISHNA (1836–1886)
Gospel of Sri Ramakrishna

In all real prayer there are two persons interacting with each other: God and the finite mind. The individual is meeting the conditions for finding God, and God is finding the opportunity to enter into a kind of relationship with the individual otherwise not possible. For in prayer at its best both God and man meet, both to foster the creation of new values in and through each other and to enjoy mutual fellowship for its own sake.

PETER A. BERTOCCI (1910–)
Introduction to the Philosophy of Religion

Here is the Heart that broods over His children with unutterable love. How alert that divine ear is to listen, none of us can know. It does not need a formal prayer; the most stumbling and broken cry—a sigh, a whisper, anything that tells the heart's loneliness and need and penitence—can find its way to Him.   PHILLIPS BROOKS (1835–1893)
The More Abundant Life

To pray is to desire; but it is to desire what God would have us desire.

FRANÇOIS FÉNELON (1651–1715)
Advice Concerning Prayer

Men who come to God not to dictate but to receive have approached prayer from the right angle. They have seen that prayer is giving God an opportunity to bestow what he is more willing to give than we are to welcome. As a sixteenth-century mystic said, "Prayer is not to ask what we wish of God, but what God wishes of us."

HARRY EMERSON FOSDICK (1878–1969)
Meaning of Prayer

To worship is to quicken the conscience by the holiness of God, to feed the mind with the truth of God, to purge the imagination by the beauty of God, to open the heart to the love of God, to devote the will to the purpose of God.

WILLIAM TEMPLE (1881–1944)
The Church and Its Teaching Today

The Prophet's words, "The man at prayer is in secret converse with his Lord," are only to be predicated of that inward knowledge which belongs solely to pure souls that are abstracted and free from events in time and directions in space: they contemplate God intellectually, and behold Him with spiritual not corporeal vision. It is thus evident that true prayer is spiritual contemplation, and that pure worship is spiritual Divine love.

AVICENNA (980–1037)
On Prayer

Whoever has it in his power to pray on behalf of his neighbor, and fails to do so, is called a sinner.   *The Gemarah*

Prayer is for the soul what nourishment is for the body.

JUDAH HALEVI (c. 1085–c. 1140)
Kitab Al Khazari

Prayer at the right time is better than the whole world and everything in it.

Moroccan Proverb

Any trick used in order to attract God's attention deprives prayer of all its value.

The Talmud

We call prayer in the pregnant sense of the term that speech of man to God which, whatever else is asked, ultimately asks for the manifestation of the divine Presence, for this Presence's becoming dialogically perceivable.

MARTIN BUBER (1878–1965)
Eclipse of God

Look at me, Chief, that nothing evil may happen to me this day, made by you as you please, Great-Walking-to-and-fro-all-over-the-World, Chief. Ha.

Kwakiutl Indian Prayer

Let us invoke God Himself, not in mere form of words, but by elevating our souls to Him in prayer. And the only way truly to pray is to approach alone the One who is Alone. To contemplate that One, we must withdraw into the inner soul, as into a temple, and be still.   PLOTINUS (205–270)
Enneads

Worship does not consist in fasts and prayers, but in the offering of a pure and contrite heart. The musk is in the deer but it

thinks that the fragrance comes from outside and so hunts for it restlessly. God is in us and we have only to turn within to realize the truth.
SARVEPALLI RADHAKRISHNAN (1888–1978)
My Search for Truth

Prayer begins by talking to God, but it ends by listening to Him.
FULTON J. SHEEN (1895–1979)
The Woman

I prayed to Earthmaker. And as I prayed I was aware of something above me, and there He was! That which is called the soul, that is it, that is what one calls Earthmaker.
Winnebago Indian Prayer

O Lord our God, grant us grace to desire thee with our whole heart; that so desiring we may seek and find thee; and so finding thee, may love thee.
SAINT ANSELM (1033–1109)
Cur Deus Homo

As soon as we are with God in faith and in love, we are in prayer.
FRANÇOIS FÉNELON (1651–1715)
Maximes des Saints

All great souls have prayed receptively. "I will hear," said the psalmist, "what God the Lord will speak." Prayer is the hospitality of the soul entertaining the Most High.
HARRY EMERSON FOSDICK (1878–1969)
Riverside Sermons

Orison draws the great God into the small heart; it drives the hungry soul out to the full God. It brings together two lovers, God and the soul, into one joyful room.
MECHTILD OF MAGDEBURG (1217–1282)
The Book of the Flowing Light of the Godhead

Prayer is the responsibility to meet others with *all* I have, to be ready to encounter the unconditional in the conditional, to expect to meet God in the way, not to turn aside from the way.
JOHN A. T. ROBINSON (1919–)
Honest to God

The Divine wisdom has given us prayer, not as a means whereby to obtain the good things of earth, but as a means whereby we learn to do without them; not as a means whereby we escape evil, but as a means whereby we become strong to meet it.
FREDERICK WILLIAM ROBERTSON (1816–1853)
Sermons

"To love the Lord your God and serve Him with all your heart and soul" (Deuteronomy 11:13). What is service of the heart? This is prayer.
The Talmud

O Breath from out the Eternal Silence! blow
Softly upon our spirits' barren ground;
The precious fullness of our God bestow,
That fruits of faith, love, reverence may abound.
GERHARD TERSTEEGEN (1697–1769)
Hymns

We must not conceive of prayer as an overcoming of God's reluctance, but as a laying hold of his highest willingness.
RICHARD CHENEVIX TRENCH (1807–1886)
Notes on the Parables

In hours of crisis the soul feels for its Companion, by a natural gravitation, as the brook feels for the ocean. In times of joy and strength, it reaches out to its source of Life, as the plant does to the sun. And when it has learned the language of spiritual communion and knows its Father, praying refreshes it as the greeting of a friend refreshes one in a foreign land.
RUFUS JONES (1863–1948)
The Double Search

Every prayer—be it with or without words —that reaches its aim, namely, the reunion with the divine ground of our being, is a work of the Spirit speaking in us and through us. Prayer is a spiritual sighing and longing of a finite being to return to its origin.

PAUL TILLICH (1886–1965)
Sermons

Prayer is called mystical, because of the hidden nature of the conversation: God and the individual speak heart to heart, and what passes between them can be shared with no one else.

SAINT FRANCIS OF SALES (1567–1622)
The Love of God

When I pray for something, I do not pray; when I pray for nothing, I really pray. To pray for anything except God might be called idolatry or injustice.

MEISTER ECKHART (1260–1327)
Works

Who would stand before a blackboard, and pray the principle of mathematics to solve the problem? Shall we ask the divine Principle of all goodness to do His own work?

MARY BAKER EDDY (1821–1910)
Science and Health

There is no end to a prayer. It echoes on forever in your soul. Long after the visible demonstration has been made and forgotten, the prayer that produced it continues to work for your spiritual advancement, for the creative power of a God-thought is unlimited and eternal.   EMMET FOX (1886–1951)
Power Through Constructive Thinking

O God, whose call precedes the very first of our movements, grant me the desire to desire being—that, by means of that divine thirst which is your gift, the access to the great waters may open wide within me.

PIERRE TEILHARD DE CHARDIN (1881–1955)
The Divine Milieu

If by prayer I mean the power of words to persuade God to do things, then prayer is futile and foolish. One might utter the words of the most devout prayer that was ever breathed and yet not be praying at all. It is the attitude of the personality which is the prayer, and not the words.

HENRY NELSON WIEMAN (1884–1975)
The Issues of Life

The worship of God is not a rule of safety —it is an adventure of the spirit.

ALFRED NORTH WHITEHEAD (1861–1947)
Nature and Life

Cry hard to God for an enlightened heart, and a willing mind, and God give thee a prosperous journey!

JOHN BUNYAN (1628–1688)
The Heavenly Footman

The highest type of prayer has for its object not any material benefit, but the enlightenment and amendment of our wills, the elevation of all humanity, and the coming of the Kingdom.

SIR OLIVER LODGE (1851–1940)
The Substance of Faith

Prayer is the aspiration of our poor, struggling, heavy-laden soul toward its Eternal Father.   THOMAS CARLYLE (1795–1881)
Letters

Our vows, our prayers, we now present
Before thy throne of grace,
God of our fathers, be the God
Of their succeeding race.

PHILIP DODDRIDGE (1702–1751)
Hymns

When in prayer you clasp your hands, God opens His.   *German Proverb*

Prayer is a principal means for opening oneself to the power and love of God that is already there—in the depths of reality. He is always ready to guide, to inspire, to comfort, to accept, to heal, to enrich; such barriers as there are to His thus operating in us, with us, and through us are in each of us and in our respective situations—not in Him.

JAMES A. PIKE (1913–1969)
A Time for Christian Candor

No man's prayer is given hearing, unless when he raises his hands to heaven in prayer, he also raises his whole soul heavenward in his hands; for Scripture saith (Lamentations 3:40): "Let us lift up our heart with our hands unto God in the heavens."

The Talmud

When we pray to God, says St. Cyprian, with entire assurance, it is himself who has given us the spirit of our prayer. Then it is the Father listening to the words of his child; it is he who dwells in the depths of our hearts, teaching us how to pray.

FRANÇOIS FÉNELON (1651–1715)
On Prayer

Prayer is not to hear oneself speak, but to arrive at silence, and continue being silent; to wait till one hears God speak.

SÖREN KIERKEGAARD (1813–1855)
Journals

Prayer is not a vain attempt to change God's will: it is a filial desire to learn God's will and to share it. Prayer is not a substitute for work: it is the secret spring and ally of all true work—the clarifying of work's goal, the purifying of its motives, and the renewing of its zeal.

GEORGE ARTHUR BUTTRICK (1892–1979)
The Christian Fact and Modern Doubt

No prayer can be selfish, for God is the Father of all mankind. There are no fences of race or class in His eyes.

GEORGE ARTHUR BUTTRICK (1892–1979)
So We Believe, So We Pray

O Thou, who art the True Light, shine ever through all the blind corners of my soul.

JOSEPH HALL (1574–1656)
On Occasion When the Light's Brought In

When a man prays solely for material benefits, his prayer of supplication is wasted. It forms a material curtain between God and himself, because he has brought matter into the domain of spirit. He receives no answer whatsoever.

BAAL SHEM TOV (1700–1760)
Sayings

Pray the largest prayers. You cannot think a prayer so large that God, in answering it, will not wish you had made it larger. Pray not for crutches but for wings!

PHILLIPS BROOKS (1835–1893)
Sermons

Make every effort to pray from the heart. Even if you do not succeed, the effort is precious in the eyes of God.

RABBI NAHMAN OF BRATZLAV (1772–1811)
Sayings

At the time of prayer, clear all worldly matters out of your heart; prepare your heart before God, blessed be He, purify your senses, and consider your words before you allow them to leave your mouth.

NAHMANIDES (1195–1270)
Letter to His Son

When I stir thee to prayer, I stir thee not to the prayer that standeth in many words, but to that prayer which, in the secret chamber of the mind, in the privy closet of the soul, with very affect speaketh unto God.

GIOVANNI PICO DELLA MIRANDOLA
(1463–1494)
Letters

There be many tongues and many languages of men—but the language of prayer is one by itself, *in* all and above *all*. It is the inspiration of that Spirit that is ever working with our spirit, and constantly lifting us higher than we know.

HARRIET BEECHER STOWE (1811–1896)
The Minister's Wooing

He who prays should always believe the Divine Presence is before him, for Scripture states (Psalms 16:8): I have set the Lord always before me. *The Talmud*

God will excuse our prayers for ourselves, whenever we are prevented from them, by being occupied in such good works as to entitle us the prayers of others.

CHARLES CALEB COLTON (1780–1832)
Lacon

Take prayer out of the world and it is as if you had torn asunder the bond that binds humanity to God, and had struck dumb the tongue of the child in the presence of his Father.

GUSTAV THEODOR FECHNER (1801–1887)
Vorschule der Asthetik

The prayer of the heart is not a single act or series of acts which the soul undertakes, but the essential state in which the soul lives.

MADAME GUYON (1648–1717)
Autobiography

In true meditation a man cries to the Lord like a child to his father who is about to take his departure. There is no sadness in his weeping—only longing and yearning.

RABBI NAHMAN OF BRATZLAV (1772–1811)
Likkute Mahoran

God usually answers our prayers according rather to the measure of His own magnificence than to that of our asking; so that we often do not know His boons to be those for which we besought Him.

COVENTRY PATMORE (1823–1896)
The Rod, the Root, and the Flower

The whole confidence and glory of prayer is in its appeal to a Father who knows our necessities before we ask, who knows our thoughts before they rise in our hearts, and whose decrees, as unalterable in the eternal future as in the eternal past, yet in the close verity of visible fact, bend, like reeds, before the fore-ordained and faithful prayers of His children. JOHN RUSKIN (1819–1900)
On the Old Road

Prayer needs a joyous conscience as its preliminary. *The Talmud*

Our hopes and prayers are not directed to God in vain, for if they are just they cannot fail. Therefore, stand firm against vice and cultivate virtue. Lift up your soul to worthy hopes, and offer humble prayers to heaven. If you will face it, the necessity of virtuous action imposed upon you is very great, since all your actions are done in the sight of a Judge who sees all things.

BOETHIUS (480–524)
The Consolation of Philosophy

Prayer is similar to a communication between God and us whereby we expound to him our desires, our joys, our sighs, in a word, all the thoughts of our hearts.

JOHN CALVIN (1509–1564)
Instruction in Faith

Here lies the ground of the great efficacy of prayer, which when it is the prayer of the heart, the prayer of faith, has a kindling and creating power, and forms and transforms the soul into everything that its desires reach after: it has the key to the Kingdom of Heaven and unlocks all its treasures, it opens, extends and moves that in us which has its being and motion in and with the divine nature, and so brings us into real union and communion with God.

WILLIAM LAW (1686–1761)
The Way to Divine Knowledge

No help but prayer,
A breath that fleets beyond this iron world,
And touches Him that made it.
ALFRED LORD TENNYSON (1809–1892)
Harold

The noblest fruit of the tree of prayer is communion with God.

ISAAC ARAMA (15th century)
Akeda

The conversation which passes in prayer between God and the soul is carried on in the secret recesses of the heart; it is a communication of feelings impenetrable to all but those who speak.

SAINT FRANCIS OF SALES (1567–1622)
Treatise on the Love of God

When the soul is hungry for the light, for the truth—when its hunger has waked its higher energies, thoroughly roused the will, and brought the soul into its highest condition, that of action—its only fitness for receiving the things of God—that action is prayer. GEORGE MACDONALD (1824–1905)
Unspoken Sermons

The coldness of our love is the silence of our hearts toward God. Without this we may pronounce prayers, but we do not pray; for what shall lead us to meditate upon the laws of God, if it be not love of him who has made these laws? Let our hearts be full of love then, and they will pray.

FRANÇOIS FÉNELON (1651–1715)
Dialogues on Eloquence

This is my prayer to Thee, O Lord—
Strike, strike at the root of penury in my
    heart.
Give me the strength lightly to bear my joys
    and sorrows.
Give me the strength to make my love
    fruitful in service.
Give me the strength never to disown the
    poor or bend my knees before insolent
        might,
Give me the strength to raise my mind above
    daily trifles,
And give me the strength to surrender my
    strength to Thy will with love.

KABIR (1454–1518)
The Adi Granth

What men usually ask for when they pray to God is that two and two may not make four. *Russian Proverb*

O powerful Goodness! bountiful Father! merciful Guide! Increase in me that wisdom which discovers my truest interest. Strengthen my resolutions to perform what that wisdom dictates. Accept my kind offices to thy other children as the only return in my power for thy continual favours to me.

BENJAMIN FRANKLIN (1706–1790)
Autobiography

Prayer is an expression of man's inner yearning for a response in the awful silence of the universe. It is a unique process of discovery whereby the searching ego affirms itself in the very moment of self-negation, and thus discovers its own worth and justification as a dynamic factor in the life of the universe.

MAHOMED IQBAL (1873–1938)
The Reconstruction of Religious Thought in Islam

Prayer is not informing God of something he does not already know, or pleading with him to change his mind. Prayer is the opening of the soul to God so he can speak to us. "Prayer is not overcoming God's reluctance; it is laying hold of God's willingness."

GEORGIA HARKNESS (1891–1974)
Prayer and the Common Life

My prayers, my God, flow from what I am
    not;
I think thy answers make me what I am.

GEORGE MACDONALD (1824–1905)
Diary of an Old Soul

Prayer is more than affirmation of theism; it is encounter. The Eternal who is being sought by me is ever seeking me. We meet in prayer. It is like meeting a friend upon a busy thoroughfare. Thousands are rushing by. They do not know my name, but my friend does. There is the flash of recognition, the word of greeting. I count in the crowd. I am an individual known and knowing.

G. BROMLEY OXNAM (1891–1963)
A Testament of Faith

Prayer is the language in which the heart asks God to hear it, and to take it lovingly to His own heart.   KARL RAHNER (1904–)
Happiness Through Prayer

When a soul prays, God does not sit upright until the prayer travels immensity and climbs to his ear. In more than one place the Psalmist said He inclined His ear, by which I come to believe that God puts His ear so closely down to your lips that he can hear your faintest whisper. It is not God away off up yonder; it is God away down here, close up—so close up that when you pray to him it is not more a whisper than a kiss.
THOMAS DE WITT TALMAGE (1832–1902)
Sermons

If God already knows what we want and, more importantly, knows what we *need*, why tell Him? Because our relationship with the Father is a personal one. Even the poor human parent wants the child to open up his heart without fear or scruples, though most of what is told is already well known.
D. ELTON TRUEBLOOD (1890–)
A Place to Stand

Trying to be perfect means trying to do *your* particular best, with the particular graces God has given *you*. You cannot pray like Saint Teresa, any more than you can sing like Caruso: but how foolish if for that reason you give up trying to pray at all. What God asks of you is that you should do your best, not Saint Teresa's best.
GERALD VANN (1906–1963)
Stones or Bread?

To pray is to expose the shores of the mind to the incoming tide of God.
RALPH W. SOCKMAN (1889–1970)
Recoveries in Religion

Prayer is the soul of a man moving in the presence of God, for the purpose of communicating its joy, or sorrow, or fear, or hope, or any other conscious experience that it may have, to the bosom of a parent.
HENRY WARD BEECHER (1813–1887)
Sermons

When we pray for any virtue, we should cultivate the virtue as well as pray for it; the form of your prayers should be the rule of your life; every petition to God is a precept to man.   JEREMY TAYLOR (1613–1667)
Sermons

Praying is not standing aside from reality, dreaming and longing; on the contrary, it demands the whole person: his contemplation, the tension of his will, and the movement of his heart. There must be resolution which ensures that all this is not a passing attitude, soon to be dissipated, but a solid frame of mind which finds expression in everyday action.   ROMANO GUARDINI (1885–1968)
The Lord's Prayer

· FROM WHOM ALL BLESSINGS FLOW ·

From thee, great God, we spring, to thee we
   tend—
Path, motive, guide, original and end.
DR. SAMUEL JOHNSON (1709–1784)
Motto to the Rambler

All thy works shall give thanks to thee, O Lord.   *The Old Testament*
Psalms 145:10

If God is for us, who is against us?
The New Testament
Romans 8:31

The superior man stands in awe of three things. He stands in awe of the Mandate of Heaven; he stands in awe of great men; and he stands in awe of the sages.
CONFUCIUS (551–479 B.C.)
Analects

Let us build altars to the Blessed Unity which holds nature and souls in perfect solution, and compels every atom to serve a universal end.
RALPH WALDO EMERSON (1803–1882)
Fate

Within us, as well without us, there is a Universe; and therefore arises the praiseworthy custom of all peoples that each should call the best he knows by the name of God, *his* God; and give over heaven and earth to Him; and fear Him and, when possible, love Him.
JOHANN WOLFGANG VON GOETHE (1749–1832)
Works

Your feeling is piety insofar as it expresses the being and life common to you and to the All. Your feeling is piety insofar as it is the result of the operation of God in you by means of the operation of the world upon you.
FRIEDRICH SCHLEIERMACHER (1768–1834)
Speeches on Religion

There is a living creature in heaven which by day has "Truth" upon its forehead, by which the angels know it is day; but in the evening it has "Faith" on its forehead, whereby the angels know that night is near. Each time the living creature says, "Bless ye the blessed Lord," all the hosts above respond, "Blessed be the blessed Lord forever."
The Kabbalah

What I would ask Thee, tell me it right, O thou living God! Who holds up the earth and the clouds above it? Who made the waters and the trees of the field? Who gave to the winds and storms their wings that they so quickly run? Who governs all things in his goodness?
ZOROASTER (6th century B.C.)
Gathas

Ascription of praise to God is the utterance of the joy and gladness which the divine excellence tends to excite in us, and may be called a *caress of words*.
HENRY WARD BEECHER (1813–1887)
Sermons

We praise Thee, O God,
For whatever perspicuity of language Thou hast taught us
And whatever eloquence Thou hast inspired us with.
ABU MOHAMMED KASIM BEN ALI HARIRI
(1054–1122)
Makamet

Blessed art Thou, O Lord, our God, King of the Universe, who formest light and createst darkness; who makest peace and createst all things; who givest light in mercy to the earth and to those who live thereon, and in goodness renewest every day continually the work of creation.
Yotzer, a Traditional Hebrew Prayer

Thou art the Governor of the unseen world;
Thou art the nature of natures;
Thou nourishest nature—
The origin of the mortal,
The image of the immortal;
So that the lowest part in the world
Might obtain the other life.
SYNESIUS OF CYRENE (373–414)
Hymns

Glory be to God for dappled things—
For skies of couple-colour as a brinded cow;
For rose-moles all in stipple upon trout that swim;
Fresh-firecoal chestnut-falls; finches' wings;

Landscape plotted and pieced—fold, fallow,
  and plough;
And all trades, their gear and tackle and
trim.
                GERARD MANLEY HOPKINS (1844–1889)
                                    Pied Beauty

The song of the morning stars was really
the first hymn of praise and will be the last;
the face of nature, the breath of the hills, the
lights of the skies, are to a simple heart the
real occasions of devout feeling more than
vestries and sermon hearings; and are those
natural checks that are ever exerting an insensible influence to hold us back from fanat-
icism and keep us within sight of the true
God.
                RALPH WALDO EMERSON (1803–1882)
                                        Sermons

Great art Thou, O God; though it is in a
dark saying we know Thee and as in a mirror, yet we adore Thy goodness with wonder
—how much more must we one day extol it
when we learn to know it more fully.
                SÖREN KIERKEGAARD (1813–1855)
                            Christian Discourses

The liveliest emblem of heaven that I know
upon earth is when the people of God in the
deep sense of his excellency and bounty,
from hearts abounding with love and joy,
join together both in heart and voice in the
cheerful and melodious singing of his
praises.   RICHARD BAXTER (1615–1691)
                    The Saints' Everlasting Rest

This is the day which the Lord hath made;
we will rejoice and be glad in it.
                            The Old Testament
                                Psalms 118:24

We need not much poetry in our spirit, to
catch the song of night, and hear the spheres
as they chant praises which are loud to the
heart, though they be silent to the ear—the

praises of the mighty God who bears up the
unpillared arch of heaven, and moves the
stars in their courses.
            CHARLES HADDON SPURGEON (1834–1892)
                                        Sermons

O God, Thou art our Providence, our
  Father Thou!
We are Thy brethren, and Thou art our
  spring of life.
Thou art called Father, caring for the weak.
And, Wisest, to the simple one Thou
  teachest lore.   *The Rig-Veda*

Let no one, therefore, however humble
and insignificant he be, despairing of a better
fortune, scruple to become a suppliant of
God. Even if he can expect nothing more, let
him give thanks to the best of his power for
what he has already received. Infinite are the
gifts he has: birth, life, nature, soul, sensa-
tion, imagination, desire, reason.
                PHILO JUDAEUS (30 B.C.–A.D. 40)
                                            Works

O Thou divine Substance, from whence all
forms of life have sprung! Thou sendest
forth the word, and earth is flooded with silence, O Thou only One who didst dwell in
heaven before ever the earth and the mountains came into being.

                        Egyptian Hymn to Ra
                            (1580–1350 B.C.)
                        The Book of the Dead

Were I to live for millions of years,
  And drink the air for my nourishment,
I should still not be able to express Thy
    worth.
  How great shall I call Thy name!
                    GURU NANAK (1469–1539)
                              The Adi Granth

Ought we not, as we dig and plough and
eat, to sing the hymn to God? "Great is God
that He gave us these instruments wherewith
we shall till the earth. Great is God that He

has given us hands, and the power to grow without knowing it, and to draw our breath in sleep." At every moment we ought to sing these praises and above all, the greatest and divinest praise, that God gave us the faculty to comprehend these gifts and to use the way of reason. EPICTETUS (1st century)
Discourses

Magnified and praised by the living God;
He is, and there is no limit in time unto His
  being.
He is One, and there is no unity like unto
  His unity;
Inconceivable is He, and unending is His
  unity.
DANIEL BEN JUDAH (14th century)
Prayers

The heavens and the earth are everywhere spread above and beneath us; and the spirit of God, which fills them, which gives to man his elevation and, at the view of the glories around him, kindles up the native poetry of the heart and the understanding, extends to all its creative energies.
JOHANN GOTTFRIED HERDER (1744–1803)
The Spirit of Hebrew Poetry

God be prais'd, that to believing souls
Gives light in darkness, comfort in despair!
WILLIAM SHAKESPEARE (1564–1616)
Henry VI

The essence of the Vedas, Puranas and
  Simritis
Is to contemplate the One, the Holy Name.
He who but treasureth the Lord in his heart
  for a moment,
Who can recount his enrichment or his
  exaltation?
GURU ARJAN (1563–1606)
Hymns

Great God, we sing that mighty hand
By which supported still we stand;

The opening year thy mercy shows;
That mercy crowns it till it close.
PHILIP DODDRIDGE (1702–1751)
Hymns

Mountain Lord, we speak to thee with blissful words, so that all that is moving and living may, free from disease, have happiness of heart. *The Yajurveda*

The spacious firmament on high,
And all the blue ethereal sky,
And spangled heavens, a shining frame,
Their great Original proclaim.
JOSEPH ADDISON (1672–1719)
The Spectator

Lord of the Universe, glory to thee! Thou art the Self of All, thou art the maker of All, the enjoyer of All; thou art all life, and the lord of all pleasure and joy. Glory to thee, the tranquil, the deeply hidden, the incomprehensible, the immeasurable, without beginning and without end. *The Upanishads*

I would like to take a brush into my hand and write down in weighted notes "Credo in unum Deum."
LUDWIG VAN BEETHOVEN (1770–1827)
Letters

Thou art the framer of my nobler being;
Nor does there live one virtue in my soul,
One honorable hope, but calls thee father.
SAMUEL TAYLOR COLERIDGE (1772–1834)
Zapolya

Let me then not fail to praise my God continually, for it is his due, and it is all I can return for his many favours and great goodness to me; and let me resolve to be virtuous, that I may be happy, that I may please Him, who is delighted to see me happy.
BENJAMIN FRANKLIN (1706–1790)
Papers

All that has worth and dignity for man, all wherein he seeks his happiness, his glory, and his pride, finds its ultimate center in religion, in the thought, the consciousness and the feeling of God.

GEORG WILHELM FRIEDRICH HEGEL
(1770–1831)
Lectures on the Philosophy of Religion

Whatever a man offers to Me, whether it be a leaf, or a flower, or fruit, or water, I accept it, for it is offered with devotion and purity of mind.   *The Bhagavad Gita*

My religion consists of a humble admiration of the illimitable superior spirit who reveals himself in the slight details we are able to perceive with our frail and feeble minds.

ALBERT EINSTEIN (1879–1955)
On Zionism, the Land of Israel and the Arabs

O Thou, who art my soul's comfort in the
    season of sorrow,
O Thou, who art my spirit's treasure in the
    bitterness of death!
That which the imagination hath not
    conceived, that which the understanding
        hath not seen,
Visiteth my soul from thee; hence in
    worship I turn toward Thee.

JALAL-UD-DIN RUMI (1207–1273)
The Diwan

Great Spirit who puts us to sleep in
    darkness,
We thank thee for the silences of darkness.
Iroquois Indian Folklore Fire Ritual

I have no friend like God
Who gave me soul and body, and infused
    into me understanding.
He cherisheth and watcheth over all
    creatures;
He is wise and knoweth the secret of hearts.
The Guru is like a lake; we are his beloved
    swans;
In the water are many jewels and rubies.
God's praises are pearls, gems, and

diamonds; singing them maketh soul and body happy!

GURU NANAK (1469–1539)
The Adi Granth

To Thee all things offer praise:
Day and night, lightnings, snows,
The heavens and the aether, roots and
    growing things,
Beasts and birds and shoals of swimming
    fish.

SYNESIUS OF CYRENE (373–414)
Hymn

Now, God be thanked Who has matched us
    with His hour,
And caught our youth, and wakened us
    from sleeping,
With hand made sure, clear eye, and
    sharpened power,
To turn, as swimmers into cleanness leaping.
RUPERT BROOKE (1887–1915)
Collected Poems

Earth, with her thousand voices, praises God.
SAMUEL TAYLOR COLERIDGE (1772–1834)
Hymn Before Sunrise in the Vale of Chamouni

Of all the ways of awakening inner reverence in man, the best is the contemplation of the works of God. Their transcendent greatness must inspire awe.

ELIJAH DE VIDAS (16th century)
The Beginning of Wisdom

Do you not see how Allah compares a good word to a good tree? Its root is firm and its branches reach the sky; it yields its fruit in every season by Allah's leave. But an evil word is like an evil tree torn out of the earth and shorn of all its roots.   *The Koran*

O, tell us, poet, what do you do?—I praise.
But those dark, deadly, devastating ways,
how do you bear them, suffer them?—I
    praise.

And then the Nameless, beyond guess or
   gaze,
how can you call it, conjure it?—I praise.
            RAINER MARIA RILKE (1875–1926)
                            Later Poems

We are the flute, the music you,
The mountain we, which echoes you,
The chessmen set in line by you,
To win or lose now moved by you,
We are the flags embroidered with the lion,
The unseen wind which ripples us is you.
            JALAL-UD-DIN RUMI (1207–1273)
                          The Masnawi

In one salutation to thee, my God, let all
my senses spread out and touch this world at
thy feet. Like a flock of homesick cranes
flying night and day back to their mountain
nests let all my life take its voyage to its eternal home in one salutation to thee.
           RABINDRANATH TAGORE (1861–1941)
                             Gitanjali

What else can I do, a lame old man, but
sing hymns to God? If I were a nightingale, I
would do the nightingale's part; if I were a
swan, I would do as a swan. But now I am a
rational creature, and I ought to praise God:
this is my work; I do it, nor will I desert my
post, so long as I am allowed to keep it. I
exhort you to join me in this same song.
                  EPICTETUS (1st century)
                          Enchiridion

         Thou mastering me
     God! giver of breath and bread;
       World's strand, sway of the sea;
      Lord of living and dead;
Thou hast bound bones and veins in me,
    fastened me flesh,
and after it almost unmade, what with
    dread,
     Thy doing; and dost thou touch me
  afresh?
Over again I feel thy finger and find thee.
        GERARD MANLEY HOPKINS (1844–1889)
            The Wreck of the Deutschland

Hast thou not seen how all in the Heavens
and in the Earth uttereth the praise of God?
—the very birds as they spread their wings?
Every creature knoweth its prayer and its
praise! and God knoweth what they do.
                           The Koran

· TRUE FEAR COMES FROM FAITH ·

Everything comes from God except the
fear of God.   *Basque Proverb*

God planted fear in the soul as truly as he
planted hope or courage—It is a kind of bell
or gong which rings the mind into quick life
and avoidance on the approach of danger. It
is the soul's signal for rallying.
        HENRY WARD BEECHER (1813–1887)
                            Sermons

Being afraid of God is different from fear-
ing God. The fear of God is a fruit of love,
but being afraid of him is the seed of hatred.
Therefore we should not be afraid of God
but should fear him so that we do not hate
him whom we should love.
           MARTIN LUTHER (1483–1546)
                            Sermons

"Fear of God" never means to the Jews that
they ought to be afraid of God, but that,
trembling, they ought to be aware of his incomprehensibility. The fear of God is the
creaturely knowledge of the darkness to
which none of our spiritual powers can
reach, and out of which God reveals himself.
Therefore, "the fear of God" is rightly called
"the beginning of knowledge" (Psalms

111:10). It is the dark gate through which man must pass if he is to enter into the love of God. MARTIN BUBER (1878–1965)
Kampf um Israel

True fear comes from faith; false fear comes from doubt. True fear is joined to hope, because it is born of faith, and because men hope in the God in whom they believe. False fear is joined to despair, because men fear the God in whom they have no belief. The former fear to lose Him; the latter fear to find Him. BLAISE PASCAL (1623–1662)
Pensées

Where the Fearless One is, there is no fear
of others.
Where there is fear, there God is not.
KABIR (1454–1518)
Hymns

If you fear God, cast yourself into His arms, and then His hands cannot strike you.
SAINT AUGUSTINE (354–430)
Sermons

I think we honour God more if we gratefully accept the life he gives us with all its blessings, loving it and drinking it to the full, and also grieving deeply and sincerely when we have impaired or wasted any of the good things of life than if we are insensitive to life's blessings and may therefore also be insensitive to pain.
DIETRICH BONHOEFFER (1906–1945)
Letters and Papers from Prison

God: the coming one, imminent from all eternity, the future one, the final fruit of a tree whose leaves we are.
RAINER MARIA RILKE (1875–1926)
Letters to a Young Poet

Whoever lives piously with God for some time, maintains that only at that period of his life has he lived apart from evils and tasted something good, as if he had retired into his haven. MARSILIO FICINO (1433–1499)
Theologia Platonica

· I KNOW THAT MY REDEEMER LIVETH ·

I thank thee, O Lord,
because thine eyes watch over my soul;
thou hast rescued me from the jealousy of
the interpreter of lies,
from the congregation of those who seek
smooth things.
Thou hast redeemed the soul of the poor.
The Dead Sea Scrolls (100 B.C.–A.D. 100)

I know that my Redeemer liveth,
Though He be the last to arise upon earth!
For from within my skin, this has been
marked,
And from my flesh do I see God.
The Old Testament
Job 19:25–26

Perhaps this is the destined hour
When hell shall lose its fatal power

And heaven itself shall bend above
To hail the soul redeemed by love.
EMILY BRONTË (1818–1848)
Last Lines

Into the matrix of Life darkly divinely
resumed,
Man and his littleness perish, erased like an
error and cancelled,
Man and his greatness survive, lost in the
greatness of God.
SIR WILLIAM WATSON (1858–1935)
Hymn to the Sea

They that know Thy name will put their trust in Thee: for Thou, Lord, hast not forsaken them that seek Thee.
The Old Testament
Psalms 9:10

· THE SAVING GRACE ·

In the matter of man's salvation God is first. He comes to us self-invited—he names us by name—he isolates us from the crowd, and sheds upon us the sense of personal recognition—he pronounces the benediction, till we feel that there is a mysterious blessing on our house, and on our meal, and on our heart.

FREDERICK WILLIAM ROBERTSON (1816–1853)
Sermons

The world's salvation commenced in God's heart, and is contained in the throb of every human heart that carries in it the beat of the heavenly pulse. And when our work is finished, the value that we have been to the world will have to be estimated by the amount of love-deposit we have been able to leave in the treasury of the world's life.

CHARLES H. PARKHURST (1842–1933)
Sermons

Salvation is no bargain-counter product. We have to pay for it in full. Though God pays for the guilt of personal relations and freely offers to us full restoration to fellowship, we still have to pay for the consequences of our deeds in works of faith and love within the grace of God.

NELS F. S. FERRE (1908–1971)
Know Your Faith

There are countless places of refuge; there is only one place of salvation. But the possibilities of salvation are as numerous as all the places of refuge.

FRANZ KAFKA (1883–1924)
Reflections on Sin, Pain, Hope

God never draws anyone to Himself by force and violence. He wishes all men to be saved, but forces no one.

SAINT JOHN CHRYSOSTOM (345–407)
Sermons

God comes to self-expression through the regenerated individuals. Till the end of the cosmic process is achieved, the individuals retain their distinction though they possess universality of spirit.

SARVEPALLI RADHAKRISHNAN (1888–1975)
The Brahma-Sutra

He whose heart loveth God's order is said to have obtained salvation during life. He is ever happy, and is never separated from God.   GURU ARJAN (1563–1606)
Hymns

It is hard to dispel the mind's sorrow unless one reaches the feet of the incomparable God.   TIRUVALLUVAR (2nd century)
Kural

All men deserve to be saved, but he above all deserves immortality who desires it passionately and even in the face of reason.

MIGUEL DE UNAMUNO (1864–1936)
The Tragic Sense of Life

Drop down, ye heavens, from above, and let the skies pour down righteousness: let the earth open, and let them bring forth salvation, and let righteousness spring up together; I the Lord have created it.

*The Old Testament
Isaiah 45:8*

I believe that for every individual there is salvation, no matter how low he has sunk. "Have I any pleasure at all that the wicked should die? saith the Lord God; and not that he should return from his ways, and live?" (Ezekiel 8:23). The heart of man is bound with the divinity through the radiations of divinity. To the darkest and most horrible retreats to which men have withdrawn from the divinity, a ray of the divinity penetrates.

SHOLEM ASCH (1880–1957)
What I Believe

The cool, calm vigor of the normal human life; the making of the man to be himself; the

calling up out of the depth of his being and the filling with vitality of that self which is truly he—*that* is salvation.

PHILLIPS BROOKS (1835–1893)
Sermons

· THE GLORY OF HOPE ·

Hope humbly then; with trembling pinions
  soar;
Wait the great teacher death, and God
  adore.
What future bliss he gives not thee to know,
But gives that hope to be thy blessing now.
Hope springs eternal in the human breast;
Man never is, but always to be blessed.

ALEXANDER POPE (1688–1744)
Essay on Man

Behind the clouds the starlight lurks,
Through showers the sunbeams fall;
For God, who loveth all His works,
Has left His hope with all!

JOHN GREENLEAF WHITTIER (1807–1892)
A Dream of Summer

O God! we came deficient in work;
We came empty of hand, but hopeful.

SAADI (1184–1291)
Bustan

This, therefore, is the sum of it: cling to hope, let no one take that away from you; and if what we hope for may well be large, they are large matters to us; to God nothing is large before Whom "our substance is as if nothing," and before Whose eyes "a thousand years are as yesterday when it passes."

PETRARCH (1304–1374)
Secret Conflict of My Cares

Hope teaches us the art of wise forgetting; of dropping the superfluous, the outgrown,

the trivial. It cleanses the mind from all those half-realities which impede the total concentration of our love and will on God; and lifts up all the rest of our experience into the eternal light, saying: "Even though I do not see the meaning, yet I know all this is conditioning my growth, purifying my spirit, taking me towards You; and nothing matters but that.

EVELYN UNDERHILL (1875–1941)
Concerning the Inner Life

In this vale of Death, God girds us round; and over our gloom, the sun of Righteousness still shines a beacon and a hope.

HERMAN MELVILLE (1819–1891)
Moby Dick

Within us we have a hope which always walks in front of our present narrow experience; it is the undying faith in the infinite in us.

RABINDRANATH TAGORE (1861–1941)
Sadhana

This is a direct act of hope: to look through the cloud and look for a beam of the light from God.

JEREMY TAYLOR (1613–1667)
Holy Living

We are saved by hope; but hope that is seen is not hope: for what a man seeth, why doth he yet hope for? But if we hope for that we see not, then do we with patience wait for it.

The New Testament
Romans 8:24–25

Hope is the thing with feathers
That perches in the soul
And sings the tune without the words
And never stops at all.

EMILY DICKINSON (1830–1886)
Complete Poems

Hope deifies man; it is the apotheosis of the soul; the prophecy and fulfilment of her destinies.   BRONSON ALCOTT (1799–1888)
Orphic Sayings

When stern Duty wakes to watch,
Then His hand is on the latch.
But when Hope thy song doth rouse,
Then the Lord is in the house.

GEORGE MACDONALD (1824–1905)
Approaches

Be not afraid to pray—to pray is right.
   Pray, if thou canst, with hope, but ever
      pray,
Though hope be weak, or sick with long
      delay;
Pray in the darkness, if there be no light.

HARTLEY COLERIDGE (1796–1849)
Collected Poems

Through love, through hope, and faith's
   transcendent dower,
We feel that we are greater than we know.

WILLIAM WORDSWORTH (1770–1850)
After-Thought

We do not believe that the human enterprise will have a tragic conclusion; but the ground of our hope lies not in human capacity but in divine power and mercy, in the character of the ultimate reality, which carries the human experience.

REINHOLD NIEBUHR (1892–1971)
Beyond Tragedy

Faith is our longing for the eternal, for God; and hope is God's longing, the longing of the eternal, of the divine in us, which advances to meet our faith and raises us up.

MIGUEL DE UNAMUNO (1864–1936)
Essays and Soliloquies

Remembering Him who feeds
The pelican and ostrich of the desert,
From my own threshold I looked up to
      Heaven
And did not want glimmerings of quiet
      hope.

WILLIAM WORDSWORTH (1770–1850)
Collected Poems

To begin with, in action I adhere to the creative power of God; I coincide with it; I become not only its instrument but its living extension. And as there is nothing more personal in a being than his will, I merge myself, in a sense, through my heart, with the very heart of God.

PIERRE TEILHARD DE CHARDIN (1881–1955)
The Divine Milieu

· SEEKING GOD THROUGH WORSHIP ·

To worship is to quicken the conscience by the holiness of God, to feed the mind with the truth of God, to purge the imagination by the beauty of God, to open the heart to the love of God, to devote the will to the purpose of God.

WILLIAM TEMPLE (1881–1944)
The Hope of a New World

The world is imprisoned in its own activity except when actions are performed as worship of God. Therefore you must perform every action sacramentally and be free from any attachment to results.

The Bhagavad Gita

To worship in simplicity
The invisible God, and take for guide
The faith reformed and purified.

WILLIAM WORDSWORTH (1770–1850)
The White Doe of Rylestone

Lord! of the men who serve Thee—true in
   heart—
As God revealed; and of the men who serve,
Worshipping Thee unrevealed, Unbodied,
   Far,
Which take the better way of faith and life?

The Bhagavad Gita

Verily, this whole world is Brahma. Tranquil, let one worship it as that from which he came forth, as that unto which he will be dissolved, as that in which he breathes.

The Upanishads

The worship of God is: Honouring His gifts in other men, each according to his genius, and loving the greatest men best; those who envy or calumniate great men hate God, for there is no other God.

WILLIAM BLAKE (1757–1827)
The Marriage of Heaven and Hell

All true prayer is worship—the ascription of worth to the Eternal. Without adoration, thanksgiving may become a miserliness, petition a selfish clamor, intercession a currying of special favors for our friends, and even contemplation may turn into a refined indulgence.

GEORGE ARTHUR BUTTRICK (1892–1979)
Prayer

Be ours a religion which, like sunshine, goes everywhere; its temple, all space; its shrine, the good heart; its creed, all truth; its ritual, works of love; its profession of faith, divine living.

THEODORE PARKER (1810–1860)
Sermons

The well-spring of social unity and spiritual love in the mystical worship of the God of love should never be forgotten. Religious worship, alone of all the forces known to man, is able to perform that miracle of pity and of hope which enables him who has seen God to see not his fellow worshipers only, but all mankind, as a potential Community of Love. That miracle, I say, for the natural man lacks this vision, and the presence of traces of such a feeling toward the human race is almost universally regarded as a token of the presence and work of God in the life of man.

EDGAR S. BRIGHTMAN (1884–1953)
Religious Values

When a man says "I ought"—when love warms him—when he chooses, warmed from on high, the good and great deed—then deep melodies wander through his soul from Supreme Wisdom; then he can worship, and be enlarged by his worship, for he can never go behind this sentiment.

RALPH WALDO EMERSON (1803–1882)
Collected Essays

O People of the Book! Let us now come to agreement upon a noble principle common to all of us, namely, that we shall not worship anything but God, that we shall not associate anyone with Him, and that we shall not take one another for lords beside God.

The Koran

Repentance is not a free and fair highway to God. God prefers that you approach Him thoughtful, not penitent, though you are the chief of sinners. It is only by forgetting yourself that you draw near to Him.

HENRY DAVID THOREAU (1817–1862)
Journals

Joy shall be in heaven over one sinner that repenteth, more than over ninety and nine just persons, which need no repentance.

The New Testament
Luke 15:7

Repentance waiteth patiently at all times for the sons of men. When can a man be purified of iniquity? When he returneth to the King on High, and uttereth prayer from the depths of his heart, as Scripture saith: Out of the depths I call unto Thee.

The Zohar

· SONGS OF REVERENCE ·

The One who rules over every source,
in whom the world coheres and dissolves,
the Lord, giver of blessings, adorable God—
by revering him one goes to peace forever.

The Upanishads

Reverence for God is the thread upon which the various good qualities of men are strung like pearls. When this string is severed, the pearls scatter in all directions and are lost one by one.

JUDAH IBN KALAAZ (16th century)
Sefer ha-Musar

Two things draw me to reverence: the starry heaven above and the moral law within.   IMMANUEL KANT (1724–1804)
Metaphysical Foundations of Natural Science

He who knows God reverences Him.

LUCIUS ANNAEUS SENECA (4 B.C.–A.D. 65)
Epistolae morales ad Lucilium

The more completely a man lives, the more largely alive he is in every part of him—in brain, and heart, and hands—the more completely he will comprehend the magnitude of life, and stand in reverence before the Power that moves and governs it.

PHILLIPS BROOKS (1835–1893)
The Battle of Life

After the lights of inspirations have rayed out and their mysteries have been deposited, do not seek their continuance, for you have in God one who enables you to dispense with everything; but nothing enables you to dispense with God.

IBN 'ATA'ILLAH (died 1309)
Kitab Al-Hakim

God sent his Singers upon earth
With songs of sadness and mirth,
That they might touch the hearts of men,
And bring them back to heaven again.

HENRY WADSWORTH LONGFELLOW
(1807–1882)
The Singers

Thou knowest my tongue, O God,
Fain would it bring a precious gift—
The songs thou makest me sing!

SOLOMON IBN GABIROL (1021–1058)
The Crown of the Kingdom

I will sing with knowledge,
And all my music shall be for the glory of
    God;
my lyre and harp shall be for his holy fixed
    order,
and the flute of my lips I shall raise in his
    just circles.

The Dead Sea Scrolls (100 B.C.–A.D. 100)

God! sing, ye meadow-streams, with
    gladsome voice!
Ye pine-groves, with your soft and soul-like
    sounds!
And they too have a voice, yon piles of
    snow,
And in their perilous fall shall thunder,
    God!

SAMUEL TAYLOR COLERIDGE (1772–1834)
Hymn Before Sunrise in the Vale of Chamouni

IV · The Attributes of God

Should I not call God the Beautiful,
Who daily showeth himself so to me in his
gifts?
RALPH WALDO EMERSON

THE GOD SEEKERS are only too well aware of their limitations in putting into words or any other symbol an all-encompassing definition or representation of God. Perhaps not so much out of a feeling of frustration, but rather out of piety and awe and love for the Divine Force that created the universe and all who dwell in it, the God Seekers contemplate the totality of the Creator in terms of attributes they feel can best personify him, concepts such as his beauty, his eternality, his magnitude, and his mercy.

John Ruskin wrote that we ought to be happy when we consider "how much more beauty God has made, than human eyes can ever see." To Balzac, beauty was nothing less than the signature of God written on the work in which He has put his soul. In "Fra Lippo Lippi," Robert Browning looked at "the beauty and the wonder and the power, the shapes of things, their colours, lights and shades, changes, surprises" and marveled at the thought that God made it all. Yet, as Maurice Maeterlinck observed in *The Treasure of the Humble*, although this beauty and grandeur are everywhere and plainly visible to all people, it seems that "only when fortune or death lashes them do they grope around the wall of life in search of the crevices through which God may be seen."

Father Gerald Vann, the contemporary English priest who explored with sensitivity the entire spectrum of our link with God, must surely have loved John Keats' familiar lines: "A thing of beauty is a joy forever: its loveliness increases; it will never pass into nothingness." As Vann explains in *The Divine Pity,* what to us may seem only a fleeting moment of beauty is always present in God. If we are to reach the fullest range of our spiritual sensibilities, Vann tells us, we must strive to understand the permanence of God's beauty, and "to have, under all the pain that time inflicts, a deep sense of the abidingness of things."

In the attempt to describe God, no symbol appears more often in the varied scriptures of the world's religions than that of light. We have noted its dramatic role in the theophanies of some of the greatest prophets—Moses, Zoroaster, Gautama Buddha, Saint Paul, to name only a few. Poets as diverse as Dante, Jalal-ud-din Rumi, Angelus Silesius, and Alfred Lord Tennyson also have symbolized the Creator in terms of light. Shelley, in one of his most felicitous poetic images, refers to "that Light whose smile kindles the Universe." Milton, in *Paradise Regained,* maintained that anyone who received light from above, from God, the fountain of light, would need no other doctrine.

Meister Eckhart speaks of an uncreated and uncreatable light that is in our souls, a light that discloses "God unveiled and unmanifested as He is in Himself." This is reiterated by Johannes Tauler, who refers to God's supernatural, divine light shining into the deepest recesses of a man's heart. To Benjamin Whichcote, the leader of the seventeenth-century Cambridge Platonists, the soul per se is the candle of God, a candle that He has lit and placed within each of us.

Another dominant theme in this section is that God and truth are one and the same. Saint Augustine, in his *Confessions,* said, "For where I found truth, there I found my God, who is Truth itself." Frederick William Robertson, whose sermons were among the most widely read throughout the nineteenth century, also felt that God is truth, and "to be true, to hate every form of falsehood, to live a brave, true, real life—that is to love God." Meister Eckhart was so certain of this that he claimed, "If God were able to backslide from truth, I would prefer to cling to truth and let God go." The great German dramatist Gotthold Lessing voiced this bold notion in a similar way: "If God should hold enclosed in his right hand all truth, and in his left hand only the ever-active impulse after truth, although with the condition that I must always and forever err, I would with humility turn to his left hand and say, 'Father, give me this: pure truth is for Thee alone.' "

To Mohandas Gandhi, everything that has been created is a spark of truth and the sum of these sparks, although indescribable, is nothing less than the "as-yet-unknown Truth, which is God." Moreover, noting that he had never found a double meaning in connection with truth, and that not even atheists demurred to its necessity and power, Gandhi concluded, "I saw that rather than say God is Truth I should say Truth is God."

The founder of Hasidism, Israel ben Eliezer, known as the Baal Shem Tov, during one of his discourses quoted Psalm 85, "Truth shall spring out of the earth," and then asked his listeners, "Surely it must be easy to find Truth?" Answering his own question, he added, "Yes, it is easy, but no one wants to bend down; no one is willing to stoop to pick up a little Truth."

"I believe that only in broken gleams has the Sun of Truth yet shown on men," is the way Helen Keller put it in *The Open Door.* She envisioned the day when love would establish the Kingdom of God on earth, a kingdom whose cornerstones would be truth, liberty, brotherhood, and service.

In describing God's magnitude, another major theme in this section, William Ralph Inge, dean of London's Saint Paul's, paraphrased what the Greek philosopher Empedocles had observed in the fifth century B.C. In Inge's words, "God, whose center is everywhere and His circumference nowhere, cannot be fitted into a diagram." In every grand religious scripture, from the Rig-Veda and Upanishads of India, the Adi Granth of the Sikhs, the Old and New Testaments, and the Koran, we find the God Seekers declaring their wonderment and awe at the inconceivable immensity, the incalculable complexity of God.

Thomas Carlyle, in his *Sartor Resartus,* pictured God as the author of "a mighty drama, enacted on the theater of Infinitude, with suns for lamps, and Eternity as a background." When Archbishop Fénelon looked at the sky above him with its countless number of stars, he wondered, what if all these stars were worlds like the earth we inhabit? If, indeed, this were so, Fénelon said, "how wise and powerful must be He who has made worlds as innumerable as the grains of sand on the sea-shore, and who has led on in order, for so many ages, all these moving worlds, as a shepherd leads his flocks." Miguel de Unamuno, the Spanish philosopher and writer, expressed the same thought when he compared our planetary system to a mere molecule in the Milky Way, itself only a cell in the body of God.

Mark Twain was no less overwhelmed with the magnitude of God; in a letter to a friend he wrote, "How insignificant we are—with our pigmy little world!—an atom glinting with uncounted myriads of other atom worlds in a broad shaft of light streaming from God's countenance—and yet prating complacently of our speck as the Great World." Walt Whitman echoed Twain's wonderment at God's infinitude in an entry in his *Notebooks:*

All the vastness of Astronomy—and space—and systems of suns, carried in their computation to the farthest that figures are able, and then multiplied in geometrical progression ten thousand billion fold, do no more than symbolize the reflection of the reflection, of the spark thrown off a spark, from some emanation of God.

One problem that the God Seekers have always tried to solve is, in Rufus Jones' words, "to see the eternal in the midst of time, to feel and to enjoy the infinite here in the finite." Our latest scientific theories hypothesize that our *observable* universe is approximately eighteen billion years old. Whether this present universe is the only one that God created is a matter that has not been definitively settled. Whenever we try to put a time-space continuum on the Creator, who existed before these manmade definitions, we are stretching our knowledge to the breaking point.

Meister Eckhart believed that nothing so much hinders a spiritual knowledge of God as being mired in the time-space enigma: "The Now-moment in which God made the first man and the Now-moment in which the last man will disappear, and the Now-moment in which I am speaking are all one in God, in whom there is only one Now."

John Wesley, in his treatise *On Eternity,* observed that "if we consider boundless space, or boundless duration, we shrink into nothing before it." He asks us to remember that God is not a man or woman, and least of all some kind of gigantic computer that invented itself, and that a day, a minute, or even a microsecond and millions of ages, are the same with him.

In the two hundred years since Wesley's death the science of astronomy has developed to the point where today our powerful telescopes can survey the Milky Way galaxy, which we share with possibly a hundred billion other stars. The magnitude of God's creativity is further demonstrated when we consider that there may be a billion galaxies with as many stars in each of them as in our own.

To the agnostic mind as well as to those who profess atheism, it seems audacious, illogical, and impossible to conceptualize a God who is the fountainhead of this incalculable creativity—a God who maintains a link with his children on this little dot in the universe among several quadrillion stars. These modern scientific discoveries would not have dismayed Wesley, who would reiterate his faith and tell us, "Whenever you are tempted to fear lest you should be forgotten before the immense, the eternal God, remember that nothing is little or great, that no duration is long or short, before Him."

Sir Thomas Browne urges us not to be too concerned with the fact that few humans will spend even as much as one hundred years in this world, for the world itself is not so ancient. In *Christian Morals* he wrote, "The created world is but a small parenthesis in eternity and a short interposition, for a time, between such a state of duration as was before it and may be after it."

The God Seekers' perception of time in relation to eternity was epitomized by Richard Jefferies, the nineteenth-century English natural philosopher, who wrote in his *Story of My Heart* that his soul had never been, nor could ever be, dipped in time. To him, as to Meister Eckhart six hundred years before, "It is eternity now, it always was eternity, and always will be. By no possible means could I get into time if I tried."

Throughout history the various prophets have been saddened as they looked at the manner in which most of the people around them negated their God-endowed spirituality. Not that they exclude themselves, for the true God Seekers know that they, too, are, in Nietzsche's phrase, *menschliches, allzumenschliches* (human, all too human). They know only too well how strong earthly passions can grip them.

The same David who probably wrote some of that great poetry of the spirit known as the Psalms was also the world-weary king who lusted after the wife of one of his generals. Fighting an incessant battle within his own heart, the David who aspired to be "a leafy olive-tree in the house of God" was also the David who usurped Bathsheba after a single glance.

God is always sending us messages about his attributes: in the physical beauty of the world we see a glimpse of eternal beauty; in the vast compass of the stars we see a glimpse of unending magnitude. To the Hebrews of the early kingdoms, to men like David, God revealed yet another of his qualities, that He is the source of mercy and compassion. This attribute became a very important one among the Jewish, Christian, and Moslem God Seekers.

Henry Ward Beecher, although mindful and appreciative of God's power, wisdom, and justice, held these in less awe than love and mercy, which "are God's peculiar glory." John Donne, in one of his sermons from Saint Paul's altar, went even further, saying: "Let the Devil make me so far desperate as to conceive a time when there was no mercy, and he hath made me so far an Atheist, as to conceive a time when there was no God."

There is an Irish proverb that God never shuts one door without opening another. As this world approaches the final minutes on the ticking nuclear clocks, as we watch ourselves being swept into the vortex of an Armageddon that will make even the horrors of Revelation 16:16–20 seem like a mild nightmare, we need more than ever to believe that God will open another door. A door named sanity and reason is beckoning to the power-brokers of the world. It is a deathly sobering thought that today several men, the leaders of the United States and the Soviet Union, hold in their hands the power to unleash a devastating force that could destroy every human being in the world, themselves included.

Yet, as Rabindranath Tagore, the noble heir of thousands of years of Hindu philosophical wisdom and perspective, said in his book *Stray Birds:* "Every child comes with the message that God is not yet discouraged of man." Meister Eckhart recalled that the Psalmist tells us that the compassion of God is over all his works. Eckhart added, "It does not say *in* all his works, as though it went *with,* but *over* all his works, because it goes ahead and overtops them."

God, with eternal compassion and mercy for all He has created out of his infinite Self, has given us the messages through his prophets and messengers. But He also created us with the freedom to choose life over death for this planet.

If, in our world paranoia, we destroy all of humanity, God may in a few billion years allow a new breed of men and women to inhabit a detoxified Earth, and perhaps a new band of God Seekers will find his attributes of beauty, mercy, and compassion. On that day God, who sees all, hears all, and remembers everything, may recall the words of his servant, Isaiah: "For ye shall go out with joy, and be led forth with peace: the mountains and the hills shall break forth before you into singing, and all the trees of the field shall clap their hands."

· THE BEAUTY, THE WONDER, THE POWER ·

O tender God, if Thou art so loving in Thy creatures, how fair and lovely must Thou be in Thyself!   HENRY SUSO (1300–1366)
Horologium Sapientae

If you get simple beauty and nought else,
You get about the best thing God invents.
     ROBERT BROWNING (1812–1889)
Fra Lippo Lippi

Our Creator would never have made such lovely days, and have given us the deep hearts to enjoy them, above and beyond all thought, unless we were meant to be immortal.   NATHANIEL HAWTHORNE (1804–1864)
Mosses from an Old Manse

Some souls lose all things but the love of
     beauty;
And by that love they are redeemable;
For in love and beauty they acknowledge
     good;
And good is God—the great Necessity.
     PHILIP JAMES BAILEY (1816–1902)
Festus

Divinely superfluous beauty
Rules the games, presides over destinies,
     makes trees grow
And hills tower, waves fall.
The incredible beauty of joy.
     ROBINSON JEFFERS (1887–1962)
Divinely Superfluous Beauty

In the house of long life, there I wander.
In the house of happiness, there I wander.
Beauty before me, with it I wander.
Beauty behind me, with it I wander.
Beauty below me, with it I wander.
Beauty above me, with it I wander.
In old age traveling, with it I wander.
On the beautiful trail I am, with it I wander.
     Navajo Indian Chant

In beauty surpassing
     the Universe smiled,
On the morn of its birth,
     like an innocent child,
Or like the rich bloom
     of some delicate flower;
And the Father rejoiced
     in the work of His power.
     JOHN CARDINAL NEWMAN (1801–1890)
The Queen of Seasons

You ought to be glad in thinking how much more beauty God has made, than human eyes can ever see; but not glad in thinking how much more evil man has made, than his soul can ever conceive—much more, than his hands can ever heal.
     JOHN RUSKIN (1819–1900)
Ethics of the Dust

Spirit of Beauty, that dost consecrate
     With thine own hues all thou dost shine
          upon
Of human thought or form.
     PERCY BYSSHE SHELLEY (1792–1822)
Hymn to Intellectual Beauty

Oh, Beauty, old yet and ever new!
     Eternal Voice and Inward Word.
     JOHN GREENLEAF WHITTIER (1807–1892)
The Shadow and the Light

Beholding this Being—resting, rapt, in the vision and possession of so lofty a loveliness, growing to Its likeness—what beauty can the soul yet lack? For This, the Beauty supreme, the absolute and the primal, fashions Its lovers to Beauty and makes them also worthy of love.   PLOTINUS (205–270)
Enneads

Whoever takes a walk in the month of Nissan and beholds the blossoming trees should say, "Blessed art Thou Who hast made Thy world lacking in naught, and produced therein goodly creatures and lovely trees to give delight to the children of men."

The Talmud

You've seen the world—
The beauty and the wonder and the power,
The shapes of things, their colors, lights and
  shades,
Changes, surprises—and God made it all.

ROBERT BROWNING (1812–1889)
Fra Lippo Lippi

Flowers may beckon toward us, but they speak toward heaven and God.

HENRY WARD BEECHER (1813–1887)
Sermons

The Infinite has written its name on the heavens in shining stars, and on the earth in tender flowers.

JEAN PAUL RICHTER (1763–1825)
Hesperus

Flowers beyond reach are sacred to God.

Tamul Proverb

Beauty is a terrible and frightening thing. It is terrible because it has not been fathomed, and can't be fathomed, for God makes nothing but riddles. In this one, extremes meet and contraries lie down together.   NIKOLAI BERDYAEV (1874–1948)
Dostoevski

Some thoughts always find us young, and keep us so. Such a thought is the love of the universal and eternal beauty.

RALPH WALDO EMERSON (1803–1882)
The Over-Soul

I am certain of nothing but the holiness of the heart's affections and the truth of imagination—what the imagination seizes as beauty must be truth—whether it existed before or not.   JOHN KEATS (1795–1821)
Letter to Benjamin Bailey

In the long run if we think about the cosmos at all, we surrender either to its beauty or its ugliness, making one basic and the other ephemeral. . . . To surrender to the ugliness of the world our cosmic outlook seems to me as irrational as it is disheartening. Doubtless, the final truth takes both the beauty and the terror in and, in that comprehensive view which no human mind is large enough to grasp, I am confident that the secondary element will not be beauty.

HARRY EMERSON FOSDICK (1878–1969)
As I See Religion

We talked of the beauty of this world of God's and of the great mystery of it. Every blade of grass, every insect, ant and golden bee, all so amazingly know their path, though they have not intelligence, they bear witness to the mystery of God and continually accomplish it themselves.

FYODOR DOSTOEVSKY (1821–1881)
The Brothers Karamazov

Shall I not call God the Beautiful, who daily showeth himself to me in his gifts?

RALPH WALDO EMERSON (1803–1882)
Friendship

One thing have I admired of the Lord, that will I seek after; that I may dwell in the house of the Lord all the days of my life, to behold the beauty of the Lord, and to enquire in His temple.   *The Old Testament*
Psalms 27:4

Let the beauty of the Lord our God be upon us.   *The Old Testament*
Psalms 90:17

Behind the veil of self shines unseen the beauty of the Loved One.   *Persian Saying*

God passes through the thicket of the world, and wherever His glance falls He turns all things to beauty.

SAINT JOHN OF THE CROSS (1542–1591)
The Spiritual Canticle

The laws, the life, and the joy of beauty in the material world of God, are as eternal and sacred parts of His creation as, in the world of spirits, virtue; and in the world of angels, praise.
JOHN RUSKIN (1819–1900)
Modern Painters

What is all beauty in the world? The image, like quivering boughs reflected in a stream, Of that eternal Orchard which abides Unwithered in the hearts of Perfect Men.
JALAL-UD-DIN RUMI (1207–1273)
The Diwan

One music maketh its occult abode
In all things scatter'd from great
Beauty's hand;
And evermore the deepest words of God
Are yet the easiest to understand.
SIR WILLIAM WATSON (1858–1935)
Epigrams

Look at the rainbow and praise its Maker;
it shines with a supreme beauty,
rounding the sky with its gleaming arc,
a bow bent by the hands of the Most
High.
The Old Testament Apocrypha
Ecclesiasticus 43:11–12

Beauty crowds me till I die,
Beauty, mercy have on me!
But if I expire today,
Let it be in sight of thee.
EMILY DICKINSON (1830–1886)
Collected Poems

What God has resolved concerning me I know not, but this at least I know: he has instilled into me a vehement love of the beautiful.
JOHN MILTON (1608–1674)
Letter to Charles Diodati

God expects answers for the flowers he sends us, not for the sun and the earth.
RABINDRANATH TAGORE (1861–1941)
Stray Birds

O world, as God has made it! All is beauty:
And knowing this, is love, and love is duty.

What further may be sought for or declared?
ROBERT BROWNING (1812–1889)
The Guardian Angel

For the world is not painted or adorned, but is from the beginning beautiful; and God has not made some beautiful things, but Beauty is the creator of the universe.
RALPH WALDO EMERSON (1803–1882)
The Poet

Beauty is a pledge of the possible conformity between the soul and nature, and consequently a ground of faith in the supremacy of the good.
GEORGE SANTAYANA (1863–1952)
The Sense of Beauty

Ask the loveliness of the earth, the loveliness of the sea, the loveliness of the wide airy spaces, the loveliness of the sky, the order of the stars, the sun making the day light with its rays; ask the moon tempering the darkness of the night that follows, the living things which move in the waters, which tarry on land, which fly in the air; ask the souls that are hidden, the bodies that are perceptible; the visible things which must be governed, the invisible things which govern— ask all these things, and they will all answer thee, See, we are lovely. Their loveliness is their confession. And these lovely but immutable things, who has made them, save Beauty immutable?
SAINT AUGUSTINE (354–430)
Sermons

There can be no doubt but that everything in the world, by the beauty of its order, and the evidence of a determinate and beneficial purpose which pervades it, testifies that some supreme efficient Power must have pre-existed, by which the whole was ordained for a specific end.
JOHN MILTON (1608–1674)
A Treatise on Christian Doctrine

Beholding beauty with the eye of the mind brings forth, not images of beauty, but realities nourishing true virtue, to become the friend of God and be immortal.

PLATO (427–347 B.C.)
Symposium

I will say to him, "Hear me, almighty Lord ... You may decide about me according to your own judgment. But from this day on I shall build only what is most beautiful on earth."   HENRIK IBSEN (1828–1906)
The Master Builder

If God had been here this summer, and seen the things I have seen—I guess he would think His Paradise superfluous. Don't tell Him for the world, though, for after all He's said about it, I should like to see what He was building for us, with no hammer, and no stone, and no journeyman either.

EMILY DICKINSON (1830–1886)
Letters

The prophet Zechariah has a strange verse in which he tells how he brought the people who were entrusted to him to the Lord—"I took unto me two staves; the one I called Beauty and the other I called Bands." Beauty and Bands, Beauty and Duty, so God rules the world! He would rather tempt us with His beauty than bind us with His bands; it is better to be urged on by the inspirations than to be driven by the compulsions of holiness.

PHILLIPS BROOKS (1835–1893)
The More Abundant Life

In eternity without beginning, a ray of thy beauty began to gleam, when Love sprang into being, and cast flames over all nature.

HAFIZ (14th century)
The Diwan

Thou dost fashion the beauty of form
Through Thyself alone.
For Thou art the Lord of the day at its
   zenith.
And Thou art in my heart.

IKHNATON (14th century B.C.)

By God! when He showed me His beauty,
Whatever else I beheld appeared to me
   fancy.

SAADI (1184–1291)
Bustan

· GOD DWELLS IN LIGHT ·

And being thence admonished to return to myself, I entered even into my inward self, Thou being my Guide: and able I was, for Thou wert become my Helper. And I entered and beheld with the eye of my soul (such as it was), above the same eye of my soul, above my mind, the Light Unchangeable.   SAINT AUGUSTINE (354–430)
Confessions

God dwells in light which no man can approach unto.   *The New Testament*
1 Timothy 6:16

O thou immortal light and heat!
Whose hand so shines through all this
      frame,
That by the beauty of the seat,
We plainly see, who made the same.
      Seeing thy seed abides in me,
      Dwell thou in it, and I in thee.

HENRY VAUGHAN (1622–1695)
Cock Crowing

Shouldst thou come with the whole of thy being to God and be attracted to the lights of the Kingdom of God and be enkindled by the fire of the love of God, then wilt thou see that which thou canst not see today, wilt comprehend the inner significance of the Word of God and thoroughly understand the mysteries contained in the holy Books.

ABDU'L BAHA (1844–1921)
The Loom of Reality

Light, God's eldest daughter, is a principal beauty in a building.

THOMAS FULLER (1608–1661)
Holy State

O everlasting Light, surpassing all created luminaries, flash forth Thy lightning from above, piercing all the most inward parts of my heart. Make clean, make glad, make bright and make alive my spirit, with all the powers thereof, that I may cleave unto thee in ecstasies of joy.

THOMAS À KEMPIS (1380–1471)
Imitation of Christ

That Light whose smile kindles the
  Universe.
That Beauty in which all things work and
  more . . .

PERCY BYSSHE SHELLEY (1792–1822)
Adonais

Who in this mortal life would see
The Light that is beyond all light,
Beholds it best by going forth
Into the darkness of the Night.

ANGELUS SILESIUS (1624–1677)
The Cherubic Wanderer

Light, my light, the world-filling light, the eye-kissing light, heart-sweetening light.

RABINDRANATH TAGORE (1861–1941)
Gitanjali

But I lose
Myself in Him, in Light ineffable!
Come then, expressive Silence, muse His
  praise.
These, as they change, Almighty Father,
  these

Are but the varied God. The rolling year
Is full of Thee.

JAMES THOMSON (1700–1748)
Hymn

This is the light of lights; when it shines, the sun does not shine.

When Brahman shines, everything shines after him, by his light all the world is lighted.

The Mundaka Upanishad

Arise, arise!
And like old cloths fold up these skies,
This long worn veil: then shine and spread
Thy own bright self over each head,
And through thy creatures pierce and pass
Till all becomes thy cloudless glass.

HENRY VAUGHAN (1622–1695)
L'Envoy

The Divine Light is always in man, presenting itself to the senses and to the comprehension, but man rejects it.

GIORDANO BRUNO (1548–1600)
A Philosophy of the Infinite Universe

He that saith he is in the light, and hateth his brother, is in darkness even until now. He that loveth his brother abideth in the light, and there is none occasion of stumbling in him. If a man say, I love God, and hateth his brother whom he hath seen, how can he love God whom he hath not seen?

The New Testament
1 John 2:9–11; 4:20

God is the Light of the Heavens and the Earth. The similitude of His Light is as it were a niche wherein is a lamp, the lamp within a glass, the glass as though it were a pearly star. It is lit from a Blessed Tree, an olive-tree neither of the East nor the West, the oil whereof were like to shine even though no fire were applied to it; Light upon Light; God guideth to His Light whom He will.

The Koran

They are on the way to truth who apprehend God by means of the divine, Light by
the light.   PHILO JUDAEUS (30 B.C.–A.D. 40)
In Time and Eternity

Many times have I spoken of that un-
created and uncreateable Light that is in the
soul. It is this Light that discloses God unveiled and unmanifested as He is in himself;
indeed, it discloses him in his act of Self-affir-
mation.   MEISTER ECKHART (1260–1327)
German Works

God is light, that is, God is truth and verity
itself, for verity is spiritual light.
                WALTER HILTON (died 1396)
The Ladder of Perfection

The morn of blessedness hath dawned.
Morn? No, 'tis the light of God.
                JALAL-UD-DIN RUMI (1207–1273)
The Diwan

There is a light above, which visible
Makes the Creator unto every creature,
Who only in beholding Him has peace,
And it expands itself in circular form
To such extent, that its circumference
Would be too large a girdle for the sun.
                        DANTE (1265–1321)
The Divine Comedy

And God said, "Let there be light"; and
there was light. And God saw that the light
was good; and God separated the light from
the darkness.   *The Old Testament*
Genesis 1:3

Love's community is like the light of God;
whatever being we possess, from its existence
is derived.

                MAHOMED IQBAL (1873–1938)
Mysteries of Selflessness

The eye is the lamp of the body. So, if your
eye is sound, your whole body will be full of
light, but if your eye is not sound, your whole

body will be full of darkness. If then the light
in you is darkness, how great is the darkness.
                        The New Testament
Matthew 6:22–23

Lead, kindly Light, amid the encircling
    gloom;
Lead thou me on!
The night is dark, and I am far from home;
Lead thou me on!
            JOHN CARDINAL NEWMAN (1801–1890)
The Pillar of the Cloud

God stooping shows sufficient of his light
For us i' the dark to rise by. And I rise.
                ROBERT BROWNING (1812–1889)
The Ring and the Book

O you great Light who shines in the
    heavens,
You strengthen the generations of men with
    the Nile-flood
And you cause gladness in all lands, and in
    all cities, and
in all the temples.

                        The Book of the Dead

Images appear to man, but the light which
is in them is hidden in the image of the Father's light. He will reveal himself; His image
is concealed by the light.
            The Gospel According to Thomas
(4th century)

Our faith is a light, kindly coming from
our endless Day that is our Father God.
                JULIAN OF NORWICH (1343–1416)
Revelations of Divine Love

The heavenly Father wishes that we should
see, because He is a Father of light. And
therefore He speaks eternally, without mean
and without ceasing, in the secret places of
our spirit, one single unfathomable word and
nothing more. And in this word He enunci-
ates Himself and all things. And this word is
nothing else than "See."

                JAN VAN RUYSBROECK (1293–1381)
The Spiritual Espousals

If we consider Him in Himself, He dwells in inaccessible light (I Tim., 6:16). His peace surpasses all that can be imagined (Philip., 4:1). His wisdom does not have boundaries, nor His grandeur limits, and no man is able to see Him in this life (Exod., 33:29).

SAINT BERNARD OF CLAIRVAUX (1091–1153)
Canticle of Canticles

He who first filled space with lights through
  Mind,
Who through his Will created
  Righteousness,
Whereby he maintains the Good Mind—
You have increased this, O Wise One, by
  your Spirit
Which is one with you, O Lord!

ZOROASTER (6th century B.C.)
asna 31:8

Through love to light! Through light, O
  God, to thee,
Who art the love of love, the eternal light of
  light!

RICHARD WATSON GILDER (1844–1909)
The Celestial Passion

O God, as all our light is from Thee, the Father of lights, so make me no niggard of that poor rush-candle thou hast lighted in my soul; make me more happy in giving light to others than in receiving it into myself.

JOSEPH HALL (1574–1656)
On the Sight of a Dark Lantern

We cannot see divine things but in a divine light; God only, who is the true light, and in whom there is no darkness at all, can so shine out of himself upon our glassy understandings, as to beget in them a picture of himself, his own will and pleasure, and turn the soul, as the phrase is, like wax or "clay to the seal" of his own light and love.

JOHN SMITH (1616–1652)
Discourses

There is a Divine Light which shines into the very deeps of a man's heart, a supernatural Light.

JOHANNES TAULER (1300–1361)
Sermons

The spirit in man is the candle of the Lord, lighted by God, and lighting men to God.

BENJAMIN WHICHCOTE (1609–1683)
Discourses

He that in the beginning thus thought, "Let the blessed realms be filled with lights," he it is that by his wisdom created Right. Those realms that the Best Thought shall possess thou dost prosper, Mazdah, by thy spirit, which, O Ahura, is ever the same.

ZOROASTER (6th century B.C.)
Gathas

The Light of the World is a light that is saturated with the darkness which it has overcome and transfigured.

FELIX ADLER (1851–1933)
Sermons

Whoever has in him the human quality, whoever really has the spirit of man, may be a candle of the Lord. A larger measure of that spirit may make a brighter light; but there must be a light wherever any human being, in virtue of his humanness, by obedience becomes luminous with God.

PHILLIPS BROOKS (1835–1893)
Sermons

"Let there be Light!" said God; and
  forthwith Light
Ethereal, first of things, quintessence pure,
Sprung from the deep.

JOHN MILTON (1608–1674)
Paradise Lost

The light of God in the heart of man is the source of his freedom, and the spirit of man is the candle of the Lord.

GERALD A. KENNEDY (1907–)
Who Speaks for God?

Arise, shine; for thy light is come, and the glory of the Lord is risen upon thee. For, behold, the darkness shall cover the earth, and gross darkness the people: but the Lord shall arise upon thee, and his glory shall be seen upon thee.   *The Old Testament*
Isaiah 60:1–3

My light, the Torah, says God to man, is in thy hand; but thy light, the soul, is in my hand. Take care of my light, so that I may take care of thy light.   *The Midrash*

Let us concentrate as much as we can, and call upon the everlasting light to enlighten our darkness, so that we may see the image of God in ourselves, insofar as we are permitted.   SAINT AUGUSTINE (354–430)
On the Trinity

And anxious hearts have pondered here
    The mystery of life,
And prayed the eternal Light to clear
    Their doubts, and aid their strife.
          RALPH WALDO EMERSON (1803–1882)
Hymn

There is a light deposited in hearts that is nourished by the Light coming from the treasuries of the invisible realms.
          IBN 'ATA'ILLAH (died 1309)
The Book of Wisdom

If, as David professes, "the light of God's countenance more gladdens the heart than corn and wine," then, surely, they that draw nearest, and most behold it, must be fullest of these joys.   RICHARD BAXTER (1615–1691)
The Saints' Everlasting Rest

O Father, touch the east, and light
The light that shone when Hope was born.
          ALFRED LORD TENNYSON (1809–1892)
In Memoriam

It is one light which beams out of a thousand stars. It is one soul which animates all men.   RALPH WALDO EMERSON (1803–1882)
The American Scholar

Driving away evil with thy light, Agni, shine upon us—driving away evil with thy light.   *The Rig-Veda*

God is Light, and in him is no darkness at all; He is Love by nature and there is no hatred in his Essence.
          THOMAS TRAHERNE (1637–1674)
Christian Ethics

O light, in whose unbounded deeps unshook I saw the dispers'd things of space and time ingather'd all by love, as in a book.
          DANTE (1265–1321)
Paradiso

Where the ray of God's light shall fall upon my path, there will I walk and in his strength perform without inquietude the work that his providence shall set before me.
          FRANÇOIS FÉNELON (1651–1715)
Maximes des Saints

I saw that there was an ocean of darkness and death, but an infinite ocean of Light and Love which flowed over the ocean of darkness.   GEORGE FOX (1624–1691)
Journal

The riches of the Light are the Works of God which are the portion and inheritance of His sons, to be seen and enjoyed in Heaven and Earth, the Sea, and all that is therein: the Light and the Day, great and fathomless in use and excellency, true, necessary, freely given, proceeding wholly from His infinite love.   THOMAS TRAHERNE (1637–1674)
Centuries of Meditations

Of God's light I was not utterly bereft; if my as yet sealed eyes, with their unspeakable longing, could nowhere see Him, nevertheless in my heart He was present, and his heaven-written Law still stood legible and sacred there.   THOMAS CARLYLE (1795–1881)
Sartor Resartus

For I say that all the lights which shine from the Supreme Light, the Most Concealed of All, are all paths leading toward that Light.
The Kabbalah

Know the light, the eternal light of life, the little glimmerings and shinings of it in thy soul. This comes from the rock, to lead thee to the rock; and if thou wilt follow it, it will fix thee upon the rock where thou canst not be shaken.
ISAAC PENNINGTON (1616–1679)
Works

The people that walked in darkness have seen a great light: they that dwell in the land of the shadow of death, upon them the light hath shined.
The Old Testament
Isaiah 9:2

Ye that be turned to the Light walk in the Light that never changeth. Ye may come to see that which was in the beginning before the world was, where there is no shadow nor darkness.
GEORGE FOX (1624–1691)
Epistles

The true light is that Eternal Light which is God; or else it is a created light, but yet divine, which is called grace.
Theologia Germanica

Our whole teaching is nothing else than how man should kindle in himself God's light in the world.
JACOB BOEHME (1575–1624)
Six Theosophic Points

If the light is
It is because God said, "Let there be light."
DANTE GABRIEL ROSSETTI (1828–1882)
At Sunrise

And all creation is one act at once,
The birth of light.
ALFRED LORD TENNYSON (1809–1892)
The Princess

We feel thy calm at evening's hour,
Thy grandeur in the march of night;
And when the morning breaks in power,
We hear thy words, "Let there be light."
SAMUEL LONGFELLOW (1819–1892)
God of the Earth, the Sky, the Sea

"Let there be light" is the perpetual demand of Truth and Love, changing chaos into order and discord into the music of the spheres.
MARY BAKER EDDY (1821–1910)
Science and Health

When I sit in darkness, the Lord shall be a light unto me.
The Old Testament
Micah 7:8

For thou wilt light my candle: the Lord my God will enlighten my darkness.
The Old Testament
Psalms 18:28

From within or from behind, a Light shines through us upon things and makes us aware that we are nothing, but the Light is all. The little eating, sleeping, counting man we do not admire, but when the Light shines through him, then every knee bends.
RALPH WALDO EMERSON (1803–1882)
The Over-Soul

The world would be darker than it is if every human spirit, so soon as it became obedient, did not become the Lord's candle. A poor, meager, starved, bruised life, if only it keeps the true human quality and does not become inhuman, and if it is obedient to God in its blind, dull, half-conscious way, becomes a light.
PHILLIPS BROOKS (1835–1893)
Sermons

It is with man's Soul as it was with Nature: the beginning of Creation is—Light. Till eye have vision, the whole members are in bonds. Divine moment, when over the tempest-tost

Soul, as once over the wild-weltering Chaos,
it is spoken: Let there be Light!

THOMAS CARLYLE (1795–1881)
Sartor Resartus

We thank Thee for the stars wherewith Thou hast spangled the raiment of darkness, giving beauty to the world when the sun withdraws his light. All this magnificence is but a little sparklet that has fallen from Thy presence, Thou Central Fire and Radiant Light of all! These are but reflections of Thy wisdom, Thy power, and Thy glory!

THEODORE PARKER (1810–1860)
Sermons

To me every hour of the light and dark is a
    miracle,
Every cubic inch of space is a miracle.

WALT WHITMAN (1819–1892)
Miracles

In Great Eternity every particular Form
    gives forth or Emanates
Its own peculiar Light; and the Form is the
    Divine Vision
And the Light is his Garment. This is
    Jerusalem in every Man,
A tent and Tabernacle of Mutual
    Forgiveness.

WILLIAM BLAKE (1757–1827)
Jerusalem

Thou art the light hidden in this world and revealed in the world of beauty, "In the mount of the Lord it shall be seen" (Genesis 22:14).

Thou art the eternal light, and the inward eye yearns for Thee and is astonished—she shall see but the utmost part of them, and shall not see them all.

SOLOMON IBN GABIROL (1021–1058)
The Crown of the Kingdom

He who receives
Light from above, from the Fountain of
    Light,

No other doctrine needs, though granted
true.

JOHN MILTON (1608–1674)
Paradise Regained

The sunbeams, infinitely small,
    In numbers numberless,
Reveal, pervade, illumine all
    Nature's void wilderness:
But, meeting worlds upon their way,
    Wrapt in primeval night,
In language without sound, they say
    To each—"God sends you light!"

JAMES MONTGOMERY (1771–1854)
Songs of Zion

He sends forth the light, and it goes on its way; he called it, it feared him and obeyed. The stars shone at their appointed stations and rejoiced; he called them and they answered, "We are here!" Joyfully they shone for their Maker.

The Old Testament Apocrypha
Baruch 3:33–35

That Good which is above all light is called a Spiritual Light, because it is an Originating Beam and an Overflowing Radiance, illuminating with its fullness every Mind above the world around it or within it, and renewing all their spiritual powers.

DIONYSIUS THE AREOPAGITE (5th century)
Mystical Theology

We look, with blind eyes like a mole, on the majesty of God, and after that light which is shown neither in words nor miracles, but is only signified; out of curiosity and wilfulness we would behold the highest and greatest light of the celestial sun ere we see the morning star. Let the morning star, as St. Peter says, go first up in our hearts, and we shall see the sun in his noon-tide splendor.

MARTIN LUTHER (1483–1546)
Table-Talk

If the ray from the divine being touched us all, it would appear in us everywhere; not our words alone, but our deeds as well, would have the glow and luster of it. Whatever proceeded from us would be seen to be illuminated by this noble light.

MICHEL EYQUEM DE MONTAIGNE (1533–1592)
Apology for Raimond Sebond

When God said, "Let there be Light, and there was Light," no change happened to eternal light itself, nor did any light then begin to be; but the darkness of this world then only began to receive a power or operation of the eternal light upon it, which it had not before; or eternity then began to open some resemblance of its own glory in the dark elements and shadows of time.

WILLIAM LAW (1686–1761)
The Spirit of Love

The first creature of God, in the work of the days, was the light of the sense; the last was the light of reason; and His Sabbath work ever since is the illumination of His Spirit. First He breathed light upon the face of the matter, or chaos; then He breathed light into the face of man; and still He breatheth and inspireth light into the face of His chosen. FRANCIS BACON (1561–1626)
Of Truth

O light eternal who only in thyself abidest, only thyself dost understand, and to thyself, self-understood, self-understanding, turnest love and smiling! DANTE (1265–1321)
Paradiso

The light which is in everything is thine, O Lord of light. From its brilliancy everything is brilliant. GURU NANAK (1469–1539)
The Sohila

God is in me the fire, and I in Him the light,
Do we not with each other in deepest bonds unite?

ANGELUS SILESIUS (1624–1677)
The Cherubic Wanderer

If high in the heavens suddenly from a
thousand suns

Light flamed, its radiance would be like the
Lofty One's splendor.
The universe standing as one, and yet
manifoldly divided,
The son of Pandu saw in the body of the
God of gods.

The Bhagavad Gita

For thou art my lamp, O Lord; and the Lord will lighten my darkness.

*The Old Testament
2 Samuel 22:29*

Who in this mortal life would see
The Light that is beyond all light,
Beholds it best by faring forth
Into the darkness of the Night.

ANGELUS SILESIUS (1624–1677)
The Cherubic Wanderer

Thou who createst light where there was no light, and form, O men! where there was no form, hast been born together with the dawns. *The Rig-Veda*

When you have accepted the Light, O
beloved,
When you behold what is veiled without a
veil,
Like a star you will walk upon the heavens.

JALAL-UD-DIN RUMI (1207–1273)
The Masnawi

I have kindled the light, I have woven the star-strewn path. *The Book of the Dead*

All things are God's, not as being in His power—that of course—but as coming from Him. The darkness itself becomes light around Him when we think that verily He hath created the darkness, for there could have been no darkness but for the light.

GEORGE MACDONALD (1824–1905)
Unspoken Sermons

The lights of great cities go out, and there is a howling darkness to all appearance. But always since men began, the light of the pure

God-knowing human consciousness has kept alight.   D. H. LAWRENCE (1885–1930)
On Human Destiny

On that effulgent power which is God himself, and is called the Light of the radiant Sun, do I meditate; governed by the mysterious light which resides in me for the purposes of thought.   *The Rig-Veda*

In the midst of the sun is the light, in the midst of the light is truth, and in the midst of truth is the imperishable being.
The Rig-Veda

God is the light of all lights and luminous beyond all the darkness of our ignorance. He is knowledge and the object of knowledge.
The Bhagavad Gita

Do you not seek a light, ye who are surrounded by darkness?   *The Dhammapada*

At the end of woe suddenly our eyes shall be opened, and in clearness of light our sight shall be full; which Light is God.
JULIAN OF NORWICH (1343–1416)
Revelations of Divine Love

He that knows the Truth, knows what that Light is; and he that knows It, knows eternity. Love knows it. O Truth who art Eternity! and Love Who art Truth! and Eternity Who art Love! Thou art my God, to Thee do I sigh night and day.
SAINT AUGUSTINE (354–430)
Confessions

This is nature's nest of boxes: the heavens contain the earth; the earth, cities; cities, men. And all these are concentric; the common centre to them all is decay, ruin; only that is eccentric which was never made; only that place rather, which we can imagine but not demonstrate. That light, which is the very emanation of the light of God . . . only that bends not to this centre, to ruin.
JOHN DONNE (1572–1631)
Meditations

The Scriptures say: "And God said: 'Let there be light'; "and there was light." It would have sufficed to say: "And it was so." Why this repetition? In order to show us that light will once more shine on the world at the end of time.   *The Zohar*

He that has an eye and a heart can even now say: Why should I falter? Light has come into the world; to such as love Light, so as Light must be loved, with a boundless all-doing, all-enduring love.
THOMAS CARLYLE (1795–1881)
Characteristics

For with Thee is the fountain of life; in Thy light do we see light.
The Old Testament
Psalms 36:10

A steady light, swifter than thought, is stationed among the moving things, to show the way; all the devas of one mind and like wisdom proceed devoutly to that one intelligence. My ears strain to hear, my eyes to see this all-spreading light lodged within my spirit.   *The Rig-Veda*

Mind, thou art a Spark of Divine Light, so grasp the True Source of thy being.
GURU AMAR DAS (1479–1574)
Hymns

Rabbi Isaac said: At the Creation, God irradiated the world from end to end with the light, but then it was withdrawn, so as to deprive the sinners of the world of its enjoyment, and it is stored away for the righteous, as it stands written, "Light is sown for the righteous" (Psalms 97:11); then will the worlds be in harmony and all will be united into one, but until the future world is set up, this light is put away and hidden.
The Zohar

Patience! Truth! Obedience!
Be thou soul transparent! so the Light

Thou seekest, may enshrine itself within
    thee!
    SAMUEL TAYLOR COLERIDGE (1772–1834)
                         Zapolya

Blow, winds of God, awake and blow
    The mists of earth away;
Shine out, O Light Divine, and show
    How wide and far we stray!
    JOHN GREENLEAF WHITTIER (1807–1892)
                      Our Master

The light of the moral law glows from a
remote and unknown realm. Humanity has
always moved only in the glow of a *divine
light*.
    PETER YAKOVLEVICH CHAADAYEV (1794–1856)
                        Letters

One effort more, my altar this bleak sand;
That Thou O God my life has lighted,
With ray of light, steady, ineffable,
    vouchsafed of Thee
Light rare untellable, lighting the very light,
Beyond all signs, descriptions, languages.
    WALT WHITMAN (1819–1892)
                  Prayer to Columbus

· THE DOOR OF THE TRUE ·

True thinking can take place only in the
contact between the naked mind and the
naked reality which confronts it. If God be
really the Truth, then in that contact lies
His perfect opportunity. But how often is
it offered to Him?
    JOHN BAILLIE (1886–1960)
                Invitation to Pilgrimage

Truth in a man's imagination is the power
to recognize this truth of a thing; and wherever, in anything that God has made, in the
glory of it, be it sky or flower or human face,
we see the glory of God, there a true imagination is beholding a truth of God.
    GEORGE MACDONALD (1824–1905)
                Unspoken Sermons

Of all kinds of knowledge that we can ever
obtain, the knowledge of God and the knowledge of ourselves are the most important.
    JONATHAN EDWARDS (1703–1758)
                Freedom of Will

To know God and to live are one and the
same thing.   LEO TOLSTOY (1828–1910)
                My Religion

Let us lie low in the Lord's power, and
learn that truth alone makes rich and great.
    RALPH WALDO EMERSON (1803–1882)
                Spiritual Laws

To seek life in truth, then, is to seek, in the
cult of truth, to ennoble and elevate our spiritual life and not to convert truth, which is
and always must be living, into a dogma,
which usually is dead.
    MIGUEL DE UNAMUNO (1864–1936)
                Perplexities and Paradoxes

We love God only with the knowledge with
which we know Him, and as is the measure
of the knowledge, so is the measure of the
love: if little, little; if much, much.
    MAIMONIDES (1135–1204)
                Guide for the Perplexed

If a man would nourish himself on truth,
God gives him enough of it, and that is his
nourishment. God owes us our nourishment
and gives it to us in the form in which we
ourselves desire it. If we desire it in the form
of lies, even truth becomes lies in us, and we
live like liars. For God gives the liars their

nourishment just as He gives it to the truthful. He must nourish all of us, whether we be good or evil, just as he makes provision for the sun, the earth, and all creation.

PARACELSUS (1493–1541)
Works

There is for every man a statement possible of that truth which he is most unwilling to receive—a statement possible, so broad and pungent, that he cannot get away from it, but must either bend to it or die of it.

RALPH WALDO EMERSON (1803–1882)
Journal

The door of the True is covered with a golden disk. Open that, O Pushan, that we may see the nature of the True.

The Upanishads

Fight to the death for truth, and the living God will fight on your side.

*The Old Testament Apocrypha
Ecclesiasticus 4:28*

The truth of God has to run the gauntlet of all other truths. It is on trial by them and they on trial by it. Our *final* opinion about God can be settled only after all the truths have straightened themselves out together.

WILLIAM JAMES (1842–1910)
Pragmatism

In its deepest sense, *the truth* is a condition of heart, soul, mind, and strength towards God and towards our fellow—not an utterance, not even a *right* form of words; and therefore such truth coming forth in words is, in a sense, the person that speaks.

GEORGE MACDONALD (1824–1905)
Unspoken Sermons

Mercy and truth are met together; righteousness and peace have kissed each other. Truth shall spring out of the earth; and righteousness shall look down from heaven.

*The Old Testament
Psalms 80:10–11*

The soul is the ship, reason is the helm, the oars are the soul's thoughts, and truth is the port.

Turkish Proverb

The relation between the mind and matter is not fancied by some poet, but stands in the will of God, and so is free to be known by all men.   RALPH WALDO EMERSON (1803–1882)
Nature

The most ignorant among mankind have some truth in them. We are all sparks of Truth. The sum total of these sparks is indescribable, as-yet-Unknown-Truth, which is God.   MOHANDAS K. GANDHI (1869–1948)
Contemporary Indian Philosophy

The more I know of my subjectivity, the more it remains obscure to me. If I were not known to God, no one would know me. No one would know me in my truth, in my own existence. No one would know me—*me*—as subject.   JACQUES MARITAIN (1882–1973)
Existence and the Existent

The only perfect homage that can be rendered to God is the homage of truth. The kingdom of God, whose advent is mechanically exhorted every day by millions of tongues defiled by lies, is none other than the kingdom of truth.

MIGUEL DE UNAMUNO (1864–1936)
What Is Truth?

Only when men shall roll up the sky like a hide, will there be an end of misery, unless God has first been known.

The Upanishads

Man as man cries for God. He cries not for a truth, but for *truth*; not for *something* good but *the* good; not for answers but *the* answer—the one that is identical with its own question. *Man* himself is the real question, and if the answer is to be found in the *question*, he must find answer in himself: he must be the answer.

KARL BARTH (1886–1968)
The Word of God and the Word of Man

The most effective kind of prayer is that in which we place ourselves, in our hearts, before God, relinquishing all resistance, letting go of all secret irritation, opening ourselves to the truth, to God's holy mystery, saying over and over again, "I desire truth, I am ready to receive it, even this truth which causes me such concern, if it be the truth. Give me the light to know it—and to see how it bears on me."

ROMANO GUARDINI (1885–1968)
The Faith and Modern Man

God's truth may slip into men's hearts without their knowing it; it may seem to be there only in a little piece, for example in silent humility of the heart, in a nameless longing of the mind, in the resignation with which a man accepts the silent dispositions of Fate in spite of her refusal to justify them.

KARL RAHNER (1904–)
Meditations on the Sacraments

Men never *make* truths; they only recognize the value of this currency of God. They find truths, as men sometimes find bills, in the street, and only recognize the value of that which other persons have drawn.

HENRY WARD BEECHER (1813–1887)
Sermons

When the truth shines out in the soul, and the soul sees itself in the truth, there is nothing brighter than that light or more impressive than that testimony. And when the splendour of this beauty fills the entire heart, it naturally becomes visible, just as a lamp under a bowl or a light in darkness are not there to be hidden.

SAINT BERNARD OF CLAIRVAUX (1091–1153)
Sermons

The body of all Truth dies; and yet in all, I say, there is a soul which never dies; which in new and ever-nobler embodiment lives immortal as man himself! It is the way with Nature. The genuine essence of Truth never dies. That it be genuine, a voice from the great Deep of Nature, there is the point at Nature's judgment seat.

THOMAS CARLYLE (1795–1881)
Mohammed and Mohammedanism

Truth is like light: visible in itself, not distinguished by the shadows that it casts. There is something in our souls of God, which corresponds with what is of God outside us, and recognizes it by direct intuition: something in the true soul which corresponds with truth and knows it to be truth.

FREDERICK WILLIAM ROBERTSON (1816–1853)
Sermons

If there were no obscurity, man would not be sensible of his corruption; if there were no light, man would not hope for a remedy. Thus, it is not only fair, but advantageous to us, that God be partly hidden and partly revealed; since it is equally dangerous to man to know God without knowing his own wretchedness, and to know his own wretchedness without knowing God.

BLAISE PASCAL (1623–1662)
Pensées

We are made in His image to witness Him;
And were no eye in us to tell,
Instructed by no inner sense,
The light of Heaven from the dark of Hell,
That light would want its evidence.

ROBERT BROWNING (1812–1889)
Christmas Eve

Why dost thou prate of God? Whatever thou sayest of Him is untrue.

MEISTER ECKHART (1260–1327)
Works

If God should hold enclosed in his right hand all truth, and in his left hand only the ever-active impulse after truth, although with the condition that I must always and forever err, I would with humility turn to his left hand and say, "Father, give me this: pure truth is for thee alone."

GOTTHOLD EPHRAIM LESSING (1729–1781)
Anti-Gotze

Servant of God, well done! well hast thou
  fought
The better fight, who single hast maintain'd
Against revolted multitudes the cause
Of truth.

JOHN MILTON (1608–1674)
Paradise Lost

The Divine Truth proceeding from the Lord in the heavens appears as light, and constitutes all the light of heaven.

EMMANUEL SWEDENBORG (1688–1772)
The Divine Providence

No one can arrive at a knowledge of the Lord without knowing his own soul, his own mind, and body; for what wisdom can he possess who does not know himself?

RABBI BEN EZRA (1092–1167)
Commentaries

Truth is like a vast tree which yields more and more fruit, the more you nurture it. The deeper the search in the mine of Truth, the richer the discovery of the gems buried there in the shape of opening for an ever greater variety of service.

MOHANDAS K. GANDHI (1869–1948)
Autobiography

God has a seal, and his seal is truth.

The Midrash

Hast thou wonder at the travelers of the
  path of God,
That they should be immersed in the sea of
  Truth?

SAADI (1184–1291)
Bustan

When the awareness of God comes in— how He entered, one does not know—one is certain that He has been there all the time.   HOWARD THURMAN (1899–1981)
Meditations of the Heart

No thought that ever dwelt honestly as true in the heart of man but was an honest insight into God's truth on man's part, and has an essential truth in it which endures through all changes, an everlasting possession for us all.   THOMAS CARLYLE (1795–1881)
On Heroes and Hero-Worship

The one essential condition of human existence is that man should always be able to bow down before something infinitely great. If men are deprived of the infinitely great they will not go on living and will die of despair. The Infinite and the Eternal are as essential for man as the little planet on which he dwells.

FYODOR DOSTOEVSKY (1821–1881)
The Devils

To get at the core of God at his greatest, one must first get into the core of himself at the least, for no one can know God who has not first known himself. Go to the depths of the soul, the secret place of the Most High, to the roots, to the heights; for all that God can do is focused there.

MEISTER ECKHART (1260–1327)
Works

If it is the knowledge of God that first gives us our human comradeship and its varied and satisfying responsiveness, the God who is the bearer of that responsiveness is not himself without response. These comrades are in a measure God's organs of response, even as Nature is God's announcement of his presence and individuality: but God has also a responsiveness of his own, and herein lies the immediate experience of the personality of God.

WILLIAM EARNEST HOCKING (1873–1966)
The Meaning of God in Human Experience

Within the cave of the mind is an
  inexhaustible treasure;
Within it resides the unknowable, Infinite,
He who Himself is manifest, unmanifest,
Yea, through the Lord's word, one loseth
  one's Self and knoweth Him.

GURU NANAK (1469–1539)
The Adi Granth

Man does not know himself truly except as
he knows himself confronted by God. Only
in that confrontation does he become aware
of his full stature and freedom and of the evil
in him.   REINHOLD NIEBUHR (1892–1971)
The Nature and Destiny of Man

We may never in all the ages comprehend
God, but the quality of God's life is present
everywhere. The sensitive soul responds to
its influence as the plant turns to the sunlight
and as flowers open to the morning dew. As
we speak of life being geotropic—orienting
itself to gravity—and heliotropic—orienting
itself to light—so we should speak of it as
theotropic—orienting itself to the divine.

JOHN ELOF BOODIN (1869–1950)
God: A Cosmic Philosophy of Religion

True and substantial wisdom principally
consists of two parts, the knowledge of God,
and the knowledge of ourselves. But, while
these two branches of knowledge are so intimately connected, which of them precedes
and produces the other, is not easy to discover.   JOHN CALVIN (1509–1564)
Institutes of the Christian Religion

The fact that the prophets equated knowledge with love and that it occurred to them
to speak of love in connection with an unapproachable God would remain inexplicable
were it not for their insight that it takes more
than knowledge to "know" God.

HERMANN COHEN (1842–1918)
Jewish Writings

All knowledge that begins not, and ends
not with God's glory, is but a giddy, but a
vertiginous circle, but an elaborate and exquisite ignorance.

JOHN DONNE (1572–1631)
Sermons

If a man has learnt the true goal of his
being and is seeking to open his heart to God
so that God may dwell in him and he in God,
he knows that he has all Time before him in
which to explore the riches of the Divine
Love which to all ages he never will exhaust.

WILLIAM TEMPLE (1881–1944)
Christus Veritas

The Truth shines in its full effulgence, and
we know ourselves—for samadhi lies potential in us all—for what we truly are, free, immortal, omnipotent, loosed from the finite,
and its contrasts of good and evil altogether,
and identical with the Atman or Universal
Soul.   SWAMI VIVEKANANDA (1863–1902)
Raja Yoga

Let him who can, hear you inwardly as you
speak to us. I will cry out boldly in words
from your oracle: "How great are your
works, O Lord; you have made all things in
wisdom!"   SAINT AUGUSTINE (354–430)
Confessions

Truth sees God, and wisdom contemplates
God, and of these two comes the third, and
that is a marvellous delight in God, which is
love. Where truth and wisdom are, truly
there is love, truly coming from them both,
and all are of God's making.

JULIAN OF NORWICH (1343–1416)
Showings

The dawn is not distant,
Nor is the night starless;
Love is eternal!
God is still God, and
His faith shall not fail us.

HENRY WADSWORTH LONGFELLOW
(1807–1882)
Tales of a Wayside Inn

God is the immediate certitude without which there is no other, the primordial light, the language we know without having learned it. He is the only one whom we cannot look for in vain, yet we can never find him fully.

MAURICE BLONDEL (1861–1949)
L'Action

He who has no intellectual cognition at all of God is like one who is in darkness and has never seen light, just as explained with regard to the dictum: "The wicked shall be put to silence in darkness."

MAIMONIDES (1135–1204)
Guide for the Perplexed

Knowledge of God takes place where there is actual experience that God speaks, that He so represents Himself to man that he cannot fail to see and hear Him, where, in a situation which he has not brought about, in which he becomes incomprehensible to himself, man sees himself faced with the fact that he lives with God and God with him, because so it has pleased God.

KARL BARTH (1886–1968)
Dogmatics in Outline

God, who, in His simple substance is all everywhere equally, nevertheless, in efficacy, is in rational creatures in another way than in the irrational, and in good rational creatures in another way than in the bad. He is in irrational creatures in such a way as not to be comprehended by them; by all rational creatures, however, He can be comprehended by knowledge; but only by the good is He also comprehended by love.

SAINT BERNARD OF CLAIRVAUX (1091–1153)
The Steps of Humility

Not to live and move and have the being in God is to be entirely ignorant of Him. If this natural feeling, this inner consciousness is lost amid a mass of sense impressions and desires, no religion has yet entered the narrow sense.

FRIEDRICH SCHLEIERMACHER (1768–1834)
On Religion

There is an absolute truth about everything, something which is certainly the fact about that thing, entirely independent of what you and I or any man may think about it. No man on earth may know that fact correctly—but the fact exists. It lies behind all blunders and partial knowledge, a calm, sure, unfound certainty, like the great sea beneath its waves, like the great sky behind its clouds. God knows it. It and the possession of it makes the eternal difference between God's knowledge and man's.

PHILLIPS BROOKS (1835–1893)
The Battle of Life

There is hardly ever a complete silence in our soul. God is whispering to us wellnigh incessantly. Whenever the sounds of the world die out in the soul, or sink low, then we hear these whisperings of God. He is always whispering to us, only we do not always hear, because of the noise, hurry and distraction which life causes as it rushes on.

FREDERICK WILLIAM FABER (1814–1863)
Sermons

We look to thee! thy truth is still the Light
Which guides the nations on their way.
Stumbling and falling in disastrous night,
Yet hoping ever for the perfect day.

THEODORE PARKER (1810–1860)
Hymns

God is Truth. To be true, to hate every form of falsehood, to live a brave, true, real life—that is to love God.

FREDERICK WILLIAM ROBERTSON (1816–1853)
Sermons

All truth must be God's, intuitively or without the discursive process by which the human understanding mostly works; so that truth may be said to belong to his nature, whereas for man it is something to be attained.

WILLIAM RITCHIE SORLEY (1855–1935)
Moral Values and the Idea of God

As regards God, if my mind were not preoccupied with prejudices, and if my thought did not find itself on all hands diverted by the continual pressure of sensible things, there would be nothing which I could know more immediately and more easily than Him. For is there anything more manifest than that there is a God, that is to say, a Supreme Being, to whose essence alone existence pertains?

RENÉ DESCARTES (1596–1650)
Meditations

Let not kindness and truth forsake thee;
Bind them about thy neck,
Write them upon the tablet of thy heart.
Then shalt thou find favor and good esteem
In the sight of God and man.

Hebrew Proverb

Truth does not, and cannot, come from ourselves. In all that is spiritual it comes from God, or from those spirits, the friends of God, on whom His light has placed it.

JOSEPH JOUBERT (1754–1824)
Pensées

It is written, "For God is light"—not the light seen by these eyes of ours, but that which the heart sees upon hearing of the words "He is Truth."

SAINT AUGUSTINE (354–430)
On the Trinity

This is Truth—eternal Reason—
That in Beauty takes its dress,
And, serene through time and season,
Stands complete in Righteousness.

JOHANN WOLFGANG VON GOETHE
(1749–1832)
Complete Verse

Men who are living here are in a dream,
And when they die then shall they be
awake;
For all this world is a mere thought—the
thought
Of Him who is the True, whose thought is
Truth.

The Hadith

We are rising to the conviction that we are a part of nature, and so a part of God; that the whole creation—the One and the Many and All-One—is travailing together toward some great end; and that now, after ages of development, we have at length become conscious portions of the great scheme, and can cooperate in it with knowledge and joy.

SIR OLIVER LODGE (1851–1940)
*Suggestions Toward the Reinterpretation
of Christian Doctrine*

The world rests upon three things: upon truth, upon justice, and upon peace. All these three are really one, for when justice is done the truth becomes an actuality, peace a reality.

The Talmud

While grasping eternal truth, ideas get into the whirlpool of consideration, and thus are raised to the sphere of pure spirit and arrive at the realm of high sublimity where the souls are resting in the shadow of Divine Majesty.

HUNEIN IBN ISHAK (809–873)
The Sayings of the Philosophers

The truth of God could be known in a great many ways. Although God is a single essence which consists of no diversity of parts or of accidents, still the Apostle says in the plural: "the invisible things of God," because the truth of God is known in many ways through things which have been made.

PETER LOMBARD (1100–1160)
Four Books of Sentences

It is clear that God is truth itself, for what can He have which appears to be and is not, He who is being itself?

GIOVANNI PICO DELLA MIRANDOLA
(1463–1494)
On Being and One

Walk in the Truth and the love of it up to God.   GEORGE FOX (1624–1691)
Epistles

All those who labor in the discovery and communication of truth, if they are actuated by a love of it and a sense of its importance to the happiness of mankind may consider themselves as workers together with God.

JOSEPH PRIESTLEY (1733–1804)
Notes on All the Books of Scriptures

Insofar as it knows the eternity of truth and is absorbed in it, the mind lives in that eternity. In caring only for the eternal, it has ceased to care for that part of itself which can die.   GEORGE SANTAYANA (1863–1952)
The Ethics of Spinoza

To say that God exceeds the powers of our comprehension is not to say that we do not know God. We know empirically the actual, present, dynamic working of creativity in our midst, progressively creating, saving and transforming the personality of man when required conditions are present. Therefore we know God and know him more intimately than any other, because he is so deeply involved in our existence. But to know God thus does not mean that we can construct in our imagination a picture of him or comprehend the depth and fullness of his being.

HENRY NELSON WIEMAN (1884–1975)
Intellectual Foundation of Faith

Man is a being who overcomes his limitations, transcends to something higher. If there is no God, as Truth and Meaning, if there is no higher Justice, then everything flattens out, and there is neither any one nor any thing to which man can rise.

NIKOLAI BERDYAEV (1874–1948)
The Realm of Spirit and the Realm of Caesar

Every man has some kind of religion: that is, a supreme Truth by which he measures all his judgments—a supreme Will by which he measures all his endeavors.

FRIEDRICH HEINRICH JACOBI (1743–1819)
Christianity and Paganism

The truth can neither be communicated nor be received except as it were under God's eyes, not without God's help, not without God's being involved as the middle term, He himself being the Truth.

SÖREN KIERKEGAARD (1813–1855)
Point of View

I don't care what they say with their mouths—everybody knows that *something* is eternal. And it ain't houses and it ain't names, and it ain't earth, and it ain't stars—everybody knows in their bones that *something* is eternal, and *that* something has to do with human beings. All the greatest people ever lived have been telling us that for five thousand years and yet you'd be surprised how people are always losing hold of it. There's something way down deep that's eternal about every human being.

THORNTON WILDER (1897–1975)
Our Town

Truth, crushed to earth, shall rise again:
  Th' eternal years of God are hers;
But Error, wounded, writhes in pain,
  And dies among his worshippers.

WILLIAM CULLEN BRYANT (1794–1878)
The Battle-Field

The name of God is Truth.

Hindu Proverb

We are born to inquire after truth; it belongs to a greater power to possess it. It is not, as Democritus said, hid in the bottom of the deeps, but rather elevated to an infinite height in the divine knowledge.

MICHEL EYQUEM DE MONTAIGNE (1533–1592)
On the Art of Conversation

This world is all a fleeting show,
  For man's illusion given;
The smiles of joy, the tears of woe,
Deceitful shine, deceitful flow—
  There's nothing true but Heaven.

THOMAS MOORE (1779–1852)
Sacred Songs

In God's own might,
We gird us for the coming fight,
And, strong in him, whose cause is ours
In conflict with unholy powers,
We grasp the weapons He has given—
The Light, the Truth, and Love of Heaven.

JOHN GREENLEAF WHITTIER (1807–1892)
The Quaker Alumni

There is an absolute truth about everything; it lies behind all blunders and all partial knowledges, a calm, sure, unfound certainty, like the great sea beneath its waves, like the great sky behind its clouds. God knows it. It and the possession of it makes the eternal difference between God's knowledge and man's. It is a beautiful and noble faith when a man thus believes in the absolute truth, unfound, unfindable perhaps by man, and yet surely existent behind and at the heart of everything.

PHILLIPS BROOKS (1835–1893)
Sermons

There is knowledge and knowledge: knowledge that resteth in the bare speculation of things, and knowledge that is accompanied with the grace of faith and love, which puts a man upon doing even the will of God from the heart.

JOHN BUNYAN (1628–1688)
The Pilgrim's Progress

Fight to the death for truth,
and the Lord God will fight on your side.

The Old Testament Apocrypha
Ecclesiasticus 4:28

Once to every man and nation comes the
  moment to decide,
In the strife of Truth with Falsehood, for
  the good or evil side.

JAMES RUSSELL LOWELL (1819–1891)
The Present Crisis

The participation that we have in knowledge of the truth, such as it is, it is not by our own powers that we have acquired it. God has taught us that plainly enough by the simple and ignorant witnesses he has chosen from the common people, who instruct us concerning his wonderful secrets; our faith is not our own acquisition; it is a pure gift from the liberality of another.

MICHEL EYQUEM DE MONTAIGNE (1533–1592)
Apology for Raimond Sebond

Truth never yet fell dead in the streets; it has such affinity with the soul of man, the seed however broadcast will catch somewhere and produce its hundredfold.

THEODORE PARKER (1810–1860)
A Discourse of Matters Pertaining to Religion

He who knows the part which the Heavenly in him plays, and also knows that which the human in him ought to play, has reached the perfection of knowledge.

CHUANG-TZU (died c. 300 B.C.)
Works

Let not the authority of him that writeth, whether he be of great name or little, change thy thought, but let the love of pure truth draw thee to the love of God.

THOMAS À KEMPIS (1380–1471)
Imitation of Christ

Truth all religion comprehends, in truth alone is justice placed, in truth the words of God are based.

> VALMIKI (3rd century B.C.)
> *The Ramayana*

The search for divine truth is like gold washing; nothing is of any value until most has been swept away.

> H. G. WELLS (1866–1946)
> *God the Invisible King*

God blesses still the generous thought,
    And still the fitting word He speeds,
And Truth, at His requiring taught,
    He quickens into deeds.

> JOHN GREENLEAF WHITTIER (1807–1892)
> *Channing*

God's truth judges created things out of love, and Satan's truth judges them out of envy and hatred. God's truth has become flesh in the world and is alive in the real, but Satan's truth is the death of all reality.

> DIETRICH BONHOEFFER (1906–1945)
> *Ethics*

Weakness never need be falseness: truth is
    truth in each degree,
Thunder-pealed by God to Nature,
    whispered by my soul to me.

> ROBERT BROWNING (1812–1889)
> *La Saisiaz*

But what is truth? T'was Pilate's question put To Truth itself, that design'd him no reply.

> WILLIAM COWPER (1731–1800)
> *The Task*

"Where art thou, O man?" our ideal says to us. "Art thou not in God? To whom dost thou speak? With whom dost thou walk? What life is this in whose midst thou livest? What are all these things that thou seemest to touch? All this is in God and of God. Thou hast never seen, or heard, or touched, or handled, or loved anything but God. Know this truth, and thy life must be transformed to thee in all its significance. Serve the whole God, not the irrationally separate part that thy delusions have made thee suppose to be an independent thing. Live out thy life in its full meaning; for behold it is God's life."

> JOSIAH ROYCE (1855–1916)
> *The Religious Aspect of Philosophy*

For where I found truth, there I found my God, Who is Truth itself.

> SAINT AUGUSTINE (354–430)
> *Confessions*

The Truth in God's breast
Lies trace upon trace on ours impressed:
Though he is so bright, and we so dim,
We are made in his image to witness him.

> ROBERT BROWNING (1812–1889)
> *Poetical Works*

It is absolutely necessary to conclude that God exists; for though the idea of substance be in my mind owing to this, that I myself am a substance, I should not, however, have the idea of an infinite substance, seeing I am a finite being, unless it were given me by some substance in reality infinite.

> RENÉ DESCARTES (1596–1650)
> *Meditations*

For me truth is the sovereign principle, the Absolute Truth, the Eternal Principle, that is God. Though the path of relative truth is straight and narrow, even my Himalayan blunders have seemed trifling, for daily the conviction is growing that He alone is real and all else is unreal.

> MOHANDAS K. GANDHI (1869–1948)
> *Autobiography*

The student of nature, if his studies have not been barren of the best fruit of the investigation of nature, will have enough sense to see that when Spinoza says: "By God I understand a being absolutely infinite, that is, a substance consisting of infinite attributes," the God so conceived is one that only a very great fool would deny even in his heart.

THOMAS HENRY HUXLEY (1825–1895)
Evolution and Ethics

Roused from every inquisitive indecision, as from a dream, by one glance at the wonders of nature and the majesty of the cosmos, reason soars from height to height till it reaches the highest; from the conditioned to conditions, till it reaches the supreme and unconditioned Author of all.

IMMANUEL KANT (1724–1804)
Critique of Pure Reason

The mind's highest good is the knowledge of God, and the mind's highest virtue is to know God.

BENEDICT SPINOZA (1632–1677)
Of Human Bondage

Wherever there is response in the hearts of men to the manifested glory of God, whether that manifestation be in nature or in history, there the Spirit of Truth is at work.

WILLIAM TEMPLE (1881–1944)
Daily Readings

Him who is without beginning and without
    end, in the midst of confusion,
The Creator of all, of manifold form,
The One embracer of the universe—
By knowing God one is released from all
    fetters.

The Upanishads

One of the supreme hours of human experience arrives when a man gets his eye on something concerning which he is persuaded that it is the eternal truth.

HARRY EMERSON FOSDICK (1878–1969)
A Great Time to Be Alive

Because Spirit, God, works in our midst and in our depths, we can and we do know Him; because God has been the first to con-

descend to us and to love us, we can arise and love him in return.

FRIEDRICH VON HÜGEL (1852–1925)
The Philosophy of Religion

Knowing the Eternal means enlightenment.
    Not knowing the Eternal, causes
            passions to arise,
        And that is evil.

LAO-TSE (604–531 B.C.)
Tao Te Ching

Every man's soul has by the law of his birth been a spectator of eternal truth, or it would never have passed into this our mortal frame.

PLATO (427–347 B.C.)
Phaedrus

How could the Truth be God, if it were for us but one possibility among others? How could we be saved by it, if it did not with compelling power urge us to hazard the leap into eternity, to dare to think what God thinks, to think freely, to think anew, and to think wholly?   KARL BARTH (1886–1968)
The Epistle to the Romans

Truth is as old as God—
His Twin identity
And will endure as long as He
A Co-Eternity.

EMILY DICKINSON (1830–1886)
Complete Poems

Acquaint thyself with God, if thou wouldst
    taste
His works. Admitted once to his embrace,
Thou shalt perceive that thou wast blind
    before.

WILLIAM COWPER (1731–1800)
The Task

It is through the intellect that the human being has the capacity of honoring God.

MAIMONIDES (1135–1204)
Commentary on the Mishnah

Truth is the beginning of every good thing both in Heaven and on earth; and he who would be blessed and happy should be from the first a partaker of the truth, for then he can be trusted.

PLATO (427–347 B.C.)
Laws

O God, always one and the same, if I know myself I shall know thee.

SAINT AUGUSTINE (354–430)
Confessions

In seeing God as Truth, i.e., the Ultimate, we see the claim on our lives as total. *"Hear, O Israel, the Lord thy God is one Lord, and thou shalt love the Lord thy God with thy whole heart, thy whole mind, thy whole soul and thy strength"* is not a "law which God decided to impose." Rather, it is a necessary corollary of the very fact that He is, that we are persons with freedom—and hence responsible for our choices.

JAMES A. PIKE (1913–1969)
What Is This Treasure?

Who knoweth God dwelleth undisturbed in
the love of God,
God abideth eternally with the man who
knoweth God,
The Name of God is the stay of the man
who knoweth God.

GURU ARJAN (1563–1606)
Hymns

The only way to really know that God made us is to let God remake, regenerate us. The only way to be sure that God gave us our physical life is to let Him give us the spiritual life which shall declare for the physical life an adequate and worthy purpose.

PHILLIPS BROOKS (1835–1893)
Sermons

By divine revelation is meant the entrance of truth into the depth of living. As long as truth does not hold sway over the whole life, cognition and life are two separate entities,

God and man are living apart from each other.

TOYOHIKO KAGAWA (1888–1960)
Meditations

In the faces of men and women I see God,
and in my own face in the glass,
I find letters from God dropped in the street
—and every one is signed by God's name,
And I leave them where they are, for I know
that others will punctually come forever
and ever.

WALT WHITMAN (1819–1892)
Song of Myself

He who sees the Infinite in all things, sees God. He who sees the Ratio only, sees himself only. Therefore, God becomes as we are that we may be as He is.

WILLIAM BLAKE (1757–1827)
Letters

Boundless the deep, because I am who fill
Infinitude, nor vacuous the space.
Though I uncircumscrib'd my self retire,
And put not forth my goodness, which is
free
To act or not, Necessitie and Chance
Approach not mee, and what I will is Fate.

JOHN MILTON (1608–1674)
Paradise Lost

There was something formlessly fashioned,
That existed before heaven and earth;
Without sound, without substance,
Dependent on nothing, unchanging,
All pervading, unfailing.
One may think of it as the mother of all
things under heaven.
Its true name we do not know;
Tao is the by-name that we give it.

LAO-TSE (604–531 B.C.)
Tao Te Ching

'Tis inward truth that Thou desirest.
Grant me wisdom in my secret heart.

The Old Testament
Psalms 51:6

Man is known as true when truth is in his
  heart,
when he bears love to the True One, when
  he knows the true way.
Truth is the medicine for all, it removes,
  and washes away, sin.

GURU NANAK (1469–1539)
The Adi Granth

Indra departed not from the truth; for
Indra is truth.

Indra said: "Understand Me Myself!

This I deem most beneficent to man—
namely, that one should understand me!"

The Upanishads

Even as the roots, shut in the darksome
  earth, share in the tree-top's joyance, and
  conceive of sunshine and wide air and
  winged things, by sympathy of nature,
So do I have evidence of Thee so far above,
  yet in and of me.

JAMES RUSSELL LOWELL (1819–1891)
The Soul's Horizon

If the knowledge of some truths be required of us by God; if the knowledge of others be useful to society; if the knowledge of
no truth be forbidden us by God, or hurtful
to us; then we have a right to know or may
lawfully know any truth.

ANTHONY COLLINS (1676–1729)
A Discourse on Free Thinking

· THE MAGNITUDE OF GOD ·

Thou knowest not thy own limits,
    Thine own mystery;
So in the blind night when the seven worlds
    Are steeped in slumber,
Curious and silent-footed thou standest in
    the sky
Lighting a million torches of star-rays.

RABINDRANATH TAGORE (1861–1941)
Gitanjali

That One, though never stirring, is swifter
than thought. Though standing still, it over-
takes those who are running. It stirs and it
stirs not. It is far, and likewise near. It is inside all this, and it is outside all this.

The Upanishads

He manifests everything because He is the
Interior, and he conceals the existence of
everything because He is the Exterior.

IBN 'ATA'ILLAH (died 1309)
Kitab Al-Hakim

The embodied spirit has a thousand heads,
a thousand eyes, a thousand feet; around on

every side, enveloping the earth; yet filling
space no larger than a span, He is himself
this very Universe; He is whatever is, has
been, shall be; He is the Lord of Immortality.

The Rig-Veda

With God there is neither day nor night,
neither far nor near.   *Shinto Proverb*

The immortal Self is the sun shining in the
sky, he is the breeze blowing in space, he is
the fire burning on the altar, he is the guest
dwelling in the house; he is in all men, he is
in the gods, he is in the ether, he is wherever
there is truth; he is the fish that is born in the
water, he is the plant that grows in the soil,
he is the river that gushes from the mountain
—he, the changeless reality, the illimitable!

The Upanishads

As from a blazing fire sparks, being like
unto fire, fly forth a thousand-fold, thus are
various beings brought forth from the Imperishable, and return thither also.

The Upanishads

All is contained in the divine breath, like the day in the morning dawn.

IBN ARABI (1165–1240)
Meccan Revelations

As puppets are to men, and dolls to children, so is man's workmanship to God's: we are the picture, he the reality.

WILLIAM PENN (1644–1718)
Some Fruits of Solitude

He sang of God—the mighty source
Of all things—the stupendous force
On which all strength depends.

CHRISTOPHER SMART (1722–1770)
A Song to David

Our mind, insofar as it understands, is an eternal mode of thinking, which is determined by another mode of thinking, and this one again by another, and so on to infinity; so that they all constitute at the same time the eternal and infinite intellect of God.

BENEDICT SPINOZA (1632–1677)
Ethics

The eye of the believer sees God's greatness in the vast expanse of space; he sees His mantle in the brightness of the firmament. And how luminous is He himself, light of all light, if the beams of the sun and the stars are His covering!

ROMANO GUARDINI (1885–1968)
The Wisdom of the Psalms

Nothing with God is something. There are no ciphers in God's arithmetic. And if we were only good enough of sight, we could see as much through a microscope as through a telescope. Those things that may be impalpable and infinitesimal to us, may be pronounced and infinite to God.

THOMAS DE WITT TALMAGE (1832–1902)
Sermons

There is one Mind. It is absolutely omnipresent, giving mentality to all things.

GIORDANO BRUNO (1548–1600)
De Monade Numero et Figura

The sea is mighty, but a mightier sways
His restless billows. Thou, whose hands have
   scooped
His boundless gulfs and built his shore, thy
   breath,
That moved in the beginning o'er his face,
Moves o'er it evermore.

WILLIAM CULLEN BRYANT (1794–1878)
A Hymn of the Sea

It must be that when God speaketh he should communicate, not one thing, but all things; should fill the world with his voice; should scatter forth light, nature, time, souls, from the center of the present thought; and new date and new create the whole.

RALPH WALDO EMERSON (1803–1882)
Self-Reliance

On life's vast ocean diversely we sail,
Reason the card, but passion is the gale;
Nor God alone in the still calm we find,
He mounts the storm and walks upon the
   wind.

ALEXANDER POPE (1688–1744)
Essay on Man

Our life is scarce the twinkle of a star
In God's eternal day.

BAYARD TAYLOR (1825–1878)
Autumnal Vespers

Why is God called by the name *Makom* meaning "place" or "space"? Because he is the space of the world, but the world is not his place.   *The Midrash*

Before anything was created there was God, and he is found everywhere, so that no one can hide from him. Why should this fill us with wonder? We could not escape from the elements of all things created, even if we had cause to wish to hide from them. Just try to flee from water and air, from the sky or from the whole of the world! We are, of necessity, caught in their compass, for no one can flee from the world. So, if we cannot hide from parts of the world, and from the world itself, how then could we hide from the presence of God?

PHILO JUDAEUS (30 B.C.–A.D. 40)
Legum Sacrarum Allegoriarum Libri

I am the chain of living things, the ring that binds the worlds, Creation's ladder and the foot that mounts it but to fall.

JALAL-UD-DIN RUMI (1207–1273)
The Masnawi

The Supreme Brahman pervades the entire universe outwardly and inwardly and shines of Itself, like the fire that permeates a red-hot iron ball both inwardly and outwardly and shines of itself.

SHANKARA (788–820)
Self-Knowledge

The light of heaven which blazeth like a fire art Thou, Thou who art strong as the earth! The path of justice approacheth Thee when Thou enterest into the house of man.

Akkadian Hymn to Ishtar

Like a bridegroom Thou risest joyful and gracious. In Thy light Thou dost reach afar to the utmost bounds of heaven. The banner of the whole wide earth art Thou. O God, the men who dwell afar do look upon Thee and rejoice.

Babylonian Hymn to Shamash, the Sun-god.

There is no word to represent that which is not God, no word for the where without God in it; for it is not, could not be.

GEORGE MACDONALD (1824–1905)
Unspoken Sermons

God, surrounding all things, is Himself not surrounded.

PHILO JUDAEUS (30 B.C.–A.D. 40)
Allegories

The imagery of the heavens as being two thousand million light-years in diameter is awesome when compared to the tiny earth, but trivial when compared to the imagery of the "hand that measured the heavens."

FULTON J. SHEEN (1895–1979)
Old Errors and New Labels

There is no place to which we could flee from God which is outside God.

PAUL TILLICH (1886–1965)
The Shaking of the Foundations

Who can search out God to perfection? None of the creatures that he has made. Only some of his attributes he hath been pleased to reveal to us in his word. Hence we learn that God is an eternal Being. "His goings forth are from everlasting," and will continue to everlasting.

JOHN WESLEY (1703–1791)
Sermons

Wise, truly, and great is his own nature,
Who held asunder spacious earth and
  heaven.
He pressed the sky, the broad and lofty,
  upward,
Aye, spread the stars, and spread the earth
  out broadly.

The Rig-Veda

A mighty drama, enacted on the theater of Infinitude, with suns for lamps, and Eternity as a background; whose author is God, and whose purport and thousandfold moral lead up to the "dark with excess of light" of the throne of God.

THOMAS CARLYLE (1795–1881)
Sartor Resartus

The life of every moment is a phenomenon of God's heart. Every task is the combustion of the flame of God.

TOYOHIKO KAGAWA (1888–1960)
Meditations

The Cosmos is all darkness. It is illumined only by the manifestation of God in it. Whoever sees the Cosmos and does not contemplate Him in it or by it or before it or after

it is in need of light and is veiled from the sun of understanding by the clouds of created things.   IBN 'ATA'ILLAH (died 1309)
The Book of Wisdom

Thou, O Lord, I imagined as environing the mass on every side and penetrating it, still infinite in every direction—as if there were a sea everywhere, and everywhere through measureless space nothing but an infinite sea; and it contained within itself some sort of sponge, huge but still finite, so that the sponge would in all its parts be filled from the immeasurable sea.
SAINT AUGUSTINE (354–430)
Confessions

Only He who made all things can gaze upon their unveiled glory. We could not behold their untempered splendour and live. That is why man is permitted to look at everything only as in a glass, darkly, and gaze only upon shadows in one small, dimly lighted chamber.
HELEN KELLER (1880–1968)
My Religion

On comets, earthquakes, lightnings, thunders, and tempests, say, "Blessed be he whose strength and might fill the world."
The Mishnah

When I consider that I dwell this moment in the eternal Now that has ever been and will be, that I am in the midst of immortal things this moment, that there probably are souls as infinitely superior to mine as mine to a piece of timber—what, then, is a "miracle"?
RICHARD JEFFERIES (1848–1887)
The Story of My Heart

O Lord, my god, Thou art very great;
Thou art clothed with glory and majesty.
Who coverest Thyself with light as with a
    garment,
Who stretchest out the heavens like a
    curtain;
Who layest the beams of Thine upper
    chambers in the waters,
Who makest the clouds Thy chariot,
Who walkest upon the wings of the wind;
Who makest winds Thy messengers,
The flaming fire Thy ministers.
The Old Testament
Psalms 104:1–5

Thou seek'st in globe and galaxy,
He hides in pure transparency;
Thou ask'st in fountains and in fires,
He is the essence that inquires.
He is the axis of the star;
He is the sparkle of the spar;
He is the heart of every creature;
He is the meaning of each feature;
And his mind is the sky
Than all it holds more deep, more high.
RALPH WALDO EMERSON (1803–1882)
Wood Notes

I looked up to the heavens once more, and the quietness of the stars seemed to reproach me. "We are safe up here," they seemed to say; "we shine, fearless and confident, for the God who gave the primrose its rough leaves to hide it from the blast of uneven spring, hangs us in the awful hollows of space. We cannot fall out of His safety. Lift up your eyes on high, and behold!"
GEORGE MACDONALD (1824–1905)
Unspoken Sermons

For all behind the starry sky,
Behind the world so broad,
Behind men's hearts and souls doth lie
    The infinite of God.
GEORGE MACDONALD (1824–1905)
Collected Poems

All life and existence in its concrete forms suggests not only sources but possibilities beyond itself. These possibilities must be implied in the source or they would not be true possibilities. God is therefore both the ultimate ground of reality and its ultimate goal.

REINHOLD NIEBUHR (1892–1971)
The Truth in Myths

What is mystery? Everything is mystery, dear; in all is God's mystery. In every tree, in every blade of grass that same mystery lies hid. Whether the tiny bird of the air is singing, or the stars in all their multitudes shine at night in heaven, the mystery is one, ever the same.

FYODOR DOSTOEVSKY (1821–1881)
A Raw Youth

What is this almost countless multitude of stars for? God has sown them in the heavens, as a magnificent prince would adorn his garments with precious stones.

But some would say, these are all worlds, like the earth we inhabit. Suppose it be so, how wise and powerful must be He who has made worlds as innumerable as the grains of sand on the sea-shore, and who has led on in order, for so many ages, all these moving worlds, as a shepherd leads his flocks.

FRANÇOIS FÉNELON (1651–1715)
On the Existence of God

In the same sense that every thing may be said to be a mystery, so also may it be said that every thing is a miracle, and that no one thing is a greater miracle than another. The elephant, though larger, is not a greater miracle than a mite; nor a mountain a greater miracle than an atom. To an almighty power it is no more difficult to make the one than the other, and no more difficult to make a million of worlds than to make one.

THOMAS PAINE (1737–1809)
The Age of Reason

God takes a large compass to bring about His great works.

BENJAMIN WHICHCOTE (1609–1683)
Moral and Religious Aphorisms

Brahman is supreme; he is self-luminous, he is beyond all thought. Subtler than the subtlest is he, farther than the farthest, nearer than the nearest. He resides in the shrine of the heart of every being.

The Upanishads

There is no place where He is not. In every movement of your soul there is God; in every reach of your thought there is God. Why, even in your misdeeds, in your sins, God is there. Wherever there is life there is the breath of God.

BAAL SHEM TOV (1700–1760)
Discourses

Of sphere harmonious linked to sphere,
 In endless bright array.
All that far-reaching Science there
 Can measure with her rod,
All powers, all laws, are but the fair
 Embodied thoughts of God.

JOHN STUART BLACKIE (1809–1895)
All Things Are Full of God

Thou, O God, who art unchangeable, Thou art always and invariably to be found, and always to be found unchanged. Whether in life or in death, no one journeys so far afield that Thou art not to be found by him, that Thou art not there, Thou who art everywhere.   SÖREN KIERKEGAARD (1813–1855)
The Unchangeableness of God

All is of God! If he but wave his hand,
The mists collect, the rain falls thick and
 loud,
Till, with a smile of light on sea and land,
 Lo! he looks back from the departing
 cloud.

HENRY WADSWORTH LONGFELLOW
(1807–1882)
The Two Angels

Our little systems have their days;
They have their day and cease to be;

They are but broken lights of thee,
And thou, O Lord, art more than they.
ALFRED LORD TENNYSON (1809–1892)
In Memoriam

A thousand worlds which roll around us
    brightly,
    Thee in their orbits bless;
Ten thousand suns which shine above us
    nightly,
    Proclaim thy righteousness.
Thou didst create the world—'twas thy
    proud mandate
    That woke it unto day;
And the same power that measured,
    weighed, and spanned it,
    Shall bid that world decay.
SIR JOHN BOWRING (1792–1872)
A Thousand Worlds

A world above man's head, to let him see
How boundless might his soul's horizon be,
How vast, yet of what clear transparency!
MATTHEW ARNOLD (1822–1888)
A Summer Night

Thee, self-begotten, who, in ether rolled
    Ceaselessly round, by mystic links dost
    blend
The nature of all things, whom veils enfold
Of light, of dark night flecked with gleams
    of gold,
    Of star-hosts dancing round thee
    without end.
EURIPIDES (485–407 B.C.)
Fragments

Let us but grant to a bit ·of moss or the smallest ant its due nature as an ontological reality, and we can no longer escape the terrifying hand that made us.
JACQUES MARITAIN (1882–1973)
The Degrees of Knowledge

See, God is great so that we cannot grasp it;
    The number of his years is
    unfathomable.
The Old Testament
Job 36:26

Every action and deed of God in both animated and inanimated nature, in nature and the Bible, are the semantic symbolic, fulfillment and revelation of the past, the germ and seal of the future.
FRANCIS XAVIER VON BAADER (1765–1841)
Die Weltalter

We can find no province of the world so low but the Absolute inhabits it. Nowhere is there even a single fact so fragmentary and so poor that to the universe it does not matter. There is truth in every idea however false, there is reality in every existence however slight; and, where we can point to reality or truth, there is the one undivided life of the Absolute.
FRANCIS HERBERT BRADLEY (1846–1924)
Appearance and Reality

What, but God?
Inspiring God! who, boundless Spirit all,
And unremitting Energy, pervades,
Adjusts, sustains, and agitates the whole.
JAMES THOMSON (1700–1748)
The Seasons

Perhaps the immense Milky Way which on clear nights we behold stretching across the heavens, this vast encircling ring in which our planetary system is itself but a molecule, is in its turn but a cell in the Universe, in the body of God.
MIGUEL DE UNAMUNO (1864–1936)
The Tragic Sense of Life

I do not know its name; I call it Tao.
If forced to give it a name, I shall call it
    Great.
Now being great means functioning
    everywhere.
Functioning everywhere means far-
    reaching.
Being far-reaching means returning to the
    original point.
Therefore Tao is great.
LAO-TSE (604–531 B.C.)
Tao Te Ching

Him on whom the sky, the earth, and the
  atmosphere
Are woven, and the mind, together with all
  the life-breaths,
Him alone know as the one Soul. Other
Words dismiss. He is the bridge to
  immortality.

                                    The Upanishads

I ask you, in the name of immortal God,
what do you see in the world that is not
unique? God is the most unique being, all his
works are unique, this angel, this man, this
sun, this stone; in short, nothing can be
found that is not a unique thing.

              PIERRE GASSENDI (1592–1655)
              Exercises Against the Aristotelians

God is not affected by our mutability: our
changes do not alter Him. When we are restless, He remains serene and calm: when we
are low, selfish, mean, or dispirited, He is still
the unalterable I AM. The same yesterday,
today, and for ever, in whom is no variable-
ness, neither shadow of turning. What God is
in Himself, not what we may chance to feel
Him in this or that moment to be, that is our
hope.

     FREDERICK WILLIAM ROBERTSON (1816–1853)
                                    Sermons

An Infinite Universe lighted with millions of
  burning suns,
Boundlessly fill'd with electrical palpitant
  world-forming ether,
Endlessly everywhere moving,
  concentrating, welling-forth power,
Life into countless shapes drawn upward,
  mystical spirit
Born, that man—even we—may commune
  with God Most High.

              WILLIAM ALLINGHAM (1824–1889)
                     Songs, Ballads and Stories

Look then how lofty and how huge in
  breadth

The eternal might, which, broken and
  dispersed
Over such countless mirrors, yet remains
Whole in itself and one, as at the first.

                        DANTE (1265–1321)
                        The Divine Comedy

I see all the gods in Your body, O God, as
also the various hosts of beings, the Lord
Brahma enthroned on a lotus-seat and all the
seers and divine serpents. Wearing the crown
and bearing the mace and the discus, a mass
of splendor radiating on all sides, I see you—
hard to gaze at—all around me, possessing
the radiance of a blazing fire and sun, incomprehensible.   *The Bhagavad Gita*

Though earth and man were gone,
And suns and universes ceased to be,
And Thou were left alone
Every existence would exist in Thee.

              EMILY BRONTË (1818–1848)
                     Legends of Angria

The excellency of God is magnified; He is
not glorified in one, but in numberless suns,
not in one earth nor in one world, but in ten
hundred thousand, of infinite globes.

              GIORDANO BRUNO (1548–1600)
              A Philosophy of the Infinite Universe

Apart from Thee, Lord, naught can exist.
If then, Thine essence pervade all things, so
also doth Thy sight, which is Thine essence.
For even as no created thing can escape from
its own proper essence, so neither can it from
Thine essence, which giveth essential being
to all beings.

              NICHOLAS OF CUSA (1401–1464)
                        The Vision of God

The knowing Self is never born; nor does
he die at any time. He sprang from nothing
and nothing sprang from him. He is unborn,
eternal, abiding and primeval. Smaller than

the small, greater than the great, the Self is set in the heart of every creature. The unstriving man beholds Him, freed from sorrow. Through the tranquility of the mind and the senses one sees the greatness of the Self.   *The Upanishads*

There is a glory which thou canst not see,
There is a music which thou canst not hear;
But if the spaces of Infinity
Unrolled themselves unto thine eye and ear,
Thou wouldst behold the crystal dome
    above
Lighted with living splendours, and the
    sound
Of their great voices uttering endless love
    Would sink forever thro' the vast
        profound.
            FREDERICK TENNYSON (1807–1898)
                            Shorter Poems

Without beginning, middle or end, of
    infinite power,
Of infinite arms, whose eyes are the sun and
    the moon,
I see Thee, whose face is flaming fire,
Burning this whole universe with Thy
    radiance.
                        The Bhagavad Gita

All are but parts of one stupendous whole,
Whose body Nature is, and God the soul.
            ALEXANDER POPE (1688–1744)
                            Essay on Man

I see, smell, taste, hear, feel, that everlasting Something to which we are allied, at once our maker, our abode, our destiny, our very Selves.
            HENRY DAVID THOREAU (1817–1862)
    A Week on the Concord and Merrimack Rivers

When once one understands that in oneself
The Self has become all beings,
When once one has seen the unity,

What room is there for sorrow, what room
    for perplexity?
                        The Upanishads

In the vast and the minute we see
The unambiguous footsteps of the God
Who gives its luster to an insect's wing,
And wheels His throne upon the whirling
    worlds.
            WILLIAM COWPER (1731–1800)
                            The Task

Ye storms howl out His greatness; let your thunders roll like drums in the march of God's armies! Let your lightning write His name in fire on the midnight darkness; let the illimitable void of space become one mouth for song; and let the unnavigated ether, through its shoreless depths, bear through the infinite remote the name of Him whose goodness endureth forever!
            CHARLES HADDON SPURGEON (1834–1892)
                            Sermons

Before there was an earth at all, or sun, or stars in the splashed heavens, before matter came into being, for endless eternities before, as Genesis puts it in four initial words, "in the beginning God," He has seen kingdoms and civilizations and earths and solar systems rise and wane. He, and He alone, knows the secret of history, the meaning of the mystery called Time. Shall He not know the hearts of men and women?
            BERNARD IDDINGS BELL (1886–1958)
                            Religion for Living

And, Thou, Lord, in the beginning has laid the foundation of the earth; and the heavens are the works of thine hands: they shall perish but Thou remainest; and they shall wax as old as doth a garment; and as vesture shalt thou fold them up, and they shall be changed: but Thou art the same, and Thy years shall not fail.   *The New Testament*
                            Hebrews 1:10–11

The sun and moon, O Lord, are thy lamps;
  the firmament
thy salver and the oils of the stars the pearls
  set therein.
The perfume of the sandal tree is thy
  incense; the wind is
thy fan, all the forests are thy flowers, O
  Lord of light.
                    GURU NANAK (1469–1539)
                            The Adi Granth

God certainly creates what lies beyond the
reach of human imagination but it does not
follow that it lies beyond the reach of God's
imagination.
          HENRY NELSON WIEMAN (1884–1975)
              Intellectual Foundation of Faith

God is perpetually the same. He is not
composed of any substance or material, but
is spirit—pure, essential, and ethereal spirit
—and therefore he is immutable. He remains
everlastingly the same. There are no furrows
on his eternal brow. No age has palsied him;
no years have marked him with the memen-
toes of their flight; he sees ages pass, but with

him it is ever *now*. He is the great I AM—the
Great Unchangeable.
        CHARLES HADDON SPURGEON (1834–1892)
                                    Sermons

All the mystery which surrounds life and
pervades life is really one mystery. It is God.
Called by His name, taken up into His being,
it is filled with graciousness.
              PHILLIPS BROOKS (1835–1893)
                      The Light of the World

Say—go through the earth and see how
God has brought forth all creation: hereafter
will He give it another birth.   *The Koran*

God's whole boundless and beautiful world
is the breath of one eternal idea, the thought
of one eternal God.
          VISSARION BELINSKI (1811–1848)
                          Literary Reveries

The Spirit of God, in countless variety of
forms, neither above, nor in any way without,
but intimately within all things, is really present, with equal integrity and fullness, in the
sunbeam ninety millions of miles long, and
the wondering drop of water as it evaporates
therein.   WALTER PATER (1839–1894)
                          Gaston de Latour

· THE GOODNESS OF GOD ·

If your heart were right, then every created thing would be a mirror to life and a
book of holy doctrine, for no creature is so
small and mean that it cannot display God's
goodness.   THOMAS À KEMPIS (1380–1471)
                        Imitation of Christ

God has made everything which He has
created most good; and began the creation of
man with clay; then ordained his progeny
from germs of life, from sorry water; then
shaped him, and breathed of His spirit unto

him, and gave you hearing and seeing and
heart: what little thanks do you return?
                                    The Koran

When a man experienceth in his soul a
feeling full of bliss, a deep calm, as it were,
and a pure light, let him know that as Goodness.   *The Code of Manu*

Hold fast to God and he will add every
good thing. Seek God and you shall find him
and all good with him. To the man who

cleaves to God, God cleaves and adds virtue. Thus, what you have sought before, now seeks you; what once you pursued, now pursues you; what once you fled, now flees you. Everything comes to him who truly comes to God, bringing all divinity with it, while all that is strange and alien flies away.

MEISTER ECKHART (1260–1327)
Sermons

Look up at the stars, study the mathematics of the heavens writ in those gorgeous diagrams of fire where all is law, order, harmony, beauty without end; look down on the anthills in the field some morning in early summer, study the ethics of the emmets, all law, order, harmony, beauty without end; do you find any sign that the first person of the Godhead is malignant or capricious, and the fourth person thereof is a devil; that hate preponderates in the world?

THEODORE PARKER (1810–1860)
*Lessons in the World of Matter and the
World of Man*

The world is the overflow of Divine Goodness. Begotten of the Goodness of God, the Goodness of God is in it.

FULTON J. SHEEN (1895–1979)
The Philosophy of Religion

Good is that which contributes to the course of ascending evolution and leads us away from the animal toward freedom. Evil is that which opposes evolution, and escapes it by regressing toward the ancestral bondage, toward the beast. In other words, and from a strictly human point of view, good is the respect of human personality; evil is the disregard of this personality. Indeed, the respect of human personality is based on the recognition of man's dignity as a worker for evolution, as a collaborator with God.

PIERRE LECOMTE DU NOUY (1883–1947)
Human Destiny

The good deeds which we perform point to the goodness of the Creator, just as smoke points to fire.

ZECHARIAH HA-YEWANI (13th century)
Sefer ha-Yeshar

The Good must be the beginning and the end even of all evil things. For the Good is the final Purpose of all things, good and bad alike.

DIONYSIUS THE AREOPAGITE (5th century)
The Divine Names

The very word "God" suggests care, kindness, goodness; and the idea of God in his infinity is infinite care, infinite kindness, infinite goodness. We give God the name of good: it is only by shortening it that it becomes God.

HENRY WARD BEECHER (1813–1887)
Sermons

God whose gifts in gracious flood
    Unto all who seek are sent,
Only asks you to be good
    And is content.

VICTOR HUGO (1802–1885)
Collected Poems

Good is no good, but if it be spend:
God giveth good for none other end.

EDMUND SPENSER (1552–1599)
The Shepheardes Calender

Expediency is man's wisdom; doing right is God's.

GEORGE MEREDITH (1828–1909)
Aphorisms

While all the powers of Good aid and attend us,
Boldly we'll face the future, be what it may.
At even, and at morn, God will befriend us,
And oh, most surely on each New Year's day.

DIETRICH BONHOEFFER (1906–1945)
Letters

Grave it on brass with adamantine pen!
'Tis God Himself becomes apparent, when

God's wisdom and God's goodness are
   displayed,
For, God of these His attributes is made.
                    MATTHEW ARNOLD (1822–1888)
                                      Divinity

There shall never be one lost good! What
   was, shall live as before;
The evil is null, is nought, is silence
   implying sound;
What was good, shall be good, with, for evil,
   so much good more;
On the earth the broken arcs; in the heaven,
   a perfect round.
                    ROBERT BROWNING (1812–1889)
                                    Abt Vogler

All our goodness is a loan; God is the
owner. God works and his work is God.
         SAINT JOHN OF THE CROSS (1542–1591)
                                         Works

We should not love goodness because it is
commanded by God, but should love God because He is good.
              WILLIAM P. MONTAGUE (1873–1953)
                             The Way of Things

God, the Great Giver, can open the whole
universe to our gaze in the narrow space of a
single lane.
             RABINDRANATH TAGORE (1861–1941)
                                   Jivan Smitri

The goodness of God knows how to use
our disordered wishes and actions, after lovingly turning them to our advantage while
always pressing the beauty of His order.
         SAINT BERNARD OF CLAIRVAUX (1091–1153)
                                       Letters

God is so good, He wears a fold
   Of heaven and earth across His face—
Like secrets kept, for love, untold.
      ELIZABETH BARRETT BROWNING (1806–1861)
                        A Child's Thought of God

O goodness infinite, goodness immense!
That all this good of evil shall produce,
And evil turn to good; more wonderful
Than that which by creation first brought
   forth
Light out of darkness!
                       JOHN MILTON (1608–1674)
                                  Paradise Lost

In the eternal goodness of the divine nature (as in a miraculous mirror) the essence
of all creatures is seen as one.
               MEISTER ECKHART (1260–1327)
                        German and Latin Works

God wills nothing but man's advantage,
man's true greatness and his ultimate dignity.
This then is God's will: *man's well-being.*
                           HANS KÜNG (1928–)
                             On Being a Christian

So many are God's kindnesses to us, that,
as drops of water, they run together; and it is
not until we are borne up by the multitude of
them, as by streams in deep channels, that we
recognize them as coming from him.
             HENRY WARD BEECHER (1813–1887)
                                       Sermons

Every day is a messenger of God.
                                 Russian Proverb

Oh God! keep me on the work of goodness;
Otherwise, no work can come from me.
                          SAADI (1184–1291)
                                        Bustan

The benevolence of God is called mercy,
because we are in debt to God, and he owes
us nothing.   *The Talmud*

For I am affection, I am the cheer-bringing
God, with hope and all-enclosing charity.
                   WALT WHITMAN (1819–1892)
                        Chanting the Square Deific

Infinite Goodness is of so communicative a
nature, that it seems to delight in the confer-
ring of existence upon every degree of perceptive being. If the scale of being rises by

such a regular progress, so high as man, we may by parity of reason suppose that it still proceeds gradually through those beings which are of a superior nature to him, since there is an infinitely greater space and room for different degrees of perfection, between the Supreme Being and man, than between man and the most despicable insect.

JOSEPH ADDISON (1672–1719)
The Spectator

· THE ETERNAL IN THE MIDST OF TIME ·

God had infinite time to give us; but how did He give it? In one immense tract of a lazy millennium? No, but He cut it up into a neat succession of new mornings, and, with each, therefore, a new idea, new inventions, and new applications.

RALPH WALDO EMERSON (1803–1882)
Journal

The time God allots to each one of us is like a precious tissue which we embroider as we best know how.

ANATOLE FRANCE (1844–1924)
The Crime of Sylvestre Bonnard

Spring returns: it returns and will go away. And God curved in time repeats himself, and passes, passes with the backbone of the universe on his shoulder.

CESAR VALLEJO (1892–1938)
The Weary Circle

You, Lord, are ever in action and ever at rest. You do not see in time nor move in time nor rest in time. Yet You make all the things we see in time, and You make both time while time is and rest when time is no more.

SAINT AUGUSTINE (354–430)
Confessions

To see the eternal in the midst of time, to feel and to enjoy the infinite here in the finite, is one of the greatest blessings life has to offer. Plato used to say that life comes to its full glory when some beautiful object, or some loved person, suddenly opens for us a window that gives a glimpse into eternal reality.

RUFUS JONES (1863–1948)
New Eyes for Invisibles

Time is the supreme illusion. It is but the inner prism by which we decompose being and life, the mode under which we perceive successively what is simultaneous in idea. Time and space are fragments of the Infinite for the use of finite creatures. God permits them that He may not be alone.

HENRI FRÉDÉRIC AMIEL (1821–1881)
Journal Intime

In God there is neither past nor future. He has loved the saints eternally as He foresaw them before the world was.

MEISTER ECKHART (1260–1327)
Sermons

We must understand that God is the measure of all reality and propriety, understand that eternity exists first and then time, and therefore the future first and then the present, as surely as the Creator exists first and then the creature.

KARL BARTH (1886–1968)
Church Dogmatics

If Infinite space is God's immensity, infinite time will be God's eternity; and therefore we must say, that what is in Space, is in God's Immensity, and consequently in his Essence; and that what is in Time is also in the Essence of God.

GOTTFRIED WILHELM VON LEIBNIZ
(1646–1716)
Monadologie

The Now-moment in which God made the first man and the Now-moment in which the last man will disappear, and the Now-moment in which I am speaking are all one in God, in whom there is only one Now.

MEISTER ECKHART (1260–1327)
Sermons

As regards *time,* it is inconceivable that the concept of time could be applied to the Creator because of the fact that He is Himself the Creator of all time. Furthermore, He existed originally alone when there was as yet no such thing as time. It is, therefore, unthinkable that time should have effected any locomotion or change in Him.

SAADIA BEN JOSEPH (882–942)
The Book of Beliefs and Opinions

If we consider boundless space, or boundless duration, we shrink into nothing before it. But God is not a man. A day, and millions of ages, are the same with Him. Therefore, whenever you are tempted to fear lest you should be forgotten before the immense, the eternal God, remember that nothing is little or great, that no duration is long or short, before Him.   JOHN WESLEY (1703–1791)
On Eternity

It is the dimension of time wherein man meets God, wherein man becomes aware that every instant is an act of creation, a Beginning, opening up new roads for ultimate realizations. Time is the presence of God in the world of space, and it is within time that we are able to sense the unity of all beings.

ABRAHAM JOSHUA HESCHEL (1907–1973)
The Sabbath

Things reduced to act in time, are known by us successively in time, but by God are known in eternity, which is above time. Whence to us they cannot be certain, forasmuch as we know future contingent things as such; but they are certain to God alone, whose understanding is in eternity above time.   SAINT THOMAS AQUINAS (1225–1274)
Summa Theologica

Past and future are what veil God from our
sight.
Burn up both of them with fire! How long
Wilt thou be partitioned by these segments
as a reed?

JALAL-UD-DIN RUMI (1207–1273)
The Masnawi

Before all time and beyond all space is the first image of God. Time and space and all that they contain are this Idea revealing itself and tied to it through free necessity.

JOSEPH GORRES (1776–1848)
Mythic History of the Ancient World

Beloved, be not ignorant of this one thing, that one day is with the Lord as a thousand years, and a thousand years as one day.

The New Testament
2 Peter 3:8

The infinite significance of every moment of time is this: in it we decide and are decided about, with respect to our eternal future.

PAUL TILLICH (1886–1965)
The Shaking of the Foundations

Time is for man, not man for time. God, the Lord of nature, will never anticipate man's choices which follow one after another in time. Man will not be able to excuse himself at the last judgment, saying to God: "You overwhelmed me with the future when I was only capable of living in the present."

Cloud of Unknowing (14th century)

Time is what keeps the light from reaching us. There is no greater obstacle to God than time.   MEISTER ECKHART (1260–1327)
Sermons

Nothing hinders the soul's knowledge of God as much as time and space, for time and space are fragments, whereas God is one! And therefore, if the soul is to know God, it must know him above time and outside of space; for God is neither this nor that, as are these manifold things. God is One!

MEISTER ECKHART (1260–1327)
Sermons

With God one day is as a thousand years and a thousand years as one day, which is to say that there is no calendar and no timepiece in the divine experience, no aging, no getting away from the beginning, nor approaching towards the end.

CHARLES H. PARKHURST (1842–1933)
Sermons

Thus yesterday, to-day, to-morrow come,
They hustle one another and they pass;
But all out hustling morrows only make
The smooth to-day of God.

MATTHEW ARNOLD (1822–1888)
The Buried Life

Eternity is in love with the productions of time.

WILLIAM BLAKE (1757–1827)
The Marriage of Heaven and Hell

When looking at space we see the products of creation; when intuiting time we hear the process of creation. Things created conceal the Creator. It is the dimension of time wherein man meets God, wherein man becomes aware that every instant is an act of creation, a Beginning, opening up new roads for ultimate realizations.

ABRAHAM JOSHUA HESCHEL (1907–1973)
The Sabbath

Time is the solemn inheritance to which every man is born heir, who has a life-rent of this world—a little section cut out of eternity and given us to do our work in: an eternity before, and eternity behind; and the small stream between, floating swiftly from one into the vast bosom of the other.

FREDERICK WILLIAM ROBERTSON (1816–1853)
Sermons

Believe what thou findest written in the sanctuaries of Man's Soul, even as all Thinkers, in all ages, have devoutly read it there. that Time and Space are not God, but creations of God; that with God as it is a universal Here, so is it an everlasting Now.

THOMAS CARLYLE (1795–1881)
Sartor Resartus

In eternity there is indeed something true and sublime. But all these times and places and occasions are now and here. God himself culminates in the present moment and will never be more divine in the lapse of the ages. Time is but the stream I go afishing in. I drink at it, but when I drink I see the sandy bottom and detect how shallow it is. Its thin current slides away but eternity remains.

HENRY DAVID THOREAU (1817–1862)
Where I Lived

The meditation of time resting in eternity, of our life flowing over God's eternal life, is something to shake the roots of our soul.

MIGUEL DE UNAMUNO (1864–1936)
Essays on Faith

God forbid that anyone should say that God loved anyone in time, for with Him nothing has passed away and also nothing is future, and He loved all the saints before the world was made, as He foresaw.

SAINT AUGUSTINE (354–430)
On the Trinity

It is the highest power of divine moments that they abolish our contritions also. I accuse myself of sloth and unprofitableness day by day; but when these waves of God flow into me I no longer reckon time.

RALPH WALDO EMERSON (1803–1882)
Circles

God is said to be in time, because He is absent from no time or because he is in the simplicity of eternity, from which all time flows, according to the following: Thou who commands time to go from eternity.

ROBERT GROSSETESTE (1175–1253)
On the Knowledge of God

Think not thy time short in this world, since the world itself is not long. The created world is but a small parenthesis in eternity and a short interposition, for a time, between such a state of duration as was before it and may be after it.

SIR THOMAS BROWNE (1605–1682)
Christian Morals

· A LIGHT THAT IS NEVER DARKENED ·

Hast thou not known? hast thou not heard, that the everlasting God, the Lord, the Creator of the ends of the earth, fainteth not, neither is weary? there is no searching of his understanding.   *The Old Testament*
Isaiah 40:28–29

I will fly in the greatness of God as the
  marsh-hen flies
In the freedom that fills all the space 'twixt
  the marsh and the skies;
By so many roots as the marsh-grass sends
  in the sod
I will heartily lay me a-hold on the greatness
  of God.   SIDNEY LANIER (1842–1881)
The Marshes of Glynn

Nature was silent and at rest when the Decalogue was proclaimed on Sinai. No animal made a sound, no fowl flew, the very angels kept silent and desisted from praises before God. The billows of the sea became calm and at rest, and no creature uttered a sound whilst the words were uttered by the living God saying, "I am the Lord thy God."

The Midrash

The greatness both of God towards us, and of ourselves towards Him, we ought always as much as possible to retain in our understanding. And when we cannot effectually keep it alive in our senses, to cherish the memory of it in the centre of our hearts, and do all things in the power of it.

THOMAS TRAHERNE (1637–1674)
Centuries of Meditations

Mankind, as well as other creatures, being formed with such exquisite and wonderful skill that human wisdom is utterly insufficient to imitate the most simple fiber, vein, or nerve, much less a finger, it is perfectly evident, that all these things must originally have been made by an omnipotent and omniscient Being, for "He who formed the ear, shall He not hear; and He who made the eye, shall He not see?"

CAROLUS LINNAEUS (1707–1778)
The Study of Nature

Our ideas, not only of the almightiness of the Creator, but of his wisdom and his beneficence, become enlarged in proportion as we contemplate the extent and the structure of the universe.   THOMAS PAINE (1737–1809)
The Age of Reason

Supreme beyond the power of speech to express, Brahman may yet be apprehended by the eye of pure illumination. Pure, absolute and eternal Reality, this is Brahman and "thou art That."   SHANKARA (788–820)
Viveka-Chudamani

Who hath measured the waters in the hollow of his hand, and meted out heaven with the span, and comprehended the dust of the earth in a measure, and weighed the mountains in scales, and the hills in a balance?

The Old Testament
Isaiah 40:12

Make love thy pen, and thy heart the writer,
    and write as thy Guru instructs.
Write thou His name and His praises.
Write that He is without limit and
    fathomless.

GURU NANAK (1469–1539)
The Adi Granth

How can we little crawling creatures, so utterly helpless as He has made us, how can we possibly measure His greatness, His boundless love, His infinite compassion, such that He allows man insolently to deny Him, wrangle about Him, and cut the throat of his fellow men? How can we measure the greatness of God who is "so forgiving, so divine"?

MOHANDAS K. GANDHI (1869–1948)
Young India

All this universe is strung upon me as rows of jewels upon a string. I am the taste in water, the light in sun and moon, the AUM in the Vedas, manhood in man. The might of the mighty and the heat of the fire, the wisdom of the wise, the splendour of the magnificent. From me come the moods of goodness, fire, and melancholy. I am not in them but they are in me. And bewildered by these three moods the whole universe fails in understanding that I sit above them and am changeless. For my divine magic of moods is hard to see through, but they who cling to me transcend the magic.   *The Bhagavad Gita*

Whithersoever you turn your eyes, there is not an atom of the world in which you cannot behold some brilliant sparks at least of his glory; the exact symmetry of the universe is a mirror in which we may contemplate the otherwise invisible God.

JOHN CALVIN (1509–1564)
Institutes of the Christian Religion

God hath spoken once,
Twice have I heard this:
That strength belongeth unto God.
The Old Testament
Psalms 62:12

God is a light that is never darkened; an unwearied life that cannot die; a fountain always flowing; a garden of life; a seminary of wisdom; a radical beginning of all goodness.

FRANCIS QUARLES (1592–1644)
Emblems

There is no power but from God.
The New Testament
Romans 13:1

God is more truly imagined than expressed, and He exists more truly than is imagined.   SAINT AUGUSTINE (354–430)
On the Trinity

So Paul, standing in the middle of the Areopagus, said: "Men of Athens, I perceive that in every way you are very religious. For as I passed along and observed the objects of your worship, I found also an altar with this inscription, 'To an unknown god.' What therefore you worship as unknown, this I proclaim to you. The God who made the world and everything in it, being Lord of heaven and earth, does not live in shrines made by man, nor is he served by human hands, as though he needed anything, since he himself gives to all men life and breath and everything. And he made from one every nation of men to live on all the face of the earth, having determined allotted periods and the boundaries of their habitation, that they should seek God, in the hope that they might feel after him and find him. Yet he is not far from each of us, for 'In him we live and move and have our being'; as even some of your poets have said, 'For we are indeed his offspring.'"

The New Testament
Acts 17:22–28

He holds in his power the soul of every living thing, and the breath of each man's body.   *The Old Testament*
Job 12:10

A mighty fortress is our God, a bulwark
   never failing,
Our helper he amid the flood of mortal ills
   prevailing.

MARTIN LUTHER (1483–1546)
A Mighty Fortress Is Our God

Father of all! in every age,
In every clime adored,
By saint, by savage, and by sage,
Jehovah, Jove or Lord!

ALEXANDER POPE (1688–1744)
The Universal Prayer

Whither shall I go from Thy spirit? or
whither shall I flee from Thy presence? If I
ascend up into heaven, Thou art there; if I
make my bed in the nether world, behold,
Thou art there. If I take the wings of the
morning, and dwell in the uttermost parts of
the sea; even there would Thy hand lead me,
and Thy right hand would hold me.

The Old Testament
Psalms 139:7–12

Nothing in the world is single,
All things by a law divine
In one spirit meet and mingle.

PERCY BYSSHE SHELLEY (1792–1822)
Love's Philosophy

There is nothing which God cannot do.

MARCUS TULLIUS CICERO (106–43 B.C.)
De Divinatione

God is abroad, and wondrous in his ways,
The rise of empires, and their fall surveys.

JOHN DRYDEN (1631–1700)
Britannia Rediviva

· MERCY WITHOUT MEASURE ·

Power, wisdom and justice are God's lesser
ways, and come towards that side of His
Being where there would be restriction if
anywhere; while love and mercy are God's
peculiar glory. In these He finds the most
glorious liberty of the Divine Nature.

HENRY WARD BEECHER (1813–1887)
Sermons

God excludes none, if they do not exclude
themselves.

WILLIAM GUTHRIE (1620–1665)
The Christian's Great Interest

O God, Your mercy is a boundless ocean:
A mere drop suffices for me!
Even if the filth of all the sins of mankind
Were to be thrown into that ocean all at
   once,
It would still not be darkened for a moment;
Rather, all earthly labor is transformed into
   light!

SHARAFUDDIN MANERI (14th century)
The Hundred Letters

I know thy justice is thyself; I know,
Just God, thy very self is mercy too;
If not to thee, where? whither should I go?

FRANCIS QUARLES (1592–1644)
Oh, Whither Shall I Fly?

God giveth his wrath by weight, but his
mercy without measure.

THOMAS FULLER (1654–1734)
Gnomologia

For Mercy, Pity, Peace and Love
Is God, our Father dear,
And Mercy, Pity, Peace and Love
Is man, His child and care.

WILLIAM BLAKE (1757–1827)
The Divine Image

Even in the dark hour after he has become guilty against his brother, man is not abandoned to the force of chaos. God Himself seeks him out, and even when he comes to call him to account, His coming is salvation.

MARTIN BUBER (1878–1965)
At the Turning

There's a wideness in God's mercy
Like the wideness of the sea;
There's a kindness in his justice,
Which is more than liberty.

FREDERICK WILLIAM FABER (1814–1863)
Hymns

I have blotted out, as a thick cloud, thy transgressions, and, as a cloud, thy sins; return unto Me, for I have redeemed Thee.

*The Old Testament
Isaiah 44:22*

The Lord thy God is a merciful God; he will not forsake thee, nor destroy thee, nor forget the covenant of thy fathers which he swore unto them. *The Old Testament
Deuteronomy 4:31*

Our faults are like a grain of sand beside the great mountain of the mercies of God.

SAINT JEAN BAPTISTE MARIE VIANNEY (1786–1859)
Sermons

The Goddess of Mercy has a thousand hands—and needs them all.

Japanese Proverb

There is nothing on earth that does not show either the wretchedness of man, or the mercy of God; either the weakness of man without God, or the strength of man with God. BLAISE PASCAL (1623–1662)
Pensées

Whom the heart of man shuts out,
Sometimes the heart of God takes in.

JAMES RUSSELL LOWELL (1819–1891)
The Forlorn

And God who gave his mercies, takes his mercies,
And God who gives beginnings, gives the end.
A rest for broken things too broke to mend.

JOHN MASEFIELD (1878–1967)
The Widow in the Bye Street

It is said that mercy is the attribute that God shows forth in all His works; therefore a merciful person is a truly God-like man. The true friends of God are much more merciful and more ready to believe in the sinful and suffering than those who are not loving. Mercy is born of that love which we ought to exercise towards each other.

JOHANNES TAULER (1300–1361)
Sermons on the Inner Way

Whoever falls from God's right hand
Is caught into his left.

EDWIN MARKHAM (1852–1940)
The Divine Strategy

Mercy imitates God, and disappoints Satan.

SAINT JOHN CHRYSOSTOM (345–407)
Homilies

When all Thy face is dark,
And Thy just angers rise;
From Thee I turn to Thee,
And find love in Thine eyes.

SOLOMON IBN GABIROL (1021–1058)
Sources of Life

Give both the infinitudes their due—
Infinite mercy, but I wish,
As infinite a justice too.

ROBERT BROWNING (1812–1889)
The Heretic's Tragedy

Mercy and compassion are the great virtues which bring with them their own rewards, for they are recompensed with mercy

and loving-kindness from the mercy-seat of
God.   *The Midrash*

May the World-Creator have mercy on thee!
Whatever more I may say is empty talk and
  wind.

                              SAADI (1184–1291)
                                         Bustan

O brother who art in distress! be not dis-
heartened; for God hath many hidden mercies. Repine not at the versatility of fortune;
for patience is bitter, but the fruit is sweet.

                              SAADI (1184–1291)
                                        Gulistan

Thy malice may be measured, but God's
mercy cannot be defined; thy malice is cir-
cumscribed, his mercies infinite.

           SAINT JOHN CHRYSOSTOM (345–407)
                                        Sermons

As the sun does not set to any nation, but
withdraws itself, and returns again; God, in
the exercise of his mercy, does not set to thy
soul, though he benight it, with an affliction.

                      JOHN DONNE (1572–1631)
                                        Sermons

That it may please thee to have mercy
upon all men; We beseech thee to hear us,
good Lord.   *The Book of Common Prayer*
                                      The Litany

For a brief moment I forsook you,
but with great compassion I will gather you.
In overflowing wrath for a moment I hid my
  face from you,
but with everlasting love I will have
  compassion on you,
saith the Lord, your Redeemer.
                                The Old Testament
                                     Isaiah 54:7–8

But as for me, I am like a leafy olive-tree
in the house of God; I trust in the mercy of
God for ever and ever.   *The Old Testament*
                                     Psalms 52:10

Surely goodness and mercy shall follow me
all the days of my life; and I will dwell in the
house of the Lord forever.
                                The Old Testament
                                      Psalms 23:6

What is man and what use is he?
What do his good or evil deeds signify?
His span of life is at the most a hundred
  years;
compared with endless time, his few years
are like one drop of sea-water or a single
  grain of sand.
That is why the Lord is patient with them,
lavishing his mercy upon them.
                      The Old Testament Apocrypha
                             Ecclesiasticus 18:8–12

The greatest attribute of heaven is mercy;
And 'tis the crown of justice, and the glory,
Where it may kill with right, to save with
  pity.

                     JOHN FLETCHER (1579–1625)
                               The Lover's Progress

If God were not willing to forgive sin
Heaven would be empty.   *German Proverb*

On this mountain the Lord will swallow up
that veil that shrouds all the peoples,
the pall thrown over all the nations;
he will swallow up death for ever.
Then the Lord God will wipe away the tears
  from every face
and remove the reproach of his people from
  the whole earth.
                                The Old Testament
                                     Isaiah 25:7–8

But mercy is above the sceptred sway;
It is enthroned in the hearts of kings,
It is an attribute to God himself;
And earthly power doth then show likest
  God's,
When mercy seasons justice.
                 WILLIAM SHAKESPEARE (1564–1616)
                               The Merchant of Venice

Who is a God like unto thee, that pardoneth
   the iniquity,
And passeth by the transgression of the
   remnant of His heritage?
He retaineth not His anger for ever,
Because He delighteth in mercy.
                        The Old Testament
                        Micah 7:18–19

We implore the mercy of God, not that He
may leave us in peace in the midst of our
vices, but that He deliver us from them.
            BLAISE PASCAL (1623–1662)
                        Pensées

What humanity needs is not the promise of
scientific immortality, but compassionate pity
in this life and infinite mercy on the Day of
Judgment.   JOSEPH CONRAD (1857–1924)
                Notes on Life and Letters

Blessed are the merciful, for they shall obtain mercy.   *The New Testament*
                        Matthew 5:7

God hath two wings, which He doth ever
   move,
The one is Mercy, and the next is Love:
Under the first the Sinners ever trust;
And with the last he still directs the Just.
            ROBERT HERRICK (1591–1674)
                        Mercy and Love

Before He brought on the flood, God Himself kept seven days of mourning, for He was
grieved at heart (Genesis 6:6).
                        The Mishnah

· AND COMPASSION WITHOUT BOUNDS ·

When a man has compassion for others,
God has compassion for him.   *The Talmud*

There is no thought, feeling, yearning, or
desire, however low, trifling, or vulgar we
may deem it, which, if it affects our real interest or happiness, we may not lay before
God and be sure of his sympathy. His nature
is such that our often coming does not tire
him. The whole burden of the whole life of
every man may be rolled onto God and not
weary him, though it has wearied the man.
            HENRY WARD BEECHER (1813–1887)
                        Sermons

But God is not like human kind;
Men cannot read the Almighty mind;
Vengeance will never torture thee,
Nor hunt thy soul eternally.
            EMILY BRONTË (1818–1848)
                        Collected Poems

O Lord, in Mercy grant my soul to live,
And patience grant, that hurt I may not
   grieve:
How shall I know what thing is best to seek?
Thou only knowest: what Thou knowest,
   give!
            SHEIKH 'ABDULLAH ANSARI (1005–1090)
                        Munajat

If God is what people say there can be no
one in the universe so unhappy as He; for
He sees unceasingly myriads of His creatures
suffering unspeakable miseries—and besides
this foresees how they are going to suffer
during the remainder of their lives. One
might well say: "As unhappy as God."
            MARK TWAIN (1835–1910)
                        Notebook

He is God; and yet he picks his steps more
carefully than if angels guided them, not to

prevent his feet from stumbling against a stone, but lest he trample human beings in the dust, in that they are offended at him. He is God; and yet his eye surveys mankind with anxious care, for the tender shoots of an individual life may be crushed as easily as a blade of grass.

SÖREN KIERKEGAARD (1813–1855)
Philosophical Fragments

Compassion is the root of religion; pride the root of sin.   TULSI DAS (1543–1623)
Ramcaritmanas

Nothing makes the world so precious, so little barren, and so rich, nothing so takes away its sordidness, as the knowledge of God's solicitude concerning it, and his care over it.

HENRY WARD BEECHER (1813–1887)
Sermons

There are problems which only the heart's knowledge, piercing to the heart of things where God's pity abides, can solve; and to solve them is to be grateful to God, for the solution is the pity.

GERALD VANN (1906–1963)
The Divine Pity

Not wholly lost, O Father! is this evil world
    of ours;
Upward, through its blood and ashes, spring
    afresh the Eden flowers;
From its smoking hell of battle, Love and
    Pity send their prayer.

JOHN GREENLEAF WHITTIER (1807–1892)
The Angels of Buena Vista

We sometimes fear to bring our troubles to God, because they must seem so small to Him who sitteth on the circle of the earth. But if they are large enough to vex and endanger our welfare, they are large enough to touch His heart of love. For love does not measure by a merchant's scales, nor with a surveyor's

chain. It hath a delicacy which is unknown in any handling of material substances.

HENRY WARD BEECHER (1813–1887)
Sermons

Oh, it is hard to work for God,
    To rise and take his part,
Upon this battlefield of earth,
    And not sometimes lose heart.

FREDERICK WILLIAM FABER (1814–1863)
Hymns

"I am that I am," said God to Moses, by which He intimated that He created the world in mercy, and will always rule the world in mercy.   *The Midrash*

Always and everywhere, man is encompassed by an eternal certainty, embraced by the arms of eternity. He is therefore never forsaken and never lost, nowhere alone, nowhere condemned forever. He is never surrendered or wholly abandoned to anyone. Rather, he is always supported by the One, the unfathomable.

LEO BAECK (1873–1956)
This People Israel

If I totter, the covenant love of God is my eternal salvation, and if I stumble in the crookedness of my flesh, my justification depends on the righteousness of God, which is eternal.

The Dead Sea Scrolls (100 B.C.–A.D. 100)

O God, thou knowest how foolish I am,
And my guilty deeds are not hidden from
    thee.

The Old Testament
Psalms 69:5

In a moment the Lord reveals Himself, if a
    man cries to Him.
Beholding the humble in distress, He is
    greatly moved.   DADU (1554–1603)
The Bani

The Lord is nigh unto them that are of a broken heart and saveth such as are of a contrite spirit.
The Old Testament
Psalms 34:18

If we wish to adhere to the true law of love, our eyes must chiefly be directed, not to man, the prospect of whom would impress us with hatred more frequently than with love, but to God, who commands that our love to him be diffused among all mankind; so that this must always be a fundamental maxim with us, that whatever be the character of a man, yet we ought to love him because we love God.
JOHN CALVIN (1509–1564)
Institutes of the Christian Religion

Look from thy sphere of endless day,
O God of mercy and of might!
In pity look on those who stray,
Benighted in this land of light.
WILLIAM CULLEN BRYANT (1794–1878)
Collected Verse

God's transcendent power is not so much displayed in the vastness of the heavens, or the luster of the stars, or the orderly arrangement of the universe or his perpetual watching over it, as in his condescension to our weak nature. We marvel at the way the sublime entered a state of lowliness.
SAINT GREGORY OF NYSSA (331–396)
Address on Religious Instruction

There is no life so humble that, if it be true and genuinely human and obedient to God, it may not hope to shed some of His light. There is no life so meager that the greatest and wisest of us can afford to despise it. We cannot know at all at what sudden moment it may flash forth with the life of God.
PHILLIPS BROOKS (1835–1893)
Sermons

The compassion of man is for his neighbor, but the compassion of the Lord is for all living beings.   *The Old Testament Apocrypha*
Ecclesiasticus 18:13

Is it My desire that a wicked man shall die? says the Lord God. It is rather that he shall turn back from his ways and live.
The Old Testament
Ezekiel 18:23

The Holy One, praised be He, does not qualify any creature; He accepts everyone. The gates are always open, and whoever wants to enter may enter.   *The Talmud*

When the Evil Power stands before the Holy One, praised be He, to accuse the world for its evil deeds, the Holy One, praised be He, shows compassion for the world and gives mankind counsel by which it can escape the Evil Power, so that it will not dominate neither them nor their deeds.   *The Zohar*

Praised be my Lord for all those who pardon one another for his love's sake, and who endure weakness and tribulation.
SAINT FRANCIS OF ASSISI (1182–1226)
The Canticle of the Sun

He, our Father, He hath shown His mercy unto me.
In peace I walk the straight road.
Cheyenne Indian Hymn

God says, "Wherever there is a spark of grace lighted in the soul, if it flickers so that the breath of the person who carries it, or the least motion of his hand, is in danger of putting it out, I will deal so gently with him as not to quench that spark. I will treat it with such infinite tenderness that it shall grow into a flame which will burn on forever." And these are the symbols by which God measures his wonderful gentleness.
HENRY WARD BEECHER (1813–1887)
Sermons

Lord, I believe were sinners more
Than sands upon the ocean shore,

Thou hast for all a ransom paid,
For all a full atonement made.
COUNT NIKOLAUS LUDWIG VON ZINZENDORF
(1700–1760)
Hymns

The holiest soul, pitying the brother-soul which has fallen into vilest vice, gains, while it keeps its own purity unsoiled, something of the sight of that other side of God, the side where justice and forgiveness blend in the opal mystery of grace, which it would see as if only the soul that looked up out of the depths of guilt could see.
PHILLIPS BROOKS (1835–1893)
Sermons

It is for God to say, "to know all is to pardon all." It is for God to say that He saw us all the way; that "He knoweth our frame, He remembereth that we are dust." It is for Him to have pity on us; it is never for us to cultivate pity for ourselves.
JOHN A. HUTTON (1868–1947)
On Accepting Ourselves

A Dervish, in his prayer, said, "O God! show pity towards the wicked, for on the good thou hast already bestowed mercy by having created them virtuous."
SAADI (1184–1291)
Gulistan

God does not wish us to remember what He is willing to forget.
GEORGE ARTHUR BUTTRICK (1892–1979)
Prayer

If the orphan weeps, who buys for his
    consolation?
Beware! that he weeps not; for the great
    throne of God
Keeps trembling when the orphan weeps.
SAADI (1184–1291)
Bustan

When God created the creation he wrote a book, which is near him upon the sovereign throne; and what is written in it is this: "Verily my compassion overcometh my wrath."
The Sunan

A new heart I will give you, and a new spirit I will put within you; and I will take out of your flesh the heart of stone and give you a heart of flesh.
The Old Testament
Ezekiel 36:26–28

If the compassion of God is so great that He instructs us to our benefit, even when He hides Himself, what light ought we not to expect from Him when He reveals Himself?
BLAISE PASCAL (1623–1662)
Pensées

Man may dismiss compassion from his heart,
But God will never.
WILLIAM COWPER (1731–1800)
The Task

Have compassion on man, O man, and God will have compassion on you. You are a man and the other is a man: two who are unhappy. God is not unhappy; He is merciful. If the unhappy have not compassion on the unhappy, how can he ask for mercy from Him Who shall never know unhappiness?
SAINT AUGUSTINE (354–430)
The City of God

Man is not worthy of God, but he is not incapable of being made worthy.
It is unworthy of God to unite Himself to wretched man; but it is not unworthy of God to pull him out of his misery.
BLAISE PASCAL (1623–1662)
Pensées

· MAKE A JOYFUL NOISE UNTO THE LORD ·

My desire for knowledge is intermittent; but my desire to commune with the spirit of the universe, to be intoxicated even with the fumes, call it, of divine nectar, to bear my head through atmospheres and over heights unknown to my feet, is perennial and constant.   HENRY DAVID THOREAU (1817–1862)
Journals

The more exalted a saint is, the greater his joy; but the joy of them all put together amounts to as little as a bean when compared to the joy of God over good deeds. For truly, God plays and laughs in good deeds, whereas all other deeds, which do not make for the glory of God, are like ashes before him. Thus he says: "Rejoice, O Heavens! For the Lord hath comforted his people!"
        MEISTER ECKHART (1260–1327)
Works

In the future, the Holy One will arrange a dance for the righteous in the Garden of Eden. He will sit in their midst, and each of them will point to Him and declare (Isaiah 25:9): "Lo, this is our God, for Whom we have waited, that He might save us; this is the Lord for Whom we have waited, and we will be glad and rejoice in His salvation."
                                The Talmud

Here is what I have discovered: it is meet and proper for a man to eat, drink, and enjoy himself in return for the toil he undergoes under the sun in the scant years God has given him, for that is man's portion, and not long will he remember the days of his life.
                        The Old Testament
                        Ecclesiastes 5:17–18

Live while you live, the Epicure would say,
And seize the pleasures of the present day;

Live while you live, the sacred preacher cries,
And give to God each moment as it flies,
Lord, in my view let both united be;
I live in pleasure when I live to Thee.
        PHILIP DODDRIDGE (1702–1751)
Epigram on His Family Motto

I know not in whose hands are laid
    To empty upon earth
From unsuspected ambuscade
    The very Urns of Mirth:

Who bids the Heavenly Lark arise
    And cheer our solemn round—
The Jest beheld with streaming eyes
    And grovelings on the ground;

No creed hath dared to hail him Lord,
    No raptured choirs proclaim,
And Nature's strenuous Overword
    Hath nowhere breathed his
        name.

Yet may it be, on wayside jape,
    The selfsame Power bestows
The selfsame power as went to shape
    His Planet or His Rose.
        RUDYARD KIPLING (1865–1936)
The Necessitarian

Laughing, from my earthy bed
Like a tree I lift my head,
For the Fount of living mirth
Washes round my earth.
        JALAL-UD-DIN RUMI (1207–1273)
The Masnawi

Man could direct his ways by plain reason, and support his life by tasteless food; but God has given us wit, and flavour, and brightness, and laughter, and perfumers, to enliven the days of man's pilgrimage, and to

"charm his pained steps over the burning marle." SYDNEY SMITH (1771–1845)
The Dangers and Advantages of Wit

Earthly language is entirely insufficient to describe what there is of joy, happiness, and loveliness contained in the inner wonders of God. JACOB BOEHME (1575–1624)
The Threefold Life of Man

It is God's will, not merely that we should *be* happy, but that we should *make* ourselves happy. This is true morality.
IMMANUEL KANT (1724–1804)
Works

I say it is not enough to be drawn by will; you are drawn even by delight. What is it to be drawn by delight? "Delight yourself in the Lord and he shall give you the desires of your heart" [Psalms 37:4]. There is a pleasure of the heart to which that bread of heaven is sweet. SAINT AUGUSTINE (354–430)
Works

And the ransomed of the Lord shall return, and come to Zion with songs and ever-lasting joy upon their heads: they shall obtain joy and gladness, and sorrow and sighing shall flee away. *The Old Testament*
Isaiah 35:10

Mirth is the sweet wine of human life. It should be offered sparkling with zestful life unto God.
HENRY WARD BEECHER (1813–1887)
Sermons

O God, animate us to cheerfulness; may we have a joyful sense of our blessings, learn to look on the bright circumstances of our lot, and maintain a perpetual contentedness under Thy allotments.
WILLIAM ELLERY CHANNING (1780–1842)
Sermons

Serve the Lord with gladness; come into His presence with singing.
The Old Testament
Psalms 100:2

The Root of prayer is that the heart rejoices in the love of the Holy One, as it is written: "Let the heart of them rejoice that seek the Lord," which is why David used to play on the harp.
RABBI ELEAZAR OF WORMS (1165–1230)
Sefer Raziel

God is the creator of laughter that is good.
PHILO JUDAEUS (30 B.C.–A.D. 40)
The Worse Attacks the Better

He who has found God in his heart is happy in mind and body.
GURU ARJAN (1563–1606)
Hymns

For I am affection, I am the cheer-bringing God, with hope and all enclosing charity.
WALT WHITMAN (1819–1892)
Chanting the Square Deific

What joy can we render to God again for all the joy wherewith we joy?
The New Testament
I Thessalonians 3:9

True joy is not a thing of moods, not a capricious emotion, tied to fluctuating experiences. It is a state and condition of the soul. It survives through pain and sorrow and, like a subterranean spring, waters the whole life. It is intimately allied and bound up with love and goodness, and so is deeply rooted in the life of God. RUFUS JONES (1863–1948)
The Inner Life

Our loving God wills that we eat, drink, and be merry.
MARTIN LUTHER (1483–1546)
Table-Talk

Restore unto me the joy of thy salvation;
and uphold me with thy free Spirit.
                    The Old Testament
                    Psalms 51:12

God tastes an infinite joy
In infinite ways—one everlasting bliss,
From whom all being emanates, all
          power
Proceeds; in whom is life for evermore,
Yet whom existence in its lowest form
Includes.
          ROBERT BROWNING (1812–1889)
                    Paracelsus

We are not sanctioned either by the Torah
or by the divine philosophers to assert that
the angels, the stars, and the spheres enjoy
no delights. In truth they have exceeding
great delight in respect of what they comprehend of the Creator, glorified be He. This to
them is an everlasting felicity without a
break.   MAIMONIDES (1135–1204)
                    Hilkhot Teshuvah

God made Heaven and Earth for joy He
    took in a rhyme,
Made them, and filled them full of the
    strong red wine of His mirth,
The splendid joy of the stars, the joy of the
    earth.
          JOHN MASEFIELD (1878–1967)
                    Laugh and Be Merry

Make a joyful noise unto God, all ye lands.
                    The Old Testament
                    Psalms 66:1

He will through life be master of himself
and a happy man who from day to day can
have said, "I have lived": tomorrow the Father may fill the sky with black clouds or with
cloudless sunshine.   HORACE (65–8 B.C.)
                    Odes

It is a comely fashion to be glad—
Joy is the grace we say to God.
          JEAN INGELOW (1820–1897)
                    Dominion

We may say of angling as Dr. Boteler said
of strawberries: "Doubtless God could have
made a better berry, but doubtless God never
did"; and so, if I might be judge, God never
did make a more calm, quiet, innocent rec-
reation than angling.
          IZAAK WALTON (1593–1683)
                    The Compleat Angler

Joy is the realization of the truth of Oneness, the oneness of our soul with the world
and of the world-soul with the supreme
lover.
          RABINDRANATH TAGORE (1861–1941)
                    Gitanjali

If you grasp the Spirit of the Creator, you
will need no more admonishment, but you
will rejoice and be happy in this light, and
your soul will laugh and triumph with it.
          JACOB BOEHME (1575–1624)
                    Schriften

God alone keeps festival in reality, for he
alone rejoices, he alone is delighted, he alone
feels cheerfulness, and to him alone is it
given, to pass an existence of perfect peace
unmixed with war.
          PHILO JUDAEUS (30 B.C.–A.D. 40)
                    Allegories of the Sacred Laws

There is God's laughter on the hills of
space and the happiness of children, and the
soft healing of innumerable dawns and eve-
nings, and the blessing of peace.
          EUGENE O'NEILL (1883–1953)
                    Lazarus Laughed

· INTIMATIONS OF ETERNITY ·

God is withdrawn from both ends of time, for his life is not Time but Eternity, the archetype of time. And in eternity there is neither past nor future but only present.

PHILO JUDAEUS (30 B.C.—A.D. 40)
On the Creation of the World

Behind us, behind each one of us, lie Six Thousand Years of human effort, human conquest: before us is the boundless Time, with its yet uncreated and unconquered Continents and Eldorados, which we, even we, have to conquer, to create; and from the bosom of Eternity there shine for us celestial guiding stars.

THOMAS CARLYLE (1795—1881)
Characteristics

The Timeless and Eternal is the I AM towards which we reach out in spiritual regard. Thus truth, beauty, and goodness—rational, aesthetic, and ethical values—are raised to a higher status for those in whom the spiritual attitude is supervenient, since they have their ultimate being in God.

CONWAY LLOYD MORGAN (1852—1936)
Life, Mind, and Spirit

'Tis the divinity that stirs within us;
'Tis Heaven itself that points out an
  hereafter,
And intimates eternity to man.
Eternity! thou pleasing, dreadful thought!

JOSEPH ADDISON (1672—1719)
Cato

Eternity is the great atonement of finitude. The earthly is reconciled with the endless. All atonement is fundamentally this: reconciliation of the finite and the infinite.

LEO BAECK (1873—1956)
The Essence of Judaism

Life is a fragment, a moment between two eternities, influenced by all that has pre-

ceded, and to influence all that follows. The only way to illuminate it is by extent of view.

WILLIAM ELLERY CHANNING (1780—1842)
Journals

The time will come when every change shall
  cease,
This quick revolving wheel shall rest in
  peace:
No summer then shall glow, nor winter
  freeze;
Nothing shall be to come, and nothing past,
But an eternal now shall ever last.

PETRARCH (1304—1374)
The Triumph of Eternity

We perish but thou endurest. Ours is not thy eternity. But in thy eternity we would be remembered, not as blots on the face of this part of thy infinite reality, but as healthy leaves that flourished for a time on the branches of the eternal tree of life, and that have fallen, though not into forgetfulness. For to thee nothing is forgotten.

JOSIAH ROYCE (1855—1916)
The Religious Aspect of Philosophy

Thou perceivest the Flowers put forth their
  precious Odours,
And none can tell how from so small a
  center comes such sweets,
Forgetting that within that center Eternity
  expands
Its ever during doors.

WILLIAM BLAKE (1757—1827)
Milton

Life, like a dome of many-coloured glass,
Stains the white radiance of Eternity.

PERCY BYSSHE SHELLEY (1792—1822)
Adonais

· GOD WORKS IN WONDROUS WAYS ·

God offers to every mind its choice between truth and repose.

RALPH WALDO EMERSON (1803–1882)
Essays

All of God's works are signs and expressions of his attributes; and thus it seems that all of physical nature is an expression and image of the spiritual world. All finite creatures are able to perceive truth and the nature of things only in images.

JOHANN GEORG HAMANN (1730–1786)
Schriften

There is no vein by which life and being flow into us, derived from any source other than Thy workmanship, O Lord, for Thou art life and being in the highest degree.

SAINT AUGUSTINE (354–430)
Confessions

The ways of God are as the number of the souls of the sons of men.   *Persian Proverb*

As there is an infinity of possible universes in the ideas of God, and as only one of them can exist, there must be a sufficient reason for the choice of God, which determines him for one rather than for another.

GOTTFRIED WILHELM VON LEIBNIZ
(1646–1716)
Philosophical Works

The works of God are but a kind of voice or language of God to instruct intelligent beings in things pertaining to Himself.

JONATHAN EDWARDS (1703–1758)
Images

Man is in process of becoming the perfected being whom God is seeking to create. However, this is not taking place—it is important to add—by a natural and inevitable evolution, but through a hazardous adventure in individual freedom.

JOHN HICK (1922–)
Evil and the God of Love

Revelation is God's word, Creation his work, the Spirit sole seer and interpreter of both.   BRONSON ALCOTT (1799–1888)
Journals

All God's great works are silent. They are not done amid rattle of drums and flare of trumpets. Light as it travels makes no noise, utters no sound to the ear. Creation is a silent process; nature rose under the Almighty hand without clang or clamor, or noises that distract and disturb.

ANDREW MARTIN FAIRBAIRN (1838–1912)
Sermons

The universality of law means that God works everywhere and in all things by constant and unchangeable method. This is observed not only in the wide things, in the vast movements of solar systems, but in the tiniest details of nature, so that all the intricacies of the wing of a butterfly are as much the result in each detail of the universal law or method by which God works in all things as the vastest cosmic movement.

CHARLES GORE (1853–1932)
Sermons

Blind to the working of that secret power
That balances the wings of every hour,
The busy trifler dreams himself alone,
Frames many a purpose, and God works his own.

WILLIAM COWPER (1731–1800)
Expostulation

That anything may be found to be an infinite treasure, its place must be found in Eternity and in God's esteem. For as there is a time, so there is a place for all things. Everything in its place is admirable, deep, and glorious: out of its place like a wandering bird, is desolate and good for nothing. How therefore it relateth to God and all creatures must be seen before it can be enjoyed.

THOMAS TRAHERNE (1637–1674)
Centuries of Meditations

The Almighty does nothing without reason, though the frail mind of man cannot explain the reason.

SAINT AUGUSTINE (354–430)
The City of God

Today, even now, Thy work doth abide in that Thou hewest a pathway for the rivers. The hills bow down before Thee as were they friends; the wide spaces of the universe are knit together by Thee.   *The Rig-Veda*

It is very fit and becoming of God, who is infinitely wise, so to order things that there should be a voice of His in His works, instructing those that behold them and painting forth and shewing divine mysteries and things more immediately appertaining to Himself and His spiritual kingdom.

JONATHAN EDWARDS (1703–1758)
Images

It will not do for any of us to make up his mind that he cannot be any good and noble thing, until first he has asked himself whether it is as impossible in God's sight as in his.   PHILLIPS BROOKS (1835–1893)
Perennials

The first author of "speech" was God Himself, that instructed Adam how to name such creatures as He presented to his sight.

THOMAS HOBBES (1588–1679)
Leviathan

Ancient of Days! except thou deign
Upon the finished task to smile,

The workman's hand hath toiled in vain,
To hew the rock and rear the pile.

WILLIAM CULLEN BRYANT (1794–1878)
Except the Lord Build the House

What has been, already exists, and what is still to be, has already been, and God always seeks to repeat the past.   *The Old Testament
Ecclesiastes 3:15*

Be absorbed in me,
Lodge your mind in me:
Thus you shall dwell in me,
Do not doubt it,
Here and hereafter.

The Bhagavad Gita

From unreality, lead me to Reality,
From darkness, lead me unto Light,
From death, lead me to Immortality.

The Upanishads

God created man to be immortal, and made him to be an image of his own eternity.

*The Old Testament Apocrypha
The Wisdom of Solomon 2:23*

If I had been with God Almighty before He created the world, I could not have advised Him how out of nothing to make this globe, the firmament, and that glorious sun, which in its swift course gives light to the whole earth; how, in such manner, to create man and woman, all which He did for us, without our counsel. Therefore ought we justly to give Him the honor, and leave to His divine power and goodness the new creation of the life to come, and not presume to speculate thereon.

MARTIN LUTHER (1483–1546)
Table-Talk

There is no cruelty so inexorable and unrelenting, as that which proceeds from a bigoted and presumptuous supposition of doing service to God.

CHARLES CALEB COLTON (1780–1832)
Lacon

The teacher of evil destroys the lore, he by his teachings destroys the design of life, he prevents the possession of Good Thought from being prized. These words of my spirit I wail unto you, O Mazdah, and to the Right.

ZOROASTER (6th century B.C.)
Gathas

What avails it a man to see if he does not know what he has seen? To what end has man been created except that he may learn to distinguish between good and evil and choose the good? If we have no knowledge of this, we know nothing of God.

PARACELSUS (1493–1541)
Works

An evil soul producing holy witness
Is like a villain with a smiling cheek,
A goodly apple rotten at the heart.

WILLIAM SHAKESPEARE (1564–1616)
The Merchant of Venice

The perfectibility of man is forever excluded here by the tenor of his existence. He is here, in a flood of successive generations, to make experiment of evil, to learn the worth of virtue in the loss of it, and by such knowledge to be at last confirmed in it. As long, therefore, as he is here, evil will be, and life will be a contest with it.

HORACE BUSHNELL (1802–1876)
A Discourse on the Moral Tendencies and Results of Human History

For this corruptible must put on incorruption, and this mortal must put on incorruptibility.

The New Testament
1 Corinthians 9:25

I swear I think there is nothing but immortality,
That the exquisite scheme is for it, and the nebulous float is for it, and the cohering is for it!
And all preparation is for it—and identity for it—and life and materials are all together for it.

WALT WHITMAN (1819–1892)
To Think of Time

I am a better believer, and all serious souls are better believers, in immortality than we can give grounds for.

RALPH WALDO EMERSON (1803–1882)
Immortality

Though inland far we be,
Our souls have sight of that immortal sea
Which brought us hither.

WILLIAM WORDSWORTH (1770–1850)
Intimations of Immortality

Only of this I am assured, that some time and in some way, spirit to spirit, face to face, I shall meet the great Lord of life, and falling before Him, tell my gratitude for all He has done, and implore pardon for all that I have left undone.

PAUL ELMER MORE (1864–1937)
Journal

Here in this world He bids us come, there in the next He shall bid us Welcome.

JOHN DONNE (1572–1631)
Sermons

The soul may be trusted to the end. That which is so beautiful and attractive must be succeeded and supplanted only by what is more beautiful and so on forever.

RALPH WALDO EMERSON (1803–1882)
Love

We shall not expect to be immortal until we discover something in us that is infinitely precious and eternally worthy to be conserved in a realm to which we inherently belong—the Over-World of Spirit.

RUFUS JONES (1863–1948)
Spirit in Man

In our passing life we touch the fringe of immortality when we acknowledge God as Ultimate Substance.

CONWAY LLOYD MORGAN (1852–1936)
Life, Mind, and Spirit

When God measures men in the next world, he will not put the tape about their head, he will put it about their heart.

HENRY WARD BEECHER (1813–1887)
Sermons

The Divine Eye looks upon high and low differently from that of man. They who seem to stand upon Olympus, and high mounted unto our eyes, may be but in the valleys, and low ground unto His; for He looks upon those as highest who nearest approach His divinity, and upon those as lowest, who are farthest from it.

SIR THOMAS BROWNE (1605–1682)
Christian Morals

We never do anything so secretly but that it is in the presence of two witnesses: God and our own conscience.

BENJAMIN WHICHCOTE (1609–1683)
Moral and Religious Aphorisms

Who sees with equal eye, as God of all,
A hero perish, or a sparrow fall,
Atoms or systems into ruin hurled,
And now a bubble burst, and now a
    world.

ALEXANDER POPE (1688–1744)
Essay on Man

There is not one life which the Life-Giver ever loses out of His sight; not one which sins so that He casts it away; not one which is not so near to Him that whatever touches it touches Him with sorrow or with joy.

PHILLIPS BROOKS (1835–1893)
Sermons

The beams of glory come from God, and are something of God, and are refunded back again to their original. So that the whole

is *of* God, and *to* God, and God is the beginning, middle and end in this affair.

JONATHAN EDWARDS (1703–1758)
Two Dissertations

Who beholds a crowd of people should utter the benediction, Blessed is He Who is wise in secrets. Just as faces differ one from another, so are minds also different, but God knows them all. *The Talmud*

The prerogative, the distinction of the divine life is this: that it, and it alone, is self-enveloping. There is nothing beyond it. It is held within nothing. It holds all things within itself. There is nothing to which God is bound to be true but God.

PHILLIPS BROOKS (1835–1893)
The Mystery of Iniquity

To suppose that God did not know what events would exist in His kingdom, is to divest Him of omniscience. To suppose that He did know, and did not care—had no choice, no purpose—is to blot out His benevolence, to nullify His wisdom and convert His power into infinite indolence. To suppose that He did know, and choose, and decree, and that events do not accord with His purposes, is to suppose that God has made a world which He can not govern; has undertaken a work too vast; has begun to build, but is not able to finish. LYMAN BEECHER (1775–1863)
Sermons

God is in all things and in every place. There is not a place in the world in which He is not most truly present. Just as birds, wherever they fly, always meet with the air, so we, wherever we go, or wherever we are, always find God present.

SAINT FRANCIS OF SALES (1567–1622)
Sermons

We read at the commencement of one of the oldest of the Upanishads: "Whatever exists in this universe is to be covered with the

Lord." We have to cover everything with the Lord Himself, not by a false sort of optimism, not by blinding our eyes to evil, but by really seeing God in everything.

SWAMI VIVEKANANDA (1863–1902)
Jnana-Yoga

I believe with perfect faith that the Creator, praised be He, knows every deed of men and all their thoughts, as it is written, "He fashions the hearts of them all and observes all their deeds."

MAIMONIDES (1135–1204)
Sanhedrin

We hold that God knows what human beings are doing, and what they are going to do, what has been, what is, and how what is not would have been if it had been.

ABUL-HASSAN ALI IBN ISMAIL AL-ASHARI (873–935)
The Elucidation of Islam's Foundation

Though men may spin their cunning schemes—God knows who shall lose or win.

The Hitopadesa

We cannot think of something of God here and something else there, nor of all God gathered at some one spot; there is an instantaneous presence everywhere.

PLOTINUS (205–270)
Enneads

For God pervades all lands and regions of the sea and the deep sky; from him flocks and cattle and men and all kinds of wild beasts derive the subtle breath of life when they are born; and to him it returns in the dissolution of their bodies; and there is no room for death.

VERGIL (70–19 B.C.)
Georgics

And whatever is the seed of all beings that am I, O Arjuna. There is no being, whether moving or unmoving, that can exist without Me.

The Bhagavad Gita

Who knows? God knows: and what He
    knows
Is well and best.
The darkness hideth not from Him, but
    glows
Clear as the morning or the evening rose
    Of east or west.

CHRISTINA ROSSETTI (1830–1894)
Collected Poems

Homer with his honeyed lips sang of the bright sun's clear light; yet the sun cannot burst with his feeble rays the bowels of the earth or the depths of the sea. Not so with the Creator of this great sphere. No masses of earth can block His vision as He looks over all. With one glance of His intelligence He sees all that has been, that is, and that is to come.

BOETHIUS (480–524)
The Consolation of Philosophy

If any man hopes, in whatever he does, to escape the eye of God, he is grievously wrong.

PINDAR (522–443 B.C.)
Olympian Odes

The true doctrine of omnipresence is that God reappears with all his parts in every moss and cobweb. The value of the universe contrives to throw itself into every point.

RALPH WALDO EMERSON (1803–1882)
Compensation

As God discerns with his all-seeing eye, the real character of every action, so has he imparted to the human soul, a portion of his spirit, which gives it a similar power, and arms the decisions of conscience with a divine authority.

GEORGE RIPLEY (1802–1880)
Discourses on the Philosophy of Religion

Yet still there whispers the small voice
    within,
Heard through God's silence, and o'er
    glory's din,

Whatever creed be taught or land be trod,
Man's conscience is the oracle of God!

GEORGE GORDON, LORD BYRON (1788–1824)
Collected Verse

Men, as by a natural inspiration, have agreed to speak of conscience as the voice of God, as the Divinity within us.

WILLIAM ELLERY CHANNING (1780–1842)
Likeness

Whenever conscience speaks with a divided, uncertain, and disputed voice, it is not yet the voice of God. Descend still deeper into yourself, until you hear nothing but a clear and undivided voice, a voice that does away with doubt and brings with it persuasion, light, and serenity.

HENRI FRÉDÉRIC AMIEL (1821–1881)
Journal Intime

O Conscience! Conscience! thou divine instinct, thou certain guide of an ignorant and confined, though intelligent and free being —thou infallible judge of good and evil, who makest man to resemble the Deity.

JEAN JACQUES ROUSSEAU (1712–1778)
Emile

V · Faith in God

Teach me, O God, not to torture myself, not to make a martyr out of myself through stifling reflection, but rather teach me to breathe deeply in faith.

SÖREN KIERKEGAARD

THROUGHOUT this anthology the God Seekers have been telling us that the highest form of rapport with our spiritual Father can be achieved only with the dual realization that we are able to love him and to feel his love residing in us. Although it is patently impossible for anyone to know the totality of God, there exists within us a deep, undying desire to understand as much about our relationship with him as we can. This yearning has always led us to rely on one of God's most precious gifts, faith.

It is a gift, as John Baillie said, that we cannot give to ourselves. As he put it in his *Invitation to Pilgrimage,* "We cannot truly believe, and we ought not to try to make ourselves believe, unless that which we believe reveals itself to us as true."

Through God-given faith we possess the initial strength and purpose to look, even tentatively, for the meaning of our lives in relation to our Eternal Creator. In the passages in this portion of our anthology we see how various God Seekers have explored the boundaries of faith and how this search has elicited some of their most exalted expressions.

A connection certainly exists between faith, hope, and love. The American clergyman Frederick Brotherton Meyer compared them to a flower: "Faith is the root; hope is the stem; love the perfect flower. You may have faith without hope, and hope without love; but you cannot have love apart from faith and hope."

In some manner or other almost every person on this earth is striving to find some purpose, some unity, to his or her life. Whether we are philosophers or coal miners, each of us endeavors to find even a partial, palatable answer to such questions as who am I, why am I here, and what is the meaning of my life? For those who can detach themselves from total involvement in the minute-by-minute, day-by-day, time-encompassing details of their individual lives, faith in God becomes, in Reinhold Niebuhr's phrase, "faith in some ultimate unity of life." If we can reach into the deepest abyss of our selfhood, says Niebuhr, we may be able to find "some final comprehensive purpose which holds all the various, and frequently contradictory, realms of coherence and meaning together."

If the Eternal Creator has, indeed, planted the seed of faith in each individual, as the God Seekers keep reminding us, it takes long and painstaking cultivation to bring this seedling into a mature, viable plant. William Ralph Inge saw faith as a kind of climbing instinct within us that could pull us upward. If, at first, it seems "quite vague and undifferentiated, and partly subconscious," eventually, if we are perceptive enough to realize what *can* take place within us, this seedling plant "takes shape as a homage to, and craving after, God."

In one of the most extraordinary spiritual journals ever written, Blaise Pascal probed into the furthest reaches of sensibility to explore his relationship with God. Pascal, one of the preeminent scientific as well as religious minds of the past five hundred years, expressed deep concern with the nature of faith in his *Pensées*. To him, faith was entirely different from scientific proof, for "the one is human, the other is a gift from God. This faith that God Himself puts into the heart makes us not say I know, but I believe."

Pascal said that men fear the God in whom they have no belief, and he called this a false kind of fear, as distinguished from the true fear that comes from faith. Why a fear, albeit a "true" fear? Because those with faith fear to lose God, but those with "false" fear are afraid to find him. Pascal insisted always that faith can never come from "reasoning" but is a gift of God, perhaps one of his most precious gifts.

This thought has been restated in our time by many strong God Seekers, among whom is Gerald Vann, who infused it with renewed strength. In his book *The Heart of Man*, Vann gives us this succinct, beautiful variation on Saint Paul's summary of the greatest values—faith, hope, and love:

By faith we are led, not against reason but beyond reason, to the knowledge of God in Himself and therefore of ourselves. By hope we are kept young of heart; for it teaches us to trust in God, to work with all our energy but to leave the future to Him; it gives us poverty of spirit and so saves us from solicitude. And by love we are not told about God, we are brought to Him.

Miguel de Unamuno, in his *Nicodemus the Pharisee*, expands on another variant of this theme. If reason insists on denying there can be a "transcendental reality," Unamuno declares, "faith answers that there should be one, and since there should be one, there will be one." As a prolific creative writer, Unamuno knew that unless he had faith in his inner resources and sensibilities he could not even have attempted to be an author. In searching for God, he tells us, the stakes are far higher, "for faith does not so much consist in creating what we have not seen, but in creating what we do not *see*. And only faith can create."

Faith, say the God Seekers, is not something we experience only when things are going well. That kind of pseudofaith is merely a way of preening our egos and kidding ourselves that we are in such good graces with God that naturally He is paving our path with roses. When our "luck" or "fate" turns against us, our fair-weather faith diminishes into the barest shadow of itself. The truest measure of faith is found when, although oppressed with temporary failures and bowed over with what George Macdonald called "the weight of low thoughts, failures, neglects, and wandering forgetfulness," we can still turn to God and say, "Thou art my refuge."

Faith, in its full dimensions, involves trusting in the power *and* the goodness of God, especially when we experience a slap in the face from what seems an uncaring, impersonal force. Albert C. Knudson understood that it is only natural to be baffled when the Heavenly Father, who encompasses all goodness and compassion, has allowed such suffering to come to us, "but better a baffled faith than no faith at all."

As Karl Rahner, one of the greatest theologians of this century, wrote in *Happiness Through Prayer,* who are we to put the burden of proof on God to assure us that He is good and holy? To live in faith signifies that we do not require the "bait of constant reward to keep us faithful in our love." For most of us there are going to be times when the darkness is so impenetrable that we feel we will never see the dawn again. It is precisely then, Dr. Rahner says, that "we are called upon to love in faith—to nurse our firm belief in the stars of sweet reasonableness that continue to shine behind the darkness of events which seem to us sour and grim and beyond our understanding."

For some people, perhaps more of us than would ever admit it, even to ourselves, the mystery of Godhood is more than we can bear. Because we cannot understand his plan for the total universe, a plan in which we are a part, we alienate ourselves from the Creator by letting our fear of life or fear of death erode our brief time on earth. All the more reason to heed the words of Harry Emerson Fosdick.

Dr. Fosdick begins with the premise that no one can believe in *all* of God; so the way to start is to believe in as much of him as we can. Some of us begin to contemplate God's incomparably intricate design while listening to the call of a lark in a meadow blooming with flowers of every hue; others may discover his presence in the great scriptures his messengers have revealed; and still others may find him while listening to the exquisite strains of Beethoven's last quartets.

We should begin, Fosdick says, by asking ourselves some questions:

Could blind chance create symmetry and rhythm and light and color and melody? Or begin with the mathematics of the universe. The great mathematicians—Euclid, Newton, Einstein— did not create mathematical order; they uncovered the truth that was already there. Or begin with the great character of the men and women who have made this world a better place for the human family to live in. They too are the near range of God.

Another theme the God Seekers pursue in this section relates to the gratitude we feel toward the Master of the Universe. Phillips Brooks believed that every effort we make to live through a day, or sometimes through only the traumatic moments of an hour, is a prayer of thanks to God for life.

Faith and gratitude toward God for allowing us to be *dramatis personae* in the drama He is eternally creating, for allowing us to share the beauty of a sunrise, for countless things we take for granted even though we know that only the Master of All Things could have fashioned them—this is the central theme of the passages that follow.

As Booker T. Washington observed in his autobiography *Up from Slavery,* the word atonement, which occurs in the Bible again and again, originally meant being in accord with God, literally finding *at-one-ment* with him.

Faith signifies that even with our poor, human limitations we try to emulate the qualities and attributes we ascribe to God by letting our inner heart lead us. Faith allows us to believe, with Paracelsus, that "the heart of man is so great if it is righteous that God begrudges him nothing." Faith, in its ultimate realization, is the spiritual spaceship that transcends the bounds of the universe and leads us to our eternal destiny.

· Faith Is an Affirmation ·

Faith, hope and charity, those three virtues for whose building up is mounted all the scaffolding of the Bible, are only in the soul that believes what it sees not yet, and hopes and loves what it believes.

SAINT AUGUSTINE (354–430)
On the Trinity

Faith is an affirmation and an act
That bids eternal truth be fact.

SAMUEL TAYLOR COLERIDGE (1772–1834)
Collected Poems

No human concept of the divine is a container which encloses the truth; it is a roadway, unimaginably longer than our minds can travel, concerning whose direction we are confident—it leads out infinitely beyond our reach toward what everlastingly is so about God.

HARRY EMERSON FOSDICK (1878–1969)
In Search of God and Immortality

There are several states of mind which are incompatible with Faith. There is the merely dull and stupid temper, which takes each day as it comes, eats, drinks, and sleeps, and never thinks about the meaning of things. There is the pessimistic temper, which sees behind phenomena only an alien and hostile power. There is the skeptical temper, which refuses to admit that any clear revelation of God has been made to us through truth, beauty, and goodness.

WILLIAM RALPH INGE (1860–1954)
Faith and Its Psychology

There is no unbelief;
And day by day and night, unconsciously,
The heart lives by that faith the lips deny,
God knoweth why.

EDWARD BULWER-LYTTON (1803–1873)
Faith

Faith, not in some notions or communications about God, but in God himself, made them inheritors of His righteousness, capable of entering into His infinite love, and of losing themselves in it.

FREDERICK DENISON MAURICE (1805–1872)
What Is Revelation?

The true conclusion is to turn our backs on apprehensions, and embrace that shining and courageous virtue, Faith. Hope is the boy, a blind, headlong, pleasant fellow; Faith is the grave, experienced, yet smiling man. Hope looks for unqualified success; but Faith counts certainty a failure, and takes honourable defeat to be a form of victory.

ROBERT LOUIS STEVENSON (1850–1894)
Virginibus Puerisque

Man's faith is inadequate if his whole existence is determined by something less than ultimate. Therefore, he must always try to break through the limits of his finitude and reach what never can be reached, the ultimate itself.   PAUL TILLICH (1886–1965)
Dynamics of Faith

The soul without faith is fickle, and has no resting-place;
It is fixed on nothing sure, but flits from one thing to another.

DADU (1554–1603)
The Bani

What faith in God needs to begin with is the fair and simple assumption that great good can come to be, if we follow the call of conscience toward the heights and reach out for all possible resources in the struggle for good.

WALTER MARSHALL HORTON (1895–1966)
The God We Trust

Through love, through hope, through
faith's transcendent dower,
We feel that we are greater than we know.
WILLIAM WORDSWORTH (1770–1850)
Duddon

Faith is the possibility which belongs to
men in God, in God Himself, and only in
God, when all human possibilities have been
exhausted.   KARL BARTH (1886–1968)
The Epistle to the Romans

To stand in the darkness and yet know that
God is light; to want to know the truth about
a thousand mysteries, the answer to a thousand problems, and not find the truth, the
answers, anywhere, and yet to know beyond
a peradventure that God is not hiding from
us anything which it is possible and useful for
us to know; to stand in the darkness and yet
know that God is light,—that is a great and
noble faith, a faith to which no man can come
who does not know God.
PHILLIPS BROOKS (1835–1893)
The Light of the World

We are wiser than we know. If we will not
interfere with our thought, but will act entirely, or see how the thing stands in God, we
know the particular thing, and every thing,
and every man. For the Maker of all things
and all persons stands behind us, and casts
his dread omniscience through us over
things.
RALPH WALDO EMERSON (1803–1882)
The Over-Soul

Even such a shell the universe itself
Is to the ear of Faith; and there are times,
I doubt not, when to you it doth impart
Authentic tidings of invisible things;
Of ebb and flow, and ever-enduring power;
And central peace, subsisting at the heart
Of endless agitation.
WILLIAM WORDSWORTH (1770–1850)
The Excursion

Nothing before, nothing behind;
The steps of faith
Fall on the seeming void, and find
The rock beneath.
JOHN GREENLEAF WHITTIER (1807–1892)
Faith

Now it is faith to believe that which you do
not yet see; and the reward of faith is to see
that which you believe.
SAINT AUGUSTINE (354–430)
Sermons

What is faith? Is it to believe what appears
quite evident? No: it is evident to me that
there is a Being, necessary, eternal, supreme,
intelligent; this is not a matter of faith, but of
reason. I deserve no credit for thinking that
this eternal, infinite Being, which I perceive
as virtue and goodness itself, wishes me to be
good and virtuous.
VOLTAIRE (1694–1778)
Philosophical Dictionary

Just as the body without the spirit is dead,
so faith is dead without good deeds.
The New Testament
James 2:26

The prayer that reforms the sinner and
heals the sick is an absolute faith that all
things are possible to God,—a spiritual understanding of Him, an unselfed love.
MARY BAKER EDDY (1821–1910)
Science and Health

If faith is the pioneer that leads us to
knowledge of persons and of moral possibilities; if by faith we discover ourselves, the
outer world's existence and its unity, why
should we be surprised that faith is our road
to God?
HARRY EMERSON FOSDICK (1878–1969)
The Meaning of Faith

Wherefore, if God so clothe the grass of
the field, which today is, and tomorrow is cast

into the oven, shall he not much more clothe you, O ye of little faith?   *The New Testament*
Matthew 6:30

Man's primal faith is that God himself accepts the terms of earth. By this faith every visible thing is a word, and the whole creation the vast sign language of God.

GEORGE ARTHUR BUTTRICK (1892–1979)
Prayer

There are subjects where reason cannot take us far and we have to accept things on faith. Faith then does not contradict reason but transcends it. Faith is a kind of sixth sense which works in cases which are without the purview of reason.

MOHANDAS K. GANDHI (1869–1948)
Harijan

Any man who believes in God must realize that no scientific fact, as long as it is true, can contradict God. Otherwise, it would not be true. Therefore, any man who is afraid of science does not possess a strong faith.

PIERRE LECOMTE DU NOUY (1883–1947)
Human Destiny

He who hath faith hath wisdom; he that hath wisdom hath peace. He that hath no wisdom and no faith, whose soul is one of doubt, is destroyed.   *The Mahabharata*

Faith is an obscure communion with the infinitely luminous knowledge which the divine Abyss has of itself. Faith instructs us in the depths of God. Faith stands above any human system, no matter how valid; it is concerned with the revealed data, with that glory which cannot be named by any human name, yet has desired to make itself known to us in words which all may understand.

JACQUES MARITAIN (1882–1973)
The Range of Reason

The road that leads us to the living God, the God of the heart, and that leads us back to Him when we have left Him for the lifeless God of logic, is the road of faith, not of rational or mathematical conviction.

MIGUEL DE UNAMUNO (1864–1936)
The Tragic Sense of Life

Belief consists in accepting the affirmations of the soul; unbelief, in denying them.

RALPH WALDO EMERSON (1803–1882)
Montaigne

You call for faith:
I show you doubt, to prove that faith exists.
The more of doubt, the stronger faith, I say,
If faith o'ercomes doubt.

ROBERT BROWNING (1812–1889)
Bishop Blougram's Apology

I believe it! 'Tis Thou, God, that givest, 'tis I
    who receive;
In the first is the last, in thy will is my power
    to believe.
All's one gift; thou canst grant it moreover,
    as prompt to my prayer
As I breathe out this breath, as I open these
    arms to the air.

ROBERT BROWNING (1812–1889)
Saul

Faith in faith established evermore
Stands a sea-mark in the tides of time.

ALGERNON CHARLES SWINBURNE (1837–1909)
A Sea-Mark

Our world is the embodied material of our duty. This is the only possible confession of faith: cheerfully and unconstrainedly to do whatever duty commands, without doubt and calculation as to the results. This living and active moral order is God himself; we need no other God, and can grasp no other.

JOHANN GOTTLIEB FICHTE (1762–1814)
The Vocation of Man

Where there is faith, where there is need, there is the True God ready to clasp the hands that stretch out seeking for him into the darkness behind the ivory and gold.

H. G. WELLS (1866–1946)
God the Invisible King

We have but faith: we cannot know,
  For knowledge is of things we see;
  And yet we trust it comes from Thee,
A beam in darkness: let it grow.
    ALFRED LORD TENNYSON (1809–1892)
                In Memoriam

Faith is not built on disquisitions vain;
The things we must believe are few and
  plain.   JOHN DRYDEN (1631–1700)
                Religio Laici

If we held fast to God through the media-
tion of a lively faith; if we held fast to God
through himself, not through ourselves; if we
had a divine base and foundation, human
chances would not have the power to stagger
us as they do.
MICHEL EYQUEM DE MONTAIGNE (1533–1592)
              Apology for Raimond Sebond

I thank thee, gracious Lord, I thank thee;
because what I formerly believed by thy
bounty, I now so understand by thine illumination, that if I were unwilling to believe that
thou dost exist, I should not be able to understand this to be true.
            SAINT ANSELM (1033–1109)
                Proslogion

For not only Christians but all manner of
men do so believe in God as to hold all for
truth they hear Him say, whether they understand it or not; which is all the faith and
trust that can possibly be had in any person
whatsoever; but they do not all believe the
doctrine of the creed.
          THOMAS HOBBES (1588–1679)
                Leviathan

Faith always implies the disbelief of a lesser
fact in favor of a greater. A little mind often
sees the unbelief, without seeing the belief of
large ones.
    OLIVER WENDELL HOLMES (1809–1894)
            The Professor at the Breakfast Table

The only faith that wears well, and holds
its colors in all weathers, is that which is
woven of conviction and set with the sharp
mordant of experience.
    JAMES RUSSELL LOWELL (1819–1891)
                My Study Windows

We read in the Talmud that forty-nine
doors of understanding out of fifty were
opened to Moses. But since man aspires always to know more, how did Moses continue?
The answer is that when he found the fiftieth
door closed to him as unapproachable to the
human mind, he substituted faith and medi-
tated again upon those phases of knowledge
open to him.
          BAAL SHEM TOV (1700–1760)
                Sayings

The outward aspect of religious faith is
sometimes expressed in an absurd form, but
the light of God nevertheless abides in it.
There are seemingly absurd situations
throughout nature and existence, but the absurdity derives only from the limited vision
and the inadequate conception of the grandeur that inheres in everything small as well
as great.
    ABRAHAM ISAAC KOOK (1865–1935)
                The Moral Principles

Faith is the song of life. Woe to him who
wishes to rob life of its splendid poetry. The
whole mass of prosaic literature and knowledge is of value only when it is founded on
the perception of the poetry of life.
    ABRAHAM ISAAC KOOK (1865–1935)
                Oroth Hakodesh

Faith is allowed us as the appointed antagonist of Fear; and none are so ready with the
true courage and calmness of a man, as those
whose trust is in One that is higher than man.
        JAMES MARTINEAU (1805–1900)
            Hours of Thought on Sacred Things

Do you want a fearless faith, be careful not
to measure the comparative forces of your-

self and others; but remember that God is working for you to will and do of his own good pleasure. If He is for you, who can be against you?

FREDERICK BROTHERTON MEYER (1847–1929)
Our Daily Homily

Whoever has bread in his basket today and says, "What shall I eat tomorrow?" is to be regarded as a person who is lacking in faith.

The Talmud

And all is well, tho faith and form
    Be sundered in the night of fear;
    Well roars the storm to those that hear
A deeper voice across the storm.

ALFRED LORD TENNYSON (1809–1892)
In Memoriam

Just as the right order of going requires that we should believe the deep things of God before we presume to discuss them by reason, so it seems to me negligence if, after we have been confirmed in the faith, we do not study to understand what we believe.

SAINT ANSELM (1033–1109)
Cur Deus Homo

The first step in faith, its true quintessence, is something much more like a trust that the whole scheme of things will not play us false, that our deepest natures are not irretrievably out of tune with the deepest natures of that which holds us in its power, and that there is therefore an available way of salvation from the apparent vanity and uncertainty of life.

JOHN BAILLIE (1886–1960)
The Interpretation of Religion

The faith which Jesus required of men was neither credal adherence nor mystic ecstasy so much as the faith that is in some sort native to every pure and gentle heart—the faith in man, the faith in life, the faith in the power of love, the faith in the Unseen Love of God.

JOHN BAILLIE (1886–1960)
The Roots of Religion in the Human Soul

The hope which springs from faith is so much a part of the life of faith that one must say: the future, for which it hopes, is the present in which the believer lives.

EMIL BRUNNER (1889–1966)
Eternal Hope

Let no phantasy and imagination of faith at any time beguile you, but be sure of your faith; try it by your living; look upon the fruits that cometh of it; mark the increase of love and charity by it towards God and your neighbor; and so shall you perceive it to be a true lively faith.

THOMAS CRANMER (1489–1556)
Sermons

Belief and love—a believing love will relieve us of a vast load of care. O my brothers, God exists. There is a soul at the center of nature and over the will of every man, so that none of us can wrong the universe.

RALPH WALDO EMERSON (1803–1882)
Spiritual Laws

As is a man's meditation, so is his feeling of love.
As is a man's feeling of love, so is his gain.
And faith is the root of all.

SRI RAMAKRISHNA (1834–1886)
Gospel

No man can create faith in himself. Something must happen to him which Luther calls "the divine work in us," which changes us, gives us new birth, and makes us completely different people in heart, spirit, mind, and all our powers.

COUNT NIKOLAUS LUDWIG VON ZINZENDORF
(1700–1760)
Nine Public Lectures on Religion

Faith precedes all attempts to derive it from something else, because these attempts are themselves based on faith.

PAUL TILLICH (1886–1965)
Dynamics of Faith

Faith has to do with things that are not seen, and hope with things that are not in hand.   SAINT THOMAS AQUINAS (1225–1274)
Summa Theologica

One result of the unbelief of our day is the tragedy of trying to live a maximum life on a minimum faith. What we need is not faith in more things, but more faith in a few profound things.

RUFUS JONES (1863–1948)
The Testimony of the Soul

Give me, O God, to sing that thought,
Give me, give him or her I love, this
  quenchless faith
In thy ensemble; whatever else withheld,
  withhold not from us
Belief in plan of Thee enclosed in Time and
  Space,
Health, peace, salvation universal.

WALT WHITMAN (1819–1892)
Leaves of Grass

I will not doubt forever more,
  Nor falter from a steadfast faith,
For though the system be turned o'er,
  God takes not back the word which once
  he saith.

HENRY DAVID THOREAU (1817–1862)
Inspiration

Faith means seeking not noise but quiet, and letting God speak within—the righteous God, for there is no other. And then God works in us. Then begins in us, as from a seed, but an unfailing seed, the new basic something which overcomes unrighteousness.   KARL BARTH (1886–1968)
The Word of God and the Word of Man

In all your work believe in heartfelt faith, for this is the beginning of the commandments.   *The Old Testament Apocrypha*
The Wisdom of Jesus ben Sirach 32:23

The efficacy of faith is such that from its fruits it is very evident in whose hearts it really is.

PHILIPP MELANCHTHON (1497–1560)
Loci Communes

Faith is the soul's insight or discovery of some Reality that enables a man to stand anything that can happen to him in the universe.

JOSIAH ROYCE (1855–1916)
Sources of Religious Insight

The aim of our charge is love that issues from a pure heart and a good conscience and a faith that is unfeigned.

The New Testament
1 Timothy 1:5

Every right temper, and then all right words and actions, naturally branch out of love. In effect, you want nothing but this—to be filled with the faith that worketh by love.

JOHN WESLEY (1703–1791)
Sermons

Faith is the final assertion of the freedom of the human spirit, but also the final acceptance of the weakness of man and the final solution for the problem of life through the disavowal of any final solutions in the power of man.   REINHOLD NIEBUHR (1892–1971)
Discerning the Signs of the Times

Saving faith, fertile faith, consists in maintaining the struggle between your heart and your head, between your feelings and your intelligence, while the former cries *Yes!* and the latter says *No!*

MIGUEL DE UNAMUNO (1864–1936)
The Life of Don Quixote and Sancho

No coward soul is mine,
No trembler in the world's storm-troubled
    sphere;
  I see Heaven's glories shine,
And faith shines equal, arming me from
    fear.

EMILY BRONTË (1818–1848)
Last Lines

There is no human consciousness so depraved, that the thought of the love of God cannot occur to it, and consequently no kind of degree of abjectness from which the redeeming faith, founded on that thought, cannot uplift a man.

S. H. HODGSON (1832–1912)
The Metaphysic of Experience

To know the reasons which have moved God to choose this order of the universe, to permit sin, to dispense his salutary grace in a certain manner,—this passes the capacity of a finite mind, above all when such a mind has not come into the joy of the vision of God.

GOTTFRIED WILHELM VON LEIBNIZ
(1646–1716)
Metaphysical Discourses

I lift up mine eyes unto the hills, from whence cometh my help. My help cometh from the Lord who made heaven and earth.

The Old Testament
Psalms 121:1–2

My Soul, let your love of the Lord be like
    that of the lotus for the water,
Overcome by waves, it still flowers in love.
Living things created in the water, if taken
    out of the water, die.
My Soul, how can you be saved without
    love?

GURU NANAK (1469–1539)
The Adi Granth

I have not seen, I may not see,
    My hopes for man take form in fact,
But God will give the victory
    In due time; in that faith I act.

JOHN GREENLEAF WHITTIER (1807–1892)
The Last Walk in Autumn

If we cannot sing of faith and triumph, we will sing our despair. We will be that kind of bird. There are day owls, and there are night owls, and each is beautiful and even musical while about its business.

HENRY DAVID THOREAU (1817–1862)
Letters

Faith only exists where a "word" is accepted by the soul, or rather, where this "word" captures the soul because it comes from God, and its truth is thus self-evident.

EMIL BRUNNER (1889–1966)
The Mediator

If we honestly consider within ourselves how much our thought is blind to the heavenly secrets of God and how greatly our heart distrusts all things, we shall not doubt that faith greatly surpasses all the power of our nature and that faith is a unique and precious gift of God.   JOHN CALVIN (1509–1564)
Instruction in Faith

The look which goes from God into the soul is the beginning of faith whereby I believe things not revealed to me.

DIONYSIUS THE AREOPAGITE (5th century)
Mystical Theology

If mountains can be moved by faith,
Is there less power in love?

FREDERICK WILLIAM FABER (1814–1863)
Sermons

Faith is precisely the contradiction between the infinite passion of the individual's inwardness and the objective uncertainty. If I am capable of grasping God objectively, I do not believe, but precisely because I cannot do this I must believe.

SÖREN KIERKEGAARD (1813–1855)
Concluding Unscientific Postscript

Through the night of faith it is given us to attain in His inner life—on the testimony of His Word—the very God who will be intuitively grasped when faith gives way to vision.

JACQUES MARITAIN (1882–1973)
Approaches to God

Faith is a gift of God; do not think we say it is a gift of reasoning.

BLAISE PASCAL (1623–1662)
Pensées

Faith is a total and centered act of the personal self, the act of unconditional, infinite and ultimate concern.

PAUL TILLICH (1886–1965)
Dynamics of Faith

Faith is never self-evident, natural; it is always miraculous. The belief that God is the Father and man is the child of God is not an insight which can be gained directly—it is not an insight at all. On the contrary, it must be believed, ever and again, as the miraculous act of God. But it must be believed, truly, in faith.   RUDOLF BULTMANN (1884–1976)
Faith and Understanding

Who don't keep faith with God, won't keep it with man.   *Dutch Proverb*

Faith is a deep-seated capacity in man to forecast possibilities, a preperception of the way forward, a leap of vision which carries one beyond the verifiable courses of action.

RUFUS JONES (1863–1948)
A Call to What Is Vital

We shall be made truly wise if we be made content; content not only with what we can understand, but content with what we do not understand—the habit of mind which theologians call, and rightly, faith in God.

CHARLES KINGSLEY (1819–1875)
Sermons

Whoever has faith cannot define it, and whoever has none can only give a definition which lies under the shadow of grace withheld. The man of faith cannot speak and the man of no faith ought not to speak.

FRANZ KAFKA (1883–1924)
Conversations with Kafka

We are supposedly after the clarity of an immovable faith, but really we want an assur-

ance so unquestionable as to spare us faith and its decision. We think we seek the spirit of faith, but are only seeking the noonday of axiomatic earthly truths instead of the certainty of the spirit that dwells in the obscurity of faith.   KARL RAHNER (1904–)
Servants of the Lord

A man's real faith is never contained in his creed, nor is his creed an article of his faith. The last is never adopted. This it is that permits him to smile ever, and to live even as bravely as he does. And yet he clings anxiously to his creed, as to a straw, thinking that that does him good service because his sheet anchor does not drag.

HENRY DAVID THOREAU (1817–1862)
A Week on the Concord and Merrimack Rivers

If faith produce no works, I see
That faith is not a living tree;
Thus faith and works together grow,
No separate life they e'en can know,
They're soul and body, hand and heart—
What God hath joined, let no man part.

HENRY MORE (1614–1687)
Faith

Faith is not merely a history or a science. To have faith is nought else than for a man to make his will one with God's, and take up God's word and might in his will, so that these twain, God's will and man's will, turn to one being and substance.

JACOB BOEHME (1575–1624)
Aurora

Faith brings us home;
So that I need no more, but say
I do believe,
And my most loving Lord straightway
Doth answer, live!

HENRY VAUGHAN (1622–1695)
Faith

Faith is not an aesthetic emotion but something far higher, precisely because it has resignation as its presupposition; it is not an immediate instinct of the heart, but is the paradox of life and existence.

SÖREN KIERKEGAARD (1813–1855)
Fear and Trembling

The mysteries and secrets of the kingdom of God first seek for believing men, that they may make them understanding. For faith is understanding's step; and understanding is faith's attainment.

SAINT AUGUSTINE (354–430)
Sermons

From faith flows forth love and joy in the Lord, and from love a cheerful, willing, free spirit disposed to serve our neighbor voluntarily, without taking any account of gratitude or ingratitude, praise or blame, gain or loss. Its object is not to lay men under obligations nor does it distinguish between friends and enemies, or look to gratitude or ingratitude, but most freely and willingly spends itself and its goods, whether it loses them through ingratitude, or gains goodwill.

MARTIN LUTHER (1483–1546)
Concerning Christian Liberty

Understanding is the reward of faith. Therefore seek ye not to understand that thou mayest believe, but believe that thou mayest understand.

SAINT AUGUSTINE (354–430)
Saint Julius Gospel

If we know God, if we really understand the impulse that dominates Him, we can walk in the battle of life by faith that "He doeth all things well," though man may not.

CHARLES EDWARD GARMAN (1850–1907)
Lectures

What is faith? It is assenting to a doctrine as true, which we do not see, which we cannot prove, because God says it is true, who cannot lie. And further than this, since God says it is true, not with His own voice, but by the voice of His messengers, it is assenting to what man says, not simply viewed as a man, but to what he is commissioned to declare, as a messenger, prophet, or ambassador from God.

JOHN CARDINAL NEWMAN (1801–1890)
Discourses to Mixed Congregations

There is no doubt that every man who ennobles his soul with excellent morals and wisdom based on faith in God certainly belongs to the men of the world to come.

MAIMONIDES (1135–1204)
Letters

Our knowledge is a torch of smoky pine
That lights the pathway but one step
  ahead
Across a void of mystery and dread.
Bid, then, the tender light of faith to shine
By which alone the mortal heart is led
Unto the thinking of the thought divine.

GEORGE SANTAYANA (1863–1952)
Sonnet III

Many men have just enough faith to trust God as far as they can see Him, and they always sing as far as they can see providence go right; but true faith can sing when its possessors cannot see. It can take hold of God when they cannot discern Him.

CHARLES HADDON SPURGEON (1834–1892)
Sermons

Faith is the knowledge of the meaning of human life, in consequence of which man does not destroy himself but lives. Faith is the force of life. If a man lives he believes in something. If he did not believe there was something to live for, he would not live. If he does not see and understand the unreality of the finite, he believes in the finite; if he sees that unreality, he must believe in the infinite. Without faith it is impossible to live.

LEO TOLSTOY (1828–1910)
My Confession

Faith is to be considered as the gift of God, not on account of its being offered by God to man, to be accepted or rejected as his pleasure, but because it is in reality conferred, breathed, and infused into him.

JACOBUS ARMINIUS (1560–1609)
Remonstrance

Perfection of faith is only when you believe in God without philosophizing, with no omens and without research at all.

RABBI NAHMAN OF BRATZLAV (1772–1811)
Discourses

Faith is not a thing which one "loses," we simply cease to shape our lives by it.

GEORGES BERNANOS (1888–1948)
Diary of a Country Priest

Faith is the opening of all sides and every level of one's life to the divine inflow.

MARTIN LUTHER KING, JR. (1929–1968)
Strength to Love

Faith in God is the great loosener of bonds. It frees us of all that binds, fetters, and shackles, whether it be the fear of life or the fear of death, whether it be the fear of power of others over us or fear of the lack of power within ourselves.

ABBA HILLEL SILVER (1893–1963)
Sermons

He who would in his own person test the fact of God's presence can do so by a living faith. And since faith itself cannot be proved by extraneous evidence, the safest course is to believe in the moral government of the world and therefore in the supremacy of the moral law, the law of truth and love.

He is no God who merely satisfies the intellect, if He ever does. God to be God must rule the heart and transform it. He must express Himself in every smallest act of His votary.   MOHANDAS K. GANDHI (1869–1948)
Hindu Dharma

Every rational conception of God is in itself contradictory. Faith in God is born of love for God—we believe that God exists by force

of wishing that He may exist, and it is born also, perhaps, of God's love for us. Reason does not prove to us that God exists, but neither does it prove He cannot exist.

MIGUEL DE UNAMUNO (1864–1936)
The Tragic Sense of Life

We may well know that there is a God without knowing what He is. By faith we know His existence; in glory we shall know His nature.   BLAISE PASCAL (1623–1662)
Pensées

Faith is the only true and certain good—yea, faith in God; the consolation of life, the fulfilment of the highest hopes, the death blow to evils, the purveyor of benefits, the end of unhappiness, the knowledge of piety, the assurance of bliss, the progress of a soul which in all things rests assured upon God, the Author of all, who can do everything, but wills only what is best. It is faith alone which makes our path secure.

PHILO JUDAEUS (30 B.C.–A.D. 40)
Hymn of Faith

By faith man experiences an inward change of nature, called "regeneration," and an outward change in his relationship called "justification." By this faith we are saved from all uneasiness of mind, from the anguish of a wounded spirit, from discontent, from fear and sorrow of heart, and from that inexpressible listlessness and weariness, both of the world and ourselves, which we had so helplessly labored under for many years. In this we find that love of God and all mankind which we had elsewhere sought in vain.

JOHN WESLEY (1703–1791)
Journal

Faith is a gift of God, which man can neither give nor take away by promise of rewards or menaces of torture.

THOMAS HOBBES (1588–1679)
Leviathan

One in whom persuasion and belief
Has ripened into faith, and faith become
A passionate intuition.
WILLIAM WORDSWORTH (1770–1850)
The Excursion

Our hearts, our hopes, are all with thee,
Our hearts, our hopes, our prayers, our
tears,
Our faith triumphant o'er our fears,
Are all with thee,—are all with thee!
HENRY WADSWORTH LONGFELLOW
(1807–1882)
The Building of the Ship

Reason is our soul's left hand, Faith her
right,
By these we reach divinity.
JOHN DONNE (1572–1631)
To the Countess of Bedford

But give me, Lord, eyes to behold the truth;
A seeing sense that knows the eternal right;
A heart with pity filled, and gentlest ruth;
A manly faith that makes all darkness light.
THEODORE PARKER (1810–1860)
The Higher Good

Thy path is plain, and straight,—that light is
given:
Onward in faith,—and leave the rest to
Heaven.
ROBERT SOUTHEY (1774–1843)
The Retrospect

The sea of faith
Was once, too, at the full, and round earth's
shore
Lay like the folds of a bright girdle furl'd.
But now I only hear
Its melancholy, long, withdrawing roar,
Retreating to the breath
Of the night-wind, down the vast edges
drear
And naked shingles of the world.
MATTHEW ARNOLD (1822–1888)
Dover Beach

If we will disbelieve everything because we
cannot certainly know all things, we shall do
much—what as wisely as he who would not
use his legs, but sit still and perish, because
he had no wings to fly.
JOHN LOCKE (1632–1704)
Concerning Human Understanding

Faith is love taking the form of aspiration.
WILLIAM ELLERY CHANNING (1780–1842)
Note-books

Love needs faith, because only when an ultimate certainty takes away from man his
anxious care for himself can love be pure
love. And faith does not need love, but brings
love with it unasked through its own inner
necessity. For faith which is the life-giving
work of God in man, cannot exist without
human creative life proceeding from it.
MARTIN LUTHER (1483–1546)
Works

I stretch lame hands of faith, and grope,
And gather dust and chaff, and call
To what I feel is Lord of all,
And faintly trust the larger hope.
ALFRED LORD TENNYSON (1809–1892)
In Memoriam

They breathed in faith their well-directed
prayers
And the true God, the God of truth, was
theirs.
WILLIAM COWPER (1731–1800)
Expostulation

He it is Who sendeth down a spirit of secure repose into the hearts of the faithful,
that they might add faith to their faith.
The Koran

To the man who has no faith in God, faith
in God cannot look like righteousness; neither can we know that it is creative of all
other righteousness toward equal and inferior lives.
GEORGE MACDONALD (1824–1905)
Unspoken Sermons

Faith walking in the dark with God only prays Him to clasp its hand more closely, does not even ask Him for the lifting of the darkness so that the man may find the way himself.   PHILLIPS BROOKS (1835–1893)
Sermons

A genuine faith must recognize the fact that it is through a dark glass that we see; though by faith we do penetrate sufficiently to the heart of the mystery not to be overwhelmed by it. A genuine faith resolves the mystery of life by the mystery of God.
REINHOLD NIEBUHR (1892–1971)
Discerning the Signs of the Times

Faith summons all men to its judgment, for faith is a new dimension of thought revealing the path to the Creator. Moreover, faith is an unfathomable creative force, a great, magnificent, and incomparable gift of God.
LEV SHESTOV (1866–1938)
Athens and Jerusalem

That man is perfect in faith who can come to God in the utter dearth of his feelings and desires, without a glow or an aspiration, with the weight of low thoughts, failures, neglects, and wandering forgetfulness, and say to Him, "Thou art my refuge."
GEORGE MACDONALD (1824–1905)
Unspoken Sermons

In prayer, the flinging of our life on God in faith, is the overcoming of our deep nostalgia.
GEORGE ARTHUR BUTTRICK (1892–1979)
Prayer

It is impossible to realise perfect Truth so long as we are imprisoned in this mortal frame. We can only visualise it in our imagination. We cannot, through the instrumentality of this ephemeral body, see face to face Truth, which is eternal. That is why one has ultimately to fall back on faith.
MOHANDAS K. GANDHI (1869–1948)
Young India

I take courage from the faith that, however confused and discordant the life of this world may seem, there is ever present, like a Pilgrim Chorus, the eternal harmony of the Spirit of the Whole; and the music of this in my soul—distant and faint though it often seems—is the inspiration to strive to bring more harmony into a chaotic world.
JOHN ELOF BOODIN (1869–1950)
God: A Cosmic Philosophy of Religion

Everyone must follow the unperverted impulse of heart, conscience, reason, faith; the law of life, call it what you will.
LEO TOLSTOY (1828–1910)
Emblems

Faith is required of thee, and a sincere life, not loftiness of intellect, nor deepness in the mysteries of God.
THOMAS À KEMPIS (1380–1471)
Imitation of Christ

It is the heart that senses God, and not reason. That is what faith is, God perceptible to the heart and not to the reason.
BLAISE PASCAL (1623–1662)
Pensées

Faith is that light above our every achievement. Nothing other than the light of faith can lift us to it because it itself is most high. It pours forth over us; by it we are raised up. From this it is able to be described as closed and incomprehensible to us although it comprehends us.
MARTIN LUTHER (1483–1546)
Sermons

The mystic possesses God in his experience, the orthodox possesses Him in his system of creeds or in the book. True faith, however, is in no sense at my disposal or in my possession; it is God's free gift.
EMIL BRUNNER (1889–1966)
The Word and the World

Faith—is the Pierless Bridge
Supporting what we see
Unto the Scene that we do not.

EMILY DICKINSON (1830–1886)
Faith Is the Pierless Bridge

It is no slight achievement of faith to think of God immanent in the whole vast universe, but those who accomplish that act of faith feel him very near and mysteriously present, pulsating in their own souls in every yearning for truth and love and right.

WALTER RAUSCHENBUSCH (1861–1918)
Christianizing the Social Order

The doctrine of creation is not a speculative cosmogony, but a confession of faith, of faith in God as Lord.

RUDOLF BULTMANN (1884–1976)
Primitive Christianity

The Bhagavad Gita gives us a religion by which the rule of karma, the natural order of deed and consequence, can be transcended. There is no element of caprice or abitrary interference of a transcendent purpose within the natural order. The teacher of the Gita recognizes a realm of reality where karma does not operate, and if we establish our relations with it, we are free in our deepest being. The chain of karma can be broken here and now, within the flux of the empirical world. We become masters of karma by developing detachment and faith in God.

SARVEPALLI RADHAKRISHNAN (1888–1975)
The Bhagavad Gita

The world's great heart has proved equal to the prodigious undertaking which God set it. Rebuffed, but always persevering; self-reproached, but ever regaining faith; undaunted, tenacious, the heart of man labors toward immeasurably distant goals.

HELEN KELLER (1880–1968)
The Open Door

That God is the creator, all men could know from Nature; but what this God is in person, can be known only by special grace, is the object of a special faith.

LUDWIG FEUERBACH (1804–1872)
The Essence of Christianity

It is for the sake of the interior eyes whose blindness consists in not understanding, that hearts are purified by faith (Acts 15:9), that they may be opened and may be made more and more clear of vision. For although, unless he understand somewhat, no man can believe in God, nevertheless by the very faith whereby he believes, he is helped to the understanding of greater things.

SAINT AUGUSTINE (354–430)
Sermons

Faith itself is a mystery. It is a gift from heaven, but a gift received within ourselves.

JACQUES MARITAIN (1882–1973)
The Range of Reason

Thou canst not prove the Nameless, O my
    son,
Nor canst thou prove the world thou movest
    in,
Thou canst not prove that thou art body
    alone,
Thou canst not prove that thou art spirit
    alone,
Nor canst thou prove that thou art both in
    one:
Nor yet that thou art mortal—nay, my son,
Thou canst not prove that I, who speak
    with thee,
Am not thyself in converse with thyself,
For nothing worthy proving can be proven,
Nor yet disproven: wherefore thou be wise,
Cleave ever to the sunnier side of doubt,
Cling to Faith beyond the forms of Faith!

ALFRED LORD TENNYSON (1809–1892)
The Ancient Sage

Whatever we say about that which concerns us ultimately, whether or not we call it God, it has a symbolic meaning. It points beyond itself while participating in that to which it points. In no other way can faith express itself adequately.

PAUL TILLICH (1886–1965)
Dynamics of Faith

Faith allows the greatest latitude in philosophic speculation, allowing us without blame to think what we like about anything, and only condemning, as heretics and schismatics, those who teach opinions which tend to produce obstinacy, hatred, strife, and anger; while, on the other hand, only considering as faithful those who persuade us, as far as their reason and faculties will permit, to follow justice and charity. But as to what God may be, whether fire, or spirit, or light, or thought, or what not, this, I say, has nothing to do with faith any more than the question of how He comes to be the Exemplar of the true life, whether it be because He has a just and merciful mind, or because all things exist and act through Him, and consequently that we understand through Him, and through Him see what is truly just and good. Everyone may think on such questions as he likes.   BENEDICT SPINOZA (1632–1677)
Theologico-Political Treatise

Through the dark and stormy night
Faith beholds a feeble light
    Up the blackness streaking;
Knowing God's own time is best,
In a patient hope I rest
    For the full day-breaking!
JOHN GREENLEAF WHITTIER (1807–1892)
Barclay of Ury

Now faith is the substance of things hoped for, the evidence of things not seen. Through faith we understand that the worlds were framed by the word of God, so that things which are seen were not made of things which do appear.   *The New Testament*
Hebrews 11:1,3

All the more consoling was the lesson
That faith in God depends not on the views
We entertain of him.
GOTTHOLD EPHRAIM LESSING (1729–1781)
Nathan the Wise

Put your faith to the test of life and see whether it will not justify your confidence. If God be really what our faith assumes, we shall find him unifying our thinking, satisfying our sense of beauty or of wonder, opening out to us an enlarging and enfranchising life.   WILLIAM ADAMS BROWN (1865–1943)
The Life of Prayer in a World of Science

He will not enter hell, who hath faith equal to a single grain of mustard seed in his heart: and he will not enter paradise, who hath a single grain of pride, equal to one of mustard seed, in his heart.   *The Hadith*

To this or that form devotees present their worship, having faith, yet I myself will allocate to everyone unswerving faith.
The Bhagavad Gita

Faith cannot be made the subject of an injunction or a law; to believe does not lie within the sphere of willing. Faith, considered even as a relation between one man and another, cannot be commanded nor produced by willing but may be aroused, inspired; between man and God it is purely a gift.   RUDOLF OTTO (1869–1937)
Religious Essays

God does not deal, nor has he ever dealt with man otherwise than through a word of promise. We, in turn, cannot deal with God otherwise than through faith in the word of his promise. He does not desire works, nor has he need of them; rather we deal with men and with ourselves on the basis of works. But God has need of this: that we consider him faithful in his promises and patiently persist in this belief, and thus worship him with faith, hope and love.

MARTIN LUTHER (1483–1546)
The Babylonian Captivity of the Church

It is faith's work to claim and challenge loving-kindness out of all the roughest strokes of God.

SAMUEL RUTHERFORD (1600–1661)
Sermons

In God alone is there faithfulness, and faith in the trust that we may hold to Him, to His promise and to His guidance. To hold to God is to rely on the fact that God is there for me, and to live in this certainty.

KARL BARTH (1886–1968)
Dogmatics in Outline

Let us be like a bird for a moment perched
  On a frail branch when he sings;
Though he feels it bend, yet he sings his
    song,
  Knowing that he has wings.

VICTOR HUGO (1802–1885)
Wings

Faith in life endless, the sustaining thought
Of human Being, Eternity, and God.

WILLIAM WORDSWORTH (1770–1850)
The Prelude

Faith in itself is already a beginning of divinity. It is as though the divinity, desiring to bring salvation to man, was compelled to throw out a divine bridge from the heavenly sphere across the abyss of our earthly confinement.   SHOLEM ASCH (1880–1957)
What I Believe

Faith itself springs and has always sprung from that "reason of the heart," that migratory instinct towards a goal towards which we can go but which while we travel we can never adequately define.

GERALD HEARD (1889–1971)
The Code of Christ

A prerequisite to knowing God as the Power that makes for human self-fulfillment or happiness is the faith that human nature is capable of achieving it. To believe in God we have to exercise wisdom; to believe in man we have to exercise faith.

MORDECAI M. KAPLAN (1881–)
The Religion of Ethical Nationhood

Our beginning is faith. It may be enclosed in our hearts like a treasure in an unused shrine, and lie there, well protected, but if a poor man should come to us we should open our hearts and give him the gift that is in our heart—this gift is love.

PARACELSUS (1493–1541)
Letters to the Athenians

Without faith all that is done of us is dead before God, although the work seem never so gay and glorious before man.

THOMAS CRANMER (1489–1556)
Sermons

Not only in works, but also in faith, God has given man freedom of the will.

IRENAEUS (2nd century)
Adversus Haereses

Faith, like light, should ever be simple and unbending, while love, like warmth, should beam forth on every side and bend to every necessity of our brethren.

MARTIN LUTHER (1483–1546)
Table-Talk

Faith declares what the senses do not see, but not the contrary of what they see. It is above them, not contrary to them.

BLAISE PASCAL (1623–1662)
Pensées

It is not God Who must prove to us that He is good and holy: it is we who are called upon to show that we do not need the bait of constant reward to keep us faithful in our love. Sometimes the clouds gather and all seems impenetrably dark. It is then that we are called upon to love in faith—to nurse our firm belief in the stars of sweet reasonableness that continue to shine behind the darkness of events which seem to us sour and grim and beyond our understanding.

KARL RAHNER (1904–)
Happiness Through Prayer

Faith, in a certain sense, creates its object. And faith in God consists in creating God, and since it is God that gives us faith in Him, it is God who is continually creating Himself in us. MIGUEL DE UNAMUNO (1864–1936)
Essays and Soliloquies

Faith is the resolution to stand or fall by the noblest hypothesis. It must be a matter of the will rather than of the intellect, both because ultimate truth is beyond our reach, and because, whether consciously or unconsciously, our world is constructed out of those facts which interest us and bear upon our own needs.

WILLIAM RALPH INGE (1860–1954)
Sermons

· BELIEVE TO THE END ·

When a man says, "I believe in God," he is saying, "I have bet my life on Him."

JAMES A. PIKE (1913–1969)
A Time for Christian Candor

No iron chain, or outward force of any kind, could ever compel the soul of man to believe or disbelieve: it is his own indefeasible light, that judgement of his; he will reign and believe there by the grace of God alone!

THOMAS CARLYLE (1795–1881)
On Heroes and Hero-Worship

No man ever believes with a true and saving faith unless God inclines his heart; and no man when God does incline his heart can refrain from believing. This David well knew when he prayed, "Incline my heart, O God, unto thy testimonies."

BLAISE PASCAL (1623–1662)
Pensées

We are born believing. A man bears beliefs as a tree bears apples.

RALPH WALDO EMERSON (1803–1882)
The Conduct of Life

To believe in God our strength in the face of all seeming denial, to believe in Him out

of the heart of weakness and unbelief, in spite of numbness and weariness and lethargy; to believe in the wide-awake real, through all the stupefying, enervating, distorting dream; to will to wake, when the very being seems athirst for a godless repose—these are the broken steps up to the high fields where repose is but a form of strength, strength but a form of joy, joy but a form of love. GEORGE MACDONALD (1824–1905)
Sermons

Every believer is God's miracle.

PHILIP JAMES BAILEY (1816–1902)
Festus

If this belief from heaven be sent,
If such be Nature's holy plan,
Have I not reason to lament
What Man has made of Man?

WILLIAM WORDSWORTH (1770–1850)
Written in Early Spring

To see the world as being ruled by a divine love which sets infinite value upon each individual and includes all men in its scope, and yet to live as though the world were a realm of chance in which each must fight for his own interests against the rest, argues a very dim and wavering vision of God's rule.

JOHN HICK (1922–)
Faith and Knowledge

God is that which I must rely upon if I am to succeed in my quest for the good life; that which, when I open the flood-gates of my soul to its incoming, makes the tide of life to mount within me, till all my existence is full of meaning; that without which the tide of life begins to ebb within me, till all my existence becomes flat, stale, and unprofitable.

WALTER MARSHALL HORTON (1895–1966)
Theism and the Modern Mood

And the scribe said unto him, Well, Master, thou hast said the truth: for there is one God; and there is none other but he: And to love him with all the heart and with all the understanding, and with all the soul, and with all the strength, and to love his neighbor as himself, is more than all whole burnt offerings and sacrifices.   *The New Testament*
Mark 12:32-33

Believe to the end, even if all men went astray and you were left the only one faithful; bring your offering even then and praise God in your loneliness.

FYODOR DOSTOEVSKY (1821–1881)
The Brothers Karamazov

I will both lay me down in peace, and sleep: for thou, Lord, only makest me dwell in safety.   *The Old Testament*
Psalms 4:8

When I say, "I believe in God," the assertion means something entirely different from the statement, "I believe in the existence of ether waves"; or, "The moon is inhabited"; or, "Human nature is always the same." It means not only that I accept the existence of God, even though it not be fully demonstrable, but it implies also a certain subjective relation to him, a going out of the affections to

him, an attitude of life; in all of which there is a peculiar mixture of faith as a kind of method of knowledge with practical impulses and feelings.   GEORG SIMMEL (1858–1918)
A Contribution to the Sociology of Religion

Theologians may puzzle their heads about dogma as they will, the religion of gratitude cannot mislead us. Of that we are sure, and gratitude is the handmaid to hope and hope the harbinger of faith. I look abroad upon Nature, I think of the best part of our species, I lean upon my friends and I meditate upon the Scriptures, especially the Gospel of St. John; and my creed rises up of itself with the ease of an exhalation, yet a fabric of adamant.   WILLIAM WORDSWORTH (1770–1850)
Letter to Sir John Beaumont

The theistic believer cannot explain *how* he knows the divine presence to be mediated through his human experience. He just finds himself interpreting his experience in this way. He lives in the presence of God, though he is unable to prove by any dialectical process that God exists.   JOHN HICK (1922–)
Faith and Knowledge

My son, keep your spirit always in such a state as to desire that there be a God, and you will never doubt it.

JEAN JACQUES ROUSSEAU (1712–1778)
Emile

Seeing God, Job forgets all he wanted to say, all he thought he would say if he could but see Him.

GEORGE MACDONALD (1824–1905)
Unspoken Sermons

To believe in the God over us and around us and not in the God within us—that would be a powerless and fruitless faith.

PHILLIPS BROOKS (1835–1893)
Sermons

Every person, of whatever religious denomination he may be, is a Deist in the first article of his Creed. Deism, from the Latin

word Deus, God, is the belief of a God, and this belief is the first article of every man's creed.   THOMAS PAINE (1737–1809)
Prospect Papers

To believe is not enough; all depends on how we believe. I may believe that there is no God, that in the economy of this world without limit my existence counts for as little as the evanescent hue of a flower—I may believe all this, in a deeply religious spirit, with the infinite throbbing within me; you may believe in one all-powerful God, who cherishes and protects you, yet your belief may be mean, and petty, and small. And if the thoughts and feelings on which my doubt re-poses have become vaster and purer than those that support your faith, then shall the God of my disbelief become mightier and of supremer comfort than the God to whom you cling. For, indeed, belief and unbelief are mere empty words; not so the loyalty, the greatness and profoundness of the reasons wherefore we believe or do not believe.

MAURICE MAETERLINCK (1862–1949)
Wisdom and Beauty

The Ten Commandments and the Sermon on the Mount contain my religion.

JOHN ADAMS (1735–1826)
Letter to Thomas Jefferson

· WE PAUSE IN GRATITUDE ·

O Lord! that lends me life,
Lend me a heart replete with thankfulness!
WILLIAM SHAKESPEARE (1564–1616)
Henry VI

Some people always sigh in thanking God.
ELIZABETH BARRETT BROWNING (1806–1861)
Aurora Leigh

To the Spirit great and good,
Felt, although not understood,—
By whose breath, and in whose eyes,
The green earth rolls in the blue skies,—
Who we know, from things that bless,
Must delight in loveliness;
And who, therefore, we believe,
Means us well in things that grieve,—
Gratitude! Gratitude!
LEIGH HUNT (1784–1859)
Hymn

An easy thing, O Power Divine,
To thank Thee for these gifts of Thine,
For summer's sunshine, winter's snow,
For hearts that kindle, thoughts that glow;

But when shall I attain to this—
To thank Thee for the things I miss?
THOMAS W. HIGGINSON (1823–1911)
The Things I Miss

His mind was a thanksgiving to the power
That made him. It was blessedness and
     love.
WILLIAM WORDSWORTH (1770–1850)
The Excursion

Thou hast given so much to me
Give one thing more—a grateful heart:
Not thankful when it pleaseth me,
As if thy blessings had spare days,
But such a heart whose Pulse may be
Thy Praise.
GEORGE HERBERT (1593–1633)
A Heart to Praise Thee

Receive every day as a resurrection from death, as a new enjoyment of life; meet every rising sun with such sentiments of God's goodness, as if you had seen it, and all things, new created upon your account: and under the sense of so great a blessing, let your joyful heart praise and magnify so good and glorious a Creator.

WILLIAM LAW (1686–1761)
A Serious Call to a Devout and Holy Life

Thank God every morning when you get up that you have something to do that day which must be done, whether you like it or not. CHARLES KINGSLEY (1819–1875)
Town and Country Sermons

The ungrateful who forget God, shall wander. GURU ARJAN (1563–1606)
Hymns

Every struggle that we make to live is a prayer to God for life. And the continuance of our existence is God's answer to our prayer. But when we first take the life which He gives us we do not know what it is. Its depth, its richness only opens to us gradually. Only gradually do we learn that God has given to us not merely the power of present being and present enjoyment, but that wrapt up and hidden in that He has given us the power of thinking, feeling, loving, living in such deep and lofty ways that we may be in connection with the great continuous unbroken thoughts and feelings and movements of the universe.

PHILLIPS BROOKS (1835–1893)
Sermons

God would not put a difficulty upon you, but he desires to purify you, and to complete His favor upon you, that you may give thanks. *The Koran*

The faith be mine,
That He who guides and governs all,
        approves
When gratitude, though disciplined to look
Beyond these transient spheres, doth wear a
        crown
Of earthly hope put on with trembling
        hand.
WILLIAM WORDSWORTH (1770–1850)
Memorials of a Tour in Italy

He who partakes of anything of the goods of this world without reciting a blessing of gratitude to God is as if he had been stealing from the Holy One, blessed is He.

The Talmud

From thy hand, O Lord, do we receive everything! Thou stretchest out Thy powerful hand and takest the wise in their foolishness. Thou openest it, Thy gentle hand, and satisfiest whatever lives with blessing. And even if it seems that Thine hand is shortened, then do Thou increase our faith and our confidence, so that we may hold Thee fast.

SÖREN KIERKEGAARD (1813–1855)
Prayer

Faith is, on one side, self-surrender. But surrender is only the first stage in the human process which corresponds to redemption; the second stage is atonement, or reconciliation. God redeems man from evil and guilt, and man feels himself reconciled to God.

WILLIAM RALPH INGE (1860–1954)
Faith and Its Psychology

The word "atonement" which occurs in the Bible again and again, means literally at-one-ment. To be at one with God is to be like God. Our real religious striving, then, should be to become one with God, sharing with Him in our poor human way His qualities and His attributes. To do this we must get the inner life, the heart right, and we shall then become strong where we have been weak, wise where we have been foolish.

BOOKER T. WASHINGTON (1856–1915)
Up from Slavery

Lord of the world, rather a bitter olive given by Thee than sweets provided by man.

The Talmud

One man may perhaps provoke another to reflect upon "the righteousness of God." But no man may bring another to the peculiar, immediate, penetrating certainty which lies behind the phrase.

KARL BARTH (1886–1968)
The Word of God and the Word of Man

The heart of man is so great if it is righteous that God begrudges him nothing. But if it not righteous and holds no goodness in it, even the Lord's Prayer is poison in such a man's mouth.   PARACELSUS (1493–1541)
Liber Principiorum

God imposeth no law of righteousness upon us which he doth not observe himself.
BENJAMIN WHICHCOTE (1609–1683)
Moral and Religious Aphorisms

For therein is the righteousness of God revealed from faith to faith: as it is written, the just shall live by faith.   *The New Testament*
Romans 1:17

Faithful is the Lord to them that love Him in
    truth,
  To them that endure His chastening,
To them that walk in the righteousness of
    His commandments,
  In the law which He commanded us
    that we might live.

The Old Testament Apocrypha
Psalms of Solomon 14:1-2

VI · The Enigma of Evil

If there is a God, whence come evils?
But whence comes good, if there is none?

BOETHIUS

Nᴇᴀʀʟʏ sixteen hundred years ago Saint Augustine confronted one of the most difficult problems mankind has ever encountered in its quest to understand God: "Either God cannot abolish evil, or He will not. If he cannot, He is not all-powerful; if He will not, He is not all-God." This troubling puzzle had been voiced before by some of the early Greek philosophers, but never with such stark directness. Dramatically voicing his anguished confusion in another passage of the *Confessions*, Augustine cried out, "Whence my ability to wish evil and to refuse the good? Who placed this in me and planted the seedling of bitterness in me, since my whole being is from my most sweet God? If the Devil is the originator, then what is the source of the Devil?"

For Augustine there had to be an answer, albeit one that provided a rationale that God, indeed, had a reason for letting both good and evil coexist in his created world. Clearly, the alternative that God did not have the power to create a world without evil in it was unthinkable. In a later work, *Enchiridion*, Augustine reasoned: "Were it not good that evil things should also exist, the omnipotent God would most certainly not allow evil to be, since beyond doubt it is just as easy for Him not to allow what He does not will, as it is for Him to do what He will." In his greatest work, *The City of God*, he reiterated this thought, reasoning that God would never have created any being whose future evil nature he foreknew "unless He had equally known to what uses in behalf of the good He could turn him."

Throughout the centuries since Saint Augustine first posed this dilemma there have been countless attempts to resolve it, generally centering on the question of how an all-powerful God, whose essence is love and compassion, could have created a world in which evil could so readily flourish. In this section of our anthology the God Seekers address the entire spectrum of evil, and in the course of their exploration face such corollaries as sin, temptation, hypocrisy, and hell and its nominal ruler, the devil.

For many of the God Seekers the problem of evil and sin is, as Nikolai Berdyaev wrote, "part and parcel of the problem of freedom." Echoing what Milton had posited in *Paradise Lost,* Berdyaev, in his study of Dostoevsky, said that unless God had created us with the option to choose good *or* evil we would be little more than puppets. He concluded, "If there were no freedom, then God alone could be responsible for evil."

To those who cannot accept this premise and who remain torn by the problem voiced by Saint Augustine, this rationale has a major flaw. The atheist can argue that if

God is omniscient, if, indeed, his plan for this world existed from eternity in himself, then God *knew* before He created men and women that they would often choose evil. Freedom, yes, but a freedom that was little more than a truism if God already knew what the choice would be.

As Berdyaev also pointed out in *The Destiny of Man*, this dilemma causes the good as well as the wicked to rebel against God. Whereas many good people, including some who may call themselves atheists, cannot reconcile themselves to the existence of evil and are ready to question God or even vent their anger toward him, the wicked hate God because He often prevents them from doing evil.

Why God allowed evil into his world will always be a difficult mystery to solve. Yet, we seldom, if ever, ask ourselves why He allowed the opposite of evil, goodness, into his world, taking it for granted that this is an attribute of God. Perhaps our best course lies, as Meister Eckhart says, in accepting that there never will be a time in this life when we are entirely safe from an evil outcome of events. However, in his words, "because the rats have gotten into the wheat once is no reason to throw away the good wheat as well."

Closely allied with the modality of evil, the theme of sin has also engaged the scrutiny of God Seekers. Few have defined it more forcefully than John Bunyan, proclaiming in one of his sermons that "sin is the dare of God's justice, the rape of His mercy, the jeer of His patience, the slight of His power, and the contempt of His love."

To the Talmudic scholars, sin was "an obstruction in the heart, an inability to feel and comprehend all that is noble, true, and great, and to take part in the good." Father Gerald Vann, in *Stones or Bread,* took this thought one step further by reading sin as an "arrogation to ourselves of the sovereignty of God." By this he meant that we have the ominous power of opposing, and thus negating, God's will by consciously choosing to abjure the more noble aspects of our existence.

In his treatise *De Domo Disciplinae*, Saint Augustine once again revealed his deep insight into why people act against themselves: "Truly, he who loveth iniquity hateth his own soul. Therefore, if you love iniquity, you hate yourself." Although we are enjoined by scripture to love our neighbor as ourself, what kind of love can we offer when we lack the will or strength to reach beyond our self-indulgence? Saint Augustine ironically adds, "If you love yourself in such a way that you compass your own destruction, I have no wish to see you loving anyone as much as you love yourself."

The worldly obsession with acquiring wealth and material goods is a theme that also troubles the God Seekers in this section. Kierkegaard stated it succinctly in one of his *Journal* entries: "Man must choose between God and Mammon. This is the eternal, unchangeable condition of choice, which can never be evaded—no, not to all eternity."

Martin Luther, in one of the homilies in his *Table-Talk,* said that God gives us many gifts—some physical, such as beauty or healthy, graceful physiques; or gifts of the mind, such as understanding or wisdom. But worldly wealth is "the least worthy gift which God can give man." Why, then, do we toil for it day and night without rest or peace of mind, Luther asks. His answer is that "God commonly gives riches to foolish people, to whom he gives nothing else."

Mammon, he said elsewhere in *Table-Talk,* is a double-headed, deceiving idol. This prince of materialism makes us feel secure when everything is going well with us, so secure that we give little thought to God, if indeed we don't put him completely from our minds. On the other hand, as Luther points out, "when it goes ill with us, then we tempt God, fly from Him, and seek after another God."

In one of his sharpest aphorisms, Benjamin Whichcote observed, "It is a very great evil to make God a means, and the world an end; to name God, and to intend the world." As the God Seekers verify throughout this section, there have always been people who make a great show of external practices while, in Eckhart's words, they "cling to their selfish I."

The etymology of the word hypocrite, derived from the Greek *hypokritēs,* which means actor, describes what Benjamin Franklin meant when he wrote that "serving God is doing good to man, but praying is thought an easier Service, and therefore more generally chosen." Or as the Koran notes, "They say with their mouths what is not in their hearts, but God knows best what they hide."

Charles Lamb must have ruminated a long time on the words of the Sermon on the Mount before he wrote a terse, brilliant quatrain on how most people see the mote in their neighbor's eye but can never conceive of the beam in their own. In his poem "On the Lord's Prayer," Lamb said,

> You pray that your "trespasses may be forgiven,
> As you forgive those that are done unto you."
> Before this you say to the God that's in heaven,
> Consider the words which you speak—Are they true?

As William Penn observed, "In his prayers he says, Thy will be done, but means his own. At least acts so." In a world that places so much emphasis on material success, on becoming a celebrity, a world in which actors seem more real to us than our very selves, hypocrisy becomes a suit of clothes we too readily don.

Concomitant with the presence of evil as the sum force of mankind's negativity, the concept of the devil has from earliest times played an integral part in religious thought. Although men and women probably had their personal demons from the very beginning of their perplexity about the nature of their existence, it wasn't until Zoroaster named the evil force Ahriman that the devil became a central part of a religion.

If it seems strange that men had to learn to hate the devil before they could learn to love God, perhaps it was because Zoroaster could not conceptualize a better way to focus primitive thought on the need to recognize and overcome evil. We know now that Zoroaster's demonic adversary, Ahriman, later called Satan in the Old Testament and Prince of the World by Jesus, finally became the devil of medieval Christians, the "ancient foe," as Luther termed him in his great hymn "A Mighty Fortress Is Our God."

The consensus is that just as each man and woman finds God in a unique, individual way, so the devil can tailor himself to fit our individual personalities. Asserting that even in our holiest moments our personal devil stands close by with a smirk, Henry David Thoreau wrote, "He is a very busy devil. It gains vice some respect, I must confess, thus to be reminded of how indefatigable it is."

The God Seekers offer us some good advice on how to avoid the adversary, this Satan who seems doomed throughout eternity to be what Goethe called "the spirit of negation." The Baal Shem Tov suggested that when we perceive that Satan is trying to get us to commit an evil deed we should realize that he is only endeavoring to do his duty *as he conceives it.* Therefore, says the Baal Shem Tov, "Learn from him diligence in performing your bounded duty—namely to battle and overcome his persuasion." Indeed, Satan is the master of persuasion, which is why the Talmudists warned that when the devil tells you, "Go ahead, sin if you want to, God will forgive you," don't believe him!

Throughout the centuries, the devil has been called, among other things, a slanderer, a blasphemer, and a flatterer, but one of the most fascinating depictions comes from the pen of the anonymous writer of that fourteenth-century gem of German mysticism, *Theologia Germanica:* "The devil thinks he is God, or would like to be God or regarded as God Himself, or he lets himself be deluded into this kind of thinking. He is so deluded that he firmly believes he is not deluded."

John Milton's stirring portrait of the devil in *Paradise Lost* found its source in the Old Testament, probably in that memorable passage from the book of the prophet Isaiah wherein that preeminent master of narration recreated the drama of Satan's rebellion against God. "How art thou fallen from heaven, O Lucifer, son of the morning! How art thou cut down to the ground, which didst weaken the nations! For thou hast said in thine heart, I will ascend into heaven, I will exalt my throne above the stars of God."

The Devil's greatest act of evil may have occurred when he induced Adam to eat the apple from the Tree of Knowledge. Right from the beginning man was impatient to know all of God's secrets, to know the absolute dynamics of good and evil, which cost Adam dearly. As Montaigne put it, "The first temptation that came to human nature on the part of the devil, his first poison, insinuated itself into us by the promises he made us of learning and knowledge."

The nature and locus of hell is another theme that has intrigued the God Seekers as they explore the dimensions of evil. Although hell traditionally has been described as a region beneath the earth in which the devil holds court over a fiery prison, the term is often used metaphorically as well. Sir Thomas Browne, for example, in his *Religio Medici*, said that the devil dwells in the human heart, and "I feel sometimes a hell within myself." When Father Zossima in Dostoevsky's *Brothers Karamazov* is asked the question "What is hell?" he replies: "I maintain that it is the suffering of being unable to love."

Dean William Ralph Inge maintained that heaven and hell are not two discrete places but rather two ends of a ladder of values, and the mystic Johannes Tauler would probably have agreed, for he wrote, "I would rather be in hell and possess God, than be in heaven without God." Angelus Silesius, née Johannes Scheffler, the seventeenth-century physician who became intoxicated with the joy of his mystic rapprochement with God, would also agree:

> In you is hell's abyss, in you is heaven's grace,
> What you elect and want you have in any place.

The prophet Muhammad took one of the most optimistic views on the diminution of evil; in the Hadith the founder of Islam said, "Surely a day will come over Hell, when it will be like a field of corn that has dried up after flourishing for a while—a day when there shall not be a single human being in it."

When it comes to the point where no evasions and no equivocations can be made, men and women *do* create their own individual hells or heavens even during their short sojourn in life. Consider the Hindu and Buddhist concept of karma, a Sanskrit word meaning act or deed, with its root in the verb *karoti* (to make, to do). It recognized that people's actions, whether good or evil, during the successive phases of their life determined their destiny.

God, through a continuous succession of those prophets and kindred men and women of great spiritual sensibilities whom we have termed the God Seekers, has given a clear ethical plan to his children. But, as Saint Paul so aptly put it in his Epistle to the Galatians (6:7), "Make no mistake about this: God is not to be fooled; a man reaps what he sows."

The final theme in this section is the evil consequences of pride. There is a tale told in the Midrash that when King David had completed the Book of Psalms he felt inordinately proud and addressed God, asking, "Hast Thou a creature who has proclaimed more praises on Thee than I?" Whereupon God sent a frog to appear before the King with this message: "David, don't take such a pride in yourself. I chant the praises of my Creator as much as you do. Moreover, I perform a great virtue in that when it comes my time to die I go down to the sea and permit myself to be swallowed up by one of its creatures. So, even my death is a deed of kindness."

The Baal Shem Tov always enjoined his followers to avoid thinking that any one of them was superior to any fellow creature in devotion to God, remarking, "A worm may be as important as you in the eyes of the Creator, since it serves him with all the strength granted to it."

No one can know whether the concept of evil is exclusive to this world. Perhaps, as Saint Augustine and many other God Seekers have thought, God has allowed evil into this piece of his universe as a trial of our faith in him, and He would not have given us this challenge without also giving us the strength to overcome evil and change it into good.

· But Deliver Us from Evil ·

Doubtless the long passage through the experience of good and evil could be made much shorter and easier by limiting or even entirely suppressing human liberty. But what is the value of men coming entirely to God otherwise than by the road of freedom and after having experienced the harmfulness of evil?   NIKOLAI BERDYAEV (1874–1948)
Dostoevski

Prophecy is God's voice, speaking to us respecting the issue in all times of that great struggle which is the real interest of human life, the struggle between good and evil. Beset as we are by evil within us and without, it is the natural and earnest question of the human mind, What shall be the end at last? And the answer is given by Prophecy, that it shall be well at last; that there shall be a time when good shall perfectly triumph.
          THOMAS ARNOLD (1795–1842)
Sermons

God permits the wicked, but not for ever.
          THOMAS FULLER (1654–1734)
Gnomologia

Innumerable attempts have been made to try to solve the puzzle: How can a God of love who is all-powerful permit conditions in which evil and sin are ever able to emerge at all? In respect of sin, Saint Augustine provided an answer that was indeed very perspicacious in its way. He argued that, because God wants his creatures to love him freely, he must allow them freedom of choice: to love him or to hate him. Love that is forced is not the kind of love he wants, and for the kind he wants the creature must be free to choose whether he will give that love or withhold it.   GEDDES MACGREGOR (1909–)
He Who Lets Us Be

The most hateful evil in the world is the evil that dresses itself in such a way that men can not hate it. The men that make wickedness beautiful are the most utterly to be hated.
          HENRY WARD BEECHER (1813–1887)
Sermons

If there be a pain which devils might pity man for enduring, it is the death-bed reflection that we have possessed the power of doing good, but we have abused and perverted it to the purposes of ill.
          CHARLES CALEB COLTON (1780–1832)
Lacon

The belief in a supernatural source of evil is not necessary; men alone are quite capable of every wickedness.
          JOSEPH CONRAD (1857–1924)
Under Western Eyes

We have to carry on the struggle against the evil that is in mankind, not by judging others, but by judging ourselves. Struggle with oneself and veracity towards oneself are the means by which we influence others. We quietly draw them into our efforts to attain the deep spiritual self-realization which springs from reverence for one's own life.
          ALBERT SCHWEITZER (1875–1965)
Philosophy of Civilization

Roaming in thought over the Universe, I
    saw the little that is Good steadily
    hastening towards immortality,
And the vast that is Evil I saw hastening to
    merge itself and become lost and dead.
          WALT WHITMAN (1819–1892)
Roaming in Thought After Reading Hegel

Learned men have taught us that not only with a choice of evils we should choose the least, but that from the evil we should endeavor to extract some good.

MARCUS TULLIUS CICERO (106–43 B.C.)
De Officiis

To prefer evil to good is not in human nature; and when a man is compelled to choose one of two evils, no one will choose the greater when he might have the less.

PLATO (427–347 B.C.)
Protagoras

Let us not look about and say, "How does evil get into the world?" for that question will only be answered when you can tell why God preferred to make men as he did make them, the sum of nothing, with the capacity to develop into infinite power in infinite directions.

HENRY WARD BEECHER (1813–1887)
Sermons

When we talk about evil persons, this may give rise to evil thoughts, and hence, God forbid, to bringing evil into the world. Therefore, let us talk only about the good ways of righteous men, and so bring good into the world.

RABBI ZECHARIAH MENDEL OF JAROSLAV
(18th century)
Darke Zedek

God will say to the prince of Hell, "I from above and thou from below shall judge and condemn the slanderer."   *The Talmud*

The more deeply we become aware of the reality of evil, the less we can explain it. Sin is something which we cannot explain, something which will not fit into any reasonable scheme at all. For it is the primal fact of non-reason. The more we try to explain evil, the more we deny its reality, and the more superficial we become. The more anyone knows what evil is, the more inexplicable it becomes.

EMIL BRUNNER (1889–1966)
The Mediator

Our attitude towards concrete evils is entirely different in a world where we believe there are none but finite demanders, from what it is in one where we joyously face tragedy for an infinite demander's sake. Every sort of energy and endurance, of courage and capacity for handling life's evils, is set free in those who have religious faith.

WILLIAM JAMES (1842–1910)
The Moral Philosopher and the Moral Life

Our primary need is not to control our passions by our purpose, but to direct our purpose itself to the right end. It is the form taken by our knowledge of good and evil that perverts our nature. We know good and evil, but know them amiss. We take them into our lives, but we mis-take them.

WILLIAM TEMPLE (1881–1944)
Nature, Man and God

And so evil is not in God and is not divine. Nor cometh it of God. For either He is not good, or else He worketh goodness and bringeth good things unto existence.

DIONYSIUS THE AREOPAGITE (5th century)
The Divine Names

The wicked are like the troubled sea, when it cannot rest, whose waters cast up mire and dirt. There is no peace, saith my God, for the wicked.   *The Old Testament*
Isaiah 57:20–21

Do men relish health enough or thank God enough for it, without having ever been sick? And is it not most often necessary that a little evil render the good more discernible, that is to say, greater?

GOTTFRIED WILHELM VON LEIBNIZ
(1646–1716)
Theodicy

The only admissable moral theory of creation is that the Principle of Good cannot at once and altogether subdue the powers of evil, either physical or moral.

JOHN STUART MILL (1806–1873)
Three Essays on Religion

If evil is merely called finite error, this finite error remains none the less, as a fact of human experience, an evil. One has only changed the name. The reality remains what it was.   JOSIAH ROYCE (1855–1916)
The World and the Individual

I have always felt that the reason why the mystery of evil is so baffling is because we so resolutely think of evil as of something inimical to the very nature of God; and yet evil must derive its vitality from him. The one thing that is impossible to believe is that, in a world ruled by an all-powerful God, anything should come into existence which is in opposition to his Will.

ARTHUR CHRISTOPHER BENSON (1862–1925)
The Thread of Gold

There is not only good in man but also evil, just as there is not only truth in the world but also falsehood. Man's finite endeavors may be swayed by the influence of evil, and his finite intellect may fall prey to the lures of falsehood. But though he be susceptible to evil and error—for inadequacy and finiteness are part of the human conditon—man is not evil by nature, that is, not by divine intent. . . . Though he may indeed go wrong, man is not innately evil; he always remains a creature of God, who is the Originator and Guarantor of the good on earth.

HERMANN COHEN (1842–1918)
Jewish Writings

That man is good or evil is not indifferent to God; no! He has a lively, profound interest in man's being good; he wills that man should be good, happy—for without goodness there is no happiness.

LUDWIG FEUERBACH (1804–1872)
The Essence of Christianity

Woe unto them that seek deep to hide their counsel from the Lord, and their words are in the dark, and they say, Who seeth us? and who knoweth us?   *The Old Testament
Isaiah 29:15*

If we assure our heart let us do so in God's presence. For if our heart feel evil, that is, charges us inwardly of not acting with the right intention, "God is greater than our heart and knoweth all things." You may hide your heart from man: hide it from God if you can.   SAINT AUGUSTINE (354–430)
Homilies on 1 John

If evil is not something directly willed by God and not something wholly outside of his control, but something in his good world which he has temporarily permitted to exist while he calls for volunteers to oppose and correct it, then the task of overcoming evil is never a hopeless one.

WALTER MARSHALL HORTON (1895–1966)
The God We Trust

Where there appears to be an irreconcilable contradiction between the omnipotence and the goodness of God, there our finite wisdom has come to the end of its tether, and we do not understand the solution which yet we believe in.

RUDOLF HERMANN LOTZE (1817–1881)
Microcosmos

My son, the world is dark with griefs and
    graves,
So dark that men cry out against the
    Heavens.
Who knows but that the darkness is in man?
ALFRED LORD TENNYSON (1809–1892)
Ancient Sage

If God is all powerful He must be the Creator of evil as well as of good. All the suffering of the world would seem to be finally attributed to Him. If the suffering is due to disharmonies in the order of the world, which God has not mastered, and to recalcitrant forces which He has not subdued, the goodness of God becomes more sharply defined; but His power is called into question. This rational contradiction lies at the heart of faith's apprehension of the Holiness of God. It is never completely resolved.

REINHOLD NIEBUHR (1892–1971)
Sermons

It is the maxim of most wicked men, that the Deity is some way or another like themselves; their souls do more than whisper it, though their lips speak it not; and though their tongues be silent, yet their lives cry it upon the house-tops and in the public streets.

JOHN SMITH (1616–1652)
Excellency and Nobleness of True Religion

As fire cannot extinguish, so evil cannot suppress evil. Good alone, confronting evil and resisting its contagion, can overcome evil. And in the inner world of the human soul, the law is as absolute as was even the law of Galileo, more absolute, more clear, more immutable.   LEO TOLSTOY (1828–1910)
My Religion

Father of Light! how blind is he
Who sprinkles the altar he rears to Thee
With the blood and tears of humanity!

JOHN GREENLEAF WHITTIER (1807–1892)
The Preacher

The evil in the world is indeed terrifyingly real, both at the subpersonal and at the personal level; but it is still part of the face of God. That is to say, love is there to be met and to be created through it and out of it.

JOHN A. T. ROBINSON (1919–)
Exploration into God

Evil in relation to man is manifold in that it takes semblance for substance, and tries to get away from the divine primal source instead of striving to unite with it.

The Zohar

Thanks to those gifts which the Creator has given him, man can emancipate himself from his Creator and make himself his own lord. That is what the Bible calls sin. We see at once that this has nothing to do with animal nature, but has a purely spiritual origin. Evil, understood like this, is much more dangerous, much more profound and alarming, than what idealistic philosophy conceives as evil.

EMIL BRUNNER (1889–1966)
The Scandal of Christianity

Let no man think of evil, saying in his heart, it will not come nigh unto me. Even by the falling of water-drops a water-pot is filled; the fool becomes full of evil even if he gather it little by little.   *The Dhammapada*

Our standard of value is the way things affect ourselves. So each of us takes his place in the centre of his own world. But I am not the centre of the world, or the standard of reference between good and bad; I am not, and God is.

WILLIAM TEMPLE (1881–1944)
Christianity and the Social Order

Good is a principle of totality, of coherence, of meaning; evil is a principle of fragmentariness, of incoherence, of mockery. Hence there is no immanent logic in evil; evil is the Satan that laughs at logic.

EDGAR S. BRIGHTMAN (1884–1953)
A Philosophy of Religion

We must never feel that God will, through some breathtaking miracle or a wave of the hand, cast evil out of the world. As long as we believe this we will pray unanswerable prayers and ask God to do things that he will never do. The belief that God will do everything for a man is as untenable as the belief that man can do everything for himself. It, too, is based on lack of faith.

MARTIN LUTHER KING, JR. (1929–1968)
Strength to Love

If you set your mind on humanity, you will be free from evil.

CONFUCIUS (551–479 B.C.)
Analects

It is difficult to explain the presence of evil in the world of a good God, but to some of us it is impossible to explain the goodness in the world on the basis of no God. The mystery of evil is very great upon the basis of a good God, but the mystery of goodness is impossible upon the basis of no God.

HARRY EMERSON FOSDICK (1878–1969)
Riverside Sermons

God set the one over against the other, good against evil, and evil against good; good out of good, and evil out of evil; good testing evil, and evil testing good; good is stored away for the good, and evil is stored away for the evil.   *The Kabbalah*

In all goodness we must see the manifestation of the divine purpose, in all evil a temporary failure in its realisation. In so far as men strive for its realisation they are ethically at one with God; in so far as they lose sight of this end they are ethically at variance with him.

WILLIAM RITCHIE SORLEY (1855–1935)
Moral Values and the Idea of God

Many men, whether it be their fate, or fond opinion, easily persuade themselves, if God would but be pleas'd a while to withdraw his just punishments from us, and to restrain what power either the devil, or any earthly enemy hath to work us woe, that then man's nature would find immediate rest and releasement from all evils.

JOHN MILTON (1608–1674)
The Doctrine and Discipline of Divorce

Wherefore take unto you the whole armour of God, that ye may be able to withstand the evil day, and having done all, to stand. Stand, therefore, having your loins girt about with truth, and having on the breastplate of righteousness; and your feet shod with the preparation of the gospel of peace. Above all, taking the shield of faith, wherewith ye shall be able to quench all the fiery darts of the wicked.

The New Testament
Ephesians 6:11–16

If I am in the grip of evil, that is, if I am tempted to despair of myself or of men or of God himself, it is not by turning in on myself that I will manage to overcome this temptation; for solipsism cannot be a liberation. My only recourse is to open myself to a wider communion, perhaps an infinite one, at the heart of which this evil which has come on me in some way changes its nature.

GABRIEL MARCEL (1889–1973)
Tragic Wisdom and Beyond

And this is the condemnation, that light is come into the world, and men loved darkness rather than light, because their deeds were evil. For every one that doeth evil hateth the light, neither cometh to the light, lest his deeds be reproved. But he that doeth truth cometh to the light, that his deeds may be made manifest, that they are wrought in God.   *The New Testament*
John 3:19–21

We are fellow-workers together with God in the actualisation of a moral order: otherwise the world were not a moral order at all. For the possibility of moral evil entering into this moral order, God, who foreknew it, is responsible: He permits, so to say, the evil in order that there may be the good. But for the actual emergence of man's moral evil we cannot say that He is responsible: our sin, when "sin" is strictly and correctly defined, is not God's act but the product of our volition, or devolved freedom.

F. R. TENNANT (1866–1957)
Philosophical Theology

Because the designs of God's providence are deeply hidden and His judgment as great deeps, it happens that some, seeing that all the evils which men do go unpunished, rashly conclude that human affairs are not governed by God's providence or even that all crimes are committed because God so wills. "Both errors are impious," says St. Augustine, "especially the latter."

SAINT ROBERT BELLARMINE (1542–1621)
On the Ascent of the Mind to God

An infinite multitude of possible worlds lay before the vision of God. Evil was involved in every one which he conceived as possible, but out of all this infinitude of possibilities he selected for realisation the best possible. As absolutely good and wise he could select no other. And this world he selected, not because of its evil, but in spite of its evil, resolved to overrule the evil, which was inseparable from created being, to its greater good and his own greater glory. The only alternatives, therefore, were not between a more and a less imperfect world, but between the best possible world and no world at all. If there was to be no evil, there must be no creation; if God chose to create, he had no choice but to create the metaphysically imperfect, that is, those capable of suffering and of doing evil.

GOTTFRIED WILHELM VON LEIBNIZ
(1646–1716)
Theological Essays

Assuredly, he, who is only kept from vice by the fear of punishment, is in no wise acted on by love, and by no means embraces virtue. For my own part, I avoid or endeavor to avoid vice, because it is at direct variance with my proper nature and would lead me astray from the knowledge and love of God.

BENEDICT SPINOZA (1632–1677)
Letters

Evil is the inseparable condition of good in the world of will, the world of which time is the form. There is no evil in the eternal world in which God dwells, and because in that world there is no time, no conflict, no contingency of any kind.

WILLIAM RALPH INGE (1860–1954)
Outspoken Essays

Whoever, then, says, "To be a man is an evil," or "To be wicked is a good," falls under the prophetic denunciation: "Woe unto them that call evil good and good evil!" For he condemns the work of God, which is the man, and praises the defect of man, which is the wickedness. Therefore every being, even if it be a defective one, in so far as it is a being is good, and in so far as it is defective is evil.

SAINT AUGUSTINE (354–430)
Enchiridion

Because judgment upon an evil deed is not executed speedily, men's hearts are encouraged to do wrong, for a sinner commits a hundred crimes and God is patient with him, though I know the answer "it will be well in the end with those who revere God and fear Him and it will be far from well with the sinner, who, like a shadow, will not long endure, because he does not fear God.

The Old Testament
Ecclesiastes 8:11–13

A good man out of the good treasure of his heart bringeth forth that which is good; and an evil man out of the evil treasures of his heart bringeth forth that which is evil: for of the abundance of the heart his mouth speaketh.

The New Testament
Luke 6:45

We will never comprehend why the infinite will, in order to realize its completion, requires the incomplete, or how evil can result in good. No forced attempt to reason out these events can give us the peace of God. There is a different way, a way born from inward experience. We may not have been given the privilege of understanding how events are expressing the will of God. But one thing we do know, and on that knowledge all else depends—the will of God is directed only toward one thing: the spiritual.

ALBERT SCHWEITZER (1875–1965)
Reverence for Life

No religion which faces facts can minimize the evil in the world, not merely the moral evil, but the pain and the suffering. The book of Job is the revolt against the facile solution, so esteemed by fortunate people, that the sufferer is the evil person.

ALFRED NORTH WHITEHEAD (1861–1947)
Religion in the Making

I cannot account for the existence of evils by any rational method. To want to do so is to be co-equal with God. I am therefore humble enough to recognize evil as such. And I call God long-suffering and patient precisely because He permits evil in the world. I know that he has no evil.

MOHANDAS K. GANDHI (1869–1948)
Young India

Never did any public misery
Rise of itself: God's plagues still grounded are
On common stains of our humanity;
And, to the flame which ruineth mankind,
Man gives the matter, or at least gives wind.

FULKE GREVILLE (1554–1628)
Treaty of Wars

What you mean when you say that evil in this temporal world ought not to exist, and ought to be suppressed, is simply what God means by seeing that evil ought to be and is endlessly thwarted, endured, but subordinated. In the natural world you are the minister of God's triumph. Your deed is his.

JOSIAH ROYCE (1855–1916)
Studies of Good and Evil

Evil is a reality, and deserves only to be fought. But the means are given to do this.

For there is a Power for good that works not only side by side with man, but also in him and through him, flowering in that freedom which is given to his reason to get at truth, to his emotions, to love the beautiful, the good, and the true, and detest the ugly, the evil, and the false, and to his will and manhood to engage in the struggle.

EDWARD G. SPAULDING (1873–1940)
The New Rationalism

The kingdom of heaven is not the isolation of good from evil. It is the overcoming of evil by good. God has in his nature the knowledge of evil, of pain, and of degradation, but it is there as overcome with what is good.

ALFRED NORTH WHITEHEAD (1861–1947)
Religion in the Making

If ye look to your beginning and your author, which is God, is any man degenerate or base but he who by his own vices cherishes and leaves that beginning which was his?

BOETHIUS (480–524)
The Consolation of Philosophy

Not in the sky, not in the midst of the sea, not if we enter into the clefts of the mountains, is there known a spot in the whole world where a man might be freed from an evil deed. By oneself the evil is done, by oneself one suffers; by oneself evil is left undone, by oneself one is purified. Purity and impurity belong to oneself, no one can purify another.

GAUTAMA BUDDHA (563–483 B.C.)
The Dhammapada

I do not argue that God may commit evil, that good may come of it; but that he may will that evil should come to pass, and permit that it may come to pass, that good may come of it. It is in itself absolutely evil, for any being to commit evil that good may come of it; but it would be no evil, but good, if he had wisdom sufficient to see certainly that good would come of it, or that more good would come to pass that way than any other.

JONATHAN EDWARDS (1703–1758)
Concerning the Divine Decrees

The solution of the mystery called evil had better be left in God's own hands, to be given in his own good time.

LEIGH HUNT (1784–1859)
The Religion of the Heart

The soul itself its awful witness is.
Say not in evil doing, "No one sees."

JOHN GREENLEAF WHITTIER (1807–1892)
The Inward Judge

Good is the opposite of evil, and life of
  death;
yes, and the sinner is the opposite of the
  godly.
Look at all the works of the Most High:
they go in pairs, one the opposite of the
  other.

The Old Testament Apocrypha
Ecclesiasticus 33:14–15

Men never do evil so fully and so happily as when they do it for conscience' sake.

BLAISE PASCAL (1623–1662)
Pensées

The divine miracle par excellence consists surely in the apotheosis of grief, the transfiguration of evil by good. The work of creation finds its consummation, and the eternal will of the Infinite Mercy finds its fulfillment only in the restoration of the free creature to God and of an evil world to goodness, through love.   HENRI FRÉDÉRIC AMIEL (1821–1881)
Journal Intime

O mighty God, thou whose eyes are too pure to look upon evil, and who canst not countenance wrongdoing, why dost thou countenance the treachery of the wicked? Why keep silent when they devour men more righteous than they?   *The Old Testament*
Habakkuk 1:13

The righteous perish, and no man lays it to heart; and merciful men are taken away, no one considering that the righteous is taken away from the evil to come.

The Old Testament
Isaiah 57:1

A good End cannot sanctify evil Means; nor must we ever do Evil, that Good may come of it.   WILLIAM PENN (1644–1718)
Some Fruits of Solitude

Providence hath left man at liberty, not that he should do evil, but good by choice. . . . His powers, however, are at the same time so limited and confined, that the use he makes of his liberty is not of importance enough to disturb the general order of the universe. The evil done by man falls upon his own head, without making any change in the system of the world—without hindering the human species from being preserved in spite of themselves.

JEAN JACQUES ROUSSEAU (1712–1778)
Emile

There are in every man, at every hour, two simultaneous postulations, one towards God, the other towards Satan.

CHARLES BAUDELAIRE (1821–1867)
Mon Coeur Mis à Nu

If God is not all-powerful but existential, discovering the possibilities and limitations of His creative powers in the form of the history which is made by His creatures, then one must postulate an existential equal to God, an antagonist, the Devil, a principle of Evil whose signature was the concentration camps, whose joy is to waste substance, whose intent is to prevent God's conception of Being from reaching its mysterious goal.

NORMAN MAILER (1923–)
The Presidential Papers

There were two spirits, two parties, or, as Saint Augustine called them, two cities in the

world. The City of Satan, whatever its arti-
fices in art, war, or philosophy, was essentially corrupt and impious. Its joy was but a
comic mask and its beauty the whitening of a
sepulchre. It stood condemned before God
and before man's better conscience by its vanity, cruelty, and secret misery, by its ignorance of all that it truly behoved a man to
know who was destined to immortality.

GEORGE SANTAYANA (1863–1952)
The Life of Reason

The candor of science is the glory of the
modern. It does not hide and repress; it confronts, turns on the light. Does it not under-
mine the old religious standards? Yes, in
God's truth, by excluding the devil from the
theory of the universe—by showing that evil
is not a law in itself, but a sickness, a perversion of the good, and the other side of the
good—that in fact all of humanity, and of
everything, is divine in its bases.

WALT WHITMAN (1819–1892)
A Memorandum at a Venture

If God be good, how came he to create—
or, if he did not create, how come he to permit—the devil? The evil facts must be explained as seeming: the devil must be
whitewashed, the universe must be disinfected, if neither God's goodness nor his
unity and power are to remain impugned.

WILLIAM JAMES (1842–1910)
The Will to Believe

Epicurus' old questions are yet unan-
swered. Is he willing to prevent evil, but not
able? then is he impotent. Is he able, but not
willing? then is he malevolent. Is he both able
and willing? whence then is evil?

DAVID HUME (1711–1776)
Dialogues Concerning Natural Religion

God makes all things good; man meddles
with them and they become evil.

JEAN JACQUES ROUSSEAU (1712–1778)
Emile

The world is full of wickedness and misery
precisely because it is based on freedom—yet
that freedom constitutes the whole dignity of
man and of his world. Doubtless at the price
of its repudiation evil and suffering could be
abolished, and the world forced to be "good"
and "happy"; but man would have lost his
likeness to God, which primarily resides in
his freedom.

NIKOLAI BERDYAEV (1874–1948)
Dostoevski

Who spits against heaven, it falls in his
face.   GEORGE HERBERT (1593–1633)
Jacula Prudentum

Misfortune floods the earth. What shall we
infer from our weak rationalizations? That
there is no God? But it has been demonstrated to us that He exists. Shall we say that
God is wicked? But this idea is absurd and
contradictory. Shall we suspect that God is
powerless, and that He who has so well organized all the stars could not effectively or-
ganize mankind? This supposition is no less
intolerable. Shall we say that there is a bad
principle that alters the accomplishments of
a beneficent principle, or that produces from
it execrable works? But why does not this evil
principle upset the order of the rest of nature? Why should it persist in tormenting
some weak animals upon so puny a globe
while it would respect its worst enemy? Why
would it not attack God in those millions of
worlds that revolve regularly in space? Why
would two gods, enemies of one another,
each be equally necessary to the Being? How
would they exist together?

VOLTAIRE (1694–1778)
Homilies

The moral evil in the world is due to man's
alienation from the deepest truth, from the
springs of spiritual life within himself, to his
alienation from God.

THOMAS MERTON (1915–1968)
Christian Action in World Crisis

When God punishes sinners, He does not inflict His evil on them, but leaves them to their own evil.

SAINT AUGUSTINE (354–430)
Enarrationes in Psalms

When men shall roll up space,
  As if it were a piece of leather,
Then will there be an end of evil
  Apart from knowing God.

The Upanishads

The darkness knows neither the light nor itself; only the light knows itself and the darkness also. None but God hates evil and understands it.

GEORGE MACDONALD (1824–1905)
Unspoken Sermons

Evil is the brute motive force of fragmentary purpose, disregarding the eternal vision.

ALFRED NORTH WHITEHEAD (1861–1947)
Religion in the Making

If we accept good from God, shall we not accept evil?   *The Old Testament*
Job 2:10

By the light of grace, it is inexplicable how God can damn him who by his own strength can do nothing but sin and become guilty. Both the light of nature and the light of grace here insist that the fault lies not in the wretchedness of man, but in the injustice of God; nor can they judge otherwise of a God who crowns the ungodly freely, without merit, and does not crown, but damns another, who is perhaps less, and certainly not more, ungodly. But the light of glory insists otherwise, and will one day reveal God, to whom alone belongs a judgment whose justice is incomprehensible, as a God whose justice is most righteous and evident—provided only that in the meanwhile we *believe* it.

MARTIN LUTHER (1483–1546)
The Bondage of the Will

If every action, which is good or evil in man at ripe years, were to be under pittance and prescription and compulsion, what were virtue but a name, what praise would then be due to well-doing? Many there be that complain of Divine Providence for suffering Adam to transgress; foolish tongues! When God gave him reason, He gave him freedom to choose, for reason is but choosing.

JOHN MILTON (1608–1674)
Areopagitica

The fragmentary character of human life is not regarded as evil in Biblical faith because it is seen from the perspective of a center of life and meaning in which each fragment is related to the plan of the whole, to the will of God. The evil arises when the fragment seeks by its own wisdom to comprehend the whole or attempts by its own power to realize it.

REINHOLD NIEBUHR (1892–1971)
The Nature and Destiny of Man

God made the world in such manner that these partial evils would take place; and they take place with his infinite knowledge, and under His infinite providence. So when we see these evils, we know that though immense, they are partial evils compensated by constants somewhere, and provided for in the infinite engineering of God, so that they shall be the cause of some ultimate good.

THEODORE PARKER (1810–1860)
Theism, Atheism and the Popular Theology

In the face of evil there are three kinds of souls: There are those who do evil and deny that there is evil and call it good. "Yea, the hour cometh, that whosoever kills you, will think he doth a service to God" (John 16:2). There are also those who see evil in others, but not in themselves, and who flatter their own "virtue" by criticizing the sinful. "Thou hypocrite, cast out first the beam out of thine own eye, and then shalt thou see to cast the mote out of thy brother's eye" (Matthew 7:5). Finally, there are those who carry the burden of another's woe and sin as their own.

FULTON J. SHEEN (1895–1979)
Peace of Soul

The kingdom of heaven is not the isolation of good from evil. It is the overcoming of evil by good. This transmutation of evil into good enters into the actual world by reason of the inclusion of the nature of God, which includes the ideal vision of each actual evil so met with a novel consequent as to issue in the restoration of goodness.

ALFRED NORTH WHITEHEAD (1861–1947)
Religion in the Making

He that strives t'invert
The Universal's course with his poor way,
Not only dust-like shivers with the sway,
But, crossing God is his great work, all earth
Bears not so cursed and so damn'd a birth.

GEORGE CHAPMAN (1559–1634)
The Revenge of Bussy D'Ambois

In order that freedom should remain in nature and that evil be eliminated, God's wisdom devised the idea of letting man go in the direction he wished, to the end that after he had tasted the evils he desired, his desire would bring him back to his initial beatitude.

SAINT GREGORY OF NYSSA (331–396)
Sermons

Let no man say when he is tempted, I am tempted of God: for God cannot be tempted with evil, neither tempteth he any man.

The New Testament
James 1:13

It is not those innocent of evil who are fullest of the life of God, but those who in their own case have experienced the triumph over evil.

JOSIAH ROYCE (1855–1916)
Studies in Good and Evil

The existence of evil is not so much an obstacle to faith in God as a proof of God's ex-

istence, a challenge to turn towards that in which love triumphs over hatred, union over division, and eternal life over death.

NIKOLAI BERDYAEV (1874–1948)
Dream and Reality

That every struggle of the people of God against evil in this world must be fired with eternal principles, must be instinct with thoroughness and with justice; that is the plain prosaic meaning of the word of God to Isaiah which declared, "My sword shall be bathed in heaven."

PHILLIPS BROOKS (1835–1893)
Sermons

Two opposing mysteries are in the world —goodness and evil. If we *deny* God, then *goodness* is a mystery, for no one has ever suggested how spiritual life could rise of an unspiritual source, how souls could come from dust. If we *affirm* God, then *evil* is a mystery, for why, we ask, should love create a world with so much pain and sin? Our task is not to solve insoluble problems. It is to balance these alternatives—no God and the mystery of man's spiritual life, against God and the mystery of evil.

HARRY EMERSON FOSDICK (1878–1969)
The Meaning of Being a Christian

God knew beforehand that the world would contain both righteous and wicked men, and there is an allusion to this in the story of creation. "The earth without form," means the wicked, and the words, "and there was light," refers to the righteous.

The Midrash

Thus Evil, what we call Evil, must ever exist while man exists: Evil, in the widest sense we can give it, is precisely the dark, disordered material out of which man's Freewill has to create an edifice of order and Good.

THOMAS CARLYLE (1795–1881)
Characteristics

God has created a world which is not the best possible, but which contains the whole

range of good and evil. We are also at the point where it is as bad as possible. For beyond is the stage where evil becomes innocence.   SIMONE WEIL (1909–1943)
Notebooks

God would never have created a single angel—not even a single man—whose future wickedness He foresaw, unless, at the same time, He knew of the good which could come out of this evil. It was as though He meant the harmony of history, like the beauty of a poem, to be enriched by antithetical elements.   SAINT AUGUSTINE (354–430)
The City of God

All things come from that one source, from that ruling Reason of the Universe, either under a primary impulse from it or by way of consequence. And therefore the gape of the lion's jaws and poison and all noxious things, such as thorns and mire, are but after-results of the grand and beautiful. Look not then on these as alien to that which thou dost reverence, but turn thy thoughts to the one source of all things.
MARCUS AURELIUS (121–180)
Meditations

Upon supposition that God exercises a moral government over the world, the analogy of His natural government suggests and makes it credible that this moral government must be a scheme quite beyond our comprehension; and this affords a general answer to all objections against the justice and goodness of it.
JOSEPH BUTLER (1692–1752)
Analogy of Religion

Deliberation, judgment, necessarily presuppose the notion of good and evil. If you take this notion away from man, he will not deliberate, he will not judge, he will no longer be a rational being. Thus, God could

not let us live a single instant without it; He made us this way.
PETER YAKOVLEVICH CHAADAYEV (1796–1856)
Philosophical Letters

To explain evil would be to give a "reason" for it and thus to justify it.
SIMON L. FRANK (1877–1950)
The Unfathomable

The locus of the unconditional first-birth of evil is that portion of reality in which reality, although it is born of God and has its being in God, ceases to be God. Evil is generated in an unutterable abyss which lies, as it were, on the threshold between God and "not-God."   SIMON L. FRANK (1877–1950)
The Unfathomable

With minor variations it is a common theme in the teaching of an Athenian aristocrat like Plato, an Indian nobleman like Buddha, and a humble Jew like Spinoza; in fact, wherever men have thought carefully about the problem of evil and of what constitutes a good life, they have concluded that an essential element in any human philosophy is renunciation.

WALTER LIPPMANN (1889–1974)
Preface to Morals

If it is an extraordinary blindness to live without investigating what we are, it is a terrible one to live an evil life, while believing in God.   BLAISE PASCAL (1623–1662)
Pensées

Not in the sky, not in the midst of the sea, not if we enter into the clefts of the mountains, is there known a spot in the whole world where a man might be freed from an evil deed.   *The Dhammapada*

And for trial will We test you with evil and with good.   *The Koran*

In good years the children of the people are most of them good, while in bad years the most of them abandon themselves to evil. It is not owing to their natural powers conferred by Heaven that they are thus differ-ent. The abandonment is owing to the circumstances through which they allow their minds to be ensnared and drowned in evil.

MENCIUS (371–289 B.C.)
Meng-tzu

· THE DILEMMA OF SIN ·

They are ignorant and malicious who say that God is the author of sin, since all things are done by his will or ordination; for they do not distinguish between the manifest wickedness of men and the secret judgments of God.

JOHN CALVIN (1509–1564)
Theological Treatises

St. Augustine teaches us that there is in every man a serpent, an Eve and an Adam. The serpent is the senses and our nature, the Eve is the concupiscible appetite, and the Adam is the reason. Nature tempts us continually, concupiscible appetite often fills us with desires, but the sin is not consummated if reason does not consent. Let the serpent and the Eve therefore act if we cannot hinder it; but let us pray to God that His grace may so strengthen our Adam that he may remain victorious.

BLAISE PASCAL (1623–1662)
Letters

If a man sins in secret, God takes pity on him. If he repents, God forgives and forgets his sin. But if he does not repent, God causes his transgression to be known in public.

The Zohar

Earth cannot show so brave a sight,
As when a single soul does fence
The batteries of alluring sense
And Heaven views it with delight.

ANDREW MARVELL (1621–1678)
*A Dialogue Between the Resolved Soul
and Created Pleasure*

When wicked persons have gone on in a course of sin, and find they have reason to fear the just judgment of God for their sins, they begin at first to wish that there were no God to punish them; then by degrees they persuade themselves that there is none; and then they set themselves to study for arguments to back their opinion.

JOHN BUNYAN (1628–1688)
Visions of Heaven and Hell

Though a man be soiled with the sins of a
    lifetime,
Let him but love me, rightly resolved, in
    utter devotion:
I see no sinner; that man is holy.

The Bhagavad Gita

If a man repeats God's name, his body, mind, and everything become pure. Why should one talk only about sin and hell and such things? Say but once, "O Lord, I have undoubtedly done wicked things, but I won't repeat them." And have faith in His name.

SRI RAMAKRISHNA (1836–1886)
Gospel

This alone I have found, that God, when he made man, made him straightforward, but man invents endless subtleties of his own.

*The Old Testament
Ecclesiastes 7:29*

He that falls into sin is a man; that grieves at it is a saint; that boasts of it is a devil.

THOMAS FULLER (1608–1661)
Holy and Profane States

Man's sin, while essentially rebellion, against God, results in moral and social injustice in his relation to man. As a selfish sinner, he supremely loves neither God nor his neighbor but himself and his self-centered world. REINHOLD NIEBUHR (1892–1971)
The Nature and Destiny of Man

For my own part, I cannot admit that sin and evil have any positive existence, far less than anything can exist, or come to pass, contrary to the will of God. On the contrary, not only do I assert that sin has no positive existence, I also maintain that only in speaking improperly, or humanly, can we say that we sin against God, as in the expression that men offend God.
BENEDICT SPINOZA (1632–1677)
Letters

God accepts repentance for all sins, except the sin of imposing a bad name upon another. *The Zohar*

He that is without sin among you, let him cast the first stone. *The New Testament John 8:7*

You may say you are far from hating God; but if you live in sin you are among God's enemies, you are under Satan's standard and enlisted there; you may not like it, no wonder; you may wish to be elsewhere; but there you are, an enemy to God.
GERARD MANLEY HOPKINS (1844–1889)
Sermons

What if God were to say to Adam: "I created you for sinning, and you can no more abstain from it than you can abstain from getting hungry. But take care that you do not sin. For if you sin, you will die." Could a more absurd thing be thought? If man has been created in the image of God, then he has certainly been created for righteousness and not for sin.
SEBASTIAN CASTELLIO (1515–1563)
Of Predestination

He whose wickedness is very great brings himself down to that state where his enemy wishes him to be, as a creeper does with the tree which it surrounds.
The Dhammapada

Rabbi Akiba said: "In the beginning, sin is like a thread of a spider's web; but in the end, it becomes like the cable of a ship."
The Midrash

Rabbi Johanan ben Berokah said: "He who profanes God in secret will be punished in the open, and this is true whether he commits the profanation out of ignorance or malice."
The Mishnah

Even God in His mercy can bring about reconciliation only for that individual who, consciously striving for the good, recognizes sin for what it is and tries to liberate himself from it. Without my own moral effort and repentance even God cannot redeem me. God has given me my share of the good; it is, therefore, incumbent upon me to rid myself of my share of evil.
HERMANN COHEN (1842–1918)
Jewish Writings

We find in the prophet Isaiah, that the fire with which each one is punished is described as his own; for he says, "Walk in the light of your own fire, and in the flame which ye have kindled." By these words it seems to be indicated that every sinner kindles for himself the flame of his own fire, and is not plunged into some fire which has already been kindled by another, or was in existence before himself. ORIGEN (185–253)
De Principiis

Here we have an answer to the problem why God should have created men He foresaw would sin. It was because both in them and by means of them He could reveal how much was deserved by their guilt and condoned by his grace, and, also, because the harmony of the whole of reality which God

has created and controls cannot be marred by the perverse discordancy of those who sin.
SAINT AUGUSTINE (354–430)
Confessions

There must be something in "the nature of things" to render impossible the creation of a race of free beings who would never sin, even though they were free to do so. If it were possible, God would have created them. The impossibility must lie in the very nature of God.   EDGAR S. BRIGHTMAN (1884–1953)
The Finding of God

Man's apostasy from God is not simply something which happened once and for all, and is over and done with; man is doing it continually. The contradiction is not a fatal tragic disaster which has taken place behind us and an equally disastrous quality within us. The contradiction remains—how could it ever be anything else?—contradiction, turning away, apostasy.
EMIL BRUNNER (1889–1966)
Man in Revolt

It would, no doubt, have been possible for God to remove by miracle the results of the first sin ever committed by a human being; but this would not have been much good unless He was prepared to remove the results of the second sin, and of the third, and so on forever.   C. S. LEWIS (1898–1963)
The Problem of Pain

God has given man a thrilling responsibility for this world. But man has not fulfilled his assignment. God has placed the tiller of history in man's hand, but man has gone to his hammock and let the winds and tides sweep his ship along. Man has done things he ought not to have done, but even more importantly he has not done those things he ought to have done. He has refused to live up to the full stature of his manhood and has abdicated his crucial place in the scheme of things. This is what biblical tradition has called "sin."   HARVEY COX (1929–)
God's Revolution and Man's Responsibility

Only he who understands that sin in inexplicable knows what it is. Sin—human sin, and not only satanic sin—is the one great negative mystery of our existence, of which we know only one thing, that we are responsible for it, without the possibility of pushing the responsibility on to anything outside ourselves.   EMIL BRUNNER (1889–1966)
Man in Revolt

The guilt of sin means: all is not well between you and God, hence all is not well with you yourself: for the spiritual health of your being is dependent on your relationship to God. Your true life flows from your potential communion with God. If you are separated from Him, then evil gnaws at the roots of your life.   EMIL BRUNNER (1889–1966)
The Great Invitation

We argue conveniently that the devil is tormented more than man, because the devil fell from God without any other tempter than himself, but man had a tempter. So may it be not inconveniently argued too that man may be more tormented than he, because man continued and relapsed in his rebellions to God, after so many pardons offered and accepted, which the devil never had.
JOHN DONNE (1572–1631)
Sermons

Men conceive they can manage their sins with secrecy; but they carry about them a letter, or book rather, written by God's finger, their conscience bearing witness to all their actions.   THOMAS FULLER (1608–1661)
Sermons

What could begin this evil will but pride, that is the beginning of all sin? And what is pride but a perverse desire of height, in forsaking Him to whom the soul ought solely to cleave, as the beginning thereof, to make the self seem the beginning.

SAINT AUGUSTINE (354–430)
The City of God

Fight with your own sin, and let that fight keep you humble and full of sympathy when you go out into the world and strike at the sin of which the world is full. Fight with the world's sin, and let the needs of that fight make you aware of how much is wrong, and make you eager that everything shall be right within yourself.

PHILLIPS BROOKS (1835–1893)
The Mystery of Iniquity

When washed in the river of the heart the
  mind, from being black, becomes white.
Living in fellowship with the Lord, with ease
  it is made pure.

DADU (1554–1603)
The Bani

Most men, finding themselves the authors of their own disgrace, rail the louder against God or destiny.

ROBERT LOUIS STEVENSON (1850–1894)
Memories and Portraits

Anyone who sins must return to God the honor which has been withdrawn from him, and that is the satisfaction which every sinner owes to God.   SAINT ANSELM (1033–1109)
Cur Deus Homo

You who keep my commandments and precepts, says the Lord God, do not let your sins pull you down, or your iniquities prevail over you. Woe to those who are choked by their sins and overwhelmed by their iniquities, as a field is choked with underbrush and its path overwhelmed with thorns, so that no one can pass through.

The Old Testament Apocrypha
2 Esdras 16:76–77

Man is no helpless invalid left in a valley of total depravity until God pulls him out. Man

is rather an upstanding human being whose vision has been impaired by the cataracts of sin and whose soul has been weakened by the virus of pride, but there is sufficient vision left for him to lift his eyes unto the hills, and there remains enough of God's image for him to turn his weak and sin-battered life toward the Great Physician, the curer of the ravages of sin.

MARTIN LUTHER KING, JR. (1929–1968)
Strength in Love

The way to argue down a vice is not to tell lies about it,—to say that it has no attractions, when everybody knows that it has,—but rather to let it make out its case just as it certainly will in the moment of temptation, and then meet it with the weapons furnished by the Divine armory.

OLIVER WENDELL HOLMES (1809–1894)
The Autocrat of the Breakfast-Table

All wickedness is weakness; that plea
  therefore
With God or man will gain thee no
  remission.

JOHN MILTON (1608–1674)
Samson Agonistes

Sin is apostasy, rebellion, because it is not the primary element, but the reversal of the primary element. The primary element is the creation in the Word of God, but the second is the contradiction of this creation. Sin is not a "not yet" but a "no longer."

EMIL BRUNNER (1889–1966)
*The Christian Doctrine of Creation
and Redemption*

He that has led a wicked life, is afraid of his own memory.

THOMAS FULLER (1654–1734)
Gnomologia

Why didn't God create the universe without sin? There is only one answer: He could have done so, and man would have been but a pawn upon a chessboard. Pawns are not responsible for moves of the great Player. We must be free to be persons, and being free, we are charged with making decisions.

G. BROMLEY OXNAM (1891–1963)
A Testament of Faith

Sin is an affair of the will. It is not "a vestige of our animal inheritance." That trivial notion comes from an unexamined, too-quickly swallowed doctrine of evolution. Why blame the brute creation? No self-respecting wolf would be guilty of our modern wars.

GEORGE ARTHUR BUTTRICK (1892–1979)
God, Pain and Evil

Saint Augustine! well hast thou said
    That of our vices we can frame
A ladder, if we will but tread
    Beneath our feet each deed of shame.

HENRY WADSWORTH LONGFELLOW
(1807–1882)
Birds of Passage

What mortal aberration
    Hath so estranged mankind
That from God's destination
    He turns, abandoned, blind,
To follow mocking shade and empty rind?

FRAY LUIS PONCE DE LEÓN (1528–1591)
The Night Serene

The spiritual communion of men the world over did not operate in our favour. But had we stood for that communion of men, we should have saved the world and ourselves. In that task, we failed. Each is responsible for all. Each is by himself responsible. I understand now for the first time the mystery of the religion whence was born the civilization I claim as my own: "To bear the sins of man." Each man bears the sins of all men.

ANTOINE DE SAINT-EXUPÉRY (1900–1945)
Flight to Arras

We used to say that we were punished for our sins, as though God were a judge on a bench who passed on the case and meted out

penalty. The truth goes far deeper than that. We are not punished for our sins, but by them. It is our sins themselves that rise to slay us.   HARRY EMERSON FOSDICK (1878–1969)
Sermons

If we say that we have company with God, and walk in darkness, we do lie.

The New Testament
I John 1:6

He that is unjust in little is unjust in much. He that is malignant to the least is to the greatest. He who hates the earth which is God's footstool, hates yet more Heaven which is God's throne, and Him that sitteth thereon.   JOHN RUSKIN (1819–1900)
On the Old Road

Men have not been satisfied with devising infinite requirements and disguises of their follies to hide them from the world, but finding themselves open and discerned by God, have endeavoured to discover means of escaping from that eye, from which nothing can escape but innocence, and from which nothing can be hid but under the cover of mercy.   JEREMY TAYLOR (1613–1667)
Unum Necessarium

Sin is an attempt to control the immutable and unalterable laws of everlasting righteousness, goodness and truth, upon which the universe depends.

BENJAMIN WHICHCOTE (1609–1683)
Moral and Religious Aphorisms

When the thought of God does not remind him of his sin but that it is forgiven, and the past is no longer the memory of how much he did wrong, but of how much he was forgiven—then man rests in the forgiveness of sins.   SÖREN KIERKEGAARD (1813–1855)
Journals

Were I to define sin, I would call it the sinking of a man's soul from God into a sensual selfishness. All the freedom that wicked

men have is but like that of banished men—
to wander up and down in the wilderness of
this world from one den and cave to another.

JOHN SMITH (1616–1652)
Discourses

Hatred of cant and doubt of human creeds
May well be felt: the unpardonable sin
Is to deny the Word of God within!

JOHN GREENLEAF WHITTIER (1807–1892)
The Word

Sin is a defiance to the authority of God, a
contradiction to the law of righteousness, a
disturbance to the society of men, and a distraction to the soul of the sinner.

BENJAMIN WHICHCOTE (1609–1683)
Moral and Religious Aphorisms

Every sin brings about a particular type of
trembling in the soul, which does not cease
until repentance has been made. When man
repents out of love, the cosmic light of the
world of unity shines upon him and everything is joined in oneness; evil joins with the
good and raises it to even a higher value.

ABRAHAM ISAAC KOOK (1865–1935)
Oroth Hakodesh

Let no man be deterred from repenting by
knowing the great depth of his sin. Let him

bear in mind that he does not come to a
stranger but to his Heavenly Father.

The Midrash

In the Book of Poetry are three hundred
pieces, but the design of them all may be embraced in one sentence—Have no depraved
thoughts! CONFUCIUS (551–479 B.C.)
Analects

If God and man are absolutely different,
this cannot be accounted for on the basis of
what man receives from God. Their unlikeness must therefore be explained by what
man receives from himself, or by what he has
brought upon his own head. But what can
this unlikeness be? Aye, what can it be but
sin; since the unlikeness, the absolute unlikeness, is something that man has brought
upon himself.

SÖREN KIERKEGAARD (1813–1855)
Philosophical Fragments

Joy shall be in heaven over one sinner that
repenteth, more than over ninety and nine
just persons, which need no repentance.

The New Testament
Luke 15:7

To fall into sin is human, but to remain in
sin is devilish. *German Proverb*

· THE SEDUCTIVE WAYS OF MAMMON ·

Theirs is an endless road, a hopeless maze,
who seek for goods before they seek God.

SAINT BERNARD OF CLAIRVAUX (1091–1153)
On the Love of God

Men's pennies and God's promises don't
very well go together to buy heaven.

CHARLES HADDON SPURGEON (1834–1892)
Barbed Arrows

Charge them that are rich in this world,
that they be not highminded, nor trust in un-

certain riches, but in the living God, who giveth us richly all things to enjoy.

The New Testament
1 Timothy 6:17

Better to go to heaven in rags, than to hell
in embroidery. *English Proverb*

If, through the help of God, we do not
alienate ourselves from the things of the

world, the things of the world will certainly alienate us from God.

BENJAMIN WHICHCOTE (1609–1683)
Moral and Religious Aphorisms

To silence every motion proceeding from the love of money and humbly to wait upon God to know his will concerning us have appeared necessary. He alone is able to strengthen us to dig deep, to remove all which lies between us and the safe foundation, and so to direct us in our outward employments that pure universal love may shine forth in our proceedings.

JOHN WOOLMAN (1720–1772)
Journal

Let none admire
That riches grow in Hell; that soil may best
Deserve the precious bane.

JOHN MILTON (1608–1674)
Paradise Lost

Of ceremonies you should know that they are superfluous; for if we are to receive something from God, He looks into our hearts and not at the ceremonies. If we have received something of Him, He does not wish us to use it for ceremonies but works.

PARACELSUS (1493–1541)
De natura rerum

Money is not required to buy one necessity of the soul.

HENRY DAVID THOREAU (1817–1862)
Walden

We have mistaken the nature of poverty, and thought it was economic poverty. No, it is poverty of the soul, deprivation of God's recreating, loving peace.

THOMAS R. KELLY (1893–1941)
A Testament of Devotion

Everywhere man is this double thing. The living which he makes is narrow, practical, prosaic. The life which he lives is a fragment of the life of God. Now he is busy with the multiplication table to count up his income or his rent; and now he is on the summit of Sinai with Moses, taking the tables of the Eternal Law out of the hands of God.

PHILLIPS BROOKS (1835–1893)
Sermons

Those who deliberately occupy themselves with earthly business, constantly seeking worldly well-being, have not God's rest in their hearts and souls; for they love and seek their rest in this thing which is so little and in which there is no rest.

JULIAN OF NORWICH (1343–1416)
Showings

If you make money your God, 'twill plague you like a Devil.

THOMAS FULLER (1654–1734)
Gnomologia

Man, O man! you speak of divine love and at the same time are able to attend to all the vanities of the world. Are you sincere? "Where Rama is, there is no room for any desire; where desire is, there is no room for Rama. These never co-exist. Like light and darkness they are never together."

SWAMI VIVEKANANDA (1863–1902)
Bhakti-Yoga

Lord, what is man, whose thought, at times,
Up to Thy sevenfold brightness climbs,
While still his grosser instinct clings
To earth, like other creeping things!

JOHN GREENLEAF WHITTIER (1807–1892)
Chapel of the Hermits

There is a great difference between being occupied with God who gives us the contentment, and being busied with the contentment which God gives us.

SAINT FRANCIS OF SALES (1567–1622)
Treatise

The belly is the hand-fetter and foot-chain;
A belly-slave rarely worships God.

SAADI (1184–1291)
Bustan

If a man is attracted by things of this world and is estranged from his Creator, he is corrupted and he can corrupt the entire world with him. However, if he controls himself, cleaves to his Creator and makes use of the world only to the degree that it helps him in serving his Creator, he raises himself to a higher level of existence and the world rises with him. MOSES LUZZATTO (1707–1747)
The Way of the Upright

In this life two loves are striving in every trial for mastery—love of the world and love of God. The conquering love, whichever it be, puts force upon the lover and draws him after itself. SAINT AUGUSTINE (354–430)
Sermons

The money perisheth with thee, because thou hast thought that the gift of God may be purchased with money.
The New Testament
Acts 8:20

Man enters the world with closed hands, as if to say: "The world is mine." He leaves it with open hands, as if to say: "Behold, I take nothing with me." *The Midrash*

"Ye cannot serve God and Mammon. If ye love the one, ye will hate the other." Every proof that we love Mammon with all our heart and all our soul raises the presumption that we have lost the love of God and are merely going through the motions when we worship him.
WALTER RAUSCHENBUSCH (1861–1918)
Christianizing the Social Order

The golden mean is that a man should strive in moderation to obtain wealth, in proportion to the wants of his household; and he should cheerfully enjoy that which his Creator has graciously bestowed upon him, for it is "the Lord's blessing which maketh rich."
SAADIA BEN JOSEPH (892–942)
Ethical Treatises

A good name is rather to be chosen than great riches, and loving favor rather than silver and gold. The rich and poor meet together; the Lord is the Maker of them all.
The Old Testament
Proverbs 22:1–2

I know that what is called a treasure is transient, for the eternal is not obtained by things which are not eternal. *The Upanishads*

For a long time we have believed in nothing but the values arising in a mechanical, commercialized, urbanized way of life: it would be well for us to face the permanent conditions upon which God allows us to live upon this planet. And without sentimentalizing the life of the savage, we might practise the humility to observe, in some of the societies upon which we look down as primitive or backward, the operation of a social-religious-artistic complex which we should emulate upon a higher plane.
T. S. ELIOT (1888–1965)
The Idea of a Christian Society

Faith is a mockery if it teaches us not that we may construct a world unspeakably more complete and beautiful than the material world. And I, too, may construct my better world, for I am a child of God, an inheritor of a fragment of the Mind that created worlds. HELEN KELLER (1880–1968)
The Open Door

Were the earth to be studded with diamonds
  and rubies, and my couch to be similarly
  adorned,
Were fascinating damsels whose faces were
  decked with jewels to shed lustre and
  enhance the pleasure of the scene;
May it not be that on beholding them I may
  forget Thee and not remember Thy
  Name!

GURU NANAK (1469–1539)
The Japji

Who worships God as God God hears. But he who worships God for wordly goods, worships not God: he worships what he worships God for and employs God as his servant for the getting of it.

MEISTER ECKHART (1260–1327)
Sermons

If you men perceive your deeper selves,
Then reach toward Brahman, boundless,
Enduring, remote, and expansive;
And it shall follow that
Power and pleasure in the world
Will seem the obsessions of wretched fools.

BHARTRIHARI (7th century)
The Century of Love

Thou sayest, I am rich, and increased with goods, and have need of nothing; and knowest not that thou art wretched, and miserable, and poor, and blind, and naked.

The New Testament
Revelation 3:17

Rejoice thee not in riches if thou have any nor in friends if they be mighty: but in God that giveth all things and above all things desireth to give himself.

THOMAS À KEMPIS (1380–1471)
Imitation of Christ

Though God is the Creator of the materiality of this world, yet seeing He created it out of that wrath, division, and darkness which sin opened in nature, this truth stands firm, that sin alone is father, first cause, and beginner of all the materiality of this world, and that when sin is removed from nature all its materiality must vanish with it.

WILLIAM LAW (1686–1761)
The Spirit of Love

There are two ways—one the love of God, the other of Mammon; the way man treads depends on God's will.

GURU AMAR DAS (1479–1574)
Mohan Pothi

. HYPOCRITE, FIRST CAST THE BEAM .
OUT OF THINE OWN EYE

There are many persons, of combative tendencies, who read for ammunition, and dig out of the Bible iron for balls. So men turn the Word of God into a vast arsenal, filled with all manner of weapons, offensive and defensive.

HENRY WARD BEECHER (1813–1887)
Sermons

It is much easier to persuade men that God cares for certain observances, than that he cares for simple honesty and truth and gentleness and loving-kindness.

GEORGE MACDONALD (1824–1905)
Sermons

But whoso hath this world's good, and seeth his brother have need, and shutteth up

his bowels of compassion from him, how dwelleth the love of God in him?

The New Testament
1 John 3:17

There be many which say with their mouth, they love God: and if a man should ask here this multitude, whether they love God or no, they would say, "Yes, God forbid else!" But if you consider their unmercifulness unto the poor, you shall see as St. John said, "The love of God is not within them."

HUGH LATIMER (1485–1555)
A Sermon on the Lord's Prayer

Hear the verbal protestations of all men: Nothing they are so certain of as their religious tenets. Examine their lives: You will scarcely think that they repose the smallest confidence in them.

DAVID HUME (1711–1776)
The Natural History of Religion

As darkness over a deep sea, billows riding on billows, billows below and clouds above— one darkness on another darkness—so that if a man stretches out his hand he cannot behold it, thus is he to whom the light of God doth not come.   *The Koran*

In the hour of God cleanse thy soul of all self-deceit and hypocrisy and vain self-flattering that thou may look straight into thy spirit and hear that which summons it.

SRI AUROBINDO (1872–1950)
The Human Cycle

The influence of divine powers is not seen in choice phrases and raised eyebrows, in weeping and praying and uttering empty words, unsupported by charitable deeds; it is only made manifest by a pure heart and good works, which, although difficult, are performed with utmost zeal and love.

JUDAH HALEVI (1085–1142)
Kuzari

When devils will their blackest show put on, They do suggest at first with heavenly shows.

WILLIAM SHAKESPEARE (1564–1616)
Othello

We hand folks over to God's mercy, and show none ourselves.

GEORGE ELIOT (1819–1880)
Adam Bede

Why beholdest thou the mote that is in thy brother's eye, but considerest not the beam that is in thine own eye? Thou hypocrite, first cast out the beam out of thine own eye, and then shalt thou see clearly to cast out the mote out of thy brother's eye.

The New Testament
Luke 6:41

The hypocrite serves God for gain. He looks at the emoluments and profits which come in by religion; 'tis not the power of godliness the hypocrite loves, but the gain of godliness; 'tis not the fire of the altar, but the gold of the altar which he adores.

JOHN TILLOTSON (1630–1694)
Sermons

When men grow virtuous in their old age they are merely making a sacrifice to God of the devil's leavings.

JONATHAN SWIFT (1667–1745)
Thoughts on Various Occasions

Who, for the love of God, ever endures or undertakes so much as they do from thirst for human praise?

PETER ABÉLARD (1079–1142)
Glosses on Porphyry

There are people who in penitential exercises and external practices, of which they make a great deal, cling to their selfish I. May God have pity on these people who know so little of divine truth! These people are called holy because of their external appearances; but on the inside they are fools, for they do not understand at all the correct meaning of divine truth.

MEISTER ECKHART (1260–1327)
Sermons

God desires an inner living love. There is more truth in such a one than in a man who sings so lustily that his song reaches heaven; or in anything that he can do by fasting or watching or anything else that is external.

JOHANNES TAULER (1300–1361)
Sermons

For neither man nor angel can discern Hypocrisy, the only evil that walks Invisible, except to God alone.

JOHN MILTON (1608–1674)
Paradise Lost

God does not want to be loved by battalions or whole nations, ordered—one, two, three—to church parade.

SÖREN KIERKEGAARD (1813–1855)
Journals

Man sees the mote in his neighbor's eye, but knows not of the beam in his own.

The Talmud

He who professes one thing and does
   another,
In whose heart there is no love,
Shall be tried by the Lord, Who is wise,
Who knows everything, and is pleased
Not simply by outward appearances.
He Himself is free from all stratagems and
   wiles.
He thoroughly knows the ways of man's
   heart.

GURU ARJAN (1563–1606)
Hymns

What is the hope of the hypocrite, though he has gained, when God takes away his soul?

The Old Testament
Job 27:8

Nobody who is counterfeit can withstand God's touchstone.   KABIR (1459–1518)
Granthali

Those who thwart and destroy movements which spring from a conscience newly awakened are always the hangers-on of authority and of moneyed might. They are the so-called maintainers of order. They manufacture justice to suit their own advantage and coerce the people in the name of God. And of all concerned, God Himself surely is the most embarrassed.

TOYOHIKO KAGAWA (1888–1960)
Meditations

What is it but blasphemy when God is merely my means to an end? That takes its toll. If we turn God into a puppet of our desires (even when that happens by the pious route of prayer) then he shuts up his heaven and we find ourselves thrown back into the silence of our unredeemed life.

HELMUT THIELICKE (1908–)
How to Believe Again

Some people are for seeing God with their eyes, as they can see a cow (which they love for the milk, and for the cheese, and or their own profit.) Thus do all those who love God for the sake of outward riches or of inward comfort; they do not love aright, but seek only themselves and their own advantage.

MEISTER ECKHART (1260–1327)
Sermons

The righteous men take righteousness so earnestly that were God not righteous, they would not care a jot for Him.

MEISTER ECKHART (1260–1327)
Works

He who calls God to his assistance whilst he is in vicious courses is like a cut-purse who should call the law to his aid, or like those who bring forward the name of God as a witness to a lie. There are few men who would dare to exhibit openly the secret petitions which they make to God.

MICHEL EYQUEM DE MONTAIGNE (1533–1592)
Of Prayers

For there is no faithfulness in their mouth; their inward part is very wickedness; their throat is an open sepulchre; they flatter with their tongue.   *The Old Testament*
Psalms 5:9

Prate not about God, for prating about him thou dost lie.

MEISTER ECKHART (1260–1327)
Sermons

God knows, I'm no the thing I should be,
Nor am I even the thing I could be,
But twenty times I rather would be
   An atheist clean,

Than under gospel colours hid
  Just for a screen.
                    ROBERT BURNS (1759–1796)
                Espistle to the Rev. John M'Math

The hypocrite had left his mask, and stood
In naked ugliness. He was a man
Who stole the livery of the court of heaven
To serve the devil in; in virtue's guise,
Devoured the widow's house and orphan's
  bread;
In holy phrase, transacted villainies
That common sinners durst not meddle
  with.
                    ROBERT POLLOK (1798–1827)
                    The Course of Time

And lips say "God be pitiful,"
Who ne'er said "God be praised."
                ELIZABETH BARRETT BROWNING
                          (1806–1861)
                    The Cry of the Human

How can you expect to keep your powers of
hearing when you never want to listen? That
God should have time for you, you seem to
take as much for granted as that you cannot
have time for Him.
                DAG HAMMARSKJÖLD (1905–1961)
                          Markings

· THE DEVIL HATH VARIOUS WAYS ·

The character of Satan is pride and sensual
indulgence, finding in self the sole motive of
action.
        SAMUEL TAYLOR COLERIDGE (1772–1834)
                    A Course of Lectures

I think if the Devil doesn't exist, but man
has created him, he has created him in his
own image and likeness.
            FYODOR DOSTOEVSKY (1821–1881)
                The Brothers Karamazov

He that serves God for money will serve
the Devil for better wages.
            ROGER L'ESTRANGE (1616–1704)
                          Proverbs

It frequently happens that Satan puts us
on the wrong scent: to distract us from
achieving one thing he will suggest something seemingly better; then to prevent us
from bringing this to perfection, he will hold
out a third. He is quite content for us to make
any number of beginnings as long as we
never complete anything.
        SAINT FRANCIS OF SALES (1567–1622)
                    The Love of God

It is a good sign when the devil makes so
much noise and tempest round about the
will; it is a sign that he is not within.
        SAINT FRANCIS OF SALES (1567–1622)
            Letters to Persons in the World

The devil's snares are strong,
Yet have I God in need;
And if I had not God to friend,
What can the devil speed?
        RALPH WALDO EMERSON (1803–1882)
                          The Poet

Holiness, like the gastric fluid, dissolves
all evils. The Devil is ever afflicted with dys-
pepsia. His gastric juices are depraved by
intemperance.
            BRONSON ALCOTT (1799–1888)
                          Journals

Let the devil make me so far desperate as
to conceive a time when there was no mercy,
and he hath made me so far an atheist as to
conceive a time when there was no God.
                JOHN DONNE (1572–1631)
                          Sermons

The devil has various ways of leading men astray, and when he has hold of them in one place, it matters little to him if they escape him in another.

PIERRE JURIEU (1637–1713)
Tableau du Socialisme

Distrust and doubt produce a gloomy and terrible hate toward God, and that is the beginning of the eternal torments, and a rage like that of the devil.

PHILIPP MELANCHTHON (1497–1560)
Sermons

Since all the riches of this world
May be gifts from the Devil and earthly
    kings,
I should suspect that I worshipp'd the Devil
If I thank'd my God for worldly things.

WILLIAM BLAKE (1757–1827)
Gnomic Verses

From his brimstone bed at break of day
    A walking the Devil is gone,
To visit his snug little farm the earth,
    And see how his stock goes on.

SAMUEL TAYLOR COLERIDGE (1772–1834)
The Devil's Thoughts

O shame to men! devil with devil damn'd
Firm concord holds, men only disagree
Of creatures rational.

JOHN MILTON (1608–1674)
Paradise Lost

I sought only for the heart of God, therein to hide myself from the temptestuous storms of the devil.   JACOB BOEHME (1575–1624)
Aurora

How is it that the devils, having been produced wholly out of the Good, are not good in disposition? Or how is it that, if produced good from out of the Good, they became changed? What made them evil, and indeed, what is the nature of evil?

DIONYSIUS THE AREOPAGITE (5th century)
The Divine Names

If only the good spirits in our souls have gained the upper hand, so of itself the last devil still remaining behind in us flees away, for he is not secure in good society.

GUSTAV THEODOR FECHNER (1801–1887)
Life After Death

Get thee hence, Satan: for it is written, Thou shalt worship the Lord thy God, and him only shalt thou serve.

The New Testament
Matthew 4:10

I will speak out concerning the two Spirits of whom, at the beginning of existence, the Holier thus spoke to him who is evil: "Neither our thoughts, nor our teachings, nor our wills, nor our choices, nor our words, nor our deeds, nor our consciences, nor yet our souls agree.   *The Yasna*

If we summarise all that opposes the acceptance of God's Word as the power of contradiction, one has an inkling of what Scripture means by the devil. "Has God really said . . . ?" Is God's Word true? If one believes, one will snap his finger at the devil.

KARL BARTH (1886–1968)
Dogmatics in Outline

The Devil wipes his Breech with poor Folks' Pride.

BENJAMIN FRANKLIN (1706–1790)
Poor Richard's Almanack

I am a great enemy to flies; when I have a good book, they flock upon it and parade up and down upon it, and soil it. 'Tis just the same with the devil. When our hearts are purest, he comes and soils them.

MARTIN LUTHER (1483–1546)
Table-Talk

The Devil himself, which is the author of confusion and lies.

ROBERT BURTON (1577–1640)
The Anatomy of Melancholy

The Devil did grin, for his darling sin
Is pride that apes humility.
SAMUEL TAYLOR COLERIDGE (1772–1834)
The Devil's Thoughts

The devil tempts us not. It is we who tempt him, beckoning his skill with opportunity.
GEORGE ELIOT (1819–1880)
Adam Bede

Heaven sends us good meat, but the Devil sends cooks.
DAVID GARRICK (1717–1779)
Epigrams

Where the Devil can't go he sends his grandmother.
German Proverb

We paint the devil foul, yet he
Hath some good in him, all agree.
GEORGE HERBERT (1593–1633)
The Temple

The devil was piqu'd such saintship to
   behold,
And longed to tempt him like good Job of
   old;
But Satan now is wiser than of yore.
And tempts by making rich, not making
   poor.
ALEXANDER POPE (1688–1744)
Moral Essays

When the thief prays to God, the Devil steals his prayers in flight.
Russian Proverb

Since in doing what God permits the devil moves at the spur of his own malice, the power which he has may be called good, or even just, while his will is forever unjust. He receives, that is, the power from God, but his will is of himself.
PETER ABÉLARD (1079–1142)
Glosses on Porphyry

Reason may find what difficulties she will in the doctrine of a personal Satan, but she has yet to harmonize and arrange, under any other idea, the phenomenon of human sin.
PHILLIPS BROOKS (1835–1893)
The Mystery of Iniquity

If the devil ever laughs, it must be at hypocrites, for they are the greatest dupes he has. They serve him better than any others, and receive no wages; nay, what is still more extraordinary, they submit to greater mortifications to go to hell than the sincerest Christian to go to Heaven.
CHARLES CALEB COLTON (1780–1832)
Lacon

The devil too loves man, but not for man's sake—for his own; thus he loves man out of egotism, to aggrandize himself, to extend his power.
LUDWIG FEUERBACH (1804–1872)
The Essence of Christianity

How does Satan insinuate himself into the soul? Thou shalt detect him in all blameworthy conduct; his guidance is in all the deceit of this world, all inordinate love of created things, such as honors and riches, relatives and friends, and also self-love in all its forms.
JOHANNES TAULER (1300–1361)
Sermons

In nothing as much as in mockery is human badness evident; the Devil is the great mocker, he is the emperor and father of all mockers.
MIGUEL DE UNAMUNO (1864–1936)
The Life of Don Quixote and Sancho

'Tis much proved, that, with devotion's
   visage,
And pious action we do sugar o'er
The devil himself.
WILLIAM SHAKESPEARE (1564–1616)
Hamlet

It is Satan's wisdom to tell what God is, and by doing so he will draw you into the abyss.
JOHN CALVIN (1509–1564)
Institutes of the Christian Religion

At the devil's booth are all things sold,
Each ounce of dross costs its ounce of gold.
          JAMES RUSSELL LOWELL (1819–1891)
                              Collected Poems

The devil makes bold to brand God's works as lies, in order to abuse Him; he seduces those who are weak in their faith and leads them astray in order to make them desert God and cultivate false arts and grievously affront Him.   PARACELSUS (1493–1541)
                              Imitatio Theophrasti

And in he came with eyes of flame,
     The Devil, to fetch the dead;
And all the church with his presence glowed
     Like a fiery furnace red.
          ROBERT SOUTHEY (1774–1843)
                         The Old Woman of Berkeley

If the devil might have his free option, I believe he would ask nothing else but liberty to enfranchise all false religions, and to em-bondage the true.
          NATHANIEL WARD (1578–1652)
                    The Simple Cobbler of Aggavamm

The Devil is a slanderer, a sophist, a blas-phemer, and is opposed to both God and man.   JOHANN ARNDT (1555–1621)
                              True Christianity

It is easy to bid the devil to be your guest, but difficult to get rid of him.
                              Danish Proverb

When flatterers meet, the Devil goes to dinner.   *English Proverb*

When the Devil says his *Paternoster*, he means to cheat you.   *Spanish Proverb*

The devil's snare does not catch you, unless you are first caught by the devil's bait.
          SAINT AMBROSE (340–397)
                         Explanation of Psalm 118

When the devil is called the god of the world it is not because he made it, but be-cause we serve him with our worldliness.
          SAINT THOMAS AQUINAS (1225–1274)
                              Summa Theologica

But when to sin our bias'd nature leans,
The careful devil is still at hand with means.
          JOHN DRYDEN (1631–1700)
                         Absalom and Achitophel

Though Satan strive to block thy way
By all his Stratagems he may:
     Come, come though through the fire.
          EDWARD TAYLOR (1642–1729)
                              Christ's Reply

Who but the Evil One has cried "Whoa!" to mankind?
          HENRY DAVID THOREAU (1817–1862)
                              Walking

Is it not remarkable that the greatest atroc-ities of life—I think of the capitalistic order and of the war—can justify themselves on purely moral principles? The devil may also make use of morality. He laughs at the tower of Babel which we erect to him.
          KARL BARTH (1886–1968)
                    The Word of God and the Word of Man

He that has purchas'd the Devil, must make the most of him.
          THOMAS FULLER (1654–1734)
                              Gnomologia

Had Satan's theology been more accurate he could not even have contemplated his re-bellion. He did so only because he wor-shipped a false divinity and, coveting it, sought to oust it. So he hurled himself to hell. He had never even "seen" God, and he still leads the power-worshippers in their com-mon blindness. They are cosmic losers be-cause they have never known the nature of Being.   GEDDES MACGREGOR (1909–)
                              He Who Lets Us Be

There was given to me a thorn in the flesh, the messenger of Satan to buffet me, lest I should be exalted above measure.

The New Testament
2 Corinthians 12:7

The God of peace shall bruise Satan under your feet shortly.

The New Testament
Romans 16:20

When Satan cannot come himself he sends wine as a messenger.

The Talmud

Satan who looked at himself,
With his own eye, was condemned for ever.
Adam, on whom he cast an evil eye,
Craved forgiveness and was redeemed.

SHEIKH 'ABDULLAH ANSARI (1005–1090)
Invocations

Where a fly can alight there is room for Satan.

Greek Proverb

But then I sigh; and with a piece of
    Scripture,
Tell them that God bids us do good for evil:
And thus I clothe my naked villainy
With old odd ends, stolen out of holy writ;
And seem a saint, when most I play the
    devil.

WILLIAM SHAKESPEARE (1564–1616)
Richard III

Order governs the world. The Devil is the author of confusion.

JONATHAN SWIFT (1667–1745)
Letter to Stella

A sort of creeping comes over my skin when I hear the Devil quote Scripture.

SIR WALTER SCOTT (1771–1832)
Kenilworth

Whatever Book is for Vengeance for Sin and Whatever Book is Against the Forgiveness of Sins is not of the Father, but of Satan the Accuser and Father of Hell.

WILLIAM BLAKE (1757–1827)
Notes on the Illustration of Dante

The Evil Impulse seduces in this world and accuses in the next.

The Gemarah

Let the devil into a church and he will climb into the pulpit.

Latvian Proverb

He has not a little of the Devil in him who prays and bites.

JOHANN KASPAR LAVATER (1741–1801)
Aphorisms on Man

Soaring through wider zones that pricked

With memory of the old revolt from
    Awe,
He reached a middle height and at the stars,
Which are the brains of heaven, he looked
    and sank.
Around the ancient track marched, rank on
    rank.
The army of unalterable law.

GEORGE MEREDITH (1828–1909)
Lucifer in Starlight

If the Devil becomes your godfather you can go to hell easily.

Singhalese Proverb

To God one limps, to the devil one jumps.

German Proverb

The devil's despair is the most intense despair, for the devil is sheer spirit, and therefore absolute consciousness and transparency; in the devil there is no obscurity which might serve as a mitigating excuse. His despair is absolute defiance, and this is the maximum of despair.

SÖREN KIERKEGAARD (1813–1855)
Sickness

For still our ancient foe
Doth seek to work us woe;
His craft and power are great,
And armed with cruel hate,
On earth is not his equal.

MARTIN LUTHER (1483–1546)
A Mighty Fortress Is Our God

Casting out devils is mere juggling; they never cast out any but what they first cast in.

JOHN SELDEN (1584–1654)
Table Talk

Now on that same night, when I was sleeping, Satan assailed me mightily, in such sort as I shall remember as long as I am in this body. And he fell upon me, as it were, a huge rock, and I had no power over my limbs.

SAINT PATRICK (389–461)
Confessions

By the envy of Satan death entered into the
  world,
And they that belong to his realm
  experience it.

*The Old Testament Apocrypha
The Wisdom of Solomon 2:24–25*

Sarcasm I now see to be, in general, the language of the Devil; for which reason I have, long since, as good as renounced it.

THOMAS CARLYLE (1795–1891)
Sartor Resartus

Talk of the devil, and his horns appear, says the proverb.

SAMUEL TAYLOR COLERIDGE (1772–1834)
Biographia Literaria

There are God's poor and the Devil's poor.

THOMAS ADAMS (1612–1653)
Sermons

I thank God, amongst the millions of vices I do inherit and hold from Adam, I have escaped one, and that a mortal enemy to charity,—the first and father sin, not only of man, but of the Devil,—pride.

SIR THOMAS BROWNE (1605–1682)
Religio Medici

It is even a sin to lie against the Devil.

English Proverb

And as with guns we kill the crow,
  For spoiling our relief,

The devil so must we o'erthrow,
  With gunshot of belief.

GEORGE GASCOIGNE (1525–1577)
Good-Morrow

Patience conquers the Devil.

German Proverb

The devil divides the world between atheism and superstition.

GEORGE HERBERT (1593–1633)
Jacula Prudentum

Those saints which God loves best,
The Devil tempts not the least.

ROBERT HERRICK (1591–1674)
Noble Numbers

Abashed the Devil stood,
And felt how awful goodness is, and saw
Virtue in her shape how lovely.

JOHN MILTON (1608–1674)
Paradise Lost

Every inordinate cup is unblessed and the ingredient is a devil.

WILLIAM SHAKESPEARE (1564–1616)
Othello

Foul shame and scorn be on ye all
  Who turn the good to evil,
And steal the Bible from the Lord,
  To give it to the Devil!

JOHN GREENLEAF WHITTIER (1807–1892)
A Sabbath Scene

The free being who abandons conduct of himself, yields himself to Satan; in the moral world there is no ground without a master, and the waste lands belong to the Evil One.

HENRI FRÉDÉRIC AMIEL (1821–1881)
Journal Intime

The Devil enters the prompter's box and the play is ready to start.

ROBERT W. SERVICE (1874–1958)
The Harpy

Truth makes the Devil blush.

THOMAS FULLER (1654–1734)
Gnomologia

Gird thee as a man against the Fiend's wickedness.

THOMAS À KEMPIS (1380–1471)
Imitation of Christ

The Devil is called in scripture the prince of this world because he has great power in it, because many of its rules and principles are invented by this evil spirit, the father of all lies and falsehood, to separate us from God and prevent our return to happiness.

WILLIAM LAW (1686–1761)
A Serious Call to a Devout and Holy Life

He is damned who gives the flower of his youth to the Devil and to God the dregs of his old age.   *Polish Proverb*

The Devil has expressly created a religious soul which aspires after the infinite, to the ravishings, to the elevations, to cast it into a universe without values and without God.

JEAN-PAUL SARTRE (1905–1980)
L'Idiot de la Famille

The devil shall have his bargain; for he was never yet a breaker of proverbs.

WILLIAM SHAKESPEARE (1564–1616)
Henry IV

By the envy of the devil sin entered the world.   *The Old Testament Apocrypha*
The Wisdom of Solomon 2:24

The Devil often transforms himself into an angel to tempt men, some for their instruction and some for their ruin.

SAINT AUGUSTINE (354–430)
The City of God

The Devil, that old stager, at his trick
Of general utility, who leads
Downward, perhaps, but fiddles all the way!

ROBERT BROWNING (1812–1889)
Red Cotton Night Cap Country

Satan trembles when he sees
The weakest saint upon his knees.

WILLIAM COWPER (1731–1800)
Exhortation to Prayer

War is a fire struck in the Devil's tinder box.   JAMES HOWELL (1594–1666)
Familiar Letters

The Devil has two manners of shapes or forms, wherein he disguises himself; he either appears in the shape of a serpent, to affright and kill; or else in the form of a silly sheep, to lie and deceive; these are his two court colors.

MARTIN LUTHER (1483–1546)
Table-Talk

And if Satan rise up against himself, and be divided, he cannot stand, but hath an end.

The New Testament
Mark 3:26

Satan now is wiser than of yore,
And tempts by making rich, not making poor.

ALEXANDER POPE (1688–1744)
Moral Essays

The devil can cite Scripture for his purpose.   WILLIAM SHAKESPEARE (1564–1616)
The Merchant of Venice

He must eat with a long spoon that must eat with the devil.

WILLIAM SHAKESPEARE (1564–1616)
The Comedy of Errors

To do sin is mannish, but certes to persevere long in sin is the work of the devil.

GEOFFREY CHAUCER (1340–1400)
The Tale of Melibeus

They that worship God merely from fear,
Would worship the devil too, if he appear.

THOMAS FULLER (1654–1734)
Gnomologia

Put on the armour of God that ye may be able to stand against the wiles of the devil.

For we wrestle not against flesh and blood but against principalities, against powers, against the rulers of the darkness of this world, against spiritual wickedness in high places.
The New Testament
Ephesians 6:12

If the Devil is a thing that is once and for all opposed to God, and has absolutely nothing from God, then he is precisely identical with Nothing. If, with some, we represent him as a thinking thing that absolutely neither wills nor does any good, and so sets himself in opposition to God, then surely he is very wretched, and, if prayers could help, then one ought to pray for his conversion.
BENEDICT SPINOZA (1632–1677)
God

The Devil, had he fidelity,
Would be the finest friend—
Because he has ability,
But Devils cannot mend.
Perfidy is the virtue
That would he but resign,—
The Devil, so amended,
Were durably divine.
EMILY DICKINSON (1830–1886)
The Devil, Had He Fidelity

The Devils also believe and know abundance: But in this is the Difference, their Faith works not by Love, nor their Knowledge by Obedience; and therefore they are never the better for them.
WILLIAM PENN (1644–1718)
Some Fruits of Solitude

Be sober, be vigilant; because your adversary the devil, as a roaring lion, walketh about, seeking whom he may devour.
The New Testament
I Peter 5:8

There is no heaven with a little of hell in it —no plan to retain this or that of the devil in our hearts or our pockets. Out Satan must go, every hair and feather!
GEORGE MACDONALD (1824–1905)
Unspoken Sermons

The devil has nothing to say about the will of God. For he hates this will and categorically refuses to do its bidding. He refuses to stand "under" God. He stands "outside"—as we see—as the cunning observer, the mischief-maker and intriguer.
HELMUT THIELICKE (1908–)
Between God and Satan

If Satan were to write a book it would be in praise of virtue, because the good would purchase it for use, and the bad for ostentation.
CHARLES CALEB COLTON (1780–1832)
Lacon

"For the devil," saith the Apostle," sinneth from the beginning"; that is, was the first sinner in the universe, the author of sin, the first being who, by the abuse of his liberty, introduced evil into the creation.
JOHN WESLEY (1703–1791)
Sermons

A man is never alone, not only because he is with himself and his own thoughts, but because he is with the Devil, who ever consorts with our solitude.
SIR THOMAS BROWNE (1605–1682)
Religio Medici

Make a coward fight, and he will beat the Devil.
English Proverb

To curse is to pray to the Devil.
German Proverb

One is always wrong to open a conversation with the devil, for, however he goes about it, he always insists upon having the last word.
ANDRÉ GIDE (1869–1951)
Journals

The Devil divides the world between atheism and superstition.

GEORGE HERBERT (1593–1622)
Jacula Prudentum

We have not sent any apostle or prophet before thee among whose desires Satan injected not some wrong desire, but God shall bring to naught that which Satan had suggested.
The Koran

When the Devil preaches, the world's near an end.   ROGER L'ESTRANGE (1616–1704)
Maxims

The Devil has two occupations, to which he applies himself incessantly, and which are the foundation stones of his kingdom—lying and murder.   MARTIN LUTHER (1483–1546)
Table-Talk

Satan is like an urchin who teases his friends by asking them to guess what is in his closed hand. Each person guesses that the hand conceals whatever is particularly desirable to himself. But when the hand is opened, it is found to contain nothing.

RABBI NAHMAN OF BRATSLAV (1772–1811)
Sayings

The sons of Belial are like thorns that are thrust away; for they cannot be taken with the hand; but the man who touches them arms himself with iron and the shaft of a spear.   *The Old Testament
2 Samuel 23:6–7*

He to whom God gave no sons the Devil gives nephews.   *Spanish Proverb*

And who is this bishop? and where does he
  dwell?
Why truly 'tis Satan, archbishop of Hell.
And he was a primate and he wore a mitre
Surrounded with jewels of sulphur and
  nitre.

JONATHAN SWIFT (1667–1745)
On the Irish Bishops

God seeks comrades and claims love; the Devil seeks slaves and claims obedience.

RABINDRANATH TAGORE (1861–1941)
Fireflies

The devil is free to remain good, but there is no good in him.

SAINT THOMAS AQUINAS (1225–1274)
De Malo

The devil asks only for sadness and melancholy; and as he is sad and melancholy himself, and will be so eternally, he wishes that every one should become like him.

SAINT FRANCIS OF SALES (1567–1622)
The Love of God

If a man cast the blame of his sloth and inefficiency upon others, he will end by sharing the pride of Satan and murmuring against God.

FYODOR DOSTOEVSKY (1821–1881)
The Brothers Karamazov

What we see in Satan is the horrible coexistence of a subtle and incessant intellectual activity with an incapacity to understand anything.   C. S. LEWIS (1898–1963)
Preface to Paradise Lost

In diverse ways the devil has shown hostility to the truth. At times he has tried to shake it by pretending to defend it.

TERTULLIAN (160–230)
Against Praxeas

Death has been introduced into the world through the Devil's envy, and on this account the devil is called the author of death.

MARTIN LUTHER (1483–1546)
Table-Talk

If there were a devil, it would not be one who decided against God, but one who, in eternity, came to no decision.

MARTIN BUBER (1878–1965)
I and Thou

An idle brain is the devil's workshop.
English Proverb

When we do ill the Devil tempteth us; when we do nothing, we tempt him.

THOMAS FULLER (1654–1734)
Gnomologia

One devil often drubs another.

THOMAS FULLER (1654–1734)
Gnomologia

Thou dost believe that there is one God; Thou doest well: the devils also believe and tremble.   *The New Testament*
James 2:19

To be so wicked as to find one's pleasure and delight only in the misfortune of other people, in their lingering hunger, thirst, misery, and want, in the perpetration of nothing but bloodshed and treason, especially in the lives of those who neither have done nor could do one any harm, this is the hellish and insatiable rage and fury of the wretched devil, of which human nature is incapable.

MARTIN LUTHER (1483–1546)
Sermons

The devil knew not what he did when he made man politic; he crossed himself by't; and I cannot think but, in the end, the villainies of man will set him clear.

WILLIAM SHAKESPEARE (1564–1616)
Timon of Athens

Order governs the world. The Devil is the author of confusion.

JONATHAN SWIFT (1667–1745)
Letters

If man were composed only of the pure elements, used in the formation of Adam, he would be less disposed to sin. But it is the turbid waters, coming to mingle in the formation of bodies, which give the Devil a hold over man.   *The Zohar*

The Devil's best ruse is to persuade us he does not exist.

CHARLES BAUDELAIRE (1821–1867)
Petites Poèmes

Satan seeks to sow dissension and hatred among you by means of wine and lots, and to divert you from remembering God and prayer.   *The Koran*

When it is said that Lucifer fell from Heaven, and turned away from God and the like, it means nothing else than that he would have his own will, and would not be of one will with the Eternal will.

Theologia Germanica

In man there is something of the pig, the dog, the devil, and the saint. The pig is the appetite which is repulsive not for its form but for its lust and its gluttony. The dog is passion which barks and bites, causing injury to others. The devil is the attribute which instigates these former two, embellishing them and bedimming the sight of reason which is the divine attribute.

ABU HAMID MUHAMMAD AL-GHAZZALI
(1059–1111)
The Renovation of the Science of Religion

If man is the tonic and God the dominant, the Devil is certainly the sub-dominant and woman the relative minor.

SAMUEL BUTLER (1835–1902)
Note-Books

Mercy imitates God, and disappoints Satan.

SAINT JOHN CHRYSOSTOM (345–407)
Homilies

The Devil makes his Christmas pie of lawyers' tongues.   *English Proverb*

Temptations hurt not, though they have access;
Satan o'ercomes none but by willingness.

ROBERT HERRICK (1591–1674)
Hesperides

The devil wrestles with God, and the field of battle is the human heart.

FYODOR DOSTOEVSKY (1821–1881)
The Brothers Karamazov

Eve said to Adam, "Rise up and let us pray to God in this cause that He set us free from that devil, for thou art in this strait on my account." *Old Testament Apocrypha*
The Slavonic Book of Eve

The qualities of the Devil and all fallen angels are good qualities; they are the very same which they received from their infinitely perfect Creator, the very same which are and must be in all heavenly angels; but they are a hellish, abominable malignity in them now, because they have, by their own self-motion, separated them from the light and love which should have kept them glorious angels. WILLIAM LAW (1686–1761)
The Spirit of Prayer

God's country begins where men love to serve their fellows; the Devil's country begins where men eat men.

WALTER RAUSCHENBUSCH (1861–1918)
Christianizing the Social Order

When a man cometh into his house and remembereth God and repeateth his name at eating his meals, the devil saith to his followers, "Here is no place for you to stay in tonight, nor is there any supper for you."

The Sunan

· HELL, THE SHADOW OF A SOUL ON FIRE ·

Man cannot seek God, unless God himself teaches him; nor find him, unless He reveals himself. The believer does not seek to understand that he may believe, but he believes that he may understand: for unless he believed he would not understand.

SAINT ANSELM (1033–1109)
Proslogion

The lovely shapes and sounds intelligible
Of that eternal language which thy God
Utters, who from eternity doth teach
Himself in all, and all things in himself.
SAMUEL TAYLOR COLERIDGE (1772–1834)
Frost at Midnight

Then I saw that there was a way to hell, even from the gates of heaven.
JOHN BUNYAN (1628–1688)
Pilgrim's Progress

A fool's paradise is a wise man's hell.
THOMAS FULLER (1608–1661)
The Holy State

What hell may be I know not: this I know,
I cannot lose the presence of the Lord.
JOHN GREENLEAF WHITTIER (1807–1892)
Tauler

Where is the necessity of seeking a hell in another life, when it is to be found even in this,—in the hearts of the wicked.
JEAN JACQUES ROUSSEAU (1712–1778)
Emile

Objectively regarded, Heaven and Hell may well be identical. Each is the realisation that Man is utterly subject to the purpose of Another—of God who is Love. To the godly and unselfish soul that is Joy unspeakable; to the selfish soul it is a misery against which he rebels in vain. Heaven and Hell are the two extreme terms of our possible reactions to the Gospel of the Love of God.
WILLIAM TEMPLE (1881–1944)
Daily Readings

Hell gives us art to reach the depth of sin;
But leaves us wretched fools, when we are in.
                    JOHN FLETCHER (1579–1625)
                        The Queen of Corinth

Me miserable! which way shall I fly
Infinite wrath and infinite despair?
Which way I fly is hell; myself am hell;
And in the lowest deep a lower deep
Still threatening to devour me opens wide,
To which the hell I suffer seems a heaven.
                    JOHN MILTON (1608–1674)
                        Paradise Lost

Envy's a coal comes hissing hot from Hell.
                    PHILIP J. BAILEY (1816–1902)
                        Festus

Heaven but the Vision of fulfilled Desire,
And Hell the Shadow from a Soul on fire.
                    OMAR KHAYYÁM (died c. 1123)
                        Rubáiyát

The Hell within him, for within him Hell
He brings, and round about him, nor from
    Hell
One step no more than from himself can fly
By change of place.
                    JOHN MILTON (1608–1674)
                        Paradise Lost

Hell itself can be contained within the compass of a spark.
                    HENRY DAVID THOREAU (1817–1862)
                        Journals

For what, my small philosopher! is hell?
'Tis nothing but full knowledge of the truth,
When truth, resisted long, is sworn our foe.
And calls eternity to do her right.
                    EDWARD YOUNG (1683–1765)
                        Night Thoughts

Covetousness, envy, pride, and wrath are
the four elements of self, or nature, or Hell,
all of them inseparable from it.
                    WILLIAM LAW (1686–1761)
            A Serious Call to a Devout and Holy Life

Fear not them which kill the body, but are
not able to kill the soul, but rather fear him
which is able to destroy both soul and body
in hell.
                    The New Testament
                        Matthew 10:28

The fear o' Hell's a hangman's whip,
    To hang the wretch in order;
But where ye feed your honor's grip,
    Let that aye be your border.
                    ROBERT BURNS (1759–1796)
                        Epistle to a Young Friend

That shabby corner of God's allotment
where He lets the nettles grow, and where all
unbaptized infants, notorious drunkards,
suicides, and others of the conjecturally
damned are laid.
                    THOMAS HARDY (1840–1928)
                        Tess of the D'Urbervilles

The hell to be endured hereafter, of which
theology tells, is no worse than the hell we
make for ourselves in this world by habitually
fashioning our characters in the wrong way.
                    WILLIAM JAMES (1842–1910)
                        Principles of Psychology

Let none admire
That riches grow in hell: that soil may best
Deserve the precious bane.
                    JOHN MILTON (1608–1674)
                        Paradise Lost

And I looked, and behold a pale horse:
and his name that sat on him was Death, and
Hell followed with him. And Power was given
unto them over the fourth part of the earth,
to kill with sword, and with hunger, and with
death, and with the beasts of the earth.
                    The New Testament
                        Revelation 6:8

Even in Hell the peasant will have to serve
the landlord, for, while the landlord is boil-

ing in a cauldron the peasant will have to put wood under it. *Russian Proverb*

Easy is the descent to Hell; night and day the gates stand open; but to reclimb the slope, and escape to the outer air, this indeed is a task. VERGIL (70–19 B.C.)
Aeneid

There are depths in man that go the length of lowest Hell, as there are heights that reach highest Heaven; for are not both Heaven and Hell made out of him, made by him, everlasting Miracle and Mystery as he is?
THOMAS CARLYLE (1795–1881)
The French Revolution

It is fearful, but it is right to say it;—that if we wished to imagine a punishment for an unholy, reprobate soul, we perhaps could not fancy a greater than to summon it to heaven. Heaven would be hell to an irreligious man.
JOHN CARDINAL NEWMAN (1801–1890)
Sermons

Those who follow suggestions from hell, taking them to be inspirations from heaven, are easily known as a rule. They are men who, under a cloak of zeal, turn everything upside down, find fault with everyone, upbraid everyone, condemn everything. They are people who will not be guided, who will give way to nobody, put up with nothing; they simply gratify the passions of self-love in the name of zeal for God's honor.
SAINT FRANCIS OF SALES (1567–1622)
The Love of God

The old detestable doctrine of Hell, the idea that the stubborn and perverse spirit can defy God, and make its black choice, is simply an attempt to glorify the strength of the human spirit and to belittle the love of God. It denies the truth that God, if He chose, could show the darkest soul the beauty of ho-

liness in so constraining a way that the frail nature must yield to the appeal.
ARTHUR CHRISTOPHER BENSON (1862–1925)
The Altar Fire

Hell is in Heaven and Heaven is in Hell. But angels see only the light, and devils only the darkness.
JACOB BOEHME (1575–1624)
Aurora

And if thine eye cause thee to stumble, cast it out; it is good for thee to enter the kingdom of God with one eye, rather than having two eyes to be cast into hell.
The New Testament
Mark 9:47

When all the world dissolves,
And every creature shall be purified,
All places shall be hell that are not heaven.
CHRISTOPHER MARLOWE (1564–1593)
The Tragedy of Doctor Faustus

God has taught us, the hard way, that the supreme goal of all existence is not so quickly and easily grasped.
WALTER MARSHALL HORTON (1895–1966)
Our Christian Faith

Vishnu spake, "O Bal! take thy choice: with five wise men shalt thou enter hell, or with five fools pass into paradise." Gladly entered Bal, "Give me, O Lord, hell with the wise; for that is heaven where the wise dwell, and folly would make of heaven itself a hell!"
Hindu Fable

Out of the belly of hell cried I, and thou heardest my voice. Then I said, I am cast out of thy sight; yet will I look again toward thy holy temple. *The Old Testament*
Jonah 2:2–4

Long is the way
And hard, that out of hell leads up to light.
JOHN MILTON (1608–1674)
Paradise Lost

Nothing burns in hell but the ego.
Theologia Germanica

In Hell an ox costs only a penny, but no man has even that much.   *Yiddish Proverb*

Devoid of hope, I reach the gates of hell,
And laden with desire arrive at heaven:
Thus am I subject to eternal opposites,
And, banished both from heaven and hell,
No pause nor rest my torments know,
Because between two running wheels I go,
Of which one here, the other there compels.
GIORDANO BRUNO (1548–1600)
Ethical Poems

Many a man leaves heaven for hell just to be stubborn.   *Yiddish Proverb*

Hell is where no one has anything in common with anybody else except the fact that they all hate one another and cannot get away from one another and from themselves.
THOMAS MERTON (1915–1968)
Seeds of Contemplation

There are moments when, even to the sober eye of Reason, the world of our sad humanity must assume the aspect of Hell.
EDGAR ALLAN POE (1809–1849)
Marginalia

I can hardly think there was any scared into Heaven; they go the fairest way to Heaven that would serve God without a Hell; other mercenaries, that crouch into Him in fear of Hell, though they term themselves the servants, are indeed but the slaves, of the Almighty.
SIR THOMAS BROWNE (1605–1682)
Religio Medici

What is there in us, mortals, that has not come to us from God? He who teaches us the eternal also teaches us the perishable; for both spring from God.
PARACELSUS (1493–1541)
Manual of the Philosopher's Stone

Men may teach the grammar and rhetoric, but God teaches the divinity.
JOHN SMITH (1616–1652)
Discourses

Remember, God is teaching you always just as much truth as you can learn. If you are in sorrow at your ignorance then, still you must not despair. Be capable of more knowledge and it shall be given to you.
PHILLIPS BROOKS (1835–1893)
Sermons

· GOD'S WRATH ·

Throw away thy rod,
Throw away thy wrath,
    O my God,
Take the gentle path.
GEORGE HERBERT (1593–1633)
Discipline

His way is in whirlwind and storm, and the clouds are the dust of his feet. He rebukes the sea and makes it dry. . . . The mountains quake at Him, and the hills melt; and the earth is upheaved at His presence, yea, the

world and all that dwell therein. Who can stand before His indignation?
*The Old Testament
Nahum 1:3–6*

As long as one fulfills God's purpose, or tries to do so, He is a dear and helpful friend; but if one denies the very condition of one's being alive at all, and continues to defy God, He will quite properly break that one as a potter breaks a defective vessel, as an artist casts aside a blistered canvas or a tube of hardened paint. If that sounds cruel or dreadful, so much the worse for our reported sanity.

BERNARD IDDINGS BELL (1886–1958)
Religion for Living

Because I believe in a God of absolute and unbounded love, therefore I believe in a loving anger of His which will and must devour and destroy all which is decayed, monstrous, abortive in the Universe till all enemies shall be put under His feet, and God shall be all in all. CHARLES KINGSLEY (1819–1875)
Sermons

O soul, be changed into little water drops,
And fall into the ocean, ne'er be found:
My God, my God, look not so fierce on me.
CHRISTOPHER MARLOWE (1564–1593)
The Tragedy of Doctor Faustus

God's anger is not a tempest in a void full of mystery and dread. The world is dark, and human agony is excruciating, but the prophet casts a light by which the heart is led into the thinking of the Lord's mind. God does not delight in unleashing anger.

ABRAHAM JOSHUA HESCHEL (1907–1973)
The Prophets

Make not a person like unto myself ruler
over me;
If I bear punishment it is best from Thy
hand.

SAADI (1184–1291)
Bustan

Judge from your own feelings how God, with his infinite sensibility, must feel when he sees men rising up against their fellow men; performing gross deeds of cruelty on every hand; waging wars that cause blood to flow like rivers throughout the globe; when, in short, he sees them devastating society by every infernal mischief that their ingenuity can invent.

HENRY WARD BEECHER (1813–1887)
Sermons

Return to sobermindedness as you should, and quit sinning. For I say to your shame, some have no sense of divine Presence.

The New Testament
1 Corinthians 15:34

O that thou hadst hearkened to my commandments! Then had thy peace been as a river, and thy righteousness as the waves of the sea. *The Old Testament*
Isaiah 48:18

If "anger" and "wrath" are taken to mean the emotional reaction of an irritated self-concern, there is no such thing in God. But if God is holy love, and I am in any degree given to uncleanness or selfishness, then there is, in that degree, stark antagonism in God against me.

WILLIAM TEMPLE (1881–1944)
Daily Readings

Many would like religion as a sort of lightning rod to their houses, to ward off, by and by, the bolts of divine wrath.

HENRY WARD BEECHER (1813–1887)
Sermons

And from the prophet even unto the priest every one dealeth falsely. They have healed also the hurt of my people lightly, saying: "Peace, peace," when there is no peace.

The Old Testament
Jeremiah 6:13–14

Thou shalt neither rise up by day
Nor lie down by night;
Would God it were dark! thou shalt say;
Would God it were light!
And the sight of thine eyes shall be made
As the burning of fire;
And thy soul shall be sorely afraid
for thy soul's desire.
ALGERNON CHARLES SWINBURNE (1837–1909)
Poems and Ballads

Your words have been all too strong against Me saith the Lord. Yet ye say:

"Wherein have we spoken against Thee?" Ye have said: "It is vain to serve God; and what profit is it that we have kept His charge, and that we have walked mournfully because of the Lord of Hosts? And now we call the proud happy; yea, they that work wickedness are built up; yea, they that tempt God are even delivered."   *The Old Testament*
Malachi 3:13–15

And I heard a great voice out of the temple saying to the seven angels, Go your ways, and pour out the vials of the wrath of God upon the earth.   *The New Testament*
Revelation 16:1

Ah! Let Him damn me a hundred times, a thousand times, provided He exists. I believe in Thee, I believe. Our Father which art in heaven, I would rather be judged by an Infinite Being than judged by my equals.
JEAN-PAUL SARTRE (1905–1980)
The Devil and the Good Lord

It was for the chastisement of our pride, and the instruction of our wretchedness and incapacity, that God brought about the perplexity and confusion of the ancient Tower of Babel. Whatever we undertake without his assistance, whatever we behold save by the lamp of his grace, is but vanity and folly; the very essence of truth, which is unchanging and constant when fortune gives us possession of it, we corrupt and adulterate by our weakness.
MICHEL EYQUEM DE MONTAIGNE (1533–1592)
Apology for Raimond Sebond

For those whom God to ruin has design'd,
He fits for fate, and first destroys their
mind.
JOHN DRYDEN (1631–1700)
The Hind and the Panther

O foolish people, and without understanding; which have eyes and see not; which have ears, and hear not.   *The Old Testament*
Jeremiah 5:21

There are six things which the Lord hateth, yea, seven which are an abomination unto Him: haughty eyes, a lying tongue, and hands that shed innocent blood; a heart that deviseth wicked thoughts, feet that are swift in running to evil; a false witness that breatheth out lies, and he that soweth discord among brethern.   *The Old Testament*
Proverbs 6:16–19

Sow to yourselves in righteousness, reap in mercy, break up the fallow ground, for it is time to seek the Lord, 'til he come and teach you righteousness. Ye have plowed wickedness, you have reaped iniquity, ye have eaten the fruit of lies.   *The Old Testament*
Hosea 10:12–13

God hates these three: the person who says one thing with his mouth and thinks otherwise in his heart; the person who could give evidence in another's favor, but does not do so; and the person who, being alone, sees his neighbor sin, and gives unsupported testimony against him.   *The Gemarah*

Commandments there be which some minds
reckon lightly,
Yet no man knoweth whom shall befall
perdition.
The Book of Mohammed, ay, and the Book
of Moses,
The Gospel of Mary's son and the Psalms of
David,
Their bans no nation heeded, their wisdom
perished
In vain—and like to perish are all the
people.
ABU-AL-ALA AL-MA'ARRI (973–1057)
Meditations

· AND LEAD US NOT INTO TEMPTATION ·

The beginning of all temptations is inconstancy of heart and little trust in God; for as a ship without governance is stirred hitherward and thitherward with the waves so a man that is remiss and that holdeth not stedfastly his purpose is diversely tempted.

THOMAS À KEMPIS (1380–1471)
Imitation of Christ

God delights in our temptations, and yet hates them. He delights in them when they drive us to prayer; He hates them when they drive us to despair.

MARTIN LUTHER (1483–1546)
Table-Talk

If a man is tempted, he has a chance to choose and thereby become a worthier man. Temptation is thus a fork in the road, a way up or a way down; and if God is man's Unseen Ally, temptation can be a blessing.

GEORGE ARTHUR BUTTRICK (1892–1979)
So We Believe, So We Pray

God keeps faith and he will not allow you to be tested above your powers, but when the test comes he will at the same time provide a way out, by enabling you to sustain it.

The New Testament
1 Corinthians 10:13

To avoid an occasion for our virtues is a worse degree of failure than to push forward pluckily and make a fall. It is lawful to pray God that we be not led into temptation; but not lawful to skulk from those that come to us.

ROBERT LOUIS STEVENSON (1850–1894)
Virginibus Puerisque

The devil tempts that he may ruin; God tempts that He may crown.

SAINT AMBROSE (340–397)
Concerning Abraham

God is better served in resisting a temptation to evil than in many formal prayers.

WILLIAM PENN (1644–1718)
Truth Exalted

It is good and profitable to good men to be tempted and troubled, as is shown by what the prophet saith: To him that is tempted and troubled, God saith, I am with him in tribulation; I shall deliver him, and shall glorify him. Let no man think himself to be holy because he is not tempted, for the holiest and highest in life have the most temptations. How much higher a hill is, so much is the wind there greater; so, how much higher the life is, so much stronger is the temptation of the enemy.   JOHN WYCLIFFE (1320–1384)
The Poor Caitiff

· ALL MANNER OF SINS ·

It is not easy to fall out of the hands of the living God: They are so large, and they cradle so much of a man. And still through knowledge and will, he can break away, man can break away, and fall from the hands of God into himself alone, down the godless plunge of the abyss, a god-lost creature turning upon himself.

D. H. LAWRENCE (1885–1930)
Complete Poems

Alienation from self and from one's fellow men has its roots in separation from God.

Once the hub of the wheel, which is God, is lost, the spokes, which are men, fall apart.

FULTON J. SHEEN (1895–1979)
Peace of Soul

If man is not made for God, why is he only happy in God? If man is made for God, why is he so opposed to God?

BLAISE PASCAL (1623–1662)
Pensées

Whoso walketh in haughty pride repels the presence of God.   *The Talmud*

Let natural reason, let affections, let the profits or the pleasures of the world be the council-table, and can they tell you that you are able to maintain a war against God, and subsist so, without being reconciled to him? Deceive not yourselves, no man hath so much pleasure in this life, as he that is at peace with God.   JOHN DONNE (1572–1631)
Sermons

The rebel defies more than he denies. Originally, at least, he does not deny God, he simply talks to him as an equal. But it is not a polite dialogue. It is a polemic animated by a desire to conquer.

ALBERT CAMUS (1913–1960)
The Rebel

Once in a while there does come to a man some terrible revelation of himself in a great sorrow. Then in the tumult and anguish he looks for his religious faith to clothe his nakedness against the tempest; and he finds perhaps some moth-eaten old garment that profits him nothing, so that his soul miserably perished in the frost of doubt. Such a man has expected God to come to his help in every time of need; but the only god he has actually and consistently had, has been his own little contemptible private notion and dim feeling of a god, which he has never dared fairly to look at. Any respectable wooden idol would have done him better service; for then a man could know where and what his idol is.

JOSIAH ROYCE (1855–1916)
Religious Aspects of Philosophy

When I hate some one or deny that God is my father—it is not he that loses, but me: for then I have no father.

SÖREN KIERKEGAARD (1813–1855)
Journals

These two sins, hatred and pride, deck and trim themselves out, as the Devil clothed himself in the Godhead. These two are right deadly sins: hatred is killing; pride is lying.

MARTIN LUTHER (1483–1546)
Table-Talk

When you get God pulling one way, and the devil the other, each having his feet well braced,—to say nothing of the conscience sawing transversely,—almost any timber will give way.

HENRY DAVID THOREAU (1817–1862)
Letters

The Everlasting No had said: "Behold, thou art fatherless, outcast, and the Universe is mine, the Devil's"; to which my whole Me now made answer: "I am not thine, but Free, and forever hate thee!"

THOMAS CARLYLE (1795–1881)
Sartor Resartus

The Rationalist makes himself his own centre, not His Maker; he does not go to God, but he implies that God must come to him.

JOHN CARDINAL NEWMAN (1801–1890)
Essays Critical and Historical

Who art thou O man that disputest against God? Shall the thing formed say to him that formed it, Why hast thou made me thus? Must God come down to the bar of man, to render an account of the reason for his works?   RICHARD BAXTER (1615–1691)
Sermons

The soul of the covetous is far removed from God, as far as his memory, understanding and will are concerned. He forgets God as though He were not his God, owing to the fact that he has fashioned for himself a god of Mammon and of temporal possessions.

SAINT JOHN OF THE CROSS (1542–1591)
The Dark Night of the Soul

Men, as always, prayed to a God of their own creation, a Divinity which only mirrored the petty minds of its worshippers. This man of wealth and power prayed devoutly and absentmindedly to his conception of God, a being of unlimited wealth, plastered with diamonds, fat, vulgar, and, through his wealth, able to dictate the lives of countless millions of creatures, scattered throughout a boundless universe.

WALTER WHITE (1893–1955)
Flight

Reason is not given us to know God, but to know the world. Where reason pretends to know God, it creates a reason-God, and that always is an idol.

EMIL BRUNNER (1889–1966)
The Word and the World

For the love of money is the root of all evil: which while some coveted after, they have erred from the faith, and pierced themselves through with many sorrows. But thou, O man of God, flee these things; and follow after righteousness, godliness, faith, love, patience, meekness.
The New Testament
1 Timothy 6:10–12

By denying the existence, or providence of God, men may shake off their ease but not their yoke.   THOMAS HOBBES (1588–1679)
Leviathan

Men are not flattered by being shown that there has been a difference of purpose between the Almighty and them. To deny it,

however, in this case, is to deny that there is a God governing the world.

ABRAHAM LINCOLN (1809–1865)
Letter to Thurlow Weed

It is the maxim of most wicked men that the Deity is some way or other like themselves; their souls do more than whisper it, though their lips speak it not; and though their tongues be silent, yet their lives cry it upon the housetops and in the public streets.

JOHN SMITH (1616–1652)
Discourses

Whom the Lord loveth he chasteneth.
The New Testament
Hebrews 12:6

To the covetous man life is a nightmare, and God lets him wrestle with it as best he may.   HENRY WARD BEECHER (1813–1887)
Sermons

This light and darkness in our chaos join'd,
What shall divide? The God within the
    mind.

ALEXANDER POPE (1688–1744)
Essay on Man

No one is cast into the abyss unless he has first rejected, freed his heart from the terrible, yet gentle, hand of God. No one is abandoned unless he has first committed the fundamental sacrilege and denied God not in his justice but in his love.

GEORGE BERNANOS (1888–1948)
L'Imposture

The unstruck drum of eternity is sounded
    within me, but my deaf ears cannot hear
    it.
So long as man clamors for the *I* and the
    mine hid works are as naught:
When all love of the *I* and the *mine* is dead,
    then the work of the Lord is done.

KABIR (1440–1518)
Works

How often we are told what God can do for us; how rarely what God can do with us! God no longer the cosmic policeman of the fiery furnace religion, is now a sort of cosmic bellhop, ready to do anything to make life pleasant and safe without asking for anything more than a reasonable tip.

WILLIAM SLOANE COFFIN, JR. (1924–)
Sermons

The very mastery with which God has created the world gives occasion to the danger that the world misunderstands itself and thinks it can venture to do without God. That would be sin, and this sin has happened, and is happening all the time.

ROMANO GUARDINI (1885–1968)
The Lord's Prayer

When we come to believe that we are in possession of our God because we belong to some particular sect it gives us such a complete sense of comfort, that God is needed no longer except for quarelling with others whose idea of God differs from ours in theoretical details.

RABINDRANATH TAGORE (1861–1941)
Thought Relics

It is the greatest folly in Babel that the devil has made the world argue about religion so that they argue about self-made ideas, about the letter. The kingdom of God does not consist of any idea but of power and love.

JACOB BOEHME (1575–1624)
The Way to Christ

There are men who boast of their deeds, doing little and saying much. There are men who, when they work, sound loud bells so that the report of their goodness be heard afar. To such the heavens have no voice.

ISAAC ARAMA (15th century)
Akeda

The great seductions are: through belief in God to withdraw from men; through supposed knowledge of the absolute truth to justify one's isolation; through supposed possession of Being itself to fall into a state of complacency that is in truth lovelessness.

KARL JASPERS (1883–1969)
The Perennial Scope of Philosophy

Whoso walketh in haughty pride repels the presence of God.   *The Talmud*

He who hates not in himself his self-love and that instinct which leads him to make himself a God, is indeed blind.

BLAISE PASCAL (1623–1662)
Pensées

Thus says the Lord: Let not the wise man glory in his wisdom, let not the mighty man glory in his might, let not the rich man glory in his riches; but let him who glories glory in this, that he understands and knows Me, that I am the Lord who practises kindness, justice, and righteousness on the earth, for in these things I delight, says the Lord.

*The Old Testament
Jeremiah 9:22–23*

Of all evil traits, none vulgarizes a person more than pride, so that he cannot rise toward the majesty of the spiritual. Whoever yearns for the light of God to illumine his soul must despise pride so that he will literally feel its defilement.

ABRAHAM ISAAC KOOK (1865–1935)
The Moral Principles

He who cherishes pride in his heart, and sets himself above all creatures, is a rebel against the kingdom of heaven, for he flaunts the raiment of the Omnipresent.

NAHMANIDES (1195–1270)
Letter to His Son

One who is haughty causes the Divine Presence to lament over him, for Scripture states (Psalms 138:6): "For though the Lord be exalted, yet regardeth He the lowly, but the haughty He knoweth from afar."

The Talmud

He who wants to know truth in himself must first get rid of the beam of pride, which prevents him from seeing the light, and then erect a way of ascent in his heart by which to seek himself in himself, and thus after the twelfth step of humility he will come to the first step of truth.

SAINT BERNARD OF CLAIRVAUX (1091–1153)
Sermons

God does not listen to the prayers of the proud.   *Hebrew Proverb*

Every day we plead in the Lord's Prayer, "Thy will be done!", yet when His will is done we grumble and are not pleased with it.

MEISTER ECKHART (1260–1327)
Sermons

Think not that pleasing God lies so much in performing good works as in performing them with good will, and without attachment and respect to persons.

SAINT JOHN OF THE CROSS (1542–1591)
Spiritual Maxims

No sooner do we believe that God loves us than there is an impulse to believe that He does so, not because He is Love, but because we are intrinsically lovable.

C. S. LEWIS (1898–1963)
The Four Loves

When a man enraptured has more clarity in his understanding with which to wonder at God than he has warmth in his will with which to love him, then he had better be on his guard; for there is a danger that this ecstasy may be false, inflating rather than edifying the spirit.

SAINT FRANCIS OF SALES (1567–1622)
On the Love of God

It is not with the motes from one's neighbor's eye that the house of God can be built, but with the beams that one takes out of one's own.   ANDRÉ GIDE (1869–1951)
Letter to Paul Claudel

Whenever a man believes that he has the exact truth from God, there is in that man no spirit of compromise. He has not the modesty born of the imperfections of human nature; he has the arrogance of theological certainty and the tyranny born of ignorant assurance.

ROBERT G. INGERSOLL (1833–1899)
Works

We are not yet clear of that unreal, man-centered religious world which is from beginning to end the creation of human pride.

EVELYN UNDERHILL (1875–1941)
The Mount of Purification

The more we are clean from the cancer of pride, the more we are filled with love; and he who is filled with love is filled with God.

SAINT AUGUSTINE (354–430)
On the Trinity

It has been said that though God cannot alter the past, historians can; it is perhaps because they can be useful to Him in this respect that He tolerates their existence.

SAMUEL BUTLER (1835–1902)
Erewhon Revisited

Here we are on this tiny island in the sky, with minds which have developed slowly through many millennia in response to practical situations demanding solution, and now, in this vast cosmos whose physical aspects are mysterious beyond our comprehension, we talk as though some idea of ours could capture the truth concerning the infinite Source behind and within it all.

HARRY EMERSON FOSDICK (1878–1969)
In Search of God and Immortality

Man is at variance with his fellow man by the force of the same pride which brings him into conflict with God.

REINHOLD NIEBUHR (1892–1971)
Gifford Lectures

And what is the origin of our evil will but pride? And what is pride but the craving for undue exaltation? And this is undue exaltation, when the soul abandons Him to whom it ought to cleave as its end, and becomes a kind of end to itself.

SAINT AUGUSTINE (354–430)
The City of God

When humanity fills the heart, when its gentleness renders susceptible its thoughts and feelings, the softest breath of God's Spirit can bend it earthward to help the needy, and downward to supplicate and welcome heaven's grace. But when it is frozen through and through with pride, it coldly resists the overtures of mercy, and in its deadness is apathetic even to the storm of wrath.

GEORGE C. LORIMER (1838–1904)
Sermons

He that serves on God's altar must be free from haughtiness and false pride.

The Midrash

Thank God when thou art in prosperity,
For disappointment comes from pride.

SAADI (1184–1291)
Bustan

If God created us in his own image, we have more than reciprocated.

VOLTAIRE (1694–1778)
Le Sottisier

How many deeds, with which the world has
  rung,
From pride, in league with ignorance, have
  sprung!
But God o'errules all human follies still,
And bends the tough materials to his will.

WILLIAM COWPER (1731–1800)
Charity

There is one kind of religion in which the more devoted a man is, the fewer proselytes he makes: the worship of himself.

GEORGE MACDONALD (1824–1905)
Unspoken Sermons

If ever a man becomes proud, let him remember that a mosquito preceded him in the divine order of creation!   *The Talmud*

A certain king said to a religious man, "Do you ever think of me?" He answered, "Yes, whenever I forget God."

SAADI (1184–1291)
Gulistan

If you say that man is too little for God to speak to him, you must be very big to be able to judge.   BLAISE PASCAL (1623–1662)
Pensées

What is our reason for saying in sorrow that God does not heed us, when we ourselves do not heed Him? What is our reason for muttering that God does not look down towards earth, when we ourselves do not look up towards Heaven?

SALVIANUS (5th century)
The Governance of God

Everyone who deifies his own will is an enemy of God's will and cannot enter into the Kingdom of God.

GREGORY SAVVICH SKOVORODA (1722–1794)
Works

The pretender sees no one but himself
Because he has the veil of conceit in front.
If he were endowed with a God-discerning
  eye
He would see that no one is weaker than
  himself.

SAADI (1184–1291)
Gulistan

Count not thyself better than others, lest perchance thou appear worse in the sight of God, who knoweth what is in man. Be not proud of thy good works, for God's judgments are of another sort than the judgments of man, and what pleaseth man is ofttimes displeasing to Him.

THOMAS À KEMPIS (1380–1471)
Imitation of Christ

We know of some very religious people who came to doubt God when a great misfortune befell them, even though they themselves were to blame for it; but we have never yet seen anyone who lost his faith because an undeserved fortune fell to his lot.

ARTHUR SCHNITZLER (1862–1931)
Notebook

Talk no more so exceeding proudly; let no arrogancy come out of your mouth: for the Lord is a God of knowledge, and by him actions are weighed.   *The Old Testament*
I Samuel 2:3

There is not one of us who is as much displeased to see himself compared with God as he is to see himself brought down to the level of the other animals; so much more jealous are we of our own interests than of that of our creator.

MICHEL EYQUEM DE MONTAIGNE (1533–1592)
Apology for Raimond Sebond

All the wants which disturb human life, which make us uneasy to ourselves, quarrelsome with others, and unthankful to God, which weary us in vain labors and foolish anxieties, which carry us from project to project, from place to place in a poor pursuit of we don't know what, are the wants which neither God, nor nature, nor reason hath subjected us to, but are solely infused into us by pride, envy, ambition, and covetousness.

WILLIAM LAW (1686–1761)
A Serious Call to a Devout and Holy Life

O God of earth and altar,
  Bow down and hear our cry,
Our earthly rulers falter,
  Our people drift and die;
The walls of gold entomb us,
  The swords of scorn divide:

Take not thy thunder from us,
  But take away our pride.

G. K. CHESTERTON (1874–1936)
O God of Earth and Altar

Nor must you say to yourselves, "My own strength and energy have gained me this wealth," but remember the Lord your God; it is he that gives you strength to become prosperous, so fulfilling the covenant guaranteed by oath with your forefathers, as he is doing now.   *The Old Testament*
Deuteronomy 8:17–18

If in the beginning God did make man in his image, man has been busy ever since making God in his image, and the deplorable consequences are everywhere to be seen.

HARRY EMERSON FOSDICK (1878–1969)
Christianity and Progress

Your chief maladies are pride, which takes you away from God, and lust, which binds you to earth. What a chimera then is man! What a novelty! What a monster, what a chaos, what a contradiction, what a prodigy! Judge of all things, imbecile worm of the earth; depository of truth, a sink of uncertainty and error; the pride and refuse of the universe! Know then, proud man, what a paradox you are to yourself.

BLAISE PASCAL (1623–1662)
Pensées

The sinner's bleeding heart in anguish sighs,
The saint upon his piety relies,
Doth he not know that God resisteth pride,
But takes the low in spirit to His side?
Humility in His sight is more meet
Than strict religious forms and self-conceit;
Thy self-esteem but proves how bad thou
  art,
For egotism with God can have no part.

SAADI (1184–1291)
Tayyibat

VII · SUFFERING AND GOD

If you want to endure the world, equip yourself with a heart that can withstand suffering.
THE MIDRASH

IF, as we have seen, reconciling evil in a world the Lord of the Universe has made is a great enigma to the God Seekers, it is no less troubling to them to consider the prevalence of suffering. But they can no more evade its implications than they can the problem of evil. Unlike Voltaire's Dr. Pangloss in *Candide,* the God Seekers have always known that all is *not* the best in the best of all possible worlds. Thus, from the dawn of religious sensibility they have felt compelled to understand, as best they could, the reason for suffering. In this section of our anthology we find a representation of some of their deepest thoughts on this difficult question.

The supreme articulation of the God-man dialogue on suffering came from the unknown writer of the Book of Job in the Old Testament. In his torment, Job was driven to ask such agonizing questions as: Is man by his very nature God's enemy? Is God more pleased to destroy than to create? Is God nothing more than naked, irrational power? Can justice only be what God wills it to be?

Job's suffering almost leads him to an advocacy relationship with Satan, who is extremely adept in framing casuistic questions. In the end Job rejects this line of questioning and affirms God's justice, even though he cannot understand it. He realizes that the universe, of which he is only one small almost infinitesmal part, is filled with the mystery of God's will.

Job learns that he must accept God as He is, that neither he nor any other person can write the script of life, and that a serene acceptance of God's master plan for the world is his only path to personal peace.

In an earlier Mesopotamian poem with a Job-like theme, the protagonist was also afflicted for no known reason, and since he had been faithful to the gods in his daily living he asks why they are so angry with him. Perhaps, he ponders, what man thinks is good is evil to the gods, and what he thinks is evil is pleasing to them.

In many respects the subsequent God Seekers have only amplified the lesson of the Book of Job. But sometimes it is terribly difficult for any human being, whether Job or the parent of a child born with Down's syndrome, to accept the will of God.

Why me? If we believe that each of us existed in God's mind before we were manifest on this earth, then, like Job, we have to have faith that a loving and compassionate Creator indeed has a master plan for our lives. Josiah Royce, the noted American philosopher, said we must learn to look at the "unavoidable pains of life, the downfall of cherished plans, all the cruelty of fate" as things that are opaque to us, but "to God, who knows them fully, somehow clear and rational."

What it comes down to, the God Seekers tell us, is the choice of believing that God has a reason for our suffering or thinking that God acts imperiously, willfully, or even with cruel disdain of the world He has created. Albert Camus despaired because since human beings had emerged on this planet "the sum-total of evil has not diminished in the world" and because there is injustice in all suffering. William James would have countered this argument by reaffirming his belief that since God created this world, "tragedy is only provisional and partial, shipwreck and dissolution not the absolutely final things."

Were Dr. James still living today he might shudder at the deadly strides the nations of the world are making toward a nuclear holocaust, a genocide of all humanity. Like the billions who cannot move their seats from under this atomic sword of Damocles hovering above us, he would wonder how and why we can come to such a pass.

Yes, as Dr. James wrote nearly a century ago, a world created by God could indeed burn up or freeze; other stars whose magnitude would make our solar system seem small in comparison have died when they had finished their role in God's plan. But if we "think of Him as still mindful of the old ideals," then, James believed, God will "bring them elsewhere to fruition."

Another theme explored in this section is that we have turned this world into one that makes God himself sorrow to look at it. In his *Letters from Prison*, Dietrich Bonhoeffer, as he contemplated the horror that had enveloped his country, wrote: "Man is summoned to share in God's sufferings at the hands of a godless world. He must therefore really live in the godless world, without attempting to gloss over or explain its ungodliness in some religious way or other." Meister Eckhart had expressed a similar thought in a sermon nearly seven hundred years earlier: "No matter how great a sorrow may be, if it comes by way of God, God has already suffered it."

Job's initial rebellion, once he was beset by all of his suffering, was to think of God as some imperious sovereign far removed in the most infinite realms of infinity, a spiteful God who got pleasure from the suffering of his creatures. Josiah Royce, in concordance with Eckhart, would have assured Job that his suffering was also God's suffering, for he believed that no chasm divides us from God.

If God is always *here*, then He cannot be remote from us, even in eternity. As Royce put it in his *Studies of Good and Evil*, "His eternity means merely the completeness of his experience. But that completeness is inclusive; your sorrow is one of the included facts."

But Dr. George Arthur Buttrick is troubled with such an interpretation, and in *God, Pain, and Evil* wonders whether, if God enters into our suffering and shares it with us,

He is not then limited and distorted by evil. On the other side of the dilemma, however, as Buttrick adds, "if He is lifted above our pain in an eternal Passivity, which seems to us an eternal callousness, can he be God?"

Two hundred years before the author of the Book of Job composed his classic, unparalleled search into the abyss of human suffering, a great religious figure in India formulated some equally remarkable thoughts. Prince Sakyamuni of the Guatama clan had led a sheltered life behind opulent castle walls until he was twenty-nine years old. Legend has it that his father, King Suddhodana, had kept all knowledge of sorrow and despair from Sakyamuni, who did not know that poverty, misery, and death even existed. When Sakyamuni one day decided to ride his horse, Kanthaka, outside of the castle walls his father sent hundreds of his vassals ahead to remove any person from the wayside who was not happy and in the prime of life. But the plans, we are told, went awry and the prince saw four sights he had never even conceptualized before: a sick man, an old man, a corpse, and a religious ascetic.

These sights of human suffering, perhaps more than any other single event, made Sakyamuni leave his palatial trappings, his beautiful wife, and baby son, and seek his enlightenment. After self-mortification and many other approaches, Sakyamuni, a true Bodhisattava, achieved his sought-after enlightenment under the Bodhi tree in a grove in Bodh Gaya. What were the three cornerstones of his message to the world?

One, that all of living involves pain. Two, that worldly suffering is caused by craving and desire, and three, release from suffering comes only when desire ends. Thereafter, the Buddha, starting with his famous first sermon, the Sutra of Turning the Wheel of Doctrine, defined a remarkable system of ethical behavior he called the eightfold path, which he offered as the way to the cessation of suffering.

Although the Buddha made no allusions to prayer or ceremony and did not address himself to a God, either personal or impersonal, it would be manifestly wrong to exclude him from the company of the greatest of God Seekers. The Lord of the Universe works in many ways to give people the lessons that could bring them to great peace and rapport during their brief time on earth. So, whether he knew, or even cared, Gautama Buddha was a true and great prophet of God.

There is another dominant theme in this section—that only by suffering does mankind achieve wisdom, and suffering prepares us and makes us worthy for the eternity we shall reenter after our earthly sojourn. In one of his letters, the gifted nineteenth-century Russian novelist Nikolai Gogol wrote that God makes us wise "by that very grief which we flee and from which we seek to hide ourselves." Suffering, he says, enables us to acquire some morsels of wisdom that no book ever could provide, "but whoever has acquired one of these crumbs has not the right to conceal it from others. It is not yours but the property of God."

Ludwig van Beethoven, who was intrigued by Eastern philosophy, also held that it is necessary to be willing to suffer if one is to create something of worth. In a letter to a friend he went even further, saying that to recognize "that suffering is one of God's greatest gifts, is almost to reach a mystical solution of the problem of evil."

The God Seekers seem to be telling us, again and again, that suffering is an integral part of life, and, that we, like Job, must come to realize that God's plan for the universe, in which we too play a role, however insignificant, is beyond our understanding.

We know that eventually all physical suffering will come to an end for us and we can hope that our spirits will reenter the eternal headstream that flows into the ocean of our Creator. Each individual meets the test that suffering imposes as best he or she can, some with great fortitude and spirituality, others with hateful accusations against their fate. The gentle Saint Francis of Assisi gained surcease from his own personal sorrows by spending his life trying to relieve the pain and sorrows of others. Victor Hugo compared suffering to a fruit that grows on a tree, saying that God does not make it grow on the limbs that are too weak to hold it. Sri Ramakrishna's metaphor for suffering was that we are like iron, which must be heated repeatedly and hammered incessantly before it can become good steel. So, too, are we heated in the "furnace of tribulations and hammered with the persecutions of the world" before we can achieve the humility that fits us for the presence of God.

How can we best accept and deal with the inevitable sorrows that cast shadows on the life of almost every human being at one time or another? The Roman Stoic philosopher, Lucius Annaeus Seneca, answered that question this way: "What is the best comfort in suffering and pain? It is that a man should take all things as if he had wished for them and prayed for them. For you would have indeed have wished for them if you had known that all things happen because of, with, and in God's will.

Seneca, it will be remembered, was given the ultimate test of his own philosophy when his erstwhile protégé, Emperor Nero, ordered him to end his life by cutting his own wrists.

Meister Eckhart once wrote that if God knew *anyone* who would be willing to suffer the total configuration of human suffering, He would give it to him or her to bear. Why? So that such a person might have a greater worth in eternity.

This theme of the purification of mankind's spirit through suffering is nowhere more beautifully encapsulated than in a parable written by the fourteenth-century mystic Sharafuddin Maneri in his book *The Hundred Letters:*

When Moses spoke with God, he said: "Lord, where should I search for You?" The answer came: "In that heart which has been broken as the result of a wound inflicted by Me!" And Moses said: "O God, there is no heart that is more hopeless or broken than mine is!" And God answered, "I am where you are!"

Not long ago the world saw the enactment of virtual genocide of the Jews of Europe in what has come to be known as the Holocaust. The enormity of this calculated horror at the hands of a supposedly rational, civilized nation caused many, many people to say that God was dead, especially after the events that took place in Dachau, Buchenwald, and Auschwitz became public. How could a beneficent God have allowed such monstrosities to happen!

Most of the people who beat their breasts and proclaimed to the world that God was dead were thousands of miles from Dachau. We know now that many hundreds of these victims of Nazi psychopathia went to the gas chambers with a serenity that astounded even their cynical executioners. Following the example of the second-century Palestinian sage and martyr, Rabbi Akiba, they walked calmly to their deaths with the *shema* on their lips, that same watchword that Jewish martyrs had uttered throughout the ages as the final affirmation of faith in the one God of mankind and of their abiding love for him.

· TO SUFFER AND TO ENDURE ·

The deeper the sorrow, the less tongue it
hath.   *The Talmud*

I never found yet any religious person so
perfect but that he had sometimes absenting
of grace or some diminishing of fervor; and
there was never yet any saint so highly rapt
but that, first or last, he had some temptation.
He is not worthy to have the high gift of contemplation that hath not suffered for God
some tribulation.

THOMAS À KEMPIS (1379–1471)
Imitation of Christ

Affliction is not sent in vain, young man,
From that good God, who chastens whom he
loves.

ROBERT SOUTHEY (1774–1843)
Madoc in Wales

The rabbis have stated that the Holy One
afflicts the just in this world with physical sufferings to make them worthy of the next
world. That man who suffers, God loves him.
The Zohar

Only when men shall roll up the sky like a
hide, will there be an end to misery, unless
God has first been known.

The Upanishads

Only when grief finds its work done can
God dispense us from it. Trial then only
stops when it is useless: that is why it scarcely
ever stops. Faith in the justice and love of the
Father is the best and indeed the only support under the sufferings of this life.

HENRI FRÉDÉRIC AMIEL (1821–1881)
Journal Intime

God washes the eyes by tears until they can
behold the invisible land where tears shall
come no more.

HENRY WARD BEECHER (1813–1887)
Sermons

Endure for the sake of the Lord every
wound, every injury, every evil word and attack. If ill-requitals befall you, return them
not either to neighbor or enemy, because the
Lord will return them for you and be your
avenger on the day of the great judgment,
that there will be no avenging here among
men.   *The Old Testament Apocrypha*
Enoch 50:3–4

O God, Thy world is dark! The music of the
    spheres
    Is made of sighs and sobs no less than
        songs, I think.
Man is an atom lost in an endless vale of
    tears,
    A night wherein the good rise and the
        wicked sink.

Perchance the vast designs of Thine
    unnumbered plans
    Need that our children die,
Drowned in the eddying dark—the black
    wide swirl that spans
    The whole space of the sky?

VICTOR HUGO (1802–1885)
A Vellequier

O God, Creator of mankind, I do not aspire to comprehend You or Your creation,
nor to understand pain or suffering. I aspire
only to relieve the pain and suffering of others, and I trust in doing so, I may understand
more clearly Your nature, that You are the
Father of all mankind, and that the hairs of
my head are numbered.

SAINT FRANCIS OF ASSISI (1182–1226)
Mirror of Perfection

I was dumb with silence, I held my peace,
even from good; and my sorrow was stirred.
My heart was hot within me, while I was musing the fire burned: then spake I with my

tongue. Lord, make me to know mine end, and the measure of my days, what it is: that I may know how frail I am.

The Old Testament
Psalms 39:3–4

Why do we impute to the Creator those evils which we bring on ourselves, and those enemies we arm against our own happiness?

JEAN JACQUES ROUSSEAU (1712–1778)
Emile

God doth not promise here to man, that He
Will free him quickly from his misery;
But in His own time, and when He sees fit,
Then He will give a happy end to it.

ROBERT HERRICK (1591–1674)
Noble Numbers

The greatest of all perplexities in theology has been to reconcile the infinite goodness of God with his omnipotence. Nothing puts a greater strain upon the faith of the common man than the existence of utterly irrational suffering in the universe, and the problem which tormented Job still troubles every devout and thoughtful man who beholds the monstrous injustices of nature.

WALTER LIPPMANN (1889–1974)
Preface to Morals

If the maker of the world can do all that he will, he wills misery, and there is no escape from the conclusion.

JOHN STUART MILL (1806–1873)
Three Essays on Religion

When, to a man who understands, the Self has become all things, what sorrow, what trouble can there be to him who once beheld that unity?   *The Upanishads*

God leads human nature through no other course than that through which his own nature must pass. Participation in everything blind, dark, and suffering of God's nature is necessary in order to raise him to highest consciousness.

FRIEDRICH SCHELLING (1775–1854)
The Ages of the World

There is no remembrance more blessed, and nothing more blessed to remember, than suffering overcome in solidarity with God; this is the mystery of suffering.

SÖREN KIERKEGAARD (1813–1855)
Christian Discourses

Rabbi Jonathan, commenting on the text, "The Lord tries the righteous" (Psalm 11:5), said: "The potter does not test cracked vessels. It is useless to tap them even once, because they would break. He does, however, test the good ones, because no matter how many times he taps them they do not break. Even so, God tests not the wicked but the righteous.   *The Midrash*

Those who are afflicted, and do not afflict in return, who suffer everything for the love of God, and bear their burden with a gladsome heart, shall be rewarded according to the promise, "Those who love the Lord shall be as invincible as the rising sun in his might."   *The Talmud*

The prayer for the afflicted in King Solomon's temple was, "Thou, O Lord, knowest the heart; grant him that which in thy wisdom knowest would be best for his good, and no more!"   *The Talmud*

Just as the sun, the eye of the whole world, is not defiled by the external faults of the eye, so the One Inmost Self of every being is not defiled by the suffering of the world, but remains outside of it.   *The Upanishads*

To those who know God, pain is the supremest art. In order to enrich the stuff of our lives God has sown the earth with the seed of tears.

TOYOHIKO KAGAWA (1888–1960)
Meditations

If ye endure chastening, God deals with you as with sons, for what son is he whom the father chastens not? But if ye be without chastisement, whereof all are partakers, then are ye bastards, and not sons.

The New Testament
Hebrews 12:7–8

As faith and hope without love are only sounding brass and tinkling cymbals, so all the gladness in the world in which no sorrow is mingled is only sounding brass and tinkling cymbals, which flatter the ear but are abhorrent to the soul. But this voice of consolation, this voice that trembles in pain and yet proclaims the gladness—this the ear of the concerned hears; his heart treasures it; it strengthens and guides him even to finding joy in the depths of sorrow.

SÖREN KIERKEGAARD (1813–1855)
Edifying Discourses

Gold is tested in fire, but the man who pleases God is tested in the furnace of suffering. *The Old Testament Apocrypha*
The Wisdom of Jesus ben Sirach 2:1

Oh, merciful God, where can we find lovable people who consider that God's burden is light? Nobody wants to suffer, yet there must always be suffering and surrender, whichever way you turn.

JOHANNES TAULER (1300–1361)
Sermons

By the law of God even a slave, when his master knocked out his eye or tooth, had to be set free because of the pain he has suffered. Surely it can not be worse with God's own children when they undergo hardship, sorrow, and trouble in this life, their pain will surely purify them from the dross of iniquity, and they will inherit futurity.

The Midrash

If the world has indeed been built of sorrow, it has been built by the hands of love, because in no other way could the soul of man, for whom the world was made, reach the full stature of its perfection.

OSCAR WILDE (1854–1900)
De Profundis

Said Rabbi Eleazar ben Jacob: "When sufferings come upon him, man must utter thanks to God, for suffering draws man near unto the Holy One, blessed be He." As it saith: Whom the Lord loveth, He correcteth, even as a father correcteth the son in whom he delighteth. When griefs come upon a man, let him stand up and receive them, thus his reward will be beyond measure.

The Midrash

God's word recorded in Scripture, "Behold it is very good," refers to the suffering which occurs in the world. But how can the words "behold it is very good" be applied to suffering? Because through it men attain immortality. Go forth in life and see which path leads men to eternity; surely it is the path of sorrow.   *The Midrash*

In our moral world, the righteous can suffer without individually deserving their suffering, just because their lives have no independent Being, but are linked with all life.   JOSIAH ROYCE (1855–1916)
The World and the Individual

All who aspire after perfection must flee a thousand leagues from saying "I was in the *right.* It was not *right* for me to suffer this. They had no *right* to treat me so." God deliver us from such rights. When we receive honors, or affection or kind treatment, let us think what *right* we have to *them,* for certainly we have no right to them in this life. But when wrong is done to us, I do not know why we speak of it.

SAINT TERESA (1515–1582)
The Way of Perfection

It is not possible, or necessary, that one achieve here on earth an immediate spiritual freedom, caught as one is in the vast confusion brought about by human blindness, human willfulness. The penalty of such common calamity no one of sense, still less of honesty, would seek to avoid. Those who have caught a glimpse of God's domain will know that here, where there is no continuing city, they must pay the same tax of suffering as is paid by the rest of the world gone wrong.

BERNARD IDDINGS BELL (1886–1958)
Still Shine the Stars

What we have to do is to see as deep as we can into the truth of things, not to invent paradises of thought, sheltered gardens, from which grief and suffering shall tear us, naked and protesting; but to gaze into the heart of God, and then to follow as faithfully as we can the imperative voice that speaks within the soul.

ARTHUR CHRISTOPHER BENSON (1862–1925)
The Thread of Gold

O God, men think the heroes of tragedy great, and they admire them. But Abraham's contemporaries could not understand him. What then did he achieve? That he was true to his love. And he who loves God has no need of admiration, no need that others weep for him. He forgets his suffering in love, forgets it so thoroughly that no one even suspects his pain except thee, O God, who seest in secret, and knowest the need, and countest the tears and forgettest nothing.   SÖREN KIERKEGAARD (1813–1885)
Journals

God is always positive; He makes all things new. And the lighted window of the Father's house shine brightest in the far country where all our "blessings" have been lost. Blessed are you—not because the far country cannot take away from you the dream of home and better times to come. No, blessed are you because the door is really and truly

open and the Father's hand is stretched out to you.   HELMUT THIELICKE (1908–)
Life Can Begin Again

Only with a vision embracing eternity as well as time could we expect to read all the long purposes of God. There are many events in my life whereof we can say only with Job, "I lay my hand upon my mouth." But when suffering comes, it makes a difference whether there is a good God, an Almighty God, on whom we may rely.

GEORGIA HARKNESS (1891–1974)
Conflicts in Religious Thought

My God, my God, why hast thou forsaken me? why art thou so far from helping me, and from the words of my cries?

The Old Testament
Psalms 22:1

If God is self-sacrificing Love, and if God has taught man, not merely by precept but by example, that the right attitude towards suffering is to embrace it in order to make it serve the cause of Love, we can catch, in this vision, a glimpse of Reality that will satisfy both the Heart and the Head.

ARNOLD TOYNBEE (1889–1975)
A Historian's Approach to Religion

There is no way to depth of life, to richness of spirit, by shun-pikes that go around hard experiences. The very discovery of the nearness of God, of the sustaining power of His love, of the sufficiency of His grace, has come to men in all ages through pain, and suffering and loss.   RUFUS JONES (1863–1948)
The Inner Life

The great religious conceptions which haunt the imaginations of civilized mankind are scenes of solitariness: Prometheus chained to his rock, Mahomet brooding in the desert, the meditations of the Buddha, the solitary Man on the Cross. It belongs to

the depth of the religious spirit to have felt
forsaken, even by God.

ALFRED NORTH WHITEHEAD (1861–1947)
Religion in the Making

In times of dryness and desolation we must
be patient, and wait with resignation the return of consolation, putting our trust in the
goodness of God. We must animate ourselves
by the thought that God is always with us,
that He only allows this trial for our greater
good, and that we have not necessarily lost
His grace because we have lost the taste and
feeling of it.

SAINT IGNATIUS LOYOLA (1491–1556)
Spiritual Exercises

This is the blessing of affliction to those
who will lie still and not struggle in a cow-
ardly or a resentful way. It is God speaking
to Job out of the whirlwind, and saying, In
the sunshine and the warmth you can not
meet Me: but in the hurricane and the darkness, when wave after wave has swept down
and across the soul, you shall see My form
and hear My voice, and know that your Redeemer liveth.

FREDERICK WILLIAM ROBERTSON (1816–1853)
Sermons

The human tragedy from which there is no
escape, the dialectic of freedom, necessity
and grace finds its solution within the orbit
of the divine Mystery, within the Deity, which
lies deeper than the drama between Creator
and creature.

NIKOLAI BERDYAEV (1874–1948)
The Beginning and the End

Every human being is gloriously consti-
tuted, but what ruins so many is, among
other things, the wretched tittle-tattle between man and man about that which should
be suffered and matured in silence, this
confession before men instead of before
God, this communication between this man
and that about what ought to be secret and

exist only before God in secrecy, this impatient craving for intermediary consolation.

SÖREN KIERKEGAARD (1813–1855)
Point of View

Man should remember in his pain that God
speaks the truth and promises by Himself,
the Truth. If God were to be false to His
word, His Truth, He would be false to His
Divinity, and then He would not be God. It is
his promise that our pain shall be changed to
joy.   MEISTER ECKHART (1260–1327)
The Book of Divine Consolation

When God is taking you through the wilderness toward the promised land, never
look back, nor shrink. Bear your trouble, and
say, "Strike, God, and strike again, and as
often as needful; do anything to me and take
anything from me; but let me have Thee, and
life, and life eternal."

HENRY WARD BEECHER (1813–1887)
Sermons

Every fool thinks that life is there for his
sake alone, and as though nothing existed
but he. And so, when anything happens that
opposes his wishes, he concludes that the
whole universe is evil. But if man would regard the whole universe itself and realize
what an infinitesimal part he plays in it, the
truth would be clear and apparent to him.

MAIMONIDES (1135–1204)
Moreh Nebukim

In order to survive the supernatural night
of the spirit, which is a death and a despair
of *everything* (even of God)—a lived, not a
voluntarily suffered despair—at the heart of
which grace alone maintains a secret hope—
in order to survive such a night, divine power
is necessary.

JACQUES MARITAIN (1882–1973)
The Natural Mystical Experience and the Void

There is nothing degrading in the hum-
blest and the hardest fate; nothing much nobler in this world than a meek true soul

struggling against the narrow bounds of the sphere assigned to it, and faithful to cherish the light of God in the inglorious darkness of a bitter lot.

JAMES MARTINEAU (1805–1900)
Hours of Thought on Sacred Things

Tears are the alphabet by which God teaches us many and many a truth of wisdom that no book of philosophy gives us.

HENRY WARD BEECHER (1813–1887)
Sermons

The peace and joy that belong to deepest suffering are the miracles of faith. I find in the book of Acts one of the sublimest passages in human history. "At midnight in the prison Paul and Silas prayed and sang praises unto God."

RALPH WALDO EMERSON (1803–1882)
Sermons

Job's rebellion came from the thought that God, as a sovereign, is far off, and that, for his pleasure his creature suffers. Our own theory comes to the mourner with the assurance: "Your suffering, just as it is in you, is God's suffering. No chasm divides you from God. He is not remote from you even in eternity. He is here. His eternity means merely the completeness of his experience. But that completeness is inclusive. Your sorrow is one of the included facts."

JOSIAH ROYCE (1855–1916)
Studies of Good and Evil

Suffering is the ransom man has to pay if he would attain his glory.   *The Upanishads*

· ACCEPTING AFFLICTION COURAGEOUSLY ·

Do not despise your situation; in it you must act, suffer, and conquer. From every point on earth we are equally near to heaven and the infinite.

HENRI FRÉDÉRIC AMIEL (1821–1881)
Journal Intime

When I am in the cellar of affliction, I look for the Lord's choicest wines.

SAMUEL RUTHERFORD (1600–1661)
Sermons

It is one heart-quieting consideration in all the afflictions that befall us, that God has a special hand in them. Instruments can no more stir till God gives them a commission, than the axe can cut of itself without a hand. Job eyed God in his affliction: therefore, as Augustine observes, he does not say, "The

Lord gave, and the devil took away," but "The Lord hath taken away."

THOMAS WATSON (died 1686)
Sermons

To me it has always appeared best to bow with heartfelt humility to the inscrutable but unerring counsels of Heaven, and to remember that we can only in this life see a small portion of man's existence, and therefore can form no judgment of the whole.

WILHELM VON HUMBOLDT (1767–1835)
Letters

If we are to succeed in submitting ourselves to the will of God, we must first make a very great effort. God is not to be found indiscriminately in the things that thwart us in life or the trials we have to suffer—but solely at the point of balance between our desperate efforts to grow greater and the resistance to our domination that we meet from outside.

PIERRE TEILHARD DE CHARDIN (1881–1955)
Let Me Explain

All is best, though we oft doubt
What the unsearchable dispose
Of Highest Wisdom brings about.

JOHN MILTON (1608–1674)
Samson Agonistes

Who is honorable in the sight of the Creator? He who has met with adversity but bravely endures whatever befalls him.

SOLOMON IBN GABIROL (1021–1058)
The Choice of Pearls

VIII · GOD'S GOVERNANCE

God forces no one, for love cannot compel,
and God's service, therefore, is a thing of
perfect freedom.   JOHANNES DENCK

THE QUESTION of whether we are truly free to choose where life will take us has never permitted a simple answer. From earliest times the God Seekers have expressed their concern with whether humankind really has been given freedom of will by our Creator, and if so, what are its dimensions in God's governance of the world. In the final section of our anthology we shall find some of their answers to these and similarly formidable questions.

Essentially, the God Seekers agree that we have been granted the freedom to determine the paths our lives will follow, but whether it is a qualified or absolute freedom is a murky area. As Kierkegaard mused in his *Journals,* "The fact that God could create free beings vis-à-vis of Himself is the cross which philosophy could not carry, but remained hanging from." Robert Browning voiced almost the same thought in his dramatic monologue *Saul:* "I report, as a man may of God's work—all's love, yet all's law."

As we have seen previously, in the God Seeker's attempt to confront the problem of wordly evil, it is enormously difficult to consider our actions without looking into such matters as the extent of our freedom to act. To Albert Camus the problem of evil simply begged the question of whether we have freedom of will. In *The Myth of Sisyphus,* Camus asks us to remember the gnawing paradox, first pondered by the Greek philosophers and later by such great religious figures as Saint Augustine: either we are not free and an all-powerful God has willed evil into His plan for the world, or we are free and responsible but God is not all-powerful.

Throughout the ages the God Seekers have speculated endlessly on what kind of world the Creator intended, and more often, what role men and women should have in that world. Bishop Fulton J. Sheen, one of the most articulate of twentieth-century prelates, believed that God's intention was to create a moral world, but not one where "each and every one of us would sprout virtues as an acorn sprouts an oak." Yes, said Bishop Sheen, God could have made a world in which each of us would become saints "with the same inexorable necessity that the rain falls to embrace the earth"; He might have done this, but He didn't.

As George Arthur Buttrick pointed out in *God, Pain, and Evil,* "men who could not sin would not be men: they would be good clocks ticking out goodness." Also, Samuel Taylor Coleridge rightfully perceived that "if God created a Being with a power of choosing good, that Being must have been created with a power of choosing evil; otherwise there is no meaning in the word *choice*."

John Milton, in his classic tract the *Areopagitica*, observed that many people have railed against divine providence for allowing Adam to be tempted by the serpent in the Garden of Eden. Both in fear and anger they mutter: couldn't a God whose universe is beyond description, an all-powerful, prescient God, have created a perfect, sinless prototype of the human race? To which Milton answers, "Foolish tongues! When God gave man reason, he gave him freedom to choose, for reason is but choosing; he had been otherwise a mere artificial Adam."

God has given us ethical freedom, and even if few men or women measure up to the endless challenge of this kind of liberty, it still should be perceived as one of his greatest gifts to us. Martin Luther, in *Table-Talk*, gives us a magnificent definition of what this gift entails: "Just as no one can go to Hell or Heaven for me, so no one can believe for me and so no one can open or close Heaven or Hell for me, and no one can drive me either to believe or disbelieve."

Freedom of choice is more than a gift; it is also an obligation and a challenge. As Nikolai Berdyaev has pointed out, "God has laid upon man the *duty* of being free, of safeguarding freedom of spirit." We can never minimize how much sacrifice, and even suffering, it may require, for any freedom that is lasting and relevant never comes easily, whether it be individual freedom or that of a nation. Still, as Berdyaev wrote in *Freedom and the Spirit,* "God never forces man, never sets a limit to man's freedom."

Another brilliant contemporary religious figure, Monsignor Romano Guardini, not only agrees with Berdyaev but would go even a bit further. In *The Living God,* Guardini acknowledges that the will of God does not stand over us, nor does it ever force us to do this or that, nor tell us what kind of persons to be. Yet when we use that freedom of will that God entrusted to us to work toward the establishment of his kingdom on earth, we experience a spiritual merger of the strongest emotions of duty with an inexpressible feeling of *agape* within us.

To Guardini, the will of God is something more than a duty or claim; it is an active force, a living force that rules within us. It is "the special way in which He admonishes, urges, helps, sustains, acts and molds, struggles, overcomes and perfects, inside me." In this larger sense, then, far be it from God to give us marching orders; his will is the power that helps us to fulfill his ethical precepts. As Saint Francis of Sales viewed it, "God, when he wishes to perform in us, through us, and with us, some act of great charity, first proposes it to us by His inspiration, secondly we favor it, thirdly we consent to do it."

That most men and women will experience difficult problems in their encounter with the world outside their own solipsistic shell is a given. Sometimes when a minor crisis comes up in our work week, or something more lasting such as the severe illness of a loved one, we turn to God with a questioning approach, wondering why God has laid these burdens upon us.

Many of the God Seekers have wrestled with that enigma, too. The seventeenth-century English divine William Guthrie said that God leads us to the wilderness so that He may speak to our heart. Henry Ward Beecher went even further in one of his masterful sermons: "Difficulties are God's errands, and when we are sent upon them we should esteem it a proof of God's confidence, as a compliment of God."

But few have stated it better than Yeshua ben Sirach, about whom little is known except that he lived in Palestine some two hundred years B.C. and wrote a book, *The Wisdom of Jesus ben Sirach,* more familiarly known as *Ecclesiasticus.* That ben Sirach was a God Seeker of lasting stature is evident in his book, which interestingly enough has proven more meaningful to Christian theologians than to his fellow Jews. In his book, often read as an adjunct to the Old Testament, ben Sirach said,

My son, if you aspire to be a servant of the Lord, prepare yourself for testing. Bear every hardship that is sent you; be patient under humiliation, whatever the cost. For gold is assayed under fire, and the Lord proves me in the furnace of humiliation.

Another theme that runs throughout this section is the search for justice in the world. There is, of course, a dangerous presumption in attributing to God our earth-bound definitions of such abstract concepts as justice, truth, or goodness. Since it is often impossible to get people themselves to agree on what constitutes earthly justice, how can we at best, do more than speculate on what divine justice might be?

An Arab refugee whose forbears lived in Palestine for six hundred years prays for justice in his flimsy tent, after being again displaced from a crowded camp in southern Lebanon; a Jewish survivor of the Holocaust, whose parents were murdered at Auschwitz, lives across the border on a kibbutz where two children were recently ambushed by Arab terrorists and prays for justice. Every day hundreds of thousands of children in Ethiopia and other drought-plagued countries in Africa barely exist on the five hundred grams of grain that is their sole sustenance, slowly starving to death while affluent countries like ours spend billions for diet pills to curb our appetites. Bereaved wives and mothers, hapless survivors of the senseless violence of northern Ireland cry out for justice to God, as if there could be a Protestant God and a Catholic God refereeing the carnage from above.

God does not play favorites—not with individuals, not with nations, and not with any of the various "worlds" in his universe. Everything He has created from himself is equally precious in God's eyes.

God does rule the world with justice, even if we refuse to heed the rules He has sent to us through his intermediaries, the God Seekers in every age. Although we can, at best, intuit only a small portion of God's actualization of justice, which we can only conceptualize in symbolic language, we are remiss if we do not at least strive for whatever glimpse of these eternal attributes He chooses to reveal. John Donne's familiar apothegm, "Any man's death diminishes me, because I am involved in mankind; and therefore never send to know for whom the bell tolls; it tolls for thee," is no less meaningful today than when he voiced it from his pulpit in St. Paul's church. When we exculpate ourselves from responsibility and hide our collective shame for even *one* person dying of starvation in a world with abundant food by saying it was God's will we are committing the worst kind of blasphemy.

We cannot, in the worst flights of our guilt, blame God for our failure to recognize that *caritas* has to be more than sanctimonious lip-service and that we are our brother's keeper; we cannot blame God for our addiction to materialistic self-survival. Even the little that we can understand of the totality of God's justice will not allow us to hide under this pathetic rationalization. Through such God Seekers as the poet who wrote Psalm 10 in the Old Testament twenty-five hundred years ago, the Master of the Universe was urging us "to right the fatherless and the oppressed, that man who is of earth may be terrible no more."

Few, if any, God Seekers have better known that God rules with love and compassion and not by force than a relatively unknown Jewish carpenter from the Palestinian village of Nazareth who embarked on his ministry nearly two thousand years ago. Like the prophets Jeremiah and Isaiah before him, he saw that the religion of his day had become too concerned with excessive ritual and symbolism, that God, too often, was being obfuscated in people's minds by such casuistry as whether the Pharisees or the Sadducees were best able to interpret him.

We are told that during one of his public meetings, a lawyer approached him with the question, "Teacher, which is the greatest commandment in the Torah?" And his answer, according to one of his disciples, Matthew, was "You shall love the Lord your God with all your heart, and with all your soul, and with all your mind. This is the great and first commandment." He may have even prefaced his reference to that sixth chapter of Deuteronomy with the traditional *shema* that preceded those lines.

Then he added, "And a second is like it, you shall love your neighbor as yourself. On these two commandments depend all the law and the prophets."

· GOD FORCES NO ONE ·

God is not willing to do everything, and thus take away our free will and that share of glory which belongs to us.

NICCOLO MACHIAVELLI (1469–1527)
The Prince

Those who deny freedom to others deserve it not for themselves, and, under a just God, cannot long retain it.

ABRAHAM LINCOLN (1809–1865)
Letter to H. L. Pierce

God gave man the power to reason, which makes man capable of perfection.

MAIMONIDES (1135–1204)
Guide for the Perplexed

Love, we are in God's hand.
How strange now looks the life he makes us
    lead.
So free we seem, so fettered fast we are!

ROBERT BROWNING (1812–1889)
Andrea del Sarto

It argues surely more power in the Deity to delegate a certain degree of power to inferior creatures than to produce every thing by his own immediate volition. It argues more wisdom to contrive at first the fabric of the world with such perfect foresight that, of itself, and by its proper operation, it may serve all the purposes of providence, than if the great Creator were obliged every moment to adjust its parts, and animate by his breath all the wheels of that stupendous machine.

DAVID HUME (1711–1776)
An Enquiry Concerning Human Understanding

The most tremendous thing which has been granted to man is choice, freedom. And if you desire to save it and preserve it, there is only one way: in the very same second unconditionally and in complete resignation to give it back to God, and yourself with it. If the sight of what is granted tempts you, and if you give way to the temptation and look with egoistic desire upon the freedom of choice, then you lose your freedom. And your punishment is: to go on in a kind of confusion, priding yourself on having freedom of choice, but woe unto you, that is your judgment.

SÖREN KIERKEGAARD (1813–1855)
Journals

This emphasis on man's freedom before God is most important, since man is a being whose reality cannot be left to forces outside himself, to nature, society or events. We become real in proportion as we accept the real possibilities that are presented to us, and choose them freely and realistically for ourselves.   THOMAS MERTON (1915–1968)
Letters

No iron chain, or outward force of any kind, could ever compel the soul of a man to believe or disbelieve: it is his own indefeasible light, that judgment of his; he will reign, and believe there, by the grace of God alone.

THOMAS CARLYLE (1795–1881)
On Heroes and Hero-Worship

To produce real moral freedom, God's grace and man's will must cooperate. As God is the Prime Mover of nature, so also he creates free impulses toward himself and to all good things. Grace renders the will free that it may do everything with God's help, working with grace as with an instrument which belongs to it. So the will arrives at freedom through love, nay, becomes itself love, for love unites with God.

MEISTER ECKHART (1260–1327)
Sermons

The absolute freedom of the will, which we bring down with us from the Infinite into the world of Time, is the principle of this our life.

JOHANN GOTTLIEB FICHTE (1762–1814)
The Vocation of Man

The changes which God causes in His lower creatures are almost always from worse to better, while the changes which God allows man to make in himself are very often quite the other way.

JOHN RUSKIN (1819–1900)
Lectures on Architecture and Painting

Free will is granted to every man. If he wishes to direct himself toward the good way and become righteous, the will to do so is in his hand; and if he wishes to direct himself toward the bad way and become wicked, the will to do so is likewise in his hand.

MAIMONIDES (1135–1204)
Guide for the Perplexed

God has laid upon man the duty of being free, of safeguarding freedom of spirit, no matter how difficult that may be, or how much sacrifice and suffering it may require.

NIKOLAI BERDYAEV (1874–1948)
The Fate of Man in the Modern World

When a man enters upon the path of truth and justice God helps him forward, but when he chooses the way of sin God says, "I gave thee reason and free will, go thy way," even as the trader will wait upon the customer who purchases a good and pleasant article, while to one who desires pitch or sulphur he says, "Go, wait upon thyself."   *The Talmud*

God never forces man, never sets a limit to man's freedom. God's design for man and for the world is that man should give up his powers to God, in freedom and in love, and should carry on creative activity in the name of God.   NIKOLAI BERDYAEV (1874–1948)
Freedom and the Spirit

Reveal the primal mandate still
    Which Chaos heard and ceased to be,
Trace on mid-air th'Eternal Will
    In signs of fire: "Let man be free!"

JOHN GREENLEAF WHITTIER (1807–1892)
The Bartholdi Statue

If the infinitely perfect Being had known that were He to give existence to free creatures, they would have to be punished eternally because of their sins, He would have preferred to leave them in nothingness, or not to allow them to abuse their free will, rather than be obliged to inflict on them punishments which will never end. Common sense tells us that it is better to have no children at all than to have children who laugh at our instructions and orders, and who bring us nothing but distress and dishonor.

PIERRE BAYLE (1647–1706)
Critique Générale

In the beginning God created man and gave unto him the power of his own thinking. If you wish, you can keep his commandments, and it is his desire to be faithful. Fire and water are set before you; stretch out your hands for what you want. Before man are life and death, he will be given whichever he wishes. God orders man not to sin, and he gives no dreams to those who lie.

The Old Testament Apocrypha
The Wisdom of Jesus ben Sirach 15:11–20

Our father's God, to thee, author of liberty,
    to thee we sing:
Long may our land be bright with freedom's
    holy light;
Protect us by thy might, Great God, our King.

SAMUEL FRANCIS SMITH (1808–1895)
My Country, 'Tis of Thee

O give, great God, to Freedom's waves to ride
Sublime o'er Conquest, Avarice, and Pride.

WILLIAM WORDSWORTH (1770–1850)
Descriptive Sketches

Each man has to grow into the Divine within himself through his own individual being. Therefore a certain growing measure of freedom is a necessity of the being as it develops and perfect freedom the sign and the condition of the perfect life.

SRI AUROBINDO (1872–1950)
The Human Cycle

If God exercised compulsion by forcing obedience or by remaking the character of a self against its will, He would have abandoned omnipotence in the act which would assert it, for the will that was overridden would remain outside His control.

WILLIAM TEMPLE (1881–1944)
Nature, Man and God

Men are free to work out their purposes, and, at the same time, there is a divine purpose in the world which human history fulfills and to which the environment of nature is subordinate. Here God and man meet.

WILLIAM RITCHIE SORLEY (1855–1935)
Moral Values and the Idea of God

God creates agents with free will. He does so because the existence of such agents has of itself an infinite worth. Were there no free agents, the highest good could not be. But such agents, because they are free, can offend. The divine justice of necessity pursues such offenses with attendant evils. These evils, the result of sin, must, logically speaking, be permitted to exist, if God once creates the agents who have free will, and himself remains, as he must logically do, a just God.

JOSIAH ROYCE (1855–1916)
Studies of Good and Evil

We might do well to look at the risk God took when he made men free. That was the first great experiment and the first great affirmation of faith. If we can understand the

mind of God at all, we must thrill at his willingness to release men from the limitations of the animal world and give them the right to seek and rebel.

GERALD A. KENNEDY (1907–)
Who Speaks for God?

This is the mystery of God's nobility; that is, that He does not force His kingdom upon us, but makes it dependent on us whether we accept it or not. If we will it only in a lukewarm fashion, it comes only with difficulty and darkly. It is always we ourselves who open or close the door for Him, in all our thoughts and actions, in all we do or do not do.

ROMANO GUARDINI (1885–1968)
The Wisdom of the Psalms

God in no way hinders his creatures in their struggle for development. Not only does the sun shine upon the just and the unjust; God lets the rebellious shake their fists at him, and even deny his existence, as freely as the devout adore and praise him. He never exerts any kind of pressure upon his creatures.

GEDDES MACGREGOR (1909–)
He Who Lets Us Be

If man lost his liberty, he would be disqualified for membership in the Kingdom of God. Not even God could build a society of love out of puppets or robots. Therefore, he never defeats himself by taking away freedom of choice from man.

KIRBY PAGE (1890–1957)
The Will of God for These Days

God created free beings, beings therefore endowed with the terrible power of retreating from reality into nothingness if they so willed—for, once again, evil is privation, non-being, emptiness—and Satan is simply the first of those beings to choose this path.

GERALD VANN (1906–1963)
Stones or Bread

God made us for fulfillment through freedom. In making us for himself, he created us for unconditional and universal love. We are free only as we find this kind of love from, for, in, and through God. The anxiety of the loveless is a chain of fear.

NELS F. S. FERRE (1908–1971)
Know Your Faith

Because God wills to be and can be Lord only in this way, He places Himself face to face with an independent creature. For only an independent creature can know and acknowledge. God wills to be acknowledged as Lord in freedom, since it is by virtue of such free acknowledgement that He is Lord in the highest sense.

EMIL BRUNNER (1889–1966)
The Divine–Human Encounter

Let the free, reasonable Will, which dwells in us, as in our Holy of Holies, be indeed free, and obeyed like a Divinity, as is its right and its effort: the perfect obedience will be the silent one.

THOMAS CARLYLE (1795–1881)
Characteristics

No one is our master, and no one can become our master. We carry our charter of freedom, given and sealed by God, deep in our bosom.

JOHANN GOTTLIEB FICHTE (1762–1814)
The Vocation of Man

The dignity of man and the dignity of faith require the recognition of freedom to choose the truth, and freedom in the truth. Freedom cannot be identified with goodness or truth or perfection: it is by nature autonomous, it is freedom and not goodness.

NIKOLAI BERDYAEV (1874–1948)
Dostoevski

There is much difference between a willing act of the soul itself, and an action forced on the will, determined by another, as there is between a man that is dragged to the altar, whether he will or no, and the man that comes with all his heart with music and dancing to offer sacrifice. That God should not be able to deserve our love, unless he himself made us to love him by violence, is the greatest dishonor to him in the world. Nor is it any glory or reputation for us, who are such sorry stewards, that we cannot be entrusted with a little liberty, but we needs must abuse it.

THOMAS TRAHERNE (1637–1674)
Christian Ethics

· DIFFICULTIES ARE GOD'S ERRANDS ·

It is futile to expect God's reality to become any clearer to us so long as we continue to shut our eyes to those aspects of His reality that are already quite plainly before us, making difficult demands upon our lives.

JOHN BAILLIE (1886–1960)
Our Knowledge of God

It is a wise prayer, "Correct me, O Lord, but with judgment." Happy is the man whom God correcteth; for whom the Lord loveth He correcteth.

FREDERICK BROTHERTON MEYER (1847–1929)
Our Daily Homily

God sets the soul long, weary, impossible tasks, yet is satisfied by the first sincere proof that obedience is intended, and takes the burden away forthwith.

COVENTRY PATMORE (1812–1896)
The Rod, the Root, and the Flower

God offers to every mind its choice between truth and repose. Take which you please—you can never have both.
RALPH WALDO EMERSON (1803–1882)
Intellect

Into what great waters, not to be crossed by any swimmer, God's pale Praetorian throws us over in the end!
ROBERT LOUIS STEVENSON (1850–1894)
Aes Triplex

Good fortune and evil fortune alike serve to strengthen us with might in the inward man. But no man can give this strengthening to himself; and he who receives a testimony is not the one who gives it. The testimony itself is a gift from God, from whom all good gifts come.   SÖREN KIERKEGAARD (1813–1855)
Journals

Happy the man who can stand when he is tested, for there is none whom the Holy One, blessed be he, does not prove. He tests the rich man to see if he will be generous to the poor, and the poor man to see if he will accept suffering without complaint.
The Talmud

When God leads anyone along the highest road of obscure contemplation and aridity, such a one will think himself lost.
SAINT JOHN OF THE CROSS (1542–1590)
The Ascent of Mount Carmel

· A RIGHTEOUS JUDGE ·

God is a righteous Judge, strong and patient: and God is provoked every day.
The Old Testament
Psalms 7:12

Judge not, and ye shall not be judged: condemn not, and ye shall not be condemned: forgive, and ye shall be forgiven.
The New Testament
Luke 6:37

Man judges from a partial view,
·None ever yet his brother knew;
The Eternal Eye that sees the whole
May better read the darkened soul,
And find, to outward sense denied,
The flower upon its inmost side!
JOHN GREENLEAF WHITTIER (1807–1892)
The Pressed Gentian

If you would be honest, great is the necessity enjoined upon your goodness, since all you do is done before the eyes of an all-seeing Judge.   BOETHIUS (480–524)
The Consolation of Philosophy

And Abraham drew near, and said, Wilt thou also destroy the righteous with the wicked? Peradventure there be fifty righteous within the city: wilt thou also destroy and not spare the place for the fifty righteous that are therein? Shall not the Judge of all the earth do right? And the Lord said, If I find in Sodom fifty righteous within the city then I will spare all the place for their sakes.
The Old Testament
Genesis 18:23–26

Human beings judge one another by their external actions. God judges them by their moral choices.   C. S. LEWIS (1898–1963)
Christian Behavior

Judge me, O Lord; for I have walked in mine integrity: I have trusted also in the Lord; therefore I shall not slide.
The Old Testament
Psalms 26:1

Thou art the Judge. We are bruised thus.
But, the Judgment over, join sides with us.
                    ROBERT BROWNING (1812–1889)
                    Holy Cross Day

I said in mine heart, God shall judge the righteous and the wicked: for there is a time there for every purpose and every work.
                    The Old Testament
                    Ecclesiastes 3:17

Every globe in the remotest heaven, every chemical change from the rudest crystal up to the laws of life, every change of vegetation from the first principle of growth in the eye of a leaf, to the tropical forest and antediluvian coalmine, every animal function from the sponge up to Hercules, shall hint or thunder to man the laws of right and wrong, and echo the Ten Commandments.
                    RALPH WALDO EMERSON (1803–1882)
                    Nature

Nobody can judge men but God, and we can hardly obtain a higher or more reverent view of God than that which represents Him to us as judging men with perfect knowledge, unperplexed certainty, and undisturbed compassion.
                    FREDERICK WILLIAM FABER (1814–1863)
                    Spiritual Conferences

Let us remember that God looks in our actions only for the motive. The world judges us by appearance; God counts for nothing what is most dazzling to men. What He desires is pure intention, true docility, and a sincere self-renunciation.
                    FRANÇOIS FÉNELON (1651–1715)
                    Letters and Reflections

Before God no man stands alone. Before the All-Seeing he is surrounded by the spiritual throng of all to whom he stands related near and far, all whom he loves or hates,

whom he serves or oppresses, whom he wrongs or saves.
                    WALTER RAUSCHENBUSCH (1861–1918)
                    For God and the People

As every one of us shall give an account of himself to God, therefore let us not judge one another any more, but judge this rather, that no man put a stumbling-block in his brother's way.   *The New Testament*
                    Romans 14:12–13

And God said: This is the sign of the covenant which I make between Me and you and every living creature that is with you, for perpetual generations. I will set My bow in the clouds, and it shall be the sign of a covenant between Me and the earth. And whenever I cover the sky with clouds, My bow shall appear in the clouds, and I will remember My covenant with you and with every living creature of all flesh, and there shall be no more waters of a flood to destroy all flesh.
                    The Old Testament
                    Genesis 9:8–15

The judgment of God is the reaping that comes from sowing, and is evidence of the love of God, not proof of his wrath. The penalty of an evil harvest is not God's punishment; it is the consequence of defying the moral order which in love he maintains as the only environment in which maturity of fellowship and communion can be achieved.
                    KIRBY PAGE (1890–1957)
                    The Will of God for These Days

Each day is a kind of judgment day that settles tomorrow. What we are each day creates for us our own place in God's universe and presumably always will.
                    CHARLES H. PARKHURST (1842–1933)
                    Sermons

Only our concept of Time makes it possible for us to speak of the Day of Judgment by that name; in reality it is a summary court in perpetual session.

FRANZ KAFKA (1883–1924)
Reflections on Sin, Pain, Hope

Reflect upon three things and you will not come within the power of sin: Know what is above you—a seeing eye, and a hearing ear, and all your deeds are written in a book.

The Talmud

Heaven is above all yet; there sits a judge
That no king can corrupt.

WILLIAM SHAKESPEARE (1564–1616)
Henry VIII

When Heaven is about to confer a great responsibility on any man, it will exercise his mind with suffering, subject his sinews and bones to hard work, expose his body to hunger, put him to poverty, place obstacles in the paths of his deeds, so as to stimulate his mind, harden his nature, and improve wherever he is incompetent.

MENCIUS (371–289 B.C.)
Meng-tzu

A man's heart deviseth his way; but the Lord directeth his steps.

The Old Testament
Proverbs 16:9

It is the great God himself who drives away the flies from a tailless cow.

Yoruba Proverb

· THE WILL OF GOD ·

The will of God, when He does something, ought to satisfy us as a reason, even though we do not see why He did it. For the will of God is never irrational.

SAINT ANSELM (1033–1109)
Cur Deus Homo

That which God writes on thy forehead, thou wilt come to it.   *The Koran*

Wise to promote whatever end he means,
God opens fruitful nature's various scenes.

WILLIAM COWPER (1731–1800)
Charity

From God derived, to God by nature joined,
We act the dictates of His mighty mind;
And tho' the priests are mute, and temples still,
God never wants a voice to speak His will.

LUCAN (A.D. 39–65)
Pharsalia

I know that whatever God does remains forever—to it one cannot add and from it one cannot subtract, for God has so arranged matters that men should fear Him. What has been, already exists, and what is still to be, has already been, and God always seeks to repeat the past.   *The Old Testament*
Ecclesiastes 3:14–15

Only the man whose being has been so shaken that he has become spirit by understanding that all things are possible, only he has had dealings with God. The fact that God's will is the *possible* makes it possible for me to pray; if God's will is only the *necessary*, man is essentially as speechless as the brutes.

SÖREN KIERKEGAARD (1813–1855)
Sickness

Let man beware against going forth upon his journeyings alone. That is to say, let him obey the Divine Will so that he shall not go forth without the accompanying Presence of God —which will sustain him and deliver him in every hour of need.   *The Zohar*

The will of Heaven to me is like the compasses to the wheelwright and the square to the carpenter. The wheelwright and the carpenter measure all the square and circular objects with their square and compasses and accept those that fit as correct and reject those that do not fit as incorrect.

MO-TZU (470–391 B.C.)
Works

In great contests each party claims to act in accordance with the will of God. Both may be, and one must be, wrong. God cannot be for and against the same thing at the same time.   ABRAHAM LINCOLN (1809–1865)
Meditation on the Divine Will

Nothing, then, comes about unless God wills it so, either through permitting it to happen or Himself performing it. There is no doubt that God does well even in permitting to happen what happens ill. For He permits this only through a just judgment, and surely everything that is just is good. Therefore, although those things which are evil, insofar as they are evil, are not good, still it is good that not only good things exist but also evil. For, unless it were good that evil things also exist, they would never have been permitted to exist by the Omnipotent God.

SAINT AUGUSTINE (354–430)
Enchiridion

Whatever may happen to you was prepared for you from all eternity; and the implication of causes was from eternity spinning the thread of your being.

MARCUS AURELIUS (121–180)
Meditations

God's will is the same thing as necessity in philosophy; it is "reality."

VISSARION BELINKSI (1811–1848)
Letters

The relation between the mind and matter is not fancied by some poet, but stands in the will of God, and so is free to be known by all

men. It appears to men, or it does not appear.

RALPH WALDO EMERSON (1803–1882)
Nature

This life rests on God's providence and on your faith, since he has promised to be your God and sustain you. Therefore you should not say: No matter what I do, I cannot hinder the will of God, so that because of my conduct less happens than God has determined. For this is the language of the devil and it is forever damned.

MARTIN LUTHER (1483–1546)
Commentary on Genesis

The Lord of Hosts hath sworn, saying, Surely as I have thought, so shall it come to pass; and as I have purposed, so shall it stand.

This is the purpose that is purposed upon the whole earth: and this is the hand that is stretched out upon all the nations. For the Lord of Hosts hath purposed, and who shall disannul it?   *The Old Testament*
Isaiah 14:24, 26–27

But if the great sun move not of himself; but is as an errand boy in heaven; nor one single star can revolve, but by some invisible power; how then can this one small heart beat; this one small brain think thoughts; unless God does that beating, does that thinking, does that living, and not I. By heaven, man, we are turned round and round in this world, like yonder windlass, and Fate is the handspike.

HERMAN MELVILLE (1819–1891)
Moby Dick

The One Will is not a one-sided will. It desires the realization of all possible life, however rich, strong, ardent, courageous, manifold such life may be, if only this life can enter into that highest unity. All that has will is sacred to it, save in so far as any will refuses

to join with the others in the song and shout
of the Sons of God.

JOSIAH ROYCE (1855–1916)
Religious Aspect of Philosophy

A breath of will blows eternally through
the universe of souls in the direction of the
Right and Necessary.

RALPH WALDO EMERSON (1803–1882)
Conduct of Life

Everything is governed with supreme wisdom by the will of God. The effect which he
has ordained that a particular event, a certain
grace, should produce in us, depends on a
certain exact moment when he sees that our
heart will be favourably disposed. Earlier
than that moment would be too soon; after it
would be too late. What is useful to you today
would have been of no use yesterday and will
not be tomorrow.

JEAN NICHOLAS GROU (1730–1803)
The School of Jesus Christ

In the Will work and acquire, and thou
hast chained the wheel of chance, and shalt
always drag her after thee.

RALPH WALDO EMERSON (1803–1882)
Self-Reliance

Do that much of the will of God which is
plain to you, and "you shall know of the doctrine, whether it be of God."

FREDERICK WILLIAM ROBERTSON (1816–1853)
Sermons

Before a thought occurs to us, it has been
with God and then returned to us. What God
wills, He brings about through the spirit in
us, which is charged with performing His
work in us.   PARACELSUS (1493–1541)
Liber de Generatione Hominis

Though the Divine Will be not determined
always to this or that particular, yet it is never
bereft of eternal light and truth to act by;
and, therefore, though we cannot see a reason for all God's actions, yet we may know

they were neither done against it nor without
it.   JOHN SMITH (1616–1652)
Discourses

Only when God hath brought to light all
the hidden things of darkness, whosoever
were the actors therein, will it be seen that
wise and good were all His ways, that He saw
through the thick cloud, and governed all
things by the wise counsels of His own will,
that nothing was left to chance, or the caprice
of men, but God disposed all strongly and
sweetly, and wrought all into one connected
chain of justice, mercy and truth.

JOHN WESLEY (1703–1791)
Sermons

Our wills are ours, we know not how,
Our wills are ours to make them Thine.

ALFRED LORD TENNYSON (1809–1892)
In Memoriam

They babble and talk absurdly who, in
place of God's Providence, substitute bare
permission—as if God sat in a watchtower
awaiting chance events, and his judgment
thus depended upon human will.

JOHN CALVIN (1509–1564)
Institutes of the Christian Religion

I live my life in God, in the mysterious divine personality which I do not know as such
in the world, but only experience as mysterious Will within myself.

ALBERT SCHWEITZER (1875–1965)
Civilization and Ethics

It is when a man begins to know the ambition of his life not simply as the choice of his
own will but as the wise assignment of God's
love; and to know his relations to his brethren not simply as the result of his own impul-
sive affections but as the seeking of his soul
for these souls because they all belong to the
great Father-soul; it is then that life for that
man begins to lift itself all over and to grow

towards completion upward through all its length and breadth.

PHILLIPS BROOKS (1835–1893)
Sermons

The relation between the mind and matter is not fancied by some poet, but stands in the will of God, and so is free to be known by all men. It appears to men, or it does not appear.

RALPH WALDO EMERSON (1803–1882)
Nature

God, that sees and disposes of all things, sees also that the liberty of man in doing what he will, is accompanied by the necessity of doing that which God wills, and no more, no less.   THOMAS HOBBES (1588–1679)
Leviathan

Every man's ideas, sentiments, senses, are individual revelations of the Infinite and Spiritual. United, these are the Revealed Will and Truth of God. But then, each sees only that which his own being displays to him, and shutteth his eye to the rest.

BRONSON ALCOTT (1799–1888)
Journals

When God commands to take the trumpet, and blow a dolorous or a jarring blast, it lies not in man's will what he shall say, or what he shall conceal.

JOHN MILTON (1608–1674)
The Reason of Church Government

Just walk on uninterruptedly and very quietly; if God makes you run, He will enlarge your heart.

SAINT FRANCIS OF SALES (1567–1622)
Letters to Persons in Religion

God wills a rich harmony, not a colorless uniformity.

SARVEPALLI RADHAKRISHNAN (1888–1975)
The Hindu View of Life

· BUT GOD RULES THE STARS ·

I have lived, sir, a long time. And the longer I live, the more convincing proofs I see of this truth—that God governs in the affairs of men. And if a sparrow cannot fall on the ground without his notice, is it probable that an empire can rise without his aid?

BENJAMIN FRANKLIN (1706–1790)
Autobiography

God never repents his first decision.

LUCIUS ANNAEUS SENECA (54 B.C.–A.D. 39)
De Beneficiis

Everything is in God's hands, except the fear of God.   *The Talmud*

Thou, Lord, dost hold the thunder; the firm land
Tosses in billows when it feels thy hand;

Thou dashest nation against nation, then
Stillest the angry world to peace again.

WILLIAM CULLEN BRYANT (1794–1878)
Hymn of the Waldenses

The wisdom of God and the folly of man govern the world.   *German Proverb*

When God says "I will speak to thee from above the Mercy Seat," the mind understands the Logos of God, which is a Mean, which leaves no void in nature, but fills all things and acts as a mediator, thus creating love and unanimity.

PHILO JUDAEUS (30 B.C.–A.D. 40)
Migrat

I think also that God and nought else is meant when we speak of Necessity, which is as it were invincible being; and Fate, because His action is continuous and He cannot be stayed in His course; and Destiny, because all things have their bounds and nothing which doth exist is infinite.

ARISTOTLE (384–322 B.C.)
De Mundo

God is related to the universe, as Creator and Preserver; the laws by which He created all things are those by which He preserves them.

CHARLES DE SECONDAT MONTESQUIEU
(1689–1755)
Spirit of Laws

God ordains a revelation in this or that manner, time, and place, not because it is a justice that he cannot refuse, not because it is a matter of favor or free goodness, and therefore may be given in any manner at pleasure, but because he has the whole race of mankind, the whole order of human changes and events, the whole combination of all causes and effects of human tempers, all the actions of free agents, and all the consequences of every revelation, plainly in his sight.   WILLIAM LAW (1686–1761)
A Serious Call to a Devout and Holy Life

God who made the world so wisely, as wisely governs.

THOMAS FULLER (1654–1734)
Gnomologia

God is ever the constant foreknowing overseer, and the ever-present eternity of His sight moves in harmony with the future nature of our actions, as it dispenses rewards to the good, and punishments to the bad.

BOETHIUS (480–524)
The Consolation of Philosophy

The kingdom of God on earth is not a metaphor, not a mere spiritual state, not a dream, not an uncertain project; it is the thing before us, it is the close and inevitable destiny of mankind.

H. G. WELLS (1866–1946)
God the Invisible King

Multitudes, multitudes in the valley of decision: for the day of the Lord is near in the valley of decision.   *The Old Testament*
Joel 3:14

The years like great black oxen tread the world
And God, the hersdman, goads them on behind.

WILLIAM BUTLER YEATS (1865–1939)
The Countess Cathleen

Isn't it God alone who truly subsists through himself, since he alone is independent, absolute, and continues immutably from time immemorial? Indeed all other things have no subsistence except insofar as they are ruled by him, "with a strong hand, with a stretched out arm," as the Scriptures say. And this is so true that they do not have the power to subsist for even a moment, but would return to nothing, if he were to withdraw his hand from them in the slightest.

PIERRE GASSENDI (1592–1655)
Exercises Against the Aristotelians

The stars rule men, but God rules the stars.
Medieval Latin Proverb

The lot is cast unto the lap, but the decision is wholly from the Lord.

The Old Testament
Proverbs 16:33

God metes out justice in his own good time.
EURIPIDES (480–406 B.C.)
Electra

These are the ordinances God spoke unto them. Whatever I do is done in justice. Were I to deviate from justice but once the world would cease to exist.   *The Midrash*

All justice comes from God, he alone is the source of it; but could we receive it direct from so lofty a source, we should need neither government or laws.

JEAN JACQUES ROUSSEAU (1712–1778)
The Social Contract

There is no mediator between God's children and God. *The Talmud*

God considers not the action, but the spirit of the action. It is the intention, not the deed wherein the merit or praise of the doer consists. PETER ABÉLARD (1079–1142)
On Sin

But here is the will of God, a flash of the will
  that can,
Existent behind all laws that made them,
  and lo, they are!
And I know not if, save in this, such gift be
  allowed to man,
That out of three sounds he frame, not a
  fourth sound, but a star.

ROBERT BROWNING (1812–1889)
Abt Vogler

The economy of Heaven is dark
And wisest clerks have missed the mark.

CHARLES LAMB (1775–1834)
On an Infant Dying

Blessed are the poor in spirit, for theirs is the kingdom of heaven. Blessed are those who mourn, for they shall be comforted. Blessed are those who hunger and thirst for righteousness, for they shall be satisfied. Blessed are the merciful, for they shall obtain mercy. Blessed are the pure in heart, for they shall see God. Blessed are the peacemakers, for they shall be called sons of God.

The New Testament
Matthew 5:3–9

Just are the ways of God,
And justifiable to men.

JOHN MILTON (1608–1674)
Samson Agonistes

You shall not be partial in judgment; you shall hear the small and the great alike; you shall not be afraid of the face of man, for the judgment is God's. *The Old Testament*
Deuteronomy 1:17

Who has commanded and it came to pass, unless the Lord ordained it? Is it not from the mouth of the Most High that good and evil come? Why should a living man complain about the punishment of his sins?

The Old Testament
Lamentations 3:37–39

Foolish men imagine that because judgment for an evil thing is delayed, there is no justice, but an accidental one, here below. Judgment for an evil thing is many times delayed some day or two, some century or two, but it is as sure as life, it is sure as death.

THOMAS CARLYLE (1795–1881)
Past and Present

Since God is justice, you must embrace justice as it is in itself, as it is in God. Consequently, where justice is at work, you are at work because you could not but do the works of justice. Yes, even if hell would interfere with the course of justice, you would still do the works of justice, and hell itself would not constitute pain; hell would be joy.

MEISTER ECKHART (1260–1327)
Sermons

God's justice and love are one. Infinite justice must be infinite love. Justice is but another sign of love. The infinite rest of the "I AM" of God arises out of the harmony of His attributes.

FREDERICK WILLIAM ROBERTSON (1816–1853)
Sermons

You might write it all over the skies that God was just, but it would not burn there. It would be, at best, only a bit of knowledge, never something which it would gladden the hearts of men to know. That comes only when a human life, capable of a justice like God's, made just by God, glows with His justice in the eyes of men, a candle of the Lord.

PHILLIPS BROOKS (1835–1893)
Sermons

God never accuses anybody; He punishes him right away.   *Russian Proverb*

Justice always follows Him, and is the punisher of those who fall short of the divine law. To that law he who would be happy holds fast, and follows it in all humility and order.

PLATO (427–347 B.C.)
Laws

If His justice were such as could be adjudged just by human reckoning, it clearly would not be Divine; it would in no way differ from human justice. But inasmuch as He is the one true God, wholly incomprehensible and inaccessible to man's understanding, it is reasonable, indeed inevitable, that His justice also should be incomprehensible.

MARTIN LUTHER (1483–1546)
On the Bondage of the Will

Do you not know this from of old, since God placed men upon the earth, that the triumphing of the wicked is short, and the joy of the hypocrite but for a moment?

The Old Testament
Job 20:4

To all who are disposed to criticize you after you have decided to take a given course, because God calls you that way, you will be able to say with Paul: "With me it is a very small thing that I should be judged of you or of man's judgment. He that judgeth me is God."

WILLIAM DE WITT HYDE (1858–1917)
Sermons

God is the taker of justice for that person Who can not ask for justice from a king.

SAADI (1184–1291)
Bustan

Surely God does not do injustice to the weight of an atom. If it is a good deed, He multiplies it, and from Himself gives a great reward.   *The Koran*

God reproves with one hand and blesses with the other.   *Yiddish Proverb*

If supreme justice avenges itself on the wicked, it avenges itself on them here below. It is you and your errors, ye nations! that are its ministers of vengeance. It employs the evils you bring on each other, to punish the crimes for which you deserve them. It is in the insatiable hearts of mankind,—corroding with envy, avarice, and ambition,—that their avenging passions punish them for their vices, amidst all the false appearances of prosperity.

JEAN JACQUES ROUSSEAU (1712–1778)
Emile

The theist does not know how God punishes, how he protects, how he forgives; for he is not rash enough to flatter himself that he knows how God acts; but he knows that God does act and that he is just. The difficulties in the notion of Providence do not shake him in his faith, because they are only great difficulties and not disproofs.

VOLTAIRE (1694–1778)
Philosophical Dictionary

God is not one thing because He is, and another thing because He is just; with Him to be just and to be God are one and the same.

BOETHIUS (480–524)
De Trinitate

The judgments of the Lord are true and righteous altogether. More to be desired are they than gold, yea, than much fine gold: sweeter also than honey and the honeycomb.

The Old Testament
Psalms 19:9–10

A voice cries "In the wilderness prepare the way of the Lord, make straight in the desert a highway for our God. And the glory

of the Lord shall be revealed, and all flesh shall see it together, for the mouth of the Lord has spoken."   *The Old Testament*
Isaiah 40:3–5

For the commandment that I give you today is not beyond your powers and is not unattainable. It is not in heaven, so that you may say, "Who may go up to heaven to fetch it down for us and announce it to us so that we may fulfill it." Nor is it beyond the sea, so that you would say, "Who would go across the sea and fetch it for us so that we may act accordingly." But this word is very close to you. It has been placed in your mouth and into your heart that you may fulfill it. I call today upon heaven and earth as witnesses that I have placed before you life and death, the blessing and the curse. So choose life, so that you and your children may stay alive.
The Old Testament
Deuteronomy 30:11–19

The earth is the Lord's, and the fulness thereof; the world, and they that dwell therein: For he hath founded it upon the seas, and established it upon the floods. Who shall ascend into the hill of the Lord? or who shall stand in his holy place? He that hath clean hands, and a pure heart; who hath not lifted up his soul unto vanity, nor sworn deceitfully.   *The Old Testament*
Psalms 124:1–4

So far as practical reason has the right to serve as our guide, we shall not look upon actions as obligatory because they are the commands of God, but shall regard them as divine commands because we have an inward obligation to them.
IMMANUEL KANT (1724–1804)
Critique of Pure Reason

God does not rest content with commanding ethics. He gives it to us in our very hearts.
ALBERT SCHWEITZER (1875–1965)
Christendom

And thus, in the end, each soul may to itself,
With truth before it as its polar guide,
Become both Time and Nature, whose fixed paths
Are spiral, and when lost will find new stars,
Beyond man's unconceived infinities,
And in the Universal Movement join.
RICHARD HENRY HORNE (1803–1884)
Orion

If thy Almightiness, and all my Mite
    United be in sacred Marriage knot,
My Mite is thine: Mine thine Almighty Might.
    Then thine Almightiness my Mite hath got.
    My Quill makes thine Almightiness a String
    Of Pearls to grace the tune my Mite doth sing.
EDWARD TAYLOR (1645–1729)
The Almighty

We all know that we are bound eternally and inescapably to the Ground of our being. The abyss of separation is not always visible. But it has become more visible to our generation than to preceding generations, because of our feeling of meaninglessness, emptiness, doubt, and cynicism—all expressions of despair, of our separation from the roots and the meaning of our life.
PAUL TILLICH (1886–1965)
The Shaking of the Foundations

As there is no screen or ceiling between our heads and the infinite heavens, so there is no bar or wall in the soul where man, the effect, ceases, and God, the cause, begins.
RALPH WALDO EMERSON (1803–1882)
The Over-Soul

They say that God knows universals but not particulars. This is plain unbelief. The truth is that "there does not escape Him the weight of an atom in the heavens or in the earth" (Koran 34:3).

ABU-HAMID MUHAMMAD AL-GHAZZALI
(1058–1111)
Deliverance from Error

When the Master of the universe has points to carry in his government he impresses his will in the structure of minds.

RALPH WALDO EMERSON (1803–1882)
Letters and Social Aims

God wets you with His rain, but He also dries you with His sun.   *Slovakian Proverb*

My own hope is, a sun will pierce
The thickest cloud earth ever stretched;
That, after Last, returns the First,
Though a wide compass round be fetched;
That what began best, can't end worst,
Nor what God blessed once, prove accurst.

ROBERT BROWNING (1812–1889)
Apparent Failure

To say that everything happens according to natural laws, and to say that everything is ordained by the decree and ordinance of God, is the same thing.

BENEDICT SPINOZA (1632–1677)
Ethics

Let the dead Past bury its dead!
Act,—act in the living Present!
Heart within, and God o'erhead!

HENRY WADSWORTH LONGFELLOW
(1807–1882)
A Psalm of Life

Piety requires us to renounce no ways of life where we can act reasonably, and offer what we do to the glory of God.

WILLIAM LAW (1686–1761)
A Serious Call to a Devout and Holy Life

By giving man liberty and conscience God abdicated a part of his omnipotence in favor of his creature, and this represents the spark of God in man ("God is within you"). Liberty is real, for God Himself refused to trammel it. It is necessary, for without it man cannot progress, cannot evolve.

PIERRE LECOMTE DU NOUY (1883–1947)
Human Destiny

O Father of eternal life, and all
      Created glories under thee!
Resume thy spirit from this world of thrall
      Into true liberty.

HENRY VAUGHAN (1621–1695)
Ascension-Hymn

God does not wish that liberty, which is His word, should die.

VICTOR HUGO (1802–1885)
Funeral Oration for Louise Julien

Listen. You are free to do something. God does not know that you will do it, since you are able not to do it, and God does not know that you will not do it, since you can do it. God knows only that you are free, and just as in making man free he has freely restrained the exercise of his power in the government of the world, just so he has restrained his knowledge in relation to our acts.

JULES LEQUIER (1814–1862)
La Recherche d'une Première Vérité

Though the mills of God grind slowly, yet
      they grind exceeding small;
Though with patience He stands waiting,
      with exactness grinds He all.

FRIEDRICH VON LOGAU (1605–1655)
Sinngedichte (trans. Henry Wadsworth
Longfellow)

One on God's side is a majority.

WENDELL PHILLIPS (1811–1884)
Speech, Brooklyn, 1859

Did not your father eat and drink and do justice and righteousness? Then it was well with him. He judged the cause of the poor and needy; then it was well. Is this not to me? sayeth the Lord.   *The Old Testament*
Jeremiah 22:15

Sometimes He opens the door of obedience for you but not the door of acceptance; or sometimes He condemns you to sin, and it turns out to be a cause of arriving at Him.

IBN 'ATA'ILLAH (died 1309)
Kitab Al-Hakim

Help me, oh just and merciful God, whose light I seek, help me to understand what I say: thou art merciful because thou art just.

SAINT ANSELM (1033–1109)
Proslogion

Why are we always claiming and prophesying justice? Why does the effect rise up against the cause? Does the protest come from a puerile blindness of human vanity? No, it is the deepest cry of our being, and it is for the honour of God that the cry is uttered. Heaven and earth may pass away, but good ought to be, and injustice ought not to be. Such is the creed of the human race.

HENRI FRÉDÉRIC AMIEL (1821–1881)
Journal Intime

Justice is like the kingdom of God—it is not without us as a fact, it is within us as a great yearning.

GEORGE ELIOT (1819–1880)
Romola

There are countless paths open to God, giving him means to satisfy his justice and goodness, and the only thing one may allege against this is that we know not what way he employs; which is far from being a valid objection.

GOTTFRIED WILHELM VON LEIBNIZ (1646–1716)
Theodicy

God said unto Israel: Verily, my children, it is when you observe justice that I am most exalted.

The Midrash

Seest thou a wicked man persecuting a wicked, know thou that God is with the persecuted. If a righteous man persecutes a righteous, God is with the persecuted. And even when the righteous persecute the wicked, by the very fact of their persecution, God is still with the persecuted.

The Midrash

When Nathan the prophet brought David the message that he was not to build God's house, he prayed for his own speedy death, so that the building of God's house might be expedited. But God said that he should live out his alloted time (2 Samuel vii), because righteousness and justice, which David practised, were more acceptable to God than the building of the temple and the offering of sacrifices.

The Midrash

Set your mind on God's kingdom and his justice before anything else, and all the rest will come to you as well.

The New Testament
Matthew 6:33

Our God is just in all his ways; he reapeth not where he hath not strewed. He requireth only according to what he hath given; and where he hath given little, little is required. The glory of his justice is this, to "reward every man according to his works."

JOHN WESLEY (1703–1791)
Predestination Calmly Considered

Let this be our conclusion: to tremble with Paul at so deep a mystery; but if froward tongues clamor, not to be ashamed of this exclamation of his: "Who are you, O man, to argue with God?" For as Augustine truly contends, they who measure divine justice by the standard of human justice are acting perversely.

JOHN CALVIN (1509–1564)
Institutes of the Christian Religion

The spiritual combat is just as brutal as a human battle; but the vision of justice is the prerogative of God alone.

ARTHUR RIMBAUD (1854–1891)
A Season in Hell

It is only God who is able to see the scheme of life in such a way as to hold the scales of justice even. If man is to rise to the level of true justice, it must be because God indwells and inspires him.

WILLIAM TEMPLE (1881–1944)
Christus Veritas

O, how comely it is and how reviving
To the Spirits of just men long oppressed!
When God into the hands of their deliverer
Puts invincible might.

JOHN MILTON (1608–1674)
Samson Agonistes

The common feeling of upright men approves justice and condemns injustice. The important point is that justice has for its friend, God, while injustice has Him for an enemy; He reserves his judgments for another life, yet in such manner that He often exhibits their power in this life, and we have many examples of this in history.

HUGO GROTIUS (1583–1645)
On the Law of Peace and War

God works for all. Ye cannot hem the hope
of being free
With parallels of latitude, with mountain-
range or sea.
Put golden padlocks on Truth's lips, be
callous as ye will,

From soul to soul o'er all the world, leaps
one electric thrill.

JAMES RUSSELL LOWELL (1819–1891)
On the Capture of Certain Fugitive Slaves

There is a hard and terrible facet to justice which stands in contradiction to love. It is not, for that reason, evil. Justice is good and punishment is necessary. Yet justice alone does not move men to repentance. The inner core of their rebellion is not touched until they behold the executor of judgment suffering with and for the victim of punishment. This is the meaning of "atonement" as apprehended by faith. It is the final mystery of the relation of God to man.

REINHOLD NIEBUHR (1892–1971)
Discerning the Signs of the Times

Thou deep Base of the World, and thou
high Throne
Above the World, whoe'er thou art, unknown
And hard of surmise, Chain of Things that
be,
Or Reason of our Reason; God, to thee
I lift my praise, seeing the silent road
That bringeth justice ere the end be trod
To all that breathes and dies.

EURIPIDES (5th century B.C.)
The Trojan Women

· FORGET NOT MY LAW ·

O smooth my rugged heart, and there
Engrave thy rev'rend Law and fear;
Or make a new one, since the old
Is saplesse grown,
And a much fitter stone
To hide my dust, then thee to hold.

GEORGE HERBERT (1593–1633)
The Altar

My son, forget not my law; but let thine heart keep my commandments: for length of days, and long life, and peace, shall they add to

thee. Let not mercy and truth forsake thee: bind them about they neck; write them upon the table of thine heart: so shalt thou find favour and good understanding in the sight of God and man.   *The Old Testament*
Proverbs: 3:1–4

I will put my law in their inward parts, and write it in their hearts; and will be their God, and they shall be my people.

The Old Testament
Jeremiah 31:33

The Word of God addresses everyone clearly: the dumb, the deaf, the blind; yes, unreasoning animals, indeed, leaf and grass, stone and wood, heaven and earth, and all that is therein, in order that they might hear and do his will.

JOHANNES DENCK (1495–1527)
Whether God Is the Cause of Evil

Of Law there can be no less acknowledged than that her seat is the bosom of God, her voice the harmony of the world. All things in heaven and earth do her homage—the very least as feeling her care, and the greatest as not exempted from her power.

RICHARD HOOKER (1554–1600)
Ecclesiastical Polity

The Universal Cause
Acts not by partial, but by gen'ral laws;
And makes what happiness we justly call,
Subsist not in the good of one, but all.

ALEXANDER POPE (1688–1744)
Essay on Man

Let us acknowledge that it is an heroic obedience to observe the laws of God merely because they are the laws of God and not because He has here and there promised to reward the observer of them: to observe them even though a future reward be entirely doubted and an earthly one also is not wholly certain.

GOTTHOLD EPHRAIM LESSING (1729–1781)
The Education of the Human Race

The law of God has eminent domain everywhere. My own conscience is to declare that law to me, yours to you, before all private passions or public interests, the decisions of majorities and a world full of precedents. You cannot move out of the dominions of God, nor escape where conscience has not eminent domain.

THEODORE PARKER (1810–1860)
The Function of Conscience

Now God, in as much as He is God, acts providentially in nature, not by miraculous fits and starts, but by regular and universal laws, by constant modes of operation, and so takes care of material things without violating their constitution, acting always according to the nature of the things which He has made.

THEODORE PARKER (1810–1860)
Theism, Atheism and the Popular Theology

If we neglect the laws of health, we injure our health; if we neglect the laws of morality, we wreck our higher life. Any rational conception of the universe, any spiritual conception of God requires us to recognize the utter and unquestionable supremacy of law in shaping our conduct and character.

SARVEPALLI RADHAKRISHNAN (1888–1975)
Karma and Rebirth

A man may be able to repeat many books, but if he cannot explain them what profit is there in this? But to explain one sentence of the Law and to walk accordingly, this is the way to find supreme wisdom.

The Dhammapada

The law of his God is in his heart; none of his steps shall slide. *The Old Testament Psalms 37:31*

If you prepare your hearts, so as to sow in them the fruits of the Law, it shall protect you in that time when the Mighty One is to shake the whole creation.

The Old Testament Apocrypha 2 Baruch 32:1

No human society can exist except by virtue of the social relationship originally established between God and man, or by the truths or laws which His word made known in the beginning.

F. R. LAMENNAIS (1782–1854)
Essay on Indifference in Matters of Religion

When God sets up His law in man's thought, in his seeing and hearing and feel-

ing, the revelation of the truth is also reached about man and his reason, the revelation of man is reached, who cannot bring about of himself what is brought about simply by God Himself.　　　　KARL BARTH (1886–1968)
Dogmatics in Outline

We need to free ourselves from the idea of God's law as a statute imposed upon us from without and to substitute that of his spirit as a principle governing life from within.
WILLIAM ADAMS BROWN (1865–1943)
Beliefs That Matter

The universe is fluid and volatile. Permanence is but a word of degrees. Our globe seen by God is a transparent law, not a mass of facts.

RALPH WALDO EMERSON (1803–1882)
Circles

Let a man but realize that the purpose of his life is to fulfill the law of God, and that law will dominate him and supplant all other laws, and by its supreme dominion will in his eyes deprive all human laws of their right to command or restrict.

LEO TOLSTOY (1828–1910)
The Kingdom of God Is Within You

A noble Law, it was, in truth, that God bestowed on us, and on the tablets of each heart hath he inscribed it plain: that we should love the Lord our God with all our heart and mind, and that no creature share the love and reverence due to Him.

PETER VALDES (12th century)
The Noble Sermon

So far as we live and strive at all, our lives are various, are needed for the whole, and are unique. No one of these lives can be substituted for another. No one of us finite beings can take another's place. And all this is true just because the Universe is one significant whole.

But what is the unique meaning of my life just now? What place do I fill in God's world that nobody else fills or can fill?

JOSIAH ROYCE (1855–1916)
The Conception of Immortality

God looks forth from the high watch-tower of His Providence; He sees what suits each man, and applies to him that which suits him.

BOETHIUS (480–524)
The Consolation of Philosophy

Omnis ordo a Deo: All order is from God. We must admit that a weeping man is better than a rejoicing earthworm. But I could still expatiate in praise of the earthworm. Consider his shining complexion, his rotund body, the perfect way in which his top fits his middle, and his middle, his tail-end; how, in his humble way, all his parts strive to make up a united whole. There is no single part of him so formed as not to harmonize with the proportions of any other.

SAINT AUGUSTINE (354–430)
De Vera Religione

To each thing a term of existence is given, whether it be for good or evil purposes. The saints too have their term after which they must cease to lead their lives on earth, and the sinners too have their term.

PARACELSUS (1493–1541)
De primis tribus essentiis

If we thought men were free in the sense that in a single exception one fantastical will could prevail over the law of things, it were all one as if a child's hand could pull down the sun. If in the least particular one could derange the order of nature,—who would accept the gift of life?

RALPH WALDO EMERSON (1803–1882)
Fate

Then Job answered the Lord, I know that You can do all things and that no purpose of Yours can be thwarted. You have said, "Who is this that hides My plan without knowl-

edge?" Indeed, I have spoken without understanding, of things too wonderful for me, which I knew not. *The Old Testament*
Job 42:2-6

In the pleasant orchard closes,
'God bless all our gains,' say we;
But 'May God bless all our losses'
Better suits with our degree.
ELIZABETH BARRETT BROWNING (1806-1861)
The Lost Bower

Let me enjoy the earth no less
Because the all-enacting Might
That fashioned forth its loveliness
Had other aims than my delight.
THOMAS HARDY (1840-1928)
Let Me Enjoy

You have not measured your fingers with God's, therefore you cannot know what is in store. *Lithuanian Proverb*

The Eternal, your God, is God indeed, a faithful God, who carries out His compact of kindness to those who love Him and carry out his orders. *The Old Testament*
Deuteronomy 7:9

That thou art happy, owe to God;
That thou continuest such, owe to thyself,
That is, to thy obedience.
JOHN MILTON (1608-1674)
Paradise Lost

Thine ears shall hear a word behind thee, saying, This is the way, walk ye in it.
The Old Testament
Isaiah 30:21

God does not pay weekly, He pays at the end. *Dutch Proverb*

Happy the man who observes the heavenly and the terrestrial law in just proportion; whose every faculty, from the soles of his feet to the crown of his head, obeys the law of its level; who neither stoops nor goes on tiptoe, but lives a balanced life, acceptable to nature and God.

HENRY DAVID THOREAU (1817-1862)
Letters

To think that God acts in anything without having any reason for his willing, even if we overlook the fact that such action seems impossible, is an opinion which conforms little to God's glory. For example, let us suppose that God chooses between A and B, and that he takes A without any reason for preferring it to B. I say that this action on the part of God is at least not praiseworthy, for all praise ought to be founded upon reason which *ex hypothesi* is not present here. My opinion is that God does nothing for which he does not deserve to be glorified.

GOTTFRIED WILHELM VON LEIBNIZ
(1646-1716)
Discourse on Metaphysics

Surely God chooses His servants at birth, or perhaps even before birth.

EPICTETUS (1st century)
Discourses

Let us now praise famous men, and our fathers in their generations. The Lord apportioned to them great glory, his majesty from the beginning.

The Old Testament Apocrypha
Ecclesiasticus 44:1-2

Index of Authors' Names and Titles

Index of Selected Subjects